…zing *Mad Men*

Analyzing *Mad Men*

Critical Essays on the Television Series

Edited by
SCOTT F. STODDART

McFarland & Company, Inc., Publishers
Jefferson, North Carolina, and London

Frontispiece: Cast of *Mad Men* (2007). Standing, left to right: Aaron Staton as Ken Cosgrove, Rich Sommer as Harry Crane, Michael Gladis as Paul Kinsey, Bryan Batt as Salvatore Romano, Christina Hendricks as Joan Holloway, John Slattery as Roger Sterling, Vincent Kartheiser as Peter Campbell, Elisabeth Moss as Peggy Olson, and January Jones as Betty Draper. Seated: Robert Morse as Bertram Cooper and Jon Hamm as Don Draper (AMC/Kobal Collection).

Library of Congress Cataloguing-in-Publication Data

Analyzing Mad men : critical essays on the television series / Scott F. Stoddart [editor].
    p.   cm.
Includes bibliographical references and index.

ISBN 978-0-7864-4738-1
softcover : 50# alkaline paper ∞

1. Mad men (Television program)   I. Stoddart, Scott Frederick, 1960–
PN1992.77.M226A53   2011
791.45'75 — dc23   2011022558

British Library cataloguing data are available

On the cover: (top) Key art from Season 1 of *Mad Men*, 2007 (AMC/Photofest); (bottom) Manhattan skyline at night (Shutterstock)

Manufactured in the United States of America

McFarland & Company, Inc., Publishers
  Box 611, Jefferson, North Carolina 28640
  www.mcfarlandpub.com

For Greg ....
for helping me to take on Manhattan
to find my inner mad man.

Table of Contents

The Nostalgia of Mad Men

Acknowledgments

While working on this book was a true labor of love, there are many people I want to thank for their encouragement in making this project come to fruition. My support network is comprised of professionals, colleagues, and family who have supported me in a myriad of ways.

Professionally, I want to thank Joyce F. Brown, president of the Fashion Institute of Technology, and Reginetta Haboucha and Gretchen Bataille, vice presidents for academic affairs for supporting my research efforts. My immediate colleagues, a wonderful group of deans, support a number of my efforts, including this one: my appreciation goes to Joanne Arbuckle, Robin Sackin, Steven Zucker, Dympna Bowles and Lisa Braverman.

My staff in the School of Liberal Arts is the best I have ever worked with, and their attention to the details of our school, so I could carve out time to work on this project, is much appreciated. My thanks go to Mary Tsujimoto, Everlina Washington, Suzanne Richardson, John Chucala and Madeleine Meyerson for all of their efforts.

My immediate colleagues are avid *Mad Men* aficionados, and their concerns about the project, and their willingness to speak about each week's episode, have made for some lively exchanges. My gratitude goes to Jean Amato, Dan Beckendorf, Andrew Bodenrader, Nathan Bullock, Yasemin Celik, Tom Dennison, Howard Dillon, Brian Fallon, Patrick Knisley, Amy Lemmon, Sean Kinsell, Dan Levinson-Wilk, Kevin Martin, and Jeffrey Reinman for their willingness to talk endlessly about the weekly happenings at Sterling Cooper.

At the Picture Desk, my thanks go to Veronique Colaprete and Jamie Vuignier. They have been an endless source of support for this project.

The work presented here is the product of much effort and dedication from a series of contributors who have proven to be the most professional. My thanks for all of their efforts in making this project a reality.

Personally, my family has always supported my efforts, and I am grateful for their continued love. My parents, Jeanne F. Black and Frederick Stoddart, and their significant others, Barry Black and Barbara Marshall, support me in a number of ways. Cathy, Steve and Annie Bernard generously shared their home with me each summer while I was working on this book, providing a tranquil alternative to the city's madness.

My friend and colleague Bill Mooney has been a constant source of support for me through this and many other projects. He is a careful editor and a faithful friend who has an uncanny sixth sense about when we need to go out for a scholarly lunch.

Michael R. Schiavi served as a tireless editor of this project. He remains a committed critic and a marvelous teacher.

I met J. Benjamin Lambert as this book went into its final edit. He inspires me with his spirit and ambition; he helps me to retain my sense of humor, for which I am grateful.

Finally, I have dedicated this book to my dear friend, Gregory Kucher. I am a lucky man to have him in my corner, cheering me onward.

Introduction

On 27 July 2008, *Mad Men*'s second season debuted at 10 P.M. on American Movie Classics (AMC), the cable station that sponsors the Emmy, Golden Globe, and Peabody Award-winning series. During this particular episode, protagonist Don Draper lunched at a bar sitting next to a man reading Frank O'Hara's *Meditations in an Emergency*, a 1957 poetry collection regarding Cold War anguish. Don purchases his own copy of the slim volume and reads it throughout the episode, reading the closing lines to the poem

Jon Hamm as Don Draper in Mad Men *(2007) (AMC/Kobal Collection).*

"Meditations in an Emergency" as the episode comes to a close. Within days, Amazon.com reported that sales of this particular volume of O'Hara's poems ascended from 15,565 on their sales list to 159. Within the week, the title had sold out for the first time since O'Hara published the book fifty years before. It may appear inconceivable that a television series could foster a resurgence in popularity for a fifty-year-old literary property, but that is the cult of *Mad Men*.

In July 2007, AMC took a gamble and sponsored Matthew Weiner's *Mad Men*, the network's first foray into series television. The drama follows the career of Donald Draper, a self-made advertising genius who navigates the boardrooms of Madison Avenue's Sterling Cooper Agency, the suburbs of Ossining, New York, with his wife Betty and their two children, and the bedrooms of clients and bohemians in 1960s Manhattan. The series debuted to critical acclaim and to limited viewership; however, accolades from a variety of prestigious organizations and hosannas from cultural critics have made the series into a pop culture phenomenon. In its four seasons, the viewership has grown 34 percent, reaching 2.8 million viewers per week, and its influence is felt everywhere — from fashion merchandising to travel packaging; from furniture design to advertising. *Mad Men* has established a new craze for '60s cocktail culture. Its characters even provide dating advice and etiquette tips on their own Web sites.

What does a television series about advertising professionals set in 1960s New York City have to say about life in twenty-first-century America? Why has this series become a cultural bellwether? How can cultural theorists interpret the *Mad Men* phenomenon? These are some of the many questions the essays herein address.

I.

Each episode of AMC's *Mad Men* opens with an animated sequence: a figure in silhouette, briefcase in hand, enters a well-appointed office that gradually begins to melt away. As the credits play, the figure falls through space, the walls and floor of the office dissolving, while his tumbling body passes a variety of advertisements on the sides of office buildings. Happy families model the latest fashions; slender female legs move to-and-fro to show the shimmer of black silk stockings and garters; and smiling faces of men and women sport Pepsodent smiles and Revlon lashes. The cascading ads float in a montage as the falling figure passes through the camera's lens toward the ground. Following a cut, the show's title card appears alongside the man, now sitting confidently on his office sofa, cigarette in hand as the cool beat of

RJD2's "A Beautiful Mine" plays, preparing the viewer for another episode of this slick, provocative series. The sequence tells us that we are about to watch Don Draper, creative mastermind, navigate the daily dramas of his professional life at the Madison Avenue offices of Sterling Cooper and his personal suburban home life. Whatever the circumstance, he will end the day in control of his destiny — cool, calm, collected — the madness of the day only touching him momentarily.

In splitting its focus between the suburban anguish of Ossining and the office machinations of Madison Avenue, *Mad Men* focuses on change in America — how change affects the individual and how it affects the broader community within the historic moment. Weiner claims, "I started off writing the show as a scathing analysis of what happened to the United States ... But the more I got into Don, the more I realized this is an amazing place. Something really did change in those years" (Kaplan 18). In another interview, he describes the goal of the series: "I wanted to show what it was like to have the world change around you" (Edwards 39). The era of the late 1950s and early 1960s makes a perfect setting for understanding the cultural and personal shifts in America: Don, his family, and his company, are confronted, ultimately, with societal changes that shifted Eisenhower conservatism to Great Society liberalism through the election of 1960, the brink of nuclear invasion (via the Cuban Missile Crisis), the move from lounge music to rock 'n' roll, the elevation of the Beats over the "serious" literature of Ayn Rand, Leon Uris, and Joseph Heller, and the upward mobility of women, blacks — even closeted homosexuals — within the corporate world. Weiner feels that the series reflects his desire to monitor the effect of change: "I'm interested in how people respond to change. Are they excited by the change, or are they terrified that they'll lose everything that they know? Do people recognize that change is going on? That's what the show is all about" (Kaplan 19). In an op-ed piece for the *New York Times*, Frank Rich echoes Weiner's vision, feeling that it resonates with the audience more than one might at first believe: "It's our identification with an America that, for all its serious differences with our own, shares our growing anxiety about the prospect of cataclysmic change" (E8).

While *Mad Men* entertains its viewers, it provides fodder for cultural critics — both those who love the show and those who question its appeal. To those critics who emphasize the series' fetishizing of fashion, style, décor, and its glamorization of drinking and smoking, *Mad Men* appears to be a superficial soap opera with "an air of concerned detachment," one in which characters exude "a mood of perpetual anxiety or frustration" (Suderman 52). Part of the series' "beguiling nature," claims Richard Nalley, is its "very knowing nature about the distance between Draper's world of 1960 and ours" (99) — which he reads as simple posturing: "Don't we feel smug having eschewed smoking, in-office boozing, restrictive foundation garments and casual sexism?" (99). However, other critics pose an alternative *Mad Men* method—one that reads the series as being cognizant of its use of this particular moment in history. "Though change—beatniks, integration, feminism—percolates on its edges, *Mad Men* is mainly about people who stand outside that change" (73), says James Poniewozik, who sees that the "subtle, deliberately paced drama has a wider sense of history" (74). Anna McCarthy agrees, reading the series' deliberate blending of nostalgia and history as key to its real essence:

> It strikes me that the nostalgia that permeates *Mad Men* is not, in the end, a nostalgia for a past in which it was possible to smoke, drink and consume large amounts of cholesterol without feeling any guilt. Maybe, and perhaps wholly unconsciously, *Mad Men* signals a desire to return to a time when advertising, and the consumer culture it helped sustain, represented the vitality of Western democracy and the deeper moral meanings of capitalism [3].

McCarthy's connecting the show's audience with the current economic crisis resonates. *Mad Men* is a period drama about change just after the mid-twentieth century, which reveals a lot about our response to shifting ideological terrains in the early twenty-first.

II.

As a cultural barometer, *Mad Men* reveals another aspect of the myriad texts that comprise American popular culture. The reader of this volume will soon discover that most of the contributors to this collection subscribe to Frederic Jameson's endorsement of popular culture texts often derided by the academy as the cultural barometers of an era. This possibility is particularly important for *Mad Men* as a show that celebrates the commodity as image and as text. Jameson speaks of how popular culture texts reflect a culture while mythologizing it; it is that mythology that plays into the commodification of the cultural artifact which fulfills some desire on the part of the consumer. In this reification of a utopian ideal:

> ... the ultimate form of commodity reification in contemporary consumer society is precisely the image itself. With this universal commodification of our object world, the familiar accounts of the sexualization of our objects and activities are also given: the new model car is essentially an image for other people to have of us, and we consume, less the thing itself, than the abstract idea, open to all the libidinal investments ingeniously arrayed for us by advertising [11–12].

For Jameson, the popular text is not only a gateway for comprehending how culture intersects with the processes of capitalism, but it fulfills a deep-rooted desire for whatever it can offer. *Mad Men* celebrates a time when capitalism was king, and it apparently satisfies a desire for re-experiencing a time and place where sex roles were more clearly defined, and hedonism was celebrated in a variety of untoward behaviors.

The series' influence on contemporary culture is literally everywhere, fulfilling this nostalgic desire for '60s cocktail culture. During the show's first season, Michael Kors's clothing line made its debut on the catwalks of New York's Fashion Week, and the reviews were telling: "Thanks to Don Draper, Joan Holloway and the gang, slim suits, skinny ties, sheath dresses and pearls" began to find their way "into the closets of consumers" (Zmuda 6). Bloomingdale's quickly followed suit, featuring *Mad Men* in its windows using Kors's line to capture the feel of the 1960s era: "As far as TV shows go, [*Mad Men*] probably has the most influence [on fashion]" reported Kevin Harter, Bloomingdale's vice president of fashion direction (Zmuda 6). He believed that these fashions would continue to inspire designers and consumers alike, sparking Bloomingdale's effort to showcase the collection during 2008. Kors openly acknowledged that the series is his inspiration, and he is not alone. Banana Republic issued a "Mad About Style" fashion guide during the summer of 2009 to celebrate the series' third season and again in 2010 to celebrate its fourth season; the booklets feature photos of the series' stars wearing "The Modern Fit Two-Button Suit" (1–2), "The Pencil Skirt" (3–4), and "The Sheath Dress (7–8). The guide ends with a bonus: entry into a contest "Mad Men Casting Call" offering the lucky winner a walk-on role on the show and a $1,000 Banana Republic giftcard.

Not to be left out, Brooks Brothers, the source for many of the series' men's costumes, worked with costume designer Janie Bryant to bring a line of "*Mad Men* suits" to its retail stores in 2009. At $900 each, the two-button gray flannel sold out within three weeks of appearing on the store's Web site. Marc Jacobs' Fall 2010 collection "reconstructed femininity" (A24) by meeting the demand for "padded bras and breast implants" because of "the popularity of shows like *Mad Men*" (A24). Jacobs argued that women "want hips, phony or not"; the series had inspired his line's emphasis on "the physical — corseted breasts, bare arms and legs, womanly hips under full skirts" making "the body ... the main event" (A24). Many venues, such as *Gentlemen's Quarterly, ELLE, Glamour* and *Vanity Fair*, the Web sites Askmen.com and MarieClaire.com, and style columns in the *New York Times* tell men and women how to achieve the style and glamour of Madison Avenue gray flannel and the suburban chic of bouclé jackets and pill box hats. The *Mad Men* aesthetic appears ubiquitous.

Mad Men's retro charm is not limited to its wardrobe. A number of articles in *Entertainment Weekly* have featured the show's décor while *Advertising Age* has focused on product placement, thus spotlighting the series' commodification. The 23 June 2008 issue of *Advertising Age*, celebrating *Mad Men*'s first season on DVD, featured advertisements from the 1960s side-by-side with current ads for the same products. There are articles that "announce" Sterling Cooper as winning prized accounts at Lucky Strike, Clearasil and for the Kodak Slide Projector. There are interviews with the original Madison Avenue "Ad Women," who speak about the horrors of pervasive sexism in the office, and a fictional interview with Don Draper, outlining his thoughts on product placement and his theories as to how the industry has changed over the years: "I'd like to think that our work springs from somewhere deep in the heart of our artists. We try to be mirrors for consumers." This special issue proved to be one of *Advertising Age*'s biggest sellers.

In the 1 August 2008 issue of *Entertainment Weekly*, Lindsay Soll interviewed Emmy-nominated set designer Amy Wells for "An Office and a Gentleman," an article telling readers how to obtain items that create the look of Don Draper's office. "Don is all about appearances, and he sells himself really well," Wells says. "So anything that goes into his office would have been well made and expensive for its day" (14). The items featured include a Burke sofa ($1,500) and an Eames padded desk chair ($2,130) along with an executive day planner ($28) and a Lao table lamp ($50)—all available for purchase at a variety of Web sites. Crate & Barrel now sells a suite of furniture called "The Draper Collection," aiming to outfit homes with furniture styled along the lines of Don's office rather than the Drapers' suburban residence. In response, Stuart Elliot, an advertising critic at the *New York Times*, ponders, "Now that the home furnishings retailer is offering a 'Draper sofa,' will it be sold with ads promising shoppers that they, too, can enjoy the domestic misery that is the home life of Don Draper?" (B3).

Mad Men's efforts at commodification extend to some unlikely consumers. The *New York Times* Business page reported on 10 March 2010 that Mattel, the company responsible for making the Barbie doll a must-have for young girls since 1959, announced "a premium-price collectors' series for adults" called the Fashion Model Collection (B3). Its first collection features Don Draper, Betty Draper, Roger Sterling and Joan Holloway. While the announcement showcased the fact that "the dolls ... do a great job of embodying the series ... [and are] emblematic of the interplay between entertainment and marketing" (B3), these dolls met with a bit of derision as well:

That two of the dolls represent a relationship outside of wedlock, and Don Draper's propensity for adultery, may be firsts for the Barbie world since the brand's introduction five decades ago. But for the sake of the Barbie image, her immersion in the *Mad Men* era will only go so far: The dolls come with period accessories like hats, overcoats, pearls and padded undergarments, but no cigarettes, ashtrays, martini glasses or cocktail shakers [B3].

Given the iconography of the Barbie franchise, it might appear a little odd that a toy marketed to young girls would seek to merge with such an adult enterprise. However, series creator Matt Weiner found the merger a "realization of a fantasy" (B3)—another way to bring the series home for its audience.

Marketing executives claim that despite its popularity, *Mad Men* is a difficult series to sell. Its creators deliberately link the show to certain consumerist desires. For instance, to launch its third season, AMC craftily featured a "Mad About Town" weekend package in New York, featuring a variety of themed cocktail parties about the city, a revolving art display of 1960s advertisements on the face of the newly refurbished Museum of Decorative Arts (at Columbus Circle) and an exclusive hotel package at the St. Regis Hotel (suites starting at $895 for the week). The week culminated in a public screening of the third season opener in Times Square; many fans braved the 90-degree temperatures and populated the pedestrian park set in the middle of square to watch the episode.

In perusing the Internet sites dedicated to *Mad Men*, it is hard not to reflect on Umberto Eco's thoughts regarding popular culture and fandom. In his essay "*Casablanca*: Cult Movies and Intertextual Collage," Eco states that "the requirements for transforming a book or movie into a cult object" requires that:

> The work must be loved, obviously, but this is not enough. It must provide a completely furnished world so that its fans can quote characters and episodes as if they were aspects of the fan's private sectarian world about which one can make up quizzes and play trivia games so that the adepts of the sect recognize through each other a shared expertise [198].

The series' Web site which is filled with trivia quizzes, interviews, and blogs dedicated to the show helps to construct a community of "shared experience," encouraging fans to contribute to the weekly exchange of ideas and "become" Mad Men through the creation of avatars. A variety of entertaining fan-sites have joined AMC to cultivate a remarkable set of media dedicated to the series. For instance, Madmenunbuttoned.com, dismantles each episode and details the history behind featured advertisements by showcasing fashion trends depicted and provides historical context to key events. At the Web site What Would Dan Draper Do?, Don Draper becomes an advice columnist, and provides feedback on romance and office etiquette:

> **Dear Don Draper, I'm single and looking to hook up with the type of girl that goes out on Halloween dressed as Mystique from the first X-Men movie or another costume that only requires body paint. What should I be for Halloween?**
>
> I can't really picture what you're looking for, but I'm sure it explains why you're single. Also: I'm opposed to wearing costumes for Halloween or any

other occasion. If forced, I'll wear a tux and simple masquerade mask and stand near the bar.

Dear Don Draper, I'm a housewife and find my days depressing and empty. My husband is almost no help with the children. Should I leave him or suffer in silence?

By chance, are you almost no help with *his* job? Emptiness is a good thing. For relief. Find the depressing part(s) of your day. If it's the time you spend with your husband, then yes, leave him. If it's the children, leave them. If it's just the repetition, the routine of homemaking, hire help and get out of the house. Fill those empty parts of your day with something new: a forgotten passion, a release (have you tried a Relaxicisor?)—maybe a gun. Then return to your family and ask yourself if it's enough. And if not, must you always be full?

Dear Don Draper, Do you have any views on men using Facebook?

Yes, the same ones I have of men wearing brassieres.

Joan Holloway provides dating advice at her own Web site, What Would Joan Holloway Do?, where she answers questions sent in by loyal viewers:

Q: My workplace requires a uniform — an atrocious black polo shirt that's three sizes too big for me, khaki slacks or skirt (below the knee), and closed toe shoes. How can I make my outfit more stylish and show off my slender figure?

I would question further employment there. Any job that makes you dress this way relishes in punishing their female employees. A woman's pleasing figure is a strong asset. Any company that doesn't know that doesn't deserve your sweat.

Q: Do you think it is correct to invite the men of the office to a bridal shower? Think of all those extra gifts, not to mention the free drinks?

Having mascara slop down your face and all your girlfriends coo at your new baking dish is not a sight men at the office need to see. If you want to celebrate with the boys ask your fiancée for some extra spending cash and go with the boys for a celebratory martini. This will show them that you still know how to be a party girl even if you're not allowed to be one.

While these sites are meant to be humorous, they also indicate a discourse community, a *Mad Men* universe with its own distinct language and attitude. In essence, within the strong fan-base that the series maintains the characters live beyond Sterling Cooper's weekly drama to achieve mythic proportions — a new American saga for the millennium steeped in the traditions of the American Dream.

Given the variety of cover stories featuring the cast members in *GQ, Interview, New York Magazine, Vanity Fair* — even *Cinema Editor* — *Mad Men* appears to have struck a nerve with the public on a variety of levels.

III.

The purpose of this collection is to explore many of the political and pop cultural resonances that comprise the *Mad Men* phenomenon. *Mad Men* is a series that serves as a cultural barometer and challenges viewers to explore how a show about an advertising agency in the 1960s speaks to our current anxieties regarding capitalism, consumerism and human relations. It has raised the bar for the future of television studies as an academic discipline.

In the first section, "The Contexts of *Mad Men*," the essays seek to connect *Mad Men* to a literary pedigree. Melanie Hernandez and David Thomas Holmberg address this notion by reading Don Draper as an American archetype that stretches from Cooper's Natty Bumppo and Twain's Huck Finn to Fitzgerald's James Gatz/Jay Gatsby. Maura Grady connects the office dynamics of *Mad Men* with 1950s corporate culture, reading the first season of the series against William H. Whyte's *The Organization Man* (1956).

The essays that comprise "The Politics of *Mad Men*" examine through a Marxist lens what the series reveals about the history of capitalism. Brenda Cromb reads Don Draper and Rachel Menken's conversation regarding Utopia in "Babylon" (1:6) and the long-held belief that Utopia could be found in America's corporate climate. David P. Pierson applies the work of Fredric Jameson to the capitalist politics of Sterling Cooper, exploring what the series says more broadly about capitalism in the twentieth century, and how that might apply in the twenty-first. Examining the advertising culture of the early 1960s, Jennifer Gillan seeks to prove how the series exposes the limitations of 1960s American Dream in respect to how its products were sold.

"The Women of *Mad Men*" applies feminist theory to the series, seeking ways of reading *Mad Men*'s central women against historical trends. Tamar Jeffers McDonald sees parallels between the three key women of the series, Betty Draper, Joan Holloway and Peggy Olson and the three women key to Rona Jaffe's iconic novel *The Best of Everything* (1956), prominently featured in "Ladies Room" (1:2). Diana Davidson explores theories of motherhood as she reads Betty Draper's peculiar brand of parenting. Sara Rogers's essay reads the series through its key women, again, exposing the sexist politics at Sterling Cooper and exploring how these relate to the contemporary spectator. The episode "Maidenform" (2:6) is scrutinized by Meenasarani Linde Murugan who seeks to understand parallels drawn in Season Two between career girl Peggy Olson, party girl Joan Holloway, and housewife Betty Draper. Tonya Krouse closes this section with an essay that exposes the problem of nostalgia in her reading of the same episode (2:6), in which the sexist Paul Kinsey claims that every woman in America is either a "Jackie" or a "Marilyn."

The volume ends with "The Nostalgia of *Mad Men*" — two essays that argue that nostalgia is a central concern of the spectators who consume the series. My own essay looks at how the series uses two key American myths: the Man in the Gray Flannel Suit and Kennedy's Camelot. Christine Sprengler applies nostalgia theory to the series to reveal its reliance on *mise-en-scene*, causing the series to be read by its critics one way, and to be interpreted by its audience in quite another.

In closing, I would like to reflect on a recent use of the series to show how pervasive it has become in the cultural vernacular. In a column denouncing a blackmail attempt against David Letterman, columnist Maureen Dowd hit a nerve in October 2009 when she declared that only some things have changed since the *Mad Men* era: "The elevator operator isn't the only black face in the building. Executives no longer sip amber highballs and puff Lucky Strikes all day long" (A21). However, as Dowd notes, some things have not really changed at all: "some women still wriggle into girdles (now called Spanx). And some men still gravitate toward interns, nannies and secretaries (now called personal assistants)" (A21). As Dowd illustrates, the era of *Mad Men* is alive in spirit and practice alike. The series has hit a nerve with the American public: some nostalgically dream to recapture their lost youths; others pine away to bring back those "naughty" days of clearly delineated gender roles; still others believe that the world was simpler in an era before high-speed Internet and ubiquitous cell phone connections. As the essays in this book attest, *Mad Men* is a cultural phenomenon that reflects upon a past era, and exposes a time thought glamorous in its innocent sophistication. It celebrates a time when American consumer capitalism dominated the world discourse through brute strength. With unemployment nearly as high as it was during the Depression, with a bitter war being fought in a distant land, with a country split between conservative aggression and liberal paralysis, *Mad Men* allows us to pause and reflect on how the ebb and flow of history affects us and how change, no matter how small, is both frighteningly unnerving and assuredly inevitable.

Works Cited

Arden, Allison. "Welcome to the *Mad Men* Issue." *Advertising Age*, 23 June 2008.

Colman, David. "Dressing for Success, Again." *New York Times*, 17 December 2009: E1.

Dowd, Maureen. "Men Behaving Badly." *New York Times*, 07 October 2009: A 21.

Eagan, Timothy. "The Distant Mirror." *New York Times*, 16 August 2009: E 10.

Edwards, Gavin. "*Mad Men* in Crisis." *Rolling Stone*, 1055. 26 June 2008: 39.

Elliot, Stuart. "Mad Men Dolls in a Barbie World, But the Cocktails Stay Behind." *New York Times*, 10 March 2010: B3.

_____. "Tying Up Loose Ends with Oprah, *Mad Men*, Wine Clubs and More." *New York Times*, 30 November 2009: B3.

Fernandez, Walter. "Where the Truth Lies: Mad Men." *Cinema Editor*, September 2009: 10–18.

"Go Mad for *Mad Men*" Special Advertising section. *Vanity Fair*, August 2009: 63–4.

Hamm, Liza. "The Poetry of *Mad Men*." *People*, 18 August 2008: 48.

Handy, Bruce. "Don and Betty's Paradise Lost." *Vanity Fair*, September 2009: 268–283.

Hill, Logan. "Dangerous Curves." *New York Magazine*, 10 August 2009: 61–4.

Horyn, Cathy. "A Shift Away from Linear Thinking." *New York Times*, 12 March 2010: A24.

Kaplan, Fred. "Drama Confronts a Dramatic Decade." *New York Times*, 9 August 2009: A18.

"Mad About Style." Special Advertising section. Banana Republic. August 2009.

Martin, Brett. "Jon Hamm: Breakout." *Gentleman's Quarterly*, December 2008: 280–82.

Mazzocchi, Sherry. "TV Can Boost Book Sales, Too." *Advertising Age*, 4 August 2009: 5.

Nicholson, Jack. "January Jones." *Interview*, August 2009: 48–55.

Poniewozik, James. "The New New Frontier." *Time*, August 2008: 73–74.

Rich, Frank. "*Mad Men* Crashes Woodstock's Birthday." *New York Times*, 16 August 2009: E8.

Soll, Lindsay. "An Office and a Gentleman." *Entertainment Weekly*, 1 August 2008: 14–15.

Zmuda, Natalie. "*Mad Men* as Fashion Muse." *Advertising Age*, 4 August 2008: 6.

THE CONTEXTS OF
MAD MEN

January Jones as Betty Draper and Jon Hamm as Don Draper in Mad Men *(2007)* *(AMC/Kobal Collection).*

1. "We'll start over like Adam and Eve": The Subversion of Classic American Mythology

Melanie Hernandez and *David Thomas Holmberg*

In the beginning of Mark Twain's *The Adventures of Huckleberry Finn*, before even the second paragraph is completed, Huck complains about the Widow Douglas's attempts to "sivilize" him: "but it was rough living in the house all the time, considering how dismal regular and decent the widow was in all her ways; so when I couldn't stand it no longer, I lit out. I got in my old rags, and my sugar-hogshead again, and was free and satisfied.... all I wanted was to go somewhere; all I wanted was a change. I warn't particular" (748–9). This same sentiment of restlessness and rebellion against domesticity is echoed again in the final lines of the novel, when Huck declares his intentions to once again depart: "But I reckon I got to light out for the Territory ahead of the rest, because Aunt Sally she's going to adopt me and sivilize me and I can't stand it. I been there before" (956). The intervening story of adventure — the rafting down river with Jim, the picaresque adventures with the conmen, the rescue of Jim — does nothing to dissuade Huck from his intentions to light out; if anything, those encounters simply solidify for Huck his destination: Huck wants to be free and satisfied, something that "sivilization" can never provide.

The first we hear of Don Draper's desire to escape his life and head west — or, perhaps in this case, it is the West — is when he tries to convince Rachel Mencken to go to Los Angeles ("Nixon vs. Kennedy" 1:12). Don tells her, "We'll start over like Adam and Eve." She rebuffs him — accusing him of acting like a teenager — because she, correctly, surmises that he does not want to run away *with* her, but, like Huck, simply to run away. But Don's choice of Los Angeles as his destination is not an accident; the West has long been an important part of American mythology and has represented the site of rebirth for the frontier hero. It should not be surprising, then, that when Don, American man and modern-day frontier hero, *does* set off for the Territories — in this case, California — he does so to escape his wife, Betty Draper, and her attempts to "sivilize" him; after all, for Don, it "was rough living in the house all the time," and so, when he inevitably could no longer stand it, he "lit out." Among the most pivotal episodes of the series is Season Two's "The Jet Set" (2:11), which represents an important transitional moment for Don as frontier hero. When Don runs off with the European "jet set," he is presented, for the first time in the series (although not for the first time in his life, as Pete Campbell tells Peggy in "The Mountain King" 2:12) with an actual opportunity to start over, to escape the domesticity and social mores that ensnare him. With his luggage lost — no more "baggage" now (in fact, it winds up delivered back to his home in New York, signaling once again that absolute renewal requires a freedom from domestic tethers) — Don winds up in Palm Springs with Joy and her Euro set; his subsequent collapse from "heat exhaustion" suggests the beginning of his rebirth on the western frontier. Don's experience at the Palm Springs house carries with it an etherealness, a sense both of uncertainty and ultimate possibility, a world without form — amorphous — like that in *Genesis*, before even Adam has been created. Don's rebirth in Palm Springs allows him potentially to do anything, become anyone; at this moment in the series, the possibility that Don may never return to Betty or Sterling Cooper is very real.

From James Fenimore Cooper's Natty Bumppo retreating further and further into the frontier wilderness, to Twain's Huck on his raft escaping a broken family, to F. Scott Fitzgerald's James Gatz rechristening himself "Jay Gatsby," Don Draper emerges as another in the long line of classic American literary figures capable of continual reinvention, but also only one step from lighting out for new lands. The archetypal American narrative typically involves the reinvented man's escape from society; such is the scenario that lies at the heart of AMC's *Mad Men*, where the show's quintessential American hero, Don Draper, not only embodies the Adamic myth as famously explicated in R.W.B. Lewis's influential 1955 study *The American Adam* of "starting up again under fresh initiative" (5) but also strives repeatedly to flee the civilization that crushes down upon him. A mid-twentieth century incarnation, Don represents Adam in his new Eden, but in action and character he is also the isolated frontier hero who rejects society, even if his rebellion manifests itself less in the shape of buckskins and rifles, and more as transgressions against societal mores. By positioning Don within this regeneration narrative, *Mad Men* also hints at an impending "fortunate fall" that might allow Don to free himself from the stronghold of this supposed Eden, the Eden of our contemporary American cultural imagination: postwar America of the 1950s and early 1960s.

Although *Mad Men*'s reliance on American myths reveals itself most prominently through Don, he is far from the only character on the series whose origins can be traced to nineteenth- and early twentieth-century American literary archetypes. In Betty, Peggy, Pete, and nearly every other character in *Mad Men* can be found echoes of personas and types from American literature, and part of our chapter will focus on identifying and explaining a selection of these reverberations. But just because Don is reminiscent of the frontier hero escaping west, or because Betty so immediately invokes the Victorian Angel in the House, that still does not explain why a twenty-first-century cable television show is so indebted to these essentially nineteenth-century symbolic frameworks of cultural mythology. By exploring the series' indebtedness to these archetypes and what amounts to a national mythology of reinvention and rebirth, and the problem that gender poses to both, we hope to demonstrate that the series reveals that these myths are no longer sufficient to sustain a nation undergoing such rapid cultural changes. Whatever stories we told ourselves *about* ourselves before the 1960s are no longer viable, and a new mythology, a new set of exemplars, ephemeral by necessity, must be created to reflect these changing needs. The ease with which a twenty-first century viewing audience recognizes nineteenth century archetypes indicates the pervasive nature of this mythology in the American fancy, and *Mad Men* adeptly deploys the myth then subverts viewer expectations, calling into question the legitimacy of these forms and America's amnesiac romance with itself.

Theories of American Literary Archetypes

In the middle of the second season, a flashback reveals Don visiting Peggy Olson in the hospital after her unexpected childbirth. To the distraught and confused new mother Don explains that she must do whatever it takes to secure her release from the psychiatric ward and then to forget that any of it ever happened ("The New Girl" 2:5). This is not just Don speaking to Peggy; it is Don speaking to himself about his own (forcibly) forgotten past and self-reinvention. Indeed, Don Draper is not really Don Draper at all; he is a farm boy and "whore child" who, given an opportunity to reinvent himself, seizes it and transforms himself from a shy and frightened young man into his idea of a confident and successful adult: he wills a new self into existence. In this manner, Don inherits the qualities of the classic American frontier hero, the man who abandons his past, and often civilization in the process, to seek out new fortunes in the unsettled frontiers of the American West. Don's abandonment of his civilization is less dramatic. While he does not altogether believe in the morals and values of his own time, he still participates in the world they create — and his horizons are more limited. He must make do with forging new paths through the burgeoning world of Madison Avenue advertising, but the outlines of his actions still reflect this persistent narrative in American letters.

Before exploring Don's literary genealogy and his connection to this classic narrative, it will benefit us to take a detour through several relevant works of literary criticism that pertain to this study. Criticism on these literary archetypes is extensive, but of particular concern for this study is the myth and symbol school.[1] This focus is multipurpose. First, these critics were among the first to explicate some of the "classic" works of American literature. Second, and perhaps more importantly, their particular focus on myths and symbols — now a largely outmoded form of criticism — emerged contemporaneously to the setting of *Mad Men* in the late 1950s and early 1960s. The critics' recognition of the larger overarching mythology of America — produced and reiterated through generations of American letters, whether from the pulpit, poem, pamphlet, or penny dreadful — reveals much about the preoccupations of the postwar era, and the fixations that resurface frequently and significantly throughout the series. And as the work of many of today's critics is to deconstruct the popular analyses of the myth and symbol school, so too does *Mad Men* establish characters immediately recognizable as the progeny of archetypal traditions, only to subvert viewers' expectations by either defying or complicating their defining characteristics and, hence, the legitimacy of these icons. The decision by series creator Matthew Weiner, then, to return to this period demonstrates the resonance of these earlier concerns with issues still germane today.

Lewis' *The American Adam* theorizes a cultural mythology in which Eden reemerges from the American wilderness and that casts the colonist as its Adam. This regeneration myth preoccupies the American literary imagination by invoking such shared cultural values as rugged individualism, democracy, a Puritan work ethic, and the "get-up-and-go" spirit that invigorates generations of Americans and impels them toward progress. The Adamic myth of man's emergence from nothingness and his transition from innocence to experience is crucial for early American literature. The New World was Eden reimagined and the American male the new Adam. Casting the American in this role required a conscious rejection of the past — history, conventions, etc. — at the expense of experience. America, willfully, romantically, devoid of a history, deploys the Adam myth narrative in quest of a mythology to help mould the national character and bolster a fledgling nation against established global superpowers (which, conveniently, appear to be decaying when read in the context of a regeneration myth)—although how this narrative plays out for different authors depends upon their own internal moral positioning. Lewis argues that this Adamic myth pervades American literature:

> The American myth saw life and history as just beginning. It described the world as starting up again under fresh initiative, in a divinely granted second chance for the human race, after the first chance had been so disastrously fumbled in the darkening Old World. It introduced a new kind of hero, the heroic embodiment of a new set of ideal human attributes. America, it was said insistently from the 1820s onward, was not the end-product of a long historical process (like the Augustan Rome celebrated in the *Aeneid*); it was something entirely new [5].

This sense of America as "entirely new"—independent of history, and unlike any nation that has come before—has colored much of the nation's literature, and was certainly still present in the mid-twentieth century when American exceptionalism had not yet fully given way to more nuanced cultural perspectives. The new literary hero eventually started to undergo a transformation as the continent's true nature—a formidable and harsh expanse of unknown dangers—became known: "the isolated hero 'alone in a hostile, or at best neutral, universe' begins to replace the Adamic personality in the New World Eden" (111). He begins as an innocent, and with experience evolves into a wilderness tamer, born of and suited to the landscape he is simultaneously at odds with—and this shift is apparent along a rhetorically gendered split. He is still Adam in the sense that he is a new, self-fashioned and self-defined man uniquely adapted to this harsh environment, but there is not a suitable place for Eve in this "garden." It is a man's world—untamed, violent, antithetical to high civilization and, hence, inhospitable to genteel ladies. By necessity, the frontier hero is isolate. He might swoop in to rescue the wayward damsel in distress—he might even steal a kiss or two—but he always rides off into the sunset free of domestic entanglements.

These conceptions of the American landscape, however, are highly romanticized and problematic. Although they are consistent with the Biblical mythology, they rely heavily on Adam as an innocent, or a natural man, out of time and free from the history that had come before him. Lewis later argues in his chapter on Henry James, Sr., "The Fortunate Fall," that this state of stunted development is no paradise at all—that Adam as a perpetual innocent in Paradise is "adolescent rubbish" (58)—and that man must eventually encounter evil and fall as his passage into adulthood. Furthermore, James credits Eve for rendering this service to Adam (58), forcing his transformation from ignorance to socially responsible agent: "James looks toward a rebirth from egotism to socialized citizen. Adam's so-called 'fall' is not a loss so much as it's the uplifting of man from ignorance and complacency to the normal human level" (Lewis 60).

In *Love and Death in the American Novel*, Leslie Fiedler outlines what he believes to be the paradigmatic American narrative as that of the male hero fleeing from women and society.[2] He argues that Rip Van Winkle inaugurates this literary tradition, and that "ever since, the typical male protagonist of our fiction has been a man on the run, harried into combat — anywhere to avoid 'civilization,' which is to say, the confrontation of a man and woman which leads to the fall of sex, marriage, and responsibility" (6). Fiedler's account of the male protagonist as a "man on the run" can be seen throughout American literature — he discusses *Huck Finn, Moby Dick*, Cooper's Leatherstocking novels — and he argues that the American narrative reveals the inability or unwillingness of the male hero to accept the confines of civilization. This paradigmatic narrative points to the ongoing ambivalence displayed through American literature of the struggle between the masculine and feminine, often analogous to other binary relationships: nature/civilization, freedom/servitude, the individual/the collective, and American democracy/European aristocracy.

Richard Slotkin's *Regeneration Through Violence* argues that the American colonist had to reinvent himself as a hybrid figure in order to survive in a hostile new land. Seen as a mixture of civilization and nature (and bridging the gap), this new figure discards a corrupt aristocratic model and carries his learning and culture to a place of rebirth, but that violence is the primary means of that regeneration, however masked by rhetorics of piety and progress. Slotkin argues that the "first colonists saw in America an opportunity to regenerate their fortunes, their spirits, and the power of their church and nation" (5), but that because of (and through) the wars with the Native Americans, that "regeneration ultimately became the means of violence, and the myth of regeneration through violence became the structuring metaphor of the American experience" (5). Native Americans come to be seen as symbols of savagery, against which the new colonists could define their own sense of civilization; this in turn pushed the concept of the "frontier" to center stage, as it comes to represent, literally and figuratively, this conflict between civilization and savagery.

Out of this frontier experience emerged the self-made man, the frontier hero, and as Frederick Jackson Turner famously chronicles in his frontier thesis, "The self-made man was the Western man's ideal, was the kind of man that all men might become. Out of his wilderness experience, out of the freedom of his opportunities, he fashioned a formula for social regeneration — the freedom of the individual to seek his own" (213). Turner's 1893 speech, "The Significance of the Frontier in American History," presented at the

World's Fair in Chicago, is perhaps the most famous explication of the role of the frontier in American psychology. He argues that the frontier shaped the American character and that its "closing" marked the end of "the first period of American history" (38).[3] As he explains, "American social development has been continually beginning over again on the frontier. This perennial rebirth, this fluidity of American life, this expansion westward with its endless opportunities, its continuous touch with the simplicity of primitive society, furnish the forces dominating American character" (2–3). This is Lewis's American Adam once more, as it suggests that the landscape of the New World shapes the consciousness of its inhabitants and presents opportunities for "perennial rebirth." Although the frontier is now "closed," the idea of the West nevertheless retains this symbolic power which, in turn, continually spawns new frontiers for Americans to tame.

The Romantic Literary Genealogy of Don Draper: Natty, Huck, and Jay

All of these elements of the American mythology identified by these literary and social critics can be found encapsulated in an AMC television promotion for season three of *Mad Men* whose tagline proclaims: "This is the Wild, Wild East." In the promo, a gruff narrator intones: "In a lawless land of saloons, savages, and showdowns, one man lives by his own code." This solitary man with "his own code," of course, is Don, our lone frontier hero. The ad then cuts to a clip of Don saying, "I have a life. And it only goes in one direction: forward." While a Wild West soundtrack of whistling and trumpets accompanies, a montage of Western-themed clips from the show plays: Roger riding a woman around his office like a horse, Pete gripping his rifle, Betty on horseback, Roger telling Joan how glad he was to ride the countryside. This theme of Madison Avenue as the West is played for laughs in the ad, but it reveals the surprisingly easy and natural connection between *Mad Men* and these classic motifs of the American West, particularly Don as the frontier hero.

To assert that Don is the quintessential "frontier hero" of American literature does not mean, however, that he is merely a replica of those literary archetypes who have come before: although he shares many of their traits, he is not some amalgam of Natty, Huck, or any other frontier hero. Instead, it would seem more accurate to say that he is *conceived* by these figures, born out of and from these classic American literary archetypes and let loose into a bustling mid-twentieth-century cityscape.[4] The series hints, sometimes with a wink and sometimes with an elbow, at these classic archetypes in order to remind us of the fabric of American mythology that had clothed all previous narratives of the American experience but, at the middle of the twentieth century, were in the process of a profound and irrevocable shift.

As the quintessential frontier hero nobody better embodies the romance of the nineteenth-century American frontier than James Fenimore Cooper's Natty Bumppo. Cooper's so-called "man without a cross," free from the outdated European customs carried over to the new world, nevertheless retains the civilization of a more cultivated people, but has adapted to his new environment by appropriating some of the qualities of his "noble" savage friends and companions. He mediates both worlds and grows beyond both, viewing the native Indian on the decline and romantically lost to history and Europe as slowly decaying. America, however, was fresh and burgeoning—and he was the master of this so-called "new" world. D.H. Lawrence critiques Cooper's romantic naïveté, noting that in Bumppo's wilderness "it never rains ... it is never cold ... no one ever feels filthy, when they can't wash for a week" (60). Furthermore, Cooper's romances, *The Last of the Mohicans* (1826) in particular, deploy adventure plots that portray the American hero as knight errant, rescuing damsels in distress—a solution to the threat presented in the popular captivity narrative and gothic genres—through a sort of glorified, unreal violence that takes a back seat to Bumppo's "natural" moral integrity and chivalry. This idealized world only existed in frontier romance. In truth, the reality behind Natty Bumppo as a frontier hero means that he is "a man with a gun ... a killer, a slayer. Patient and gentle as he is, he is a slayer. Self-effacing, self-forgetting, still he is a killer" (Lawrence 59). Technically, Don might not be a "killer," but he unquestionably possesses the frontiersman's shrewdness and ruthlessness necessary for survival in an inhospitable wilderness. By the Gilded Age, the Protestant underpinnings of these traits later migrate from frontier hero to robber baron—which explains Bert Cooper's assessment that he and Don are the same type of Ayn Randian captains of industry able to make the difficult choices. Don's reinvention of himself—a metaphorical "killing" of his past—is not a simple "self-forgetting," but an active erasure of his history, an attempted regeneration of self. With James Fenimore Cooper, Lawrence notes that even the reverse narrative chronology of the Leatherstocking tales feeds the American regeneration myth: "[The Leatherstocking novels] go backwards, from old age to golden youth. That is the true myth of America. She starts old, old wrinkled and writhing in an old skin. And there is a gradual sloughing of the old skin, towards a new youth. It is the myth of America" (54). The reverse-aging process of the novels leaves us with the already Adamic Bumppo again reborn, setting off into the frontier. While Don may not have the same frontier option available, he undoubtedly attempts to engage in this "sloughing of the old skin, towards a new youth."

Like Bumppo, Huck Finn's rebirth is one born of his desire to escape civilization. When Huck initially flees down the river, he does so alone, with the sole object being (similar to Don) his escape from an abusive father. Although he ends up on a more morally courageous journey to help the runaway slave, Jim, become free, Huck's primary impulse is simply to flee; he declares at the beginning of the novel that his impetus for leaving home was a desire for change, and to escape the social suffocation he could no longer stand (Twain 748–9). Huck does not seek any particular fate, he simply does not want the one he has been dealt, and the unbridled West presents the best opportunity for a new life. Of course the levity of Huck's assertion that it was "rough living in the house all the time" belies the graver realities of Huck's life — motherless, with an alcoholic, abusive and absent father — even when he is living with the Widow Douglas. Huck may be affected by this troubled past, but if so he demonstrates a desire to look solely toward the future, and that future, for Huck, is west.

Don, however, while similarly always in the process of fleeing something — his parents, his wife, his life — has no Jim, per se, to rescue (or be rescued by), no Jim to share his experience on his existential life raft floating down the Mississippi. The scenes in the river are some of the novel's most famous: "Soon as it was night, out we shoved; when we got her out to about, the middle, we let her alone, and let her float wherever the current wanted her to; then we lit the pipes, and dangled our legs in the water and talked about all kinds of things — we was always naked, day and night, whenever the mosquitoes would let us" (831). Fiedler famously notes the homosexual overtones of Huck and Jim's relationship, particularly in moments like this one, and in an interesting way *Mad Men* deploys a more standard formulation of this dynamic to reveal its protagonist at peace: the post-coital moments with Rachel. Although superficially quite different than Jim — she is not an escaped, black, male slave — she is clearly "othered," blackened even, through her gendered and Jewish identities. Most importantly, these intimate scenes are the only moments when Don seems truly at ease, the only time when Don discusses his past with anyone; there is peace for Don in this impossible relationship, a peace he, like Huck, cannot attain through the "normal" channels presented by society.

Ultimately it is Jay Gatsby whom the series so clearly evokes through Don. The farm boy who dreams of achieving more and changes his name, an act that of self-conception that allows him to rewrite his past and enter into a world of money, women and excess that once seemed impossible: this is Don as much as it is Gatsby. Both come from nothing and, through their self-renaming, attempt to reinvent themselves: "He had changed it at the age of seventeen and at the specific moment that witnessed the beginning of his career.... It was James Gatz who had been loafing along the beach that afternoon ... but it was already Jay Gatsby who borrowed a row-boat, pulled out to the *Tuolomee* and informed Cody that a wind might catch him and break him up in half an hour" (104). James Gatz is another Midwestern country boy, but Jay Gatsby can be anything, or everything, or nothing; his new name wipes clean the slate of his past and allows Gatz/Gatsby to become whatever he desires: "the truth was that Jay Gatsby, of West Egg, Long Island, sprang from his Platonic conception of himself" (104). Gatsby's reinvention of himself is often contrasted to Daisy and Tom's old money, and we experience this revulsion even through Nick Carraway, the narrator, who regards Gatsby's self-made opulence as somehow grotesque. In fact, Don's given name, "Dick," invokes Horatio Alger's *Ragged Dick*, and comments on the discrepancy between America's romance with the self-made man — Alger's "rags to riches" mythology, steeped in Protestantism and essentialized American vigor — and the coarse reality of a nation that still fetishizes old money. This, at least, seems unchanged by the time we arrive at Don's character some thirty years later, as he is interrogated by Roger about whether or not he had a nanny ("Ladies Room" 1:2) and questioned by Betty about his family background.

Gatsby's origins are similar to Don's, but his "conception of himself" is more premeditated. Gatsby's path to success and reinvention begins as a child and is realized the moment he swims out to Cody's yacht and renames himself. Don's decision to abandon his identity is less clear, as all viewers see is him, lying wounded, exchanging dog tags with the dead lieutenant Draper. Other than his half-brother, Adam, his "family" — both of his biological parents are dead — does not seem to particularly care what happens to Don, so why bother with the renaming at all beyond a scheme for an early discharge? As Lewis articulates, it allows for a "starting up again under fresh initiative," a rebirth not possible if one still labors under one's old name. Don explains to the owner of Caldecott Farms, the dog food company that is losing sales because it is made — unsurprisingly — from horse meat that they must change the company name because it has been tainted. Don says that it will not be easy but a new name will represent a quality product ("The Gypsy and the Hobo" 3:11). Don is ever cognizant of the power of names, and renaming, be it of a dog food or a man, is a way of returning once more to the Adamic state. But despite the fact that the product inside the can remains the same, the external reforging is in a way an internal rebirth, a way of allowing both Jay and Don — and Caldecott Farm's dog food — to re-see themselves and their potential; with a new name, Don is no longer the scared private cowering in a trench, but a confident and dashing Purple Heart recipient with a whole world suddenly open before him.

While these narratives offer the promise of a fresh start, they also indicate a pattern of innocence or naïveté. James Fenimore Cooper conjures a world of unreality. Huck grapples with a moral dilemma, deciding that he would rather go to Hell for *not* returning the fugitive slave, Jim, to his master, than to do the so-called "right" thing by returning stolen property. Although he breaks society's rules, his logic indicates that, in the end, he still functions mentally within Society despite his efforts to move beyond it. An inexperienced James Gatz, likewise, "invented just the sort of Jay Gatsby that a 17-year-old boy would be likely to invent, and to this conception he was faithful to the end" (104). As Lewis and Henry James, Sr., would argue, this sort of innocence is precisely the state that precludes one's passage into adulthood. This is "paradise" simply because the subject's perception of this world is yet unaware that it is not of his own making — this world and everything in it operates within a paternal model, even if Adam does get to name all the animals himself. One need reject this model and leave the safety of the garden in order to truly begin anew.

The Gatsby model still works particularly well as a template for Don Draper since he has not yet recognized that in his alter ego there is no rebirth at all. Don Draper is merely another player on the same social stage, however different from his old life. Like Gatsby and William Faulkner's Thomas Sutpen in *Absalom, Absalom!*, becoming Don Draper is actually a backward move toward over-socialization. Contrary to the myth of westward progress and freedom, in their reinvention Gatsby, Sutpen and Don all travel *eastward* toward the immensely more rigid civilization of upper crust society. These learned standards of dress and decorum are antithetical to the "natural" man narrative central to American mythology. Gatsby and Sutpen attempt to recreate themselves as lords in a European feudal model — Gatsby by living in a lord's manor, whose original owner wanted to thatch neighboring houses into serfs' cottages; Sutpen by invoking through his God-like "Be" an agrarian plantation society with his mansion at its center. Indeed, rather than rejecting society, all three fully immerse themselves in it, and even attempt to master it; they try to "sivilize" themselves, a process which destroys Gatsby and Sutpen, and, at the very least, pushes Don to the brink of ruin.

Dick, Don, and the Two Whitmans

Like Gatsby, Don reinvents himself through a renaming process. Don Draper, of course, is not *really* Don Draper; he is Dick Whitman before his reinvention as Don Draper. But unlike Gatsby, Don's original namesake hardly seems accidental. That it would be America's most famous poet, Walt Whitman — whose *Leaves of Grass* sets forth as its task the creation and articulation of a new America and a new type of American, a new American Adam — is, if nothing else, highly fortuitous. "The fullest portrayal of the new world's representative man as a new, American Adam was given by Walt Whitman in *Leaves of Grass*— in the liberated, innocent, solitary, forward-thrusting personality that animates the whole of that long poem" (Lewis 28). As noted before, Don is, in many ways, this "liberated, innocent, solitary, forward-thrusting personality," but he also reveals the darker, more complex side of the American identity that, although Lewis ignores it, is part of the celebration of America that Whitman articulates in his poem.[5] However, this new Adam that Whitman conceives of in *Leaves of Grass* is more complex than simply "liberated" or "innocent." He is the guiltless Adam, but he is still cast off from his Eden.

Part of Whitman's task in *Leaves of Grass*— *Children of Adam* in particular — is this articulation of a new American, a type that Don represents, and crucial to the success of this American and his nation is a new national literature. In *Democratic Vistas* Whitman most clearly articulates this conception of an American literature. In this essay Whitman focuses on the future of American democracy and the future of American literature, which, he argues, are essentially intertwined: "above all previous lands, a great original literature is surely to become the justification and reliance (in some respects the sole reliance of American democracy)" (458). He proceeds to argue that in order for democracy to succeed, it needs a great literature that can produce great citizens, as "the literature, songs, aesthetics, etc., of a country are of importance principally because they furnish the materials and suggestions of personality for the women and men of that country, and enforce them in a thousand effective ways" (476). While Whitman already has faith in the masses, it is through a national literature that they will come together into a single collective and thus help achieve democracy's purpose.

In many ways, Don's profession as an ad man would seem to be the inverse of the poet Whitman's when, in fact, it shares similarities. Advertising produces desire and, like literature, it deploys a narrative to sell *affect*— which then creates a consumer market. As his name suggests, Don *is* a "draper"—a peddler, a clothier — and he drapes the American social corpus. Don peddles the types of fine wares — limbs, hairpieces, and voice boxes — as found in Poe's "The Man That Was Used Up," and just as Brevet Brigadier General John A.B.C. Smith "dons" these consumer products to suggest the illusion of a cohesive body politic, Don Draper sells Americana to a public hungry for security and prosperity. Don produces culture, and then convinces the masses that his illusion is based on reality when, actually, it is all just something imagined to sell things ("Smoke Gets in Your Eyes" 1:1). Advertising is, notoriously, an industry which produces nothing tangible: "the advertisement is unique among artworks in that its cardinal premise is falsehood, deceit, its purpose being to conceal the connection between labor and its product in order to persuade consumers to purchase *this* brand" (Trachtenberg 138). Advertising exists to persuade consumers to buy what they do not need; after all, if they really needed it, they would not need a fancy advertising campaign to convince them of that fact. Perhaps this is why all of the copy writers at Sterling Cooper dream of becoming successful creative writers, as evidenced by their jealousy over Ken Cosgrove's publication of his short story — the absurdly over-titled "Tapping a Maple on a Cold Vermont Morning" — in the *Atlantic Monthly* (Pete's own story about a talking bear, however, can only find an audience in *Boys' Life Magazine*, and that only through the machinations of his wife), and despite being part of the "Creative" department they find their profession artistically unfulfilling, albeit effective. Just as Don exploits love to sell hosiery, society uses the infinitely more romantic regeneration myth and manifest destiny to sell capitalistic imperialism — it just sounds nicer. This sentiment of manifest destiny through advertising is never articulated more clearly than when Conrad Hilton expresses his vision for international expansion. He says that by sending America around the world his business will have a positive impact, "Because we have God" ("Wee Small Hours" 3:9). Advertising serves the needs of the cultural imperialism that gives the consumer permission to go after the thing they wanted all along, be it nylons or Northern Mexico.

And yet, despite its overwhelming crassness, strangely, ironically, even absurdly, advertising *is* this fulfillment of an American literature that Whitman prophesied. Advertising does cohere the masses into a single entity — the American consumer — and it moves the masses and articulates their desires unlike any other national literature. Maybe advertising does not invent "want," maybe America already wants, hungers to appease some vague, shapeless, unnamable phantom desire — a "dumb blankness, full of meaning" that remains elusively unidentifiable, but that exposes a terrifying void that no amount of empty consumerism can fill. Advertising simply exploits this fear and longing, and suggests the next product to purchase that promises to deliver "a little more happiness" or at least to occupy one's pursuit of that happiness. Don, then, as both a "Whitman" and a successful ad man, creates a new type of American poetry — advertising — that captures the spirit and energy of, if not democracy, its driving force: capitalism. Like James Gatz conceiving Jay Gatsby, like Whitman giving birth to the New American, like Adam naming the beasts of Eden, Don is the progenitor of both himself and a new mythology — all perceived acts of self-creation. Don invents a new identity for himself, but he also creates — through advertising — an American mythology of nostalgia (perhaps best represented by his presentation of the

Kodak Carousel in "The Wheel" 1:13), the yellow spectacles that help to hue his historical mid-twentieth-century "Valley of Ashes" into an Eden. Inventing nostalgia for the past, even if it means believing in a "paradise" that never truly existed, at least creates hope that happiness *has* existed, and could exist again. Buying the newest gadget — 1960s deodorant in an aerosol can — allows the consumer to hold progress in the palm of his hand. This is the proof of continued American ingenuity, the assurance that the pursuit of happiness is far less daunting than Whitman's "A Noiseless Patient Spider" would indicate: a lonesome spider launching filament after filament into a vast void, in hopes that one "gossamer thread" might catch somewhere.

Victorian-Era Standards of Femininity

In the introduction to this essay we left Don on the shores of the continent, contemplating yet another rebirth, this time in Palm Springs with his Euro "jet set." But, of course, he *does* return. After visiting again the *real* Mrs. Draper, Don walks shirtless into the Pacific Ocean, having reached the farthest point possible in his westward journey — the tableau moment of Whitman's "Facing West from California's Shores," after millennia of human history has circled upon itself and, upon reflection, is still dissatisfied, having secured no meaningful answers to the questions that prompted its initial quest: "Now I face home again, very pleased and joyous / (But where is what I started for so long ago? / And why is it yet unfound?)" (83). This time, Don's attempt at rebirth does not end in a renaming or regeneration; it ends with his return to his family and his continued dreams of escape. It ends with the failure of the most pervasive narrative of American literature: Adam before the fall.

Don's return to his family is not surprising. As Slotkin argues, the frontier hero is a hybrid figure, a cross between high European civilization and Native American Indian know-how that allowed the colonists to evolve, to negotiate between old and new worlds without devolving to a state of so-called "savagery." Although the frontier hero moves between these two worlds, he belongs fully to neither. If the wild unknown represents rebirth and boundless opportunity, the domestic home is the opposite pole: the locus of civilization in all its constructedness, and the site of *replication*, not rebirth. This constant struggle between masculine newness and feminine replication plays out, yet again, in the naming of baby Gene after Betty's recently deceased father. In response to Don's objection, Betty snarls that this is something people do to keep hold of their memories. Later, after a frightened Sally recognizes the uncanny reemergence of Grandpa Gene through her new baby brother, Don reassures her that Gene is just a baby ... one whose identity has yet to be formed ("Guy Walks Into an Advertising Agency" 3:6).

The "marriage" of femininity to civilization is present in American frontier mythology as early as John Filson's Daniel Boone narrative, "Kentucke," which is as much speculator's propaganda as American hero myth. The relocation of Boone's wife and children to Kentucky is a symbolic gesture indicating that the "howling wilderness" of Kentucky has been tamed, and is now fit for habitation by civilized people. In large part the romance enshrouding the frontier hero exists precisely because he is a poignant loner: isolated, unfit for either world and therefore, not a suitable mate for a "lady" or the civilization she represents. Don, in this respect, represents the domesticated frontier hero. In his attempt to recreate himself as Don Draper, he inadvertently replicates a man within the very social system he'd hoped to rebuke. The frontier hero as we know him was never meant to be tied down with a wife and kids; as Fiedler notes, "the typical male protagonist of our fiction has been a man on the run, harried into combat — anywhere to avoid 'civilization,' which is to say, the confrontation of a man and woman which leads to the fall of sex, marriage, and responsibility" (6). Don runs from "sivilization" like the frontier hero, but he also represents Adam — a complex dual identity that incompatibly demands both an escape from "sivilization" and responsibility *and* the supreme responsibility of founding that "sivilization."

But if Don is our Adam — reluctantly thrust into the role of mythological hero, and the inheritor of a national literary tradition that ambivalently espouses and questions American exceptionalism, regeneration, and progress — who is his Eve? Assuming the Garden of Eden metaphor is expected to play out in American mythology, readers must recall that Eve was the first to raise doubts about whether the garden really was a "paradise" or instead a confinement disguised as a bower. While set in the 1960s and reflective of early twenty-first-century American society, in literary terms *Mad Men* harkens back to not only the classic literary masculine archetypes but also feminine models prevalent at the height of Victorian culture and that also resurge in post–World War II America. The late nineteenth century exaggerated gender roles to extremes, spawning a cast of female types: the angel in the house, the fallen woman, the madwoman, and the New Woman. Early episodes of *Mad Men* introduce characters representative of these exemplars, only to gradually reveal to both the viewers and to the characters themselves that they are, in fact, composites struggling in the wake of a stringent ideal to reconcile their competing personal desires with the largely incompatible roles into which they are compartmentalized.

The same strained ambivalence so obvious in Don's character is equally, if not more so, visible in the female characters that have fewer socially sanctioned opportunities for fulfillment. Indeed, *Mad Men's* scope is not limited to dissecting solely the masculine American archetype: behind every dissatisfied man trying to reinvent himself is an equally dissatisfied woman trying to buy "more happiness" by partaking of a consumerist panacea. In particular, Betty Draper initially represents the residual Victorian standard of femininity, "The Angel in the House" as depicted by Coventry Patmore, and as it reemerged after World War II — a nostalgic return to so-called "family values" and traditional gender assignments:

> She loves with love that cannot tire;
> And when, ah woe, she loves alone,
> Through passionate duty love springs higher,
> As grass grows taller round a stone [53].

This is an idealized image that Patmore presents in canto IX, "The Wife's Tragedy," of domesticated womanhood in which she — wife, mother, daughter — is self-sacrificing, nurturing, virtuous, chaste, and meek to the point of martyring herself in order to bolster the lives of those she loves, meanwhile yielding to a "feminine mystique" that compounds her dissatisfaction with guilt and feelings of inadequacy.[6] Episode one, "Smoke Gets in Your Eyes," immediately introduces viewers to the women (plural) in Don's life, juxtaposing Betty as the model suburban wife and mother with counterpart Midge Daniels, the first in a series of mistresses, as well as a bevy of Sterling Cooper secretaries, most with marital ambitions as pointed as their brassieres.

If the angel in the house embodies the qualities of idealized femininity, her foil is any other woman that falls beyond this rigid ideal, and these categories generally bleed into each other as they encompass all women who demonstrate "unnatural" or "depraved" behavior. Such are the women of *Mad Men*. Medically speaking, the notorious Victorian "madwoman" is an umbrella figure that runs the gamut from the psychotic murderess to the stifled woman with a nervous cough. She is Betty Draper with her numb hands, or Betty's gal-pal, Francine, who fantasizes postpartum about poisoning herself and her family as vindication for her husband's presumed infidelity. In the nineteenth century she is most commonly the "hysterical" woman, like Peggy Olson protecting her respectability by mentally repressing her full-term pregnancy with a complete psychotic break. Pedestrian rhetoric, however, is apt loosely to brand any woman who deviates from the norm as "mad." Madness, therefore, is a label that envelopes any woman who moves beyond that realm of femininity that is familiar and, thus, viewed as "natural." Just how "natural" this learned femininity is, however, is extremely suspect, as argued famously by John Stuart Mill in *The Subjection of Women*: "What is now called the nature of women is an eminently artificial thing — the result of forced repression in some directions, unnatural stimulation in others" (138). Mill argues that women's (and presumably men's) nature can not truly be known since it is manipulated and distorted from infancy into becoming the socialized, gendered creature we recognize, yet the product is so pervasive that we attribute the result to God's design instead of our own making. "Unnatural" or "monstrous" women, on the other hand, include those who are not angels. These madwomen execute revenge plots; they scream their tightly-contained discontent through hysterical symptoms; they brazenly defy social expectations by behaving in an aggressive, manly way; they are sexually promiscuous or, worse yet, have unapologetically voracious sexual appetites and, as Madonnas and whores are binary opposites, so too is the chaste angel whose virtue is heralded in contrast to her counterpart, the fallen angel.[7]

The fallen woman is a familiar warning to the Victorian reader, but the plight of this figure is much farther reaching. Peggy, for example, is merely another in a long literary tradition of fallen women. British letters alone gave rise to infamous eighteenth- and nineteenth-century examples of fallenness: Clarissa, Moll Flanders, Lady Dedlock, Tess Durbeyfield, Ruth, Esther Waters, and the Lady of Shalott (to name just a few). The fallen woman is also the frequent subject of pictorial representations, The Lady of Shalott in particular by Pre–Rahpaelite artists, as well as other mediums such as William Hogarth's popular eighteenth-century *Before* and *After* plates.[8] Beyond England, European authors contribute Emma Bovary, Anna Karenina, and Hedda Gabler. Given our shared literary heritage, America also demonstrates a clear preoccupation with women's virtue and the fallen woman. Notable non-racialized American examples of the fallen woman include Charlotte Temple, Hester Prynne, Crane's Maggie, Ellen Olenska, Edna Pontelier, Carrie Meeber and Jennie Gerhardt, Daisy Miller, and Lena Grove.[9] As the aforementioned cast of characters indicates, fallen women narratives come in a variety of plots including the seduction plot, the extramarital affair, the destitute prostitute, the sexually liberated woman, and, at the opposite extreme, the innocent girl who technically remains "intact," but who is nevertheless the victim of social innuendo to the point that her social respectability is irretrievably compromised. Consequently, most of the women of *Mad Men* are "fallen" if held to a Victorian standard, and, if not, are at least sexually loose if held to the acknowledged sexual standard of their day.

Women's virtue is often assigned the responsibility of being the glue that keeps families and cultures intact. Even if women in 1960 are on the brink of sexual revolution, remnant feelings about female respectability — being the type of girl you marry rather than the type of girl you "date" — nevertheless linger, and this tightrope walk is evident in the struggles of *Mad Men*'s women. Chastity ensures legitimate familial ties, and safeguards the proper transmission of property. While a husband's extramarital dalliances might result in a socially illegitimate (and easily ignored) bastard, a wife's infidelity imperils the entire family structure by potentially injecting a foreign male presence into the sanctity of the home, and adulterating the male bloodline; indeed, viewers are left to speculate whether Don is the biological father of their third child. With baby Gene's paternity already in question, Betty welcomes yet another foreign male presence into the Draper home through the introduction of her Victorian fainting couch as the centerpiece of the home's "hearth"—a couch that viewers recognize as the surrogate for Henry Francis, and where Betty's restless hands often wander—("Seven Twenty Three" 3:7).

Interestingly, when these images metaphorically depict the fragility of domestic harmony—as implied through subtle icons like the house of cards—this usually implies that the responsibility lies with the woman since it is her indiscretion alone that will tear the family asunder. In the Drapers' case, the threat is twofold, and not because both parties are unfaithful: aside from Betty's infidelity, the second threat is that Betty might not take Don back which, again, would result in the collapse of the family structure. This scenario, in fact, plays out at the end of Season Three when Betty blames Don for ruining everything ("The Grown-Ups" 3:12). Don, as usual, deflects responsibility, recognizing only that it is Betty who seeks to "break up" the family when she hires a divorce attorney ("Shut the Door. Sit Down." 3:13)—a last-ditch attempt to displace the final blame on her.

Finally, another often scoffed at figure of the nineteenth century is the New Woman—the product of first-wave feminism—that epitomizes the "unnatural" woman bent on infiltrating previously male-only territory and subverting normalized gender roles. Elaine Showalter writes in *Sexual Anarchy* that "the New Woman, university-educated and sexually independent, engendered intense hostility and fear as she seemed to challenge male supremacy in art, the professions, and the home.... Politically, the New Woman was an anarchic figure who threatened to turn the world upside down and to be on top in a wild carnival of social and sexual misrule" (38).[10] This figure is particularly interesting in that she is an amalgam of these "anti-angel" types. Beyond her possible sexual impropriety, her revolutionary political views are often touted as mania. This madness is not all together unfounded given the frequency with which New Women suffered from nervous conditions, which one might imagine are the result of social ostracism, frustration, and repeatedly thwarted aspirations.[11] With the exception of the angel in the house—who clings to her position by dint of her tenuous purity (or the illusion of it)—these other figures are relegated to the fringes of society if not all together disenfranchised. These women are, in a sense, defective, and do not embody the good breeding or inviolate moral integrity of the representative woman suitable for marriage, and whose social purpose is to transmit these qualities to the next generation. In this sense, "ladies" represent culture in its most constructed form. They are purposefully cloistered from the evil effects of the world, and the result is a silly, empty-headed creature obsessed with tradition, petty intrigues, and Tupperware.

Unlearning Gender Roles in *Mad Men*

Betty Draper followed society's rules; she won her prize, yet she is stifled and anxious, and suffers hysterical symptoms, which she vents in dark outbursts such as shooting the neighbor's carrier pigeons with a pellet gun — looking like Clint Eastwood with bloodshot eyes and a cigarette hanging from her lips — or creating mischief amongst the neighborhood wives. Betty recognizes, as so many Victorian paintings metaphorically depict, that the Drapers' domestic bliss is like a house of cards, tenably built on a shaky foundation, and that the livelihood of her entire family is vulnerable to a number of outside forces which she, in her position, is powerless to stop. Her only recourse is to follow the advice of her recently deceased mother that she is painting her masterpiece — "make sure to hide the brushstrokes" ("Red in the Face" 1:7). Betty continues to build her family nest inside a gilded cage — the caged bird being another popular, yet appropriate, nineteenth-century image. Betty (or "Birdie," as Don affectionately calls her) is discontent because of her helpless confinement, but also because Don cannot fully understand or anticipate her needs. Nor can he singlehandedly fill the voids in her life as she has been taught to expect of him. She is naturally enraged to discover his infidelity. She, after all, plays the dutiful housewife, and relies on Don to play the protector, not the *threat*, to the family. Meanwhile, she is largely unaware of the extent to which Don's actions actually do threaten her family: they live under an assumed family name; at one point Don offers to abandon his family for yet another fresh start, this time with Rachel; and, of course, Don flees to the "frontier" (Palm Springs) and, if only momentarily, considers never returning. He then skulks home after each indiscretion and, depending on the episode, either Betty is none the wiser or she willfully turns a blind eye in order to preserve her home life.

Don and Betty share a roof, but they lead separate lives, all the while wavering between mutual affection and resentment for not being able to complete the other. Each playing their part, Betty showers Don with care, and Don returns the favor with material wealth. He cannot understand Betty's unhappiness, always expecting that her simple mind will be appeased by bobbles and trinkets. At one point, when discussing the doctor's recommendation that Betty undergo psychotherapy, Don says, with conviction, that therapy is only for unhappy people ("Ladies Room" 1:2) — he cannot fathom that Betty might be unhappy. Don's material overtures, however, only temporarily mollify her constant concerns that their house of cards will eventually come tumbling down. Viewers recognize that Betty's hysterical symptoms are triggered by signifiers of female helplessness or domestic turbulence, such as the sight of Helen Bishop, a divorced mother of two, and the first to introduce divorce into the Drapers' homogenous suburban neighborhood. But just as Betty's needs are far more complicated than Don is able to recognize, so, too, are Don's needs. Betty fits his feminine ideal — the type of girl you marry — but in his mind, she is a wife, not a partner, hence, his continual attraction to complicated, independent and powerful women such as Midge Daniels, Rachel Menken, and Bobbie Barrett.

Compared to Betty, Midge appears to have none of the trappings of the middle class: the house in the suburbs, the social legitimacy sanctified by a wedding license, children, or wealth. She lives a modest bohemian lifestyle, writing greeting cards, accepting gifts from her lovers, and enjoying the freedoms that bourgeois respectability cannot offer. She more closely resembles the turn-of-the-century New Woman who lives on the fringe of society by defying traditional gender roles: she is happily unmarried, works outside of the home (or in her case, Greenwich Village studio apartment), and revels in her independence and sexual freedom. Taken to its extreme, however, Midge's fashionable counterculture lifestyle precludes the possibility of love and marriage as a bourgeois standard to be scorned. When last we see Midge, Don discovers — simply by reading the body language in a candid snapshot — that she actually is in love with another man, the beatnik Roy Hazelitt, but that the two bohemians are either too cynical or sophisticated to admit to such cliché emotions. Don, on the other hand, whose lips typically drip with nihilist sentiment, leaves Midge's apartment never to return, indicating an unwillingness to interfere with a young couple in love, and leaving the young pair to figure out how to cope with genuine affection inconsistent with their shared ideology — the result of a socialization process equal to, however contrary to, Don and Betty's middle class respectability. Likewise, Betty and Don grapple with the same complication of, first, locating, and second, reconciling their unfiltered selves with the social roles they have accepted — which viewers recognize as an impossibility since their entire marriage is built upon a lie.

Betty is clearly our complicated angel figure, (until Season Two) chaste and trusting. The remaining female characters are equally torn. They struggle because they are taught to want the type of domestic "bliss" Betty Draper enjoys, but they are no longer quite sure of how to achieve it. Joan, for example, is the clear equal (if not superior) to her husband in intellect, capability, and potency. Whereas his surgeon's hands have "no brains," hers save the life of visiting Londoner Guy MacKendrick — a symbol of "slight [corporate] reorganization," or the backward movement toward European dominion over America — who is gruesomely stampeded by a John Deere "iron horse"; a problem solved in true Slotkinian style ("Guy Walks Into an Advertising Agency" 3:6). Joan, nevertheless, must pin her ambitions to the future success of her husband. Socioeconomic need during World War II prompted abrupt changes in the workplace, but gender ideology still lagged years behind. On the postwar home front, these figures had to navigate through a social minefield where women increasingly worked (at least until they caught a husband), earned their own money, and experienced independence, yet this same world still touted one feminine ideal while issuing contrary sexual pressures. This created a conundrum for both sexes, as is evidenced in *Mad Men*. For example, Don seems to like and respect women, but he has a harder time taking "ladies" seriously, and this double standard places a great strain on his marriage. The series portrays Betty as a sexually-charged figure, but this appears inconsistent with Don's notions of what a wife ought to be, so he satisfies his lust for exciting sex elsewhere, without sullying his pristine wife. We also see this shifting attitude toward sex play out in scenes between Joan, a volcano of feminine sensuality, and Peggy, who hides her budding sexuality behind a girlish façade, although neither is taken seriously by the men at Sterling Cooper. Joan espouses that there is no money in virginity. Peggy counters that people say that Joan is searching for a husband and is fun, but not necessarily in that order ("Shoot" 1:9). One view demonstrates an outdated emphasis on chastity, while the other shows that certain judgments nevertheless linger, and neither woman is sure exactly what combination of sex and prudence is appropriate in this shifting world. Likewise, the men in Joan and Peggy's lives also struggle to know how to treat them. Joan's (then) fiancé is simultaneously drawn to and put off by her sexual confidence, signs which he misreads and later returns by raping her in Don's office ("The Mountain King" 2:12). Pete is equally confused about how to categorize Peggy. On the one hand, he clearly sexualizes her, having bedded her at least twice; on the other hand, his facial expressions register contempt each time she behaves flirtatiously or provocatively through dress or behavior. This gender confusion is a sign that the socially constructed categories — reflected in eighteenth- and nineteenth-century literature — that perhaps worked at one point are no longer appropriate in this changing world, and that all attempts to cling to these outdated modes — however familiar and safe they may appear — are futile and, in the end, will only create more confusion and heartbreak. Although most of the women in the series clearly do not abide by this standard (as many women of the period probably did not, either, despite protestations to the contrary) the need to uphold a respectable image persists.

In the first episode of the series, Don innocently says to Midge that he cannot decide if she has "everything, or nothing." This single unassuming statement is pregnant with the struggle Don will face for the remainder of the series. Indeed, he must decide which woman truly has "everything" or "nothing"—Betty or Midge? Is it the woman who bears the conventional markers of affluence and respectability but who is so suffocated by outmoded tradition that she ends up in psychotherapy, has a marriage on the rocks, and hears her dead mother's voice instructing her to keep up appearances? Is it the anti-establishment woman who thinks she is free from these trappings but finds herself so over-socialized in the opposite extreme that she is in a self-imposed prison of her own making, both inadmissible by "good" society and self-isolated because of her fear of appearing at all influenced by bourgeois convention? One appears to be a complete acceptance of the status quo and the other a complete rejection, and Don has to decide which of these models offers the greatest promise of happiness. Having already left Dick Whitman behind, he must now choose whether or not to value or devalue the world he has fashioned for himself as "Don Draper." But this is Don's stumbling block. He mistakenly reads Midge's life as a form of freedom instead recognizing it for what it is—another prison created within the same social framework. He sees her as outside of the system when, in fact, she is still very much caught up in it; her worldview is simply an offshoot built in opposition to—but still steeped in—the original premise. Likewise, when he reinvents himself as Don Draper, he recasts himself in a new role within the same social system he sought to escape, and then he cannot figure out why he is so dissatisfied with what he imagined to be a new life.

The characters of *Mad Men* are in the midst of their "fortunate fall" as they are tempted to leave the safety of "Eden"—in these cases, socially written scripts and schemas, whether bourgeois or bohemian—to embark on a terrifying errand of self-discovery. The series, in this sense, becomes every man's quest to reject the rules of society that no longer work, and to turn his back on empty consumerism in search of something far less mediated and infinitely more fulfilling. *Mad Men* provides the familiar bildungsroman narrative, but rather than integrating oneself into society, man unlearns his early socialization as his passage into adulthood. Rather than trying to figure out how much of a "Madonna" or "whore" each woman needs to be, the women of *Mad Men* must recognize that ascribing to these labels perpetuates this world, and that they must reject these judgments all together. Bobbie Barrett tells Peggy that there is power in being a woman ("The New Girl" 2:5). In one sense she liberates Peggy from feeling that she must contain her femininity in order to wield authority, but she also teaches Peggy to trade one gendered performance for another that is equally artificial, however more palatable. A masculine

Peggy does not work; the office boys' club will not accept her on those terms. The sex-kitten guise grants Peggy entry on other terms, but she is clearly uncomfortable playing that role. Likewise, domesticated Don is too constricted of a role; meanwhile, frontier Don is asked to sacrifice far too much for his freedom. Tensions continue to build. As the characters grow increasingly dissatisfied with their limited roles and become aware that these conceptual restrictions create their dissatisfaction, they ultimately will have to reject these limitations and question the rationale that informed these ideologies in the first place. This revolutionary shift is a step toward regeneration and away from replication. This is the Adam myth at the point of the fall where Adam grows up, where he leaves the safety of those paternal teachings that do not allow him to question the world, and where he must learn to create the world on his own according to his own needs. Like Adam and Eve exiled from Eden, each couple — Don and Betty, Pete and Peggy — must leave the thoughtless "Paradise" of prewritten gender roles and rewrite their relationships to one another on more equal terms. They must become in their daily lives the easy Don and Betty in Rome — a momentary reprieve from their social scripts that ultimately, and significantly, erupts in Betty's greater discontentment upon their return home — the first time that Betty voices her unhappiness to Don ("Souvenir" 3:8). Until now, she has been all sugar and spice, repression, hysteria, and passive-aggression. Although Don reassures her with the promise that they will go away again, the souvenir charm is the physical reminder — the threat, even — that the pattern of their life together is already formed, and that she might add another charm here and there, but that their trajectory shows very little promise of changing.

The Call of the Wild: Pete Campbell

Don Draper and the women of *Mad Men* are not the only "mad man" or "man women" whose characters are informed by these literary archetypes. Pete Campbell is, in many ways, the counterpoint to Don's self-made man: he is a man *with* a name ("New Amsterdam" 1:4) and a prestigious family (Pete's mother's family, the Dyckmans, owned everything north of 125th). There are indications throughout the first season that many of Don's actions are motivated by a petty, jealous desire to humble Pete — Roger, after Don decides to turn down Jim Hobart's offer to work at McCann Erickson, asks Don whether or not he is staying just to keep Pete in his place, and later Don's promotion of Peggy is maneuvered primarily to embarrass Pete after he lands (through nepotism, of course) the Clearasil account. This is the revenge of the self-made man against the privileged man ("Nixon vs. Kennedy" 1:12), and it is the same conflict that plays out nationally in the Kennedy vs. Nixon campaign.[12] The final moment of conflict arrives when Pete threatens to expose Don's past to Cooper; it is a conflict that, as Pete describes it, is akin to a gun battle. Don, of course, wins this particular "shootout"—he is, after all, our frontier hero — and yet nothing changes; Pete seems barely able to recognize his defeat.

Nevertheless, despite being the anti–Don — although he has the pedigree that Don does not have, he lacks Don's winning looks, easy charm, and creative ability — he similarly rebels against the standards of society being forced upon him, particularly the domesticity that his marriage to Trudy demands. In Pete's character are echoes of George Babbitt, the eponymous protagonist of Sinclair Lewis's satirical 1922 novel. Like Babbitt, Pete is the paradigm of conformity, joining in the back-slapping and male-camaraderie that should allow him entry into the all-male fraternity he desires, and yet he is nagged by an unhappiness that he does not even want to admit to himself. He, like the mass of men, leads a life of "quiet desperation." Both are pathetic characters, but we also end up sympathizing with them because we can witness them realize their true situation and also their inability, unlike previous American archetypes, to escape.

Unlike the Nattys, Hucks, Gatsbys, or Dons, the Babbitts and Petes cannot simply run from their lives of conformity and build anew. Instead, their rebellions are quieter, and ultimately, then, less rewarding. As Babbitt says, "I'd like to beat it off to the woods right now. And loaf all day.... and play poker, and cuss as much as I feel like, and drink a hundred and nine-thousand bottles of beer" (31), or again, later: "Wish I'd been a pioneer, same as my grand-dad. But then, wouldn't have a house like this. I — Oh gosh, *I don't know!*" (75). Pete's rebellions are similarly trivial, as when he returns the Chip 'n' Dip from his wedding and gets a .22-caliber rifle; later, after sighting secretaries through the scope, he asks Peggy if she has ever been hunting. Pete proceeds to tell Peggy his hunting fantasy, which, after he kills his prey, includes carrying it over his shoulders and using his hunting knife to cut off a piece of meat that a silent woman would then dutifully cook for him. Peggy, clearly reading this sexual hunting fantasy as one that links masculinity to domination, responds that it would be great ("Red in the Face" 1:7). Present in this conflation of hunting and sexuality lies the implication that masculinity is a product of frontier violence: to be masculine one must be the aggressive hunter, untamed, who responds only to the base needs of man and is not, therefore, to be restrained by the restrictions of domesticity. Trudy, of course, calls his gun — and by implication his frontier dream — a toy and demands him to return it, but it marks an important kind of rebellion for Pete. Like the true frontier heroes, there is clearly a recognition that the wilderness of cussing, poker, pioneers, and .22s is *the* path to escape domesticity. Babbitt and Pete both recognize that the frontier is their only hope to reinvigorate themselves, but the modern world that they live in — and that Don somehow is able to transcend — no longer allows this possibility; there is present in Pete the realization that these old narratives are becoming obsolete, and that new narrative possibilities must be formed for each moment in history.

There is, too, a way in which these possibilities are reflected even in the faces of Don and Pete. Don, with his "chiseled" jaw and manly physique, embodies the robust virility of the eighteenth- and nineteenth-century natural man; he is, unequivocally, male. Compared with Pete's delicate features, Don's face seems to be carved from stone. Pete is like the absurdly effeminate dandified man whose over-cultivation either causes him to lose his vigor, or prevents it from properly developing, representative of a high aristocracy on the decline. Pete's face has the softness of a child; it seems unformed and imprecise, an amorphous mass of chubby cheeks still waiting to take shape precisely because it has never been allowed to follow its own natural course of development. Stunted from the onset, Pete is, in many ways, still a child; we see this clearly as he sits on his couch, in a kid's pajamas, sifting through pictures of Don as a child on the farm ("Nixon vs. Kennedy" 1:12), and he is even further infantilized by Trudy's belief that he is looking at pornography when, in fact, he is merely looking at photos of his boss. But this interpretation of Don as über-masculine and Pete as the stunted child is not meant to simply expose Pete as infantile; in his still-forming face, his embryonic character is, in fact, an opportunity that is *not* present in Don. Ironically, unlike Don, Pete *can* still become anything because he is not yet formed, and this shapelessness is, strangely, a virtue because his identity and his future still linger undecided. One is left to wonder which of these two men is best equipped to survive in this cityscape. Until the mythology fails, Don, already formed despite his efforts at self-reinvention, will ultimately have to ride off into the sunset and occupy the liminal territory for which he is best suited. Pete, on the other hand, only partially formed can still light out on a modified path, and imagine new ways to invigorate his familiar way of life. Whereas Don — the romantic hero — is more likely to run away and start up again, Pete — the pragmatic neo-imperialist — will identify new micro niche markets to conquer. Pete will sit in his office on a hot summer afternoon reading *Ebony Magazine* ("Souvenir" 3:8), and thumb his nose at the unsavory prospect of branding Sterling Cooper a negro agency so long as there's a buck to be made. Metaphorically speaking, Pete recognizes that although the Western frontier is closed, there are lands and markets abroad to be dominated.

The End of Innocence and the
Failure of the Archetypes

Although these classic literary archetypes — both masculine and feminine — are present throughout the entire series, their presence in the first season is both clearer and more prevalent; the later seasons, however, begin to reveal the breakdown and, ultimately, the failure of these formulations. At the end of the second season, Don appears reconciled to his domestic fate, while all of the female characters — particularly Betty and Peggy — have done their best to undermine those familiar Victorian archetypes that the first season went to such lengths to suggest. The gender archetypes still linger, but nearly all are subverted or indicted. But Don's flight west, the culminating act for all great frontier heroes, fails to resolve his fate. Even the attempt at a fresh start as Sterling Cooper Draper Pryce (rather than be subsumed by McCann Erickson) seems unlikely to provide the final fulfillment of the regeneration myth unless the burgeoning enterprise can cast off the naïve notion that it is, once again, reinventing itself completely anew.

What happened? And why now (or then, as the case may be)? The first season, although obviously rooted in its historical moment, is still somehow separate from history; it floats, detached because of its ironically nostalgic and satirical commentary on America's Golden Age, America's so-called Edenic moment. The season begins as a hyper-realized version of the Post-War, as it tries to be everything we expect it to be but know, too, it was not: the romantic cigarette haze, the sexy secretaries, the fathers who know best, the grey suits and fedoras, the endless rounds of cocktails. In Season One history only invades through the Nixon-Kennedy election, an invasion that serves more as a wink to the audience — who knows only too well how the divergent histories of those two men played out — than as a serious reflection on the historical realities of the moment. Indeed, the social issues which emerge throughout the season — primarily the overt racism and sexism of Sterling Cooper — appear to be more satirical than serious. The second season onward, however, dwell increasingly on historical moments in transition: the Kennedys in the White House, for example, or Bob Dylan in Greenwich Village. This time around, history comes fast and furious: the March 1, 1962, crash of American Airlines Flight 1, Paul and Shelia's trip to Mississippi to join the freedom rides, the Cuban Missile Crisis, and the assassinations of Medgar Evers and, more prominently, JFK. Now, it is not just celebratory drinks after a successful sales pitch; it is alcoholism destroying Freddy Rumsen and "Duck" Phillips. Now, it is not Sal's repressed homosexuality; it is Kurt matter-of-factly remarking that he makes love with the men and not women ("The Jet Set" 2:11). Now, it is not just meaningless affairs; it is divorce, date rape, and failing marriages. It is Betty — scandalized in Season One that the divorcee, Helen Bishop, is moving in down the street — suddenly contemplating abortion or initiating her own divorce. History has crept ominously into the series.

The innocence, it would seem, has been lost; Lewis's fortunate fall is at last enacted, and from the gates of Eden the characters of *Mad Men* are finally cast. What does this mean for those classic literary archetypes that the series once so determinedly set forth? Like the satire and romance of Season One, these archetypes, once integral to the fabric of the series — and, therefore, arguably the series' vision of this mid-century American moment — are becoming, or have become, obsolete. *Mad Men* captures America at perhaps the most salient historical moment of deliberate world remaking since its inception. This is a moment of cultural rupture, an overt denunciation of paternalistic social values that hatched a turbulent counterculture backlash best evidenced through the Haight-Ashbury community that reached its height in 1967 San Francisco. This creates a new danger, however, the danger that the Haight-Ashbury would fall into the same trap of "rebirth" rhetoric, of trying to posture itself as a new Eden, and its hippie inhabitants as America's newest natural man, inadvertently continuing the cycle. Rather than feeding the regeneration myth — prematurely written before an actual history has unfolded, and that essentialized religion and nature into the American character, fueling a grandiose sense of achievement and entitlement long before anything has actually been accomplished or earned — the Haight-Ashbury warns that the fortunate fall is not merely an absolute rejection of the old. It is not a petulant, adolescent rebellion screaming: "Like father, like son, like Hell!" It is a passage into maturity. It is a moment of realization, an awakening to one's conditions followed by an act of agency to effect appropriate change — and that involves a thoughtful assessment of what can carry over from the paternalistic world into the modern world. What started out as an anti-establishment haven quickly became a dystopia of drug addiction, prostitution and disease overrun by runaways fleeing their parents' way of life — all nascent in *Mad Men* through the evolving character of Sally Draper and her increasing disillusionment. The problem with building a national identity around a romantic Eden myth is that it arrogantly and conveniently erases history for the sake of its own propaganda in advance of any real accomplishment — which is the type of bravado that might be necessary for a fledgling nation to survive amongst established world powers, but when continued ad infinitum, ultimately stunts its healthy growth. Constantly beginning anew sounds romantic, but it precludes the wisdom of experience; what some might romanticize as "innocence" threatens to escalate into a proud, willful ignorance. The newest incarnation of the ad agency as Sterling Cooper Draper Pryce, however, potentially could follow a different model. It does not appear merely to be a rejection of the status quo; rather, it is appropriate to its particular moment, and is neither an obstinate clinging to or outright rejection of the past. It deploys the strengths of all its members; centrally, Don's creative talent, but, more importantly, his vigor and get-up-and-go spirit — the impetus to persuade the complacent Burt and Roger to get on board. More interesting, however, is that the new agency follows the Slotkinian hybrid–American model that relies as equally on Pete's "forward-looking" imperial vision as it does on Lane Pryce's established business acumen.

Whether or not *Mad Men* overstates the intensity and novelty of those shifts of the 1960s is of course debatable, but at the very least there was a sense that things were, in fact, changing, even if they were not. As Rollo May argues in *The Cry for Myth*, "it is not by its history that the mythology of a nation is determined but, conversely, its history is determined by its mythology" (92), so if these earlier classic mythologies were perceived to have failed, then new ones must take their place in order for history to find its new direction. Perhaps Peggy and Pete — characters that are the least easy to categorize — offer that new path. Better yet, just as Quentin Compson's roommate, Shreve, hypothesizes, "the Jim Bonds are going to conquer the Western Hemisphere" (Faulkner 203), perhaps Pete and Peggy's illegitimate son will define a new model for this "modern" age. Either way, "to light out for the Territory ahead of the rest" is no longer the option it once was, no matter how appealing it might seem. The couplings of *Mad Men*— Don and Betty, Pete and Peggy, even Midge and Roy — after the fall must choose their own path and, like Adam and Eve in the final lines of Milton's *Paradise Lost*, define a new, uncertain phase of history:

> The world was all before them, where to choose
> Their place of rest, and Providence their guide:
> They hand in hand with wand'ring steps and slow,
> Through Eden took their solitary way [301].

NOTES

1. Although we will only be focusing on small selection of the myth and symbol school texts in this essay, one could easily imagine including Smith's *Virgin Land*, Marx's *The Machine in the Garden*, and Feidelson's *Symbolism and American Literature* to productively extend this discussion.

2. Fiedler's text is equally well-known for his claim that American authors fail to deal with heterosexual love, and instead flee society in homosocial friendships (Huck and Jim being the classic example).

3. Today Turner's speech is widely rebuked as simply a rationalization for colonial genocide — the violence of the frontier is glossed over in a single footnote — but it nevertheless articulates a revealing attitude towards the way that the frontier has been conceptualized throughout history.

4. Indeed, in terms of his actual family history, Don's actual history resembles more than anything the convoluted family tree of the Trasks of John Steinbeck's *East of Eden* (1952), with a prostitute mother and a brother he — inadvertently — kills (Adam Whitman in *Mad Men*, Aron Trask in *East of Eden*).

5. As Whitman writes in *Leaves of Grass*, "I am not the poet of goodness only, I do not decline to be the poet of wickedness also" (40).

6. In 1963's *The Feminine Mystique*, Betty Friedan argues that the housewives of the 1950s and 1960s suffer from a "sense of dissatisfaction, a yearning" (11), and that there is a "voice within women that says: 'I want something more than my husband and my children and my home'" (27).

7. See Showalter, Elaine. *The Female Malady: Women, Madness, and English Culture, 1830–1980.*

8. Lionel Lambourne's *Victorian Painting* (1999) provides background chapters on Pre–Raphaelite painters, and another devoted to the fallen woman.

9. In addition to these characters there is an entire cast of tragic mulatta figures whose entire genre depends on the threat of an impending fall, as well as the female slave who, technically, cannot fall since she possesses no legal claim to her own body and, therefore, is not afforded the luxuries of chastity, virtue, or respectability.

10. Although this work primarily focuses on women's shifting role in England, Showalter specifically refers to the American New Woman in this passage.

11. Josef Breuer and Sigmund Freud explain in *Studies on Hysteria* that women of uncommon intelligence often succumb to hysteria, noting that a keen and unchallenged mind is prone to "morbid introspection," which inevitably will find a way to stimulate itself when nothing else does.

12. In fact, *Mad Men* essentially rewrites this historical campaign in order to mirror the actions of its characters. In the series' formulation, Kennedy is the nouveau riche and Nixon is the "Abe Lincoln of California," it is the man with everything v. the man from nothing. This is, of course, not the way history tends to remember this particular presidential race, and therefore *Mad Men*'s rewriting of it reflects more of its own preoccupations than the realities of history.

WORKS CITED

Cooper, James Fenimore. *The Last of the Mohicans.* 1826. New York: Barnes and Noble Classics, 2003.

Faulkner, William. *Absalom, Absalom!* 1936. New York: Vintage, 1990.

Fiedler, Leslie A. *Love and Death in the American Novel.* New York: Dell Publishing, 1960.

Fitzgerald, F. Scott. *The Great Gatsby.* 1925. New York: Scribner, 1995.

Friedan, Betty. *The Feminine Mystique.* New York: Dell Publishing, 1963.

Lawrence, D.H. "Fenimore Cooper's Leatherstocking Novels." *Studies in Classic American Literature.* New York: Viking, 1968. 47–63.

Lewis, R.W.B. *The American Adam: Innocence, Tragedy, and Tradition in the Nineteenth Century.* Chicago: University of Chicago Press, 1955.

Lewis, Sinclair. *Babbitt.* 1922. New York: Signet Classic, 1961.

"*Mad Men*: This is the Wild Wild East." Advertisement. <http://www.amctv.com/videos/mad-men/.

May, Rollo. *The Cry for Myth.* New York: W.W. Norton, 1991.

Mill, John Stuart. "The Subjection of Women." *On Liberty and Other Writings.* Ed. Stefan Collini. Cambridge: Cambridge University Press, 1989. 117–217.

Milton, John. *Paradise Lost.* 1674. New York: W.W. Norton, 1993.

Patmore, Coventry. "Angel in the House." *Poems.* London: G. Bell and Sons, 1906.

Slotkin, Richard. *Regeneration Through Violence: The Mythology of the American Frontier, 1600–1860*. Norman: University of Oklahoma Press, 2000.

Trachtenberg, Alan. *The Incorporation of America: Culture and Society in the Gilded Age*. New York: Hill and Wang, 1982.

Turner, Frederick Jackson. "The Significance of the Frontier in American History." *The Frontier in American History*. 1953. New York: Dover, 1996. 1–38.

Twain, Mark. *The Adventures of Huckleberry Finn*. 1885. *The Unabridged Mark Twain*. Ed. Lawrence Teacher. Philadelphia: Running Press, 1976.

Whitman, Walt. *Democratic Vistas*. 1871. *Walt Whitman: Complete Poetry and Selected Prose*. Ed. James E. Miller, Jr. Boston: Houghton Mifflin Company, 1959.

_____. *Leaves of Grass*. 1855. *Walt Whitman: Complete Poetry and Selected Prose*. Ed. James E. Miller, Jr. Boston: Houghton Mifflin Company, 1959.

2. The Fall of the Organization Man: Loyalty and Conflict in the First Season

Maura Grady

In the summer of 2007, AMC TV premiered the original series *Mad Men*, set in the world of the early 1960s advertising business, which creator Matthew Weiner described as "a great way to talk about the image we have of ourselves, versus who we really are" (Witchell 2). *Mad Men* was singled out by critics as a show that "captures that utterly fascinating transformation as [it] explores 1960 in New York and America at large" (Goodman) and an "uncanny evocation of time and place" (Salem). The opening title card which clarifies the show's name in the first episode ("Smoke Gets in Your Eyes" 1:1) indicates that the focus is on advertising, not just advertising in general, but on the men who were possessed by a sense of self-importance and power, demarcating their masculinity in terms of their ownership of a place both real and imaginary. Madison Avenue is a real street in New York and its name is synonymous with the business of advertising, and just as Wall Street is a synecdoche for the world of finance, Mad Ave is a hotbed of imaginary ideas as well as concrete ones.

The term "Mad Men" is not only a play on words combining the abbreviation for the street ("Mad Ave") with the men who work on it, but it also denotes these men lay claim to a "mad" attitude: a wildness and free-spirited sense of creativity, making their own rules, as the series illustrates through its frequent depiction of the men drinking, smoking and womanizing with a devil-may-care attitude. Despite the title's focus on the show's male element, the press and critics generally seem to have paid the most attention to the show's female characters and its stylistic features. Less has been said about the dynamics of masculinity within the workplace organization of the advertising agency of Sterling Cooper, the show's centerpiece.

This chapter examines how conflicting definitions of American masculinity drive the narrative of the show throughout the first season, personified in the struggle between two characters: Don Draper and Pete Campbell. The conflict between the two men — one a self-made man and the other born of privilege — questions the assumed solidarity of this era's workplace organization. *Mad Men* scrutinizes the "organization man" (as defined by William H. Whyte in his landmark 1956 study) in his heyday; at a time when belonging to a corporate organization was supposed to level out class and ethnic differences, the show asks its audience to consider if these differences are instead ingrained in the capitalist superstructure at the very core of the corporate organization. If they are, the conflict and friction caused by them, resulting in competition rather than cooperation, are what keep the wheels of commerce turning. The series illustrates that the very notion of an organization man is flawed; he is a straw figure who never actually existed but rather was held out as an unattainable ideal, a subset of the equally elusive American Dream that workers reached out for but were always already unable to grasp.

Sociologist William H. Whyte's 1956 book *The Organization Man* is a study that gave this longing for belonging a name. The "organization man," according to Whyte, describes the mid-twentieth-century white male worker, who turns over his financial well-being, personal aspirations, social life and moral character to a large organization, such as a corporation. In exchange for this, he is rewarded with a secure job and a good salary. Whyte's book stayed on the best seller list until the fall of 1957 and, of the many books with a related thesis from this period (such as *The Lonely Crowd* and *The Power Elite*), it remains the most influential, with a new edition republished as late as 2002 and continuing references in popular culture.[1] Whyte was one of the first to warn against (rather than praise) the trend towards conformity in corporate life, to deconstruct the suburbs, to question the veneration of groups, and lament the growth of bureaucracy. As a former U.S. Marine, Whyte wasn't anti-organization; he merely wanted large-scale organizations such as corporations to function effectively and was one of the first to argue that conformity was the enemy of creativity and, therefore, productivity. Whyte based his study on interviews with workers in organizations in numerous fields, and his evidence suggests that only occasionally did any of his subjects question that conforming to the organization was the right thing to do.

Mad Men's cast of characters show many affiliations with Whyte's "organization men." The advertising firm of Sterling Cooper is controlled by two partners, Roger Sterling and Bert Cooper. The firm itself is not the biggest or most powerful agency in town but is a mid-sized and respectable company with some big name clients, such as Lucky Strike, Kodak and Clearasil. The big star of Sterling Cooper is undoubtedly head of creative, Don Draper. The first episode introduces his character not as the confident executive in his office but by giving the audience a glimpse of his inner panic as he struggles to come up with a solid campaign for Lucky Strike in the wake of troubling reports from the surgeon general. Still, the partners have confidence in him and the lesser members of the staff are intimidated by him.

The conflict between Don and Pete Campbell (a pompous, upper-class young account executive) will prove to be the backbone of the first season, as Don's gray-flannel-suited, middle-class work ethic conflicts with Pete's blue-suited, blue-blooded assumed privilege. Apart from head of the art department, Salvatore Romano, whom contemporary viewers will recognize as a closeted homosexual, the junior members of the staff are mostly difficult to distinguish in the premiere episode, save for Pete, who starts his day by insulting Don's new secretary, Peggy ("Smoke Gets in Your Eyes" 1:1). Though Don gently puts the copywriters, secretaries and creative team members in their place, it is with Pete that he has real confrontation and real conflict in the office.

Pete Campbell usually dresses in blue suits and is a blueblood with little but his name to recommend him; Sterling says he "redefines lack of imagination" ("Ladies Room" 1:2). Pete comes from an old and well-connected (although no longer wealthy) New York family. He is ambitious but offers little in the way of talent. He feels entitled to advancement within the firm but is rude, chauvinistic, and disrespectful to nearly everyone. Out of frustration at his lack of advancement, he will attempt to blackmail Don when he discovers that Don is not who he says he is. Though Pete claims he is only showing loyalty to the firm, he discovers that his definition of loyalty differs from the definition of the leaders of the organization. Campbell thinks he is ready to devote himself to the organization fully but the kind of mutual devotion between man and organization that Whyte describes (with faith and loyalty extending in both directions) has already begun to fade by the time we meet our characters, suggesting the security of working for a large company may be slipping away.

The men who work in the firm have accepted the parts they have been given to play in the organization. More than just work to these men, being part of Sterling Cooper means belonging to something. Though the characters might not be able to articulate it themselves, they fit Whyte's descriptions of participants in corporate hierarchies. Because Sterling Cooper is a smaller firm, it is perhaps not the epitome of Whyte's definition of the organization; Whyte defines the quintessential organization as a larger institution in corporate America, like AT&T and GM, and notes that what they have in common is a corporate philosophy that rewards conformity and discourages creativity and individual thinking, even going so far as to require personality tests of its employees so free-thinking workers could be weeded out (Nocera xiii). Sterling Cooper is a privately owned firm, not publicly traded ("Shoot" 1:9), which grants it the freedom to occasionally embrace the unconventional. Mr. Cooper is a devoted fan of Ayn Rand and frequently comments on the need to embrace and support the talented individual. For these reasons, Matt Weiner's ad agency creation is a fusion of Whyte's description of workers' needs and anxieties during this period and a fantasy of the more freewheeling corporate environment the creative enterprise of advertising required. Sterling Cooper, therefore, prompts the audience to question Whyte's assumptions and conclusions (as many have done before) while examining whether our needs and desires as workers differ significantly from Whyte's descriptive predictions. In a way, Sterling Cooper's corporate philosophy seems to be a reaction to Whyte — the firm has largely chosen to heed Whyte's warnings about surrendering too much to conformity and bureaucracy. But traces of the dangers Whyte describes still remain, leading us also to question whether it is possible to ever eliminate the worst of the organization man's tendency toward groupthink.

Although Whyte's work cannot sustain the supposition that workers within organizations did not occasionally have doubts or fears about their association with the organization, *Mad Men* shows that despite those fears, loyalty to the organization is usually strong enough to override them. What loyalty means precisely, however, differs greatly from one individual worker to the other. For Don, loyalty means giving his best work to the organization, maintaining the hierarchical structure and other internal rules of the company. He declines sexual advances from his secretary and always consults with his superiors and subordinates when appropriate.

Because he comes from humble beginnings and reinvents himself completely, Don is an embodiment of the American Dream that one does not need a name or money to be a success. He was born into poverty, the bastard child of a farmer and a prostitute, raised by his father's widow and her new husband. After serving in the Korean War, he takes the opportunity to assume the name of a dead fellow soldier in order to disappear from his old life and start a new one. Don is immensely talented. Head of Creative at Sterling Cooper, he strides around the office with supreme confidence and is of great value to the firm. He wins over clients with his gutsy, smart, and well-played marketing pitches.

According to Whyte, the organization man is not the high-flyer or the CEO, nor someone who merely works for the company but rather someone who feels he *belongs* to the company, and who derives a large part of his sense of self from his association with, and loyalty to, the organization. As Whyte clarifies,

> They are not the workers, nor are they the white-collar people in the usual, clerk sense of the word. [Those] people only work for The Organization. The ones I am talking about belong to it as well. They are the ones of our middle class who have left home, spiritually as well as physically, to take the vows of organization life, and it is they who are the mind and soul of our great self-perpetuating institutions. Only a few are top managers or ever will be. In a system that makes such hazy terminology as "junior executive" psychologically necessary, they are of the staff as much as the [assembly] line, and most are destined to live poised in a middle area that still awaits a satisfactory euphemism [3].

In these terms, *Mad Men*'s "men" fit Whyte's parameters: they are invested in identifying as ad men and operate strictly within the terms of Sterling Cooper's existing hierarchy, even when they seek advancement. But a kind of nervous energy pervades the office and its workers, suggesting they are far from the sense of security Whyte's study suggested the organization man felt he was receiving in exchange for his loyalty and abandonment of home ties.

Mad Men shows us organization men in crisis: the animated opening credits depict a man in a suit falling out of a skyscraper, suggesting a tragic and bloody demise. The silhouette of the man, carrying a briefcase, enters a corner office which quickly starts to fall away, taking the man with it, as he falls slowly past images of advertisements, whisky glasses and cigarettes. He fades out at the point of impact and is replaced by a silhouette of the back of a man's head sitting on a couch made of the words "Mad Men" with his right arm outstretched, holding a cigarette. This image is the logo of the show, and our first introduction to Don is from behind, echoing the angle of this shot. This figure is in crisis because he links his identity explicitly to the workplace. To the show's characters, masculinity is defined by their superiority to the women who work in the office and their sense of self-worth is directly connected to their success in the firm. The linking of these three elements reinforces the connection between the organization's profit and the individual worker's sense of himself as a valuable person.

The series' pilot ("Smoke Gets in Your Eyes" 1:1) follows Don through a disastrous day at the office, where all things seem to go wrong and where it seems like upstart Pete Campbell might just be getting the better of him. At the end of this day, Don's intelligence, talent and survival instincts get him through the tough situation so that he saves not only his own job but also the Lucky Strike account and the firm's reputation. Don makes a successful pitch, proving that he possesses a quality that Pete lacks: inspiration — he is able to synthesize everything he's been meditating on into a slogan that sells not only the client but everyone in the room, including himself— the smile on his face and lilt in his voice show the weight is lifted from his shoulders for at least a moment.

The Lucky Strike storyline also shows that Pete operates through deception and coasting on others' ideas. Pete's own pitch idea (stolen from Don's trash) is rejected by the client and leads to Don admonishing him, noting that he would have used it if the research was good. Immediately after this dressing-down, the "boys" go to a strip club for Pete's bachelor party and Pete is rejected again, this time by a girl at the club because he is too aggressive in propositioning her. Pete steals away to seduce a surprisingly willing Peggy at her apartment in Brooklyn. The episode ends with another shocking revelation. Don — who has spent the night with a mistress — is actually married. He has a beautiful blond wife, two cute kids, and a house in the suburbs, the "dormitory" of the organization man (Whyte 10). Whyte writes extensively about the suburbs, arguing that "the organization man is trying, quite consciously, to develop a new kind of roots to replace what he left behind" (268). Don is the perfect example of this paradigm, in that he seeks to combat his rootlessness by establishing new ties with a wife and children. Don's lack of identity is not noticed in the suburbs, as everyone there has moved in from somewhere else (Whyte 270). The suburbs in *Mad Men* are beautiful; tree-lined streets, spacious homes, lovely neighbors who come to parties and chat about local happenings. But, as with most depictions of the 'burbs these days, we learn quickly that not everything is perfect. Don's wife has a nervous condition, pregnant women smoke, and housewives gossip viciously about how the new divorcee moving in will lower property values.

Although remarkably confident at work, Don displays a marked discomfort when he is called to acknowledge job satisfaction in his personal life. At his daughter's birthday party, an awkward and already drunk Don chats with a neighbor who asks about things on "Mad Ave." The neighbor gestures around Don's spacious and comfortable middle-class home, knowing full well they have it made, yet the two men nod almost sadly to each other at this end to their conversation. If this is all there is, they seem to silently ask each other, why don't we feel happier? *Mad Men*'s Ossining, NY, is picture-perfect but the audience's contemporary eyes also see the flaws in it.

Don Draper himself is analogous to the "great package suburbs" (Whyte 267); he is beautiful to look at, but his identity is entirely constructed. Both his "new" identity and his "original" identity are tied to photographs shown in the season's final episode, when Don pitches his campaign for Kodak's slide carousel using his own family's photos. A scene of him alone in his office selecting just the right slides from a cardboard box parallels a scene from earlier in the season in which he sifts through the contents of the box from his brother Adam. Don smiles gently as he peers at the slides of his children and then reconsiders the box of photos of himself and his then-kid brother; looking through them again prompts him to phone Adam whom he had previously dismissed from his life. It is only then that he discovers Adam hanged himself the same day he sent Don the box. This devastates Don enough that he puts his head in his hands and feels the need to be more connected to his new family, ironically just at the moment his wife has begun to pull away from him and distrust him.

The pitch to the Kodak company, inspired by this look through these photos and the desire to create, through photography, the warm family connections that no longer (and perhaps never did) exist is a wild success, hailed by Pete as a win for civilization ("The Wheel" 1:13). Pete's announcement essentially validates the organization man's credo that you aren't just helping the company by working successfully; you're helping your country (Whyte viii).

The premiere episode establishes that the show, far from being a mere nostalgia trip, is a meditation on the emptiness of Don's corporate success. The season's final episode directly comments on the appeal of nostalgia, by having Don use it, showing his own personal family photos, to pitch the Kodak slide carousel. Though the episode features Don reflecting on the mistakes he's made with his family and determining to work harder to establish that place where he knows he is loved, Don's speech could easily be describing the show's chosen period. The audience, too, longs for a lost time in which a corporation would seem to value talent and creativity, rewarding its workers with decent salaries and a measure of freedom. But Don discovers when he rushes home to be with his family, only to discover that they have left for Thanksgiving celebrations without him, that that place that he longs for exists only in his imagination.

The photographs of Don's family craft an image of familial closeness, but it remains just that—an image without the substance to back it up. Matthew Weiner's comments on his show's visual style seem frequently to remind the audience not to mistake a beautiful image for inner beauty—the lovely clothes, attractive architecture, and seemingly ideal (for the men) corporate setting are not to be confused with a true satisfaction in the workplace. This uncomfortably reminds us that though we may complain about our current workplace woes and long for a past of greater security, that past never actually existed. Even at the point when things should have been perfect for the white middle class male worker, it never was so. Our nostalgia is for a past that, like Don's happy family, never existed.

As Don works on the Lucky Strike pitch, he goes to visit his mistress, Midge (a bohemian graphic artist), to vent his frustrations and fears that this will be the campaign that undoes him because he can no longer make health claims or quote smoking doctors. Despite Midge's reassurances that he has faced tougher challenges in the past, Don sounds defeated saying that when she sees him next, "young executives will be picking meat off my ribs." Don paints a picture of a workplace in which one mistake is fatal — and leads the audience to believe that we're watching a man on the brink of a career disaster. Don is painfully aware of the competition within the firm, as aggressive, younger executives are always there, nipping at his heels; his actions reveal that although the organization is supposed to be a place where "the collective" rules, it actually only masks the machinations of competitive individuals.

The competitiveness of the individuals is made evident in the behavior of the so-called "young executives." They first appear competing for the attention of the "new girl" Peggy as she enters the elevator with them on her first day. They leer at her and make inappropriate remarks while also discussing an upcoming bachelor party at a strip club. Weiner describes these junior execs as "young men trying to act like adults" (DVD commentary 1:1). They grumble and complain about their work but not about being part of the company. And despite Don's misgivings voiced to Midge, he is well respected at the firm, feared and idolized by these younger men as well as by the office's female staff.

The organization is a male-dominant zone, excluding women from the power. Whyte's use of religious metaphors such as "vows" and "salvation" suggests a monastic and militaristic devotion and solidarity, and the image thus invoked is deliberately misogynistic: defined by the exclusion of those who do not join the order. The allusion to the military is solidified early in the episode when Don, alone in his office and anxious about the Lucky Strike account, takes out a Purple Heart medal in a case with "Lt. Donald Francis Draper" printed on it. The audience is led to view him not just as a member of this corporate team but as a fighter, and a soldier, who has actually been wounded in action. His service distinguishes him from the younger executives, who went to college instead of joining the army and who try on military metaphors but are merely playing soldier as they try to fit in with the organization's structure.

The members of the organization may disagree on day-to-day policies, but feel they are on the same team and agree that the "pursuit of individual salvation through hard work, thrift, and competitive struggle is the heart of the American achievement" (Whyte 4). The contradiction between individual success and group solidarity reinforces Alexis de Tocqueville's observations about the American dream of success: namely that each individual hopes that he will be the one to "walk quick and cleave a way through the same throng which surrounds and presses him" (de Tocqueville, *Democracy in America* Chapter XIII).[2]

The hope to "cleave a way through the ... throng" is illustrated when young account executive Ken Cosgrove gets a short story published in *Atlantic Monthly*, making others feel inferior. Don is not threatened by Ken's success and congratulates him, but the other junior execs express their anxiety. For instance, Pete believes one's name and connections should lead to success; he cannot fathom how Ken managed to get published by talent alone. Pete is so discomfited by Ken's success (even though Pete had not previously tried to get anything published), he asks his wife to visit a former boyfriend (now a publisher). She secures Pete a publication in *Boys' Life* but when she fails to do more Pete humiliates her, practically asking her why she didn't sleep with the publisher to get his story in print since it was deserving of the *The New Yorker* ("5-G" 1:5). Though Pete begins his own publishing endeavor because he wants to prove he is more talented than Ken, he contradicts himself by arguing with his wife. Although Pete has an inflated sense of his own skill, he still does not believe that talent alone is what makes things happen. In Pete's mind, one's name, one's connections (such as Trudy's connection to this publisher), are what get people what they want.

When another executive apologizes for being jealous, the unassuming Ken responds by acknowledging that he has won. Clearly, everyone in this office is always competing with each other, even if they do not seem to be doing so. Ken didn't bother to brag about his magazine story the way the others might have in his place, but he is still silently keeping score.

Pete's own need to be recognized for his creativity subsequently prompts him to assert himself with a client, undermining Don's authority. Rather than encourage the client to accept Don's ideas and the artwork (Sal stands confidently beside the posters as Don pitches his idea), Pete confirms and supports the client's doubts. Later, without Don's say-so, he pitches his own ideas to the client, disrupting the organizational hierarchy. Don makes it clear to Pete that his role at Sterling Cooper is to woo the clients with his upper-class pedigree and to let Don handle the smarts and creativity. Pete is aware of the falsity of his position; he wants to contribute intellectually to the organization but feels he is being denied the opportunity, because he is both assisted and burdened by a family name.

Pete's father vehemently disapproves of Pete's choice of profession, as he reveals when Pete asks for money to buy an apartment. The scene is played in the Campbell home that is getting ready for their summer exodus — the couch is covered with a sheet, and everything is packed. Pete sits on the covered couch in his gray business suit and tie, while his father, splayed out in a chair in a yellow blazer, madras shorts and loafers, laments that when he is out in what should be the locations of a rich man's leisure, he runs into Pete "wining and whoring" his clients ("New Amsterdam" 1:4). Contrary to what might seem the larger cultural assumption, the name Pete has been given isn't helping him much at the moment, at least not from his perspective. It does prevent him from being fired when he steps out of the organizational hierarchy but he himself is not aware of that.

By contrast, Don has been given no name — he literally takes someone else's — and resents the advantages Pete seems to have. Each man looks around with envy and with regret at what he cannot achieve. They are of a kind; both are organization men though they seem to come from such different backgrounds. The dissatisfaction they feel with the hand they've been dealt draws them to the organization where they search for fulfillment for what they feel is lacking. Pete looks for validation that he does not get from his family, despite their position and Don looks for the status he never had coming from a poor background.

The organization's demand for hard work is supposed to be the equalizer. Whyte quotes Henry Clews, who noted: "You may start in business with your feet on the bottom rung of the ladder; it rests with you to acquire the strength to climb to the top.... There is always plenty of room at the top" (Whyte 14). Pete quotes Clews word-for-word to Don, but leaves out Clews's admonition that the individual must himself "acquire the strength to climb to the top." For Pete, ascending to the top of the ladder *should* happen for him simply because there is room to be filled, but he doesn't believe that he should have to do the work himself that it takes to get there. Clews's philosophy, according to Whyte, is "exuberantly optimistic," and like Ayn Rand would later do, espouses that having every individual "seeking his own self-interest automatically improves the lot of all" (Whyte 15). Rand's works *Atlas Shrugged* (mentioned favorably by Cooper several times), *The Fountainhead,* and *The Virtue of Selfishness* explicitly advocate her philosophy that "The pursuit of [man's] own rational self-interest and of his own happiness is the highest moral purpose of his life" (Aynrand.org). Rand's philosophy is frequently at odds with the ethos of the organization, which "became a standing taunt to this dream of individual success" (Whyte 17), but Don Draper manages to fuse the two together. His solitary nature and the mystique it engenders is part of what brings him success within the organization. The fear and fascination with Draper reflects Whyte's description of the organization's dislike of non-conforming behavior: "In group doctrine, the strong personality is viewed with overwhelming suspicion" (Whyte 53). Don doesn't behave in a conventional manner yet he is successful and Pete is fearful that Don has discovered some kind of secret to success that he cannot figure out.

Ultimately, the organization man is in search of the American dream — anxious because he seems to have everything one could ask for, yet he still feels unsatisfied. The organization man, Whyte argues, "seeks a redefinition of his place on Earth — a faith that will satisfy him that what he must endure has a deeper meaning than appears on the surface" (6). From the first episode, we see Don struggle to find this definition, while simultaneously despairing that he is convinced it cannot be found. It seems that Don's only comfort is found at Sterling Cooper, where the rules are more clearly defined than in his private life.

In the pilot, Don lays out the organizational structure at Sterling Cooper to Pete and disabuses him of any illusions he may have that once he's inside the organization a man can do whatever he wants whenever he wants. Don tells Pete that even if he does get his job he will never run the place because no one likes him. ("Smoke Gets in Your Eyes" 1:1). When Pete does go outside the normally approved hierarchical procedures of the organization to pitch his copy to a client, Don and Sterling approach senior partner Cooper for permission to fire him. But, while the organization and its members might wish to believe their own internal rules are paramount, they are occasionally reminded that these rules can be easily dispensed with if something valuable to the firm is at stake. It becomes clear that the Pete Campbells of the world gain entrée to the organization by virtue of their pedigree and not their abilities. Pete's mild rule-breaking is reprimanded but ultimately forgiven because his powerful family has influence in the capitalist superstructure outside the organization. Cooper reminds Don and Sterling to consider their organization works within that larger superstructure, outside the organization and its internal hierarchies. He implies that Sterling Cooper is an organization within an organization. That is, capitalism and the white-collar workers are devoted to one another, and the individual cooperation is receding in importance within that relationship.

Losing Campbell would mean a loss of connection to a wider fraternity and Cooper reminds Don that every organization knows how to play this game. Cooper knows that Pete Campbells are at every ad agency, and that retaining him is important because it keeps the firm connected to a greater power structure. Pete's mother is Dorothy Dyckman Campbell, and Cooper doesn't want her bad mouthing the firm on Fishers Island where they summer. Should the firm lose the Fishers Island crowd's goodwill, Cooper notes, they lose their access to centers of power ("New Amsterdam" 1:4). Don resents the implication that Pete is more valuable to the firm than he, but Cooper clarifies that Campbell is valuable only for his name; not for his ideas. Even as Cooper assures Don how valuable *he* is to the firm, Don's face registers the difficulty of having to continue working with Pete — he nearly chokes on it, fidgeting and gagging as he responds politely, thanking Cooper for his confidence.

Campbell's loyalty to Don is won (at least for a time) by lies — he is told that Don fought to keep him on at the firm. Roger Sterling uses military metaphor to convey to Campbell the importance of the loyalty he now owes to Don. He tells Pete that Don is his commander and that he lives and dies with him. Sterling's response indicates that while he and Don recognize that membership in the organization requires a certain level of play-acting — appropriating the brotherhood that does not actually exist — Pete's willingness to go whole-hog here implies that he misunderstands the legitimacy of that brotherhood. Pete at least pretends that the brotherhood and its associated loyalty are real, whereas Cooper and Draper openly recognize their illusory nature.

Pete is reminded of the falsity of family and corporate loyalty constantly and is distressed by it. He is especially resentful that his father-in-law is so generous with his money and support — he gives Pete and Trudy the money for their apartment that Pete's father withheld. What seems to bother Pete the most is that this support comes not from his own father and not from the organization (the two official prongs of the patriarchal hierarchy) but rather through a matriarchy — Pete knows that the support and money is via his wife and he resents this, though he seems to have no problem asking for her help when he wants his short story to be published. He bitterly comments to his wife later about the apartment, seemingly jealous that she, a woman, can be happy and get what she sets out to get but he never can. Again, the matriarchal connections are the ones to which he must be beholden, since his mother is the one with the upscale family pedigree. The only moments when people seem to be happy about Pete are when his maternal family fame comes into conversation — such as when he and his wife are meeting their new neighbors and Trudy tells her new neighbors stories of Pete's ancestor's friendship with Isaac Roosevelt. While Trudy enjoys the attention, Pete withdraws when his own identity is erased by his more significant name.

Pete constantly struggles with feelings of emasculation — exchanging a duplicate wedding gift of a chip-and-dip plate for a shotgun and concocting a Hemingway-esque fantasy of shooting an animal, dragging it back to a log cabin to drain and dress the meat and then giving it to his woman to cook it for him ("Red in the Face" 1:7). But Pete is reduced to faking power, drinking at his desk on an afternoon when no one is working because they've closed an account and gone out to celebrate, feeling he is superior to the others.

Pete still has a job despite not pulling his weight since, as Whyte explains, the organization man is often rewarded for having a "passive ambition." Like Pete, Whyte's archetype floats along in the organization, expecting the tide will simply carry him to success. But the show doesn't deny its audience the hope that merit ultimately means more than birth in America; *Mad Men* lets us keep the fantasy de Tocqueville described. Campbell is not fired for his mistakes but he is chastised and fails to get ahead in the firm — because he lacks the social graces, the natural talent, and the ability to influence clients and coworkers — so he eventually sets aside any personal loyalty for his boss and attempts to blackmail Don into giving him a promotion, threatening to expose his "true" (pre–Don Draper) identity to Cooper. Pete expects to be rewarded for what he sees as fealty to the organization, believing Cooper will appreciate it, but instead finds out that Don's financial contributions to the firm are more valued than his family connections or his misguided act of loyalty (i.e., breaking Don's "cover").

Exposing the truth might seem honorable; Midge's bohemian friend derides Don's job in advertising as bolstering lies. This describes not only work in advertising (the show's tagline is "where the truth lies") but also Don's entire life — the personal life he has fabricated in order to maintain his professional life, which lets him sleep comfortably. But even the professional coolness Don usually has on display is shaken at times. Pete relishes anything that smacks of Don's failure. When Sterling Cooper loses a client, Pete seems dismayed when Don seems not to care. Don maintains a cool exterior, refusing to give Pete satisfaction. It is so important that he maintain this façade of calm and control that Don doesn't even express the small amount of regret or dismay that would be natural, but when Pete leaves the office, Don angrily sweeps the lamps and telephone off his desk. The shot is from a low angle — the position of the lamps once they hit the floor — so that we look up at Don at the moment we see him losing control.

Precipitating the biggest confrontation between Don and Pete is a promotion that Pete is angling for towards the end of the season after Don is made a partner. As Don considers bringing in a big gun from the outside to be head of accounts, Pete tries to convince him that *he* should get the job as he has the loyalty of important clients, again alluding to his status. But Don recognizes that role has its purpose as well as its limitations. When Pete's claims of loyalty fail to persuade Don, he hypocritically switches tactics. Rather than point out *his* own loyalty, he warns that the firm needs to be careful not to lose him. Pete is "remind[ing] the organization that he is desirable to other organizations too" (Whyte 165) but Pete does this incorrectly. Rather than offering a tacit reminder, Pete acts like a spoiled child, yelling when he doesn't get his way. And Pete channels Don's dismissal of his abilities into a vindictive invasion of privacy of Don's office, where he discovers the box of photos from Don's brother Adam.

Though Don mostly maintains his cool around Pete Campbell, Season One's penultimate episode "Nixon vs. Kennedy" puts Pete in a position of power that nearly makes Don run away from everything, including his wife, children and career. Pete's power comes from his interception of a box of memorabilia sent to Don by Don's younger half-brother Adam Whitman, who has discovered Don in New York. Don at first seems suspicious of Adam's motives, but Adam's sweet demeanor indicates he is only happy to see his brother and is anxious to reestablish a relationship with him. Pete takes possession of the box, and seems to pore over it jealously before coming to the decision to blackmail Don by exposing Don's real name to Cooper, aiming to have Don give him the promotion he has failed to win by merit — as we know Pete truly believes, these things are not actually awarded on merit. Pete has even exploited his connections to gain ammunition for his threats, contacting a friend at the Department of Defense to find out that the real Don Draper should be older and that Dick Whitman died in Korea in 1950.

What Pete fundamentally fails to understand is that Draper's "deceit" ultimately is meaningless as far as the firm is concerned. For Pete, his name means everything; therefore, someone would change their name only to cover something up (like being a deserter). But Don changed his name only to disconnect from a painful past and get a fresh start. A basic fantasy of reinvention is at the root of the American Dream: immigration to a new land, where immigrants frequently adopted new "American" names at their port of entry in order to start afresh in a new capitalist nation. But in the fantasy, they don't try to hide anything criminal or otherwise shameful. As far as Bert Cooper is concerned, Don Draper is exactly who the firm needs him to be; whoever he may have been before he arrived is immaterial because he is talented. Contrast that with Cooper's assessment of Pete's value, which is intrinsically tied to his family name — a name that got Pete the job *despite* his lack of talent and frequent missteps — and it's not hard to see who will win the firm's loyalty in this power struggle.

Don is frightened by Pete's threat at first but then, after talking with Peggy, he decides to call Pete's bluff. When Pete finally does reveal Don's identity to Cooper in his attempt to get Don fired for not promoting him, Don is nervous but stands up to Pete by marching purposefully into Cooper's office ahead of him. Pete is visibly nervous; Don is fearful of what will happen to him (he had even considered running away to avoid exposure). Cooper pauses for a beat after Pete makes his revelation, then instantly diffuses the tension, shocking both Don and Pete by claiming not to care. By consciously referencing that imagined fraternity, Cooper draws Pete's and Don's attention to what is really at stake here — it isn't integrity, but rather capital. Cooper knows perfectly well that Pete has little to offer the firm beyond his name and that Don is incredibly valuable; Don's been given bonuses and raises and been made partner without the guarantee of his loyalty via a contract. Sterling Cooper *needs* Don Draper but Pete Campbell is replaceable. Far from ignoring the theme of loyalty, Cooper tells Don to fire Pete, but provides a cautious caveat, that you never know the origin of loyalty ("Nixon vs. Kennedy" 1:12). Pete seems shocked by Cooper's obvious dismissal of the importance of a name.

To the firm, Don's name is immaterial; his talent, charisma, and profitability are what matter. For Pete, this uncomfortable revelation means that his name — the thing his father calls "everything" — actually has very little intrinsic value. Don's lies about his name mean little to Cooper and this staggers Pete.

Cooper's reaction shows loyalty is a sham in the organization; it is something to be thrown away in favor of capitalist opportunism. Cooper alludes to that by referencing the history of the men who founded the country and their (probably) much worse deeds. Pete's subsequent retreat to his office, where he slumps on his couch and pours himself a drink and cries, illustrates not only his immaturity in handling defeat but also his continued bewilderment; he just cannot seem to figure out what is expected of him at Sterling Cooper. Everything that might have worked for him in the past seems ineffective in this environment.

Though the offices are not entirely private (a janitor can see the shadows of an early morning tryst through the frosted glass), the characters do feel a semblance of seclusion in them. Pete's invasion of Don's sanctum late in the season, therefore, is more than insubordination. It is a violation. And characters are frequently disturbed when non-organization interlopers appear at the office unannounced. Family visits appear to disconcert all of the office residents, as if these are aliens invading from some distant planet. The most unnerving of these is the unexpected appearance of Don's long-lost younger brother, Adam Whitman, whose appearance inadvertently provides Pete with ammunition for blackmailing Don.

When Adam first appears at Don's office, during a full staff meeting, Don is really disconcerted and exits the meeting to confront Adam. After Don first denies knowing him, he softens visibly and promises to meet him for lunch. Don walks through the office anxiously, darting glances around at everyone as if he suspects he will be found out. The sound of the office, and the music, falls away, and all he can do is look at his watch, waiting nervously for the time when he will meet his brother.

In the conversation at a small diner, Adam's face is open and warm, seeking approval, simply joyful at seeing his brother, whereas Don is very insistent on not making eye contact, not connecting with this brother or the family and past he represents. Don softens only when Adam asks plaintively if he was missed. A three-quarter close-up of Don's face makes us examine him as he waits an extra beat before replying that he did. Don sees how complicated this is going to be when Adam starts eagerly asking questions about Don's life; Don's face registers dismay at the anticipation of having to provide those answers. Would he have to introduce his brother to his wife? How would he explain him? It's clearly impossible to reconcile his brother with his constructed identity. Don's cruel abandonment of his brother is devastating, and

Adam looks utterly destroyed (catching his breath back tearfully) after Don says their meeting never happened ("5G" 1:5). The final shot after Don's exit shows Adam from behind sitting in a booth, mirroring the opening shot and series logo of Don.

A simple photograph of Don as a young soldier with his then-kid brother is sent to Don by Adam, and we see that it moves him. But at the end of the episode, Don burns the photograph before going to see his brother in Adam's squalid hotel. The scene preceding their meeting ratchets up the tension as Don places something from his desk drawer into a bag — is it a gun? As Don meets with him, he fidgets, eyes his brother suspiciously before offering him the ultimate rejection: it turns out to be money. Don tries to pay him to start over, but somewhere else and without him. Don rejects his opportunity to make a real family connection — that family connection must be severed if Don is to maintain his professional façade. Don's past cannot coincide with his present life. His present existence exists precisely because his past does not.

Don's and Pete's contrasting approaches to work and emotional belonging to the firm gives the show the opportunity to ruminate on the meaning of loyalty within the organization and to show us how the organization man looks through the lens of the new millennium. What *Mad Men* shows us is that we hunger for a workplace that doesn't care who we were before we entered the organization but praises who we've become and what we have to offer once we've arrived there. It's a throwback to the mid-twentieth-century middle-class fantasies of corporate success with some important differences and with a new millennium cynicism.

The show addresses the hunger for the security and paternal encouragement of the organization, one that recognizes and fosters talented men, even as they break the rules. Full of contradictions, the organization rewards nonconformity as much as it would seem to discourage it, as the central character of Don Draper bears out. The man in the gray flannel suit was never the anonymous drone, mindlessly obeying higher-ups in the skyscraper so he could keep his drab and empty suburban life intact — he always chafed against these boundaries. From Wilson's Tom Rath to *Mad Men*'s Don Draper, he broke the rules and was praised and rewarded for it by men who admired his bravery. What *Mad Men* gives us is a distinction with a difference — Don Draper is a liar but is unapologetic about it. Don lies to his wife, his mistresses, and his company and Don Draper is not even his real name. *Mad Men*'s conceit is that the advertising profession gives Draper the perfect environment in which to rationalize his deceit. Where, if not in advertising, is the selling of entirely fictional images more acceptable?

Masculinity in this series is organized around a lack: the lack of a construct of the organization man in its ideal form. The lack is papered over with images of manliness in the form of happy-looking marriages, assertions of sexual prowess, and dominance at the office. But both Pete and Don struggle constantly to *feel* the masculine power and control they have worked so hard to *appear* to have. When Roger advises Don to relax a little, Don replies that he is not as comfortable with being powerless. Roger knows Don well enough to conclude that Don's feelings of inadequacy are somehow connected to Pete. Though Don insists he is not competing with Pete, Roger doesn't buy it. Despite Don's clear dominance in the office environment, it seems his poor and shameful origins have left him with a hole that he hasn't figured out how to fill.

Don is usually secure enough in his confidence at work to not overtly struggle with Pete. But his obvious dislike of, frustration with, and anxiety around Pete Campbell show that in some way, Don is threatened by him. Sterling's observation is particularly astute, therefore, since he actually knows very little about Don personally. Don *is* competing with Pete, and only Pete, throughout the first season precisely because Pete has a verified and unassailable familial history, the one thing Don Draper lacks.

Don's low origins are the biggest secret he has and what he has taken the most pains to conceal. His concealment has taken its toll on him, driving him to mistresses with whom he can be more honest. The flashes of honest reve-lation of himself, the cynical dressing down of his charming persona are all found with women who are not his wife. Revealing too much about himself personally to his wife would mean breaking parts of the façade he needs to maintain to keep up the fictional persona of Don Draper. With his mistresses, and especially with Rachel Menken, he reveals a good deal about his past as Dick Whitman because there's a safety there. She has accepted him as Don Draper and because their relationship has built-in limits; there are fewer risks in revealing these personal, emotional details. Don reveals to Rachel that his mother had been a prostitute who died in childbirth and that he was raised by his father's widow and her second husband. Don's similarities to a prostitute are not coincidental — he sleeps around, and "whores" products for a living, and he seems uncomfortable whenever these comparisons are made. Don is unable to forget that the mother he never knew was not respectable and that the family that raised him did not love him. Jealous of Pete, whom Don believes has everything, Don sees an origin he never had and secretly resents the leg-up he feels it gave Pete. However, Don fails to see that the organization frowns as much on Pete Campbell as he does. Pete's sense of entitlement and distinction-by-right are at odds with a structure that venerates conformity and cooperative work. Whyte describes the ideal organization man as someone who "didn't rent the old place on the hill, but a smaller house ... drives an

Olds instead of a Caddy ... and listens more than he talks" (20). While Don
is a listener and an observer, by virtue of his feeling of being outside of happiness, normal life, and a stable identity, Pete wants to be listened *to*, refusing
to pick up on subtle cues or even more direct imperatives about his behavior
at work.

At the end of the Season One, asking ourselves why we favor Don Draper
over Pete Campbell reveals a good deal about our deeply held, though not
always acknowledged, beliefs about the American Dream. Whyte argues that
no matter how that dream may be articulated, "There is almost always the
thought that the pursuit of individual salvation through hard work, thrift,
and competitive struggle is the heart of the American achievement" (Whyte
4). Don and Pete, when examined closely, share several traits in common;
they both lie and deceive those close to them, and they both desire to rise in
their profession. But Don more closely fits Whyte's description, precisely
because he has actively and consciously set out to create a new persona that
follows what seems to be the masculine embodiment of the American Dream.
However much we may argue that the American Dream is dead (as workers
were already doing in Whyte's book), we identify more strongly with the
character that seems to embody its tenets.

Whyte's book was a warning against the power of the organization; he
feared what would happen if corporations began valuing conformity over innovation and risk-taking. And arguably, American corporations were forced to
listen to Whyte, however belatedly, when global competition and economic
downturn in the 1980s forced them to do so. As Joseph Nocera notes in his foreword to the 2002 reprint edition, corporations "jettisoned the bureaucracy. They
began to listen to dissenters in their ranks and supported corporate 'cultures'
that would spark innovation" (xvi) but 2007 TV watchers would view even
Nocera's congratulatory tone toward corporate America with cynicism. Since
this reprint, we've entered the biggest economic downturn in decades and stories
of banks suppressing and even firing workers who argued that subprime loans
were risky and short-sighted reminds us that we're not as far removed from
Whyte's warnings as we might like to think. America's dangerous embrace of
conformity and suppression of dissent came the year after this reprint when
the first "CEO president" and his "board of directors" managed to stifle any
objection towards his plan to launch a pre-emptive strike against Iraq. Weiner's
show, in which an army deserter with no name of his own is on the rise to
become one of the most influential members of a corporate environment,
therefore, offers viewers a fantasy of resistance, not just to corporate conformity but to a larger cultural oppression. We wish we could be as smart, savvy,
deviant, and successful as Don Draper, because though he might be miserable,
at least the choices that led him to his misery were his and his alone.

NOTES

1. Numerous articles aiming to get to the bottom of the current corporate climate return to Whyte's book to test the current temperature of the nation's tolerance for conformity. Bill Gates's great success, argues Michael Lewis, must surely be proof that the organization man is dead. (http://www.slate.com/id/2706/)

2. de Tocqueville's text has been translated many times with varying political intentions. I refer to the 1900 translation by Henry Reeve, full text available online at http://xroads.vir ginia.edu/~HYPER/DETOC/toc_indx.html.

WORKS CITED

Goodman, Tim. "TV Review: *Mad Men*." *San Francisco Chronicle*, 18 Jul. 2007. SFGate. com. 22 June 2009. <http://www.sfgate.com/cgibin/article.cgi?f=/c/a/2007/07/18/ DDGLNR0JHA1.DTL>.

Nocera, Joseph. "Foreword." *The Organization Man*. 1956. By William H. Whyte. Philadelphia: University of Pennsylvania Press, 2002.

Rand, Ayn. "Introducing Objectivism." Times-Mirror, 1962. 22 Jun. 2009. <http://www. aynrand.org/site/PageServer?pagename=objectivism_intro>.

Salem, Rob. "Lost in the '60s with *Mad Men*." *Toronto Star*, 19 Jul. 2007. Thestar.com. 24 May 2009. <http://www.thestar.com/entertainment/article/237469>.

Witchell, Alex. "*Mad Men* Has Its Moment." *New York Times*, 22 Jun. 2008. 15 May 2009. <http://www.nytimes.com/2008/06/22/magazine/22madmen-t.html>.

Whyte, William H. *The Organization Man*. 1956. Philadelphia: University of Pennsylvania Press, 2002.

THE POLITICS OF
MAD MEN

John Slattery as Roger Sterling and Jon Hamm as Don Draper in Mad
Men *(2007) (AMC/Kobal Collection).*

3. "The Good Place" and "The Place That Cannot Be": Politics, Melodrama and Utopia

Brenda Cromb

In *Mad Men*'s sixth episode, "Babylon," Don asks Rachel to tell him something about Israel. She replies that after living as exiles for centuries, it seems important that Jewish people finally have a land to call their own. She explains it is more like a concept than a real place. "Utopia," says Don. Rachel tells Don she learned about Utopia in college, that the Greeks defined it two ways. *Eutopos*, which means "the good place," and *utopos*, which means "the place that cannot be." The camera subtly moves forward on both their faces — while still maintaining the standard shot-reverse shot editing pattern — ratcheting up the emotional intensity of the moment. It is clear that for both of them, utopia is much a reference to their impossible relationship as to anything to do with Israel. Utopia, for them, is the idea of being together with no complications, more than a place. These two ideas of utopia — a political one and an emotional one — are intertwined in this scene, which encapsulates many of the ways *Mad Men* deals with both. On the one hand, there is the political: Rachel refers to Israel as an ideal, not knowing as twenty-first century viewers do that Israel's existence as a state and its treatment of the people its foundation displaced remains controversial. This element of the conversation is layered over and woven in our knowledge of Don and Rachel's growing mutual attraction, complicated by the fact that Don is already married. These two layers of longing inform each other and create *Mad Men*'s special brand of melodrama.

Mad Men has, to put it mildly, a complex relationship with the past. The series' portrayal of history resists both nostalgia with its dark portrayal of the social realities of the early 1960s and knee-jerk negativity with its loving cinematography emphasizing the careful production design and costuming. The show's portrayal of the characters' worldviews and the horizons of their lives shows how severely limited they are by the social conventions of the time. This historical awareness can be activated by the show to make us aware of our *own* historically bounded horizons. *Mad Men*'s focus on aspects of social life that have shown real progress — the treatment of women, racial minorities, homosexuals, for instance — creates a kind of unspoken progressive utopia, where such problems are solved completely. However this kind of historical-political *mental* calculation is always combined with an affective reaction. The show's mode of evoking emotion is purely melodramatic. This melodramatic element of the show reinforces the idea of utopia hinted at by the show's politics. All of the characters are, ultimately, searching for some kind of meaning in a world that seems meaningless.

I take the definition of utopia, not from, say, a structured, imagined world like Thomas More's, but from the concept of utopia-as-structure-of-feeling Richard Dyer writes about in "Entertainment and Utopia." Entertainment, he writes, "presents, head-on as it were, what utopia would feel like rather than how it would be organized. It thus works at the level of sensibility, by which I mean an affective code that is characteristic of, and largely specific to, a given mode of cultural production" (20). Dyer's chief examples are musicals, which present utopia with their narrative and stylistic emphases on energy, abundance, intensity, transparency, and community (22–23). What he means by most of these is fairly straightforward, but the idea of intensity is especially important to understanding *Mad Men*. Dyer describes intensity this way:

> I have in mind the capacity of entertainment to present either complex or unpleasant feelings (e.g. Involvement in personal or political events; jealousy, loss of lover, defeat) in a way that makes them seem uncomplicated, direct, vivid, not 'qualified' or 'ambiguous' as day-to-day life makes them, and without intimations of self-deception and pretence [25].

I do not claim that *Mad Men* presents this world of direct sensations and freedom from want — but rather that this is the world that its characters aspire to.

Mad Men is hardly a musical, and the world it portrays is unerringly cynical, but what the characters seem to be reaching for — what advertising is supposed to portray — is clearly related to this world of ease and clarity Dyer describes. When Don needs to explain to the Lucky Strike executives why his "It's toasted" slogan will be effective, he explains that advertising is based on happiness. He further defines happiness through material objects: "the smell of a new car" or "freedom from fear" (1:1). Don's equation between "freedom from fear" and "the smell of a new car" resonates closely with Dyer's premise that "the ideals of entertainment imply wants that capitalism itself promises to meet" (27). In Dyer's account, focusing mainly on studio-era Hollywood entertainment, works like musicals manage the contradictions in capitalism's unfulfilled promises. Since "the smell of a new car" does not actually give anyone freedom from fear or a sense of wholeness, entertainment allows viewers to imagine that these things are still possible. On *Mad Men*, it is as if the characters—none more than Don—are constantly trying to inhabit that promised world, even as they construct it. Don *knows* that love was "created by someone like him to sell nylons," but he still yearns for Rachel and her ability to understand him represents a promise that he could really be honest about himself, all parts of himself, with her—as opposed to dividing himself between his sweet wife Betty and his dangerous mistress Midge. Of course, this is not really how it works out—his affair with Rachel is short-lived once she realizes that he is not prepared to run away with her.

Don's alienation from his family is one of the show's clearest examples of the real world's failure to deliver on the promises given us by capitalism. In "The Wheel" (1:13), he uses his own family photos to sell Kodak on his campaign for their new slide projector (including a pointed speech about nostalgia). The speech is shot with a series of cuts between shots of Don talking and shots of the slides on the screen; but when he finishes, penitent adulterer Harry Crane runs unexpectedly out of the room, visibly affected. This emotional reaction emphasizes the extraordinary power of Don's pitch. At the end of the episode, it seems that Don has sold himself on this idealized, warm vision of family. Though by now the viewer knows he did not grow up with a warm or accepting home life, Don still longs to believe it might exist. The episode ends with a tease, wherein Don opens the door and tells Betty and the children he will join them for Thanksgiving after all. The scene then breaks off suddenly to show him repeating the gesture of opening the door to an empty house. He sits on the stairs, seemingly paralyzed by the chasm between what he thinks his family should be and what it actually is.

Though it has earned wide critical acclaim, one common line for *Mad Men's* detractors is that its negative image of the past leads to a complacent view of the present day. The *London Review of Books'* critic Mark Greif complains, "We watch and know better about male chauvinism, homophobia, anti-semitism, workplace harassment, housewives' depression, nutrition and smoking. We wait for the show's advertising men or their secretaries and wives to make another gaffe for us to snigger over." And Greif is perhaps right in his assessment that the show flatters the progressive politics of its viewers. After all, things really *are* better now; viewers who are shocked by the assessment that a woman coming up with a good idea is "like a dog playing the piano" cannot help but feel more enlightened than the staff of Sterling Cooper ("Babylon," 1:6). However, it does not seem necessary to understand *Mad Men* in this light, or at least not just in this light; it is just as possible to understand the series as making its viewers aware of historical context. If the show's appeal were truly to allow viewers to guffaw at how much they know better, why would it be set in the 1960s, a decade marked by cultural and political upheaval, as opposed to the 1950s, as Todd Haynes' Sirk homage *Far from Heaven* (2002) is? Central to *Mad Men's* relationship to the past is that its early 1960s setting is a moment of cultural transition and historical change. Seeing all this from the point of view of the old guard at Sterling Cooper — who look askance at Pete's observation (at a complaint that John F. Kennedy does not wear a hat) that Elvis does not either — makes the viewer all the more conscious that things are in flux. As the show progresses, as Peggy moves from secretary to copywriter, it is impossible not to feel that the world of *Mad Men* is changing.

Nonetheless, *Mad Men* works hard to remind its viewers that they are watching a show about the past — never allowing the viewer to fully suspend their disbelief, to become "lost" in the world of the show. In "The Gold Violin" (2:7) Don and Betty have a lovely family picnic, the door of Don's new Cadillac open to let music from the radio spill out, as they serenely lie on their blanket. Any bucolic nostalgia in the image is lost when Don and Betty get ready to go by throwing a beer can and just lifting their blanket and shaking off their trash. The camera lingers on the pristine landscape for a moment after they drive off in their big, beautiful, blue Cadillac to emphasize how differently people acted in everyday life in 1962. This kind of disjunction does not necessarily reflect a major social upheaval, but it is still a shock that jars viewers into remembering that the past was *different*. It seems inconceivable that *Mad Men* could have been produced in 1962, not only because of the sexual frankness, but because it seems pitched to allow viewers to compare and contrast the way things were in the 1960s with the way things are now. On the other hand, *Mad Men* is unafraid to throw in a jarringly anachronistic music choice, like the use of Bob Dylan's "Don't Think Twice, It's All Right," released in 1963, in the closing credits of "The Wheel" (1:13) the final episode of season one, set in 1960, or more jarringly, the use of the Decemberists song "The Infanta," released in 2005, in the opening montage of "Maidenform" (2:6).

These consistent reminders of the past can serve to distance the viewer, but they also produce a persistent historical awareness that *increases* emotional response. For example, in "The Mountain King" (2:12), Joan is raped by her fiancé in Don's office. The scene is filmed to focus on Joan's experience, her visceral anguish at what is happening to her, at her workplace, a space where she is used to being in control. The sounds of the couple struggling are unusually prominent in the soundtrack as Joan insists she does not want to have sex — then the camera focuses on a close-up of her face, which Greg pushes to the side. There is a shot of Don's couch from her point of view on the floor that features a subtle use of Hitchcock's dolly-in, zoom-out shot from *Vertigo,* before returning to Joan's blank face. The next scene cuts to Greg waiting for her outside the office before the two of them go off to dinner as if nothing had happened. It is painful for the viewer because it means seeing Joan, the office manager always in control of situations, have that control taken away from her. But it is also painful in another way, as Joan follows Greg out to dinner and it becomes clear that Joan will act like nothing has happened because, at the time, she would have had no other options. The kind of mental calculation a viewer has to do while watching this unfold is unavoidably colored by their awareness of the position of a woman who is raped by her fiancé in 1962. This knowledge of historical difference is accompanied with the knowledge that while things are *better* now, they are far from perfect for victims of rape. This clearly exemplifies the progressive political underpinnings of *Mad Men*: the sense that things *were* bad, but they have gotten better and that a future can be imagined where they are how they "should" be.

The gap between the way things are and the way they should be is also at the heart of another structure for thinking of Utopia, that of melodrama. Melodrama is often used as a derisive term, but I am using it in a descriptive sense here, following Peter Brooks' influential description of melodrama as a *mode* that works to produce a kind of moral clarity in the post-sacred world. In this account, the elevated emotions and clearly-stated moral coordinates produce a strong sensation of moral clarity in a world where the old rules no longer apply. The original theatrical melodramas appeared in Enlightenment France when religious orthodoxies were under fire and the divine right of the king to rule was no longer held as absolute. As Linda Williams puts it:

> ... Brooks takes it seriously as a quintessentially modern (though not modernist) form arising out of a particular historical conjuncture: the postrevolutionary, post–Enlightenment, post-sacred world where traditional imperatives of truth and morality had been violently questioned and yet in which there still a need to forge some semblance of truth and morality [51].

The cultural role of melodrama in exploring and resolving the tensions generated by the loss of moral clarity, and the sense of a need for access to some kind of absolute truth has not waned. The 1960s are an even clearer example — old hierarchies were dissolving, old assumptions about the place in society of all kinds of groups were being upended — of a time when no one knew how to relate to the world anymore. In "The Mountain King," things get explicitly post-sacred as Peggy and Salvatore use the ritual of Communion to sell Popsicles because both understand that the Catholic Church understands salesmanship. Peggy even alludes to the appeal as being "behavior, not religion." In their campaign, Popsicles represent love, family, and spiritual fulfillment: these are needs that capitalism senses, but cannot fulfill with Popsicles. This kind of desire is perhaps nowhere more clearly evoked on the show than in "Long Weekend" (1:10) when a pallid Roger has a near fatal heart attack and Don consummates his relationship with Rachel.

In characterizing *Mad Men* as a melodrama, I would take pains to distinguish it from the overwrought 1950s Douglas Sirk domestic melodramas which the term immediately evokes. As Linda Williams has argued before, melodrama is the central mode of American filmed entertainment (42). A serialized drama like *Mad Men*, with its intense emotional content and necessary tendency against finality, should be understood as upholding what Peter Brooks referred to as "melodramatic imagination." The "realism," or relative subtlety of the performances and the moral shadings that the series presents in relation to all the characters, does not necessarily preclude *Mad Men* from being understood as in the melodramatic mode. As Christine Gledhill suggests, melodrama is constantly adapting itself to forms that relate to contemporary audiences in order to establish the moral coordinates of the world:

> if the good and evil personifications of Victorian melodrama no longer provide credible articulations of conflict, modern melodrama draws on contemporary discourses for the apportioning of responsibility, guilt, and innocence — psychoanalysis, marriage guidance, medical ethics, politics, even feminism [32].

Mad Men uses these kinds of discourses to apportion blame and guilt, less on villains, more on social forces. *Mad Men*, however, shares with Victorian melodrama the impulse to work out how to live in a world where meaning is no longer automatically assumed.

One of melodrama's characteristic features is a victim-protagonist. As Williams puts it: "In cinema the mode of melodrama defines a broad category of moving pictures that move us to pathos for protagonists beset by forces more powerful than they and who are perceived as victims" (42). In classic melodramas, these forces can be social mores, like the way Cary's neighbors and children judge her in *All That Heaven Allows* (1954) or they can be natural forces, like the storm in Sjöström's *The Wind* (1928). On *Mad Men*, the powerful force that besets the characters seems to be history itself. In "The Gold Violin" (2:7) Salvatore is shown watching TV with his wife and furtively lighting a cigarette with Ken's forgotten lighter — a private moment of pleasure for a character who is hiding his true self and has to sublimate his desires because he knows he would not be accepted otherwise. The pathos of this quiet, wordless moment is heartbreaking. The "force" holding him back is a social one, but it is a social force that today's audience will recognize as historical. The reason the scene is so heartbreaking is because the viewers know that if the story were taking place today, Sal would at least be able to live openly. This wistfulness is also, as in the scene with Joan's rape, colored by the knowledge that gay men are still discriminated against in the United States, especially given the show was airing in the midst of the 2008 election campaign, which included a closely-watched battle in California over a ballot proposition that would halt the state's performing same-sex marriages. In this case, the show creates the desire for a kind of progressive utopia, a "place that cannot be" where Sal would not only not have to hide who he is, but something like full social acceptance for homosexuality could be achieved. The present becomes merely a way-station on the way to a more perfectly progressive future.

However, once *Mad Men* is defined as melodrama, it is very important to point out that it is *contemporary* melodrama, as opposed to some kind of pastiche of classic Hollywood films. While it has been compared to Todd Haynes' Sirk tribute *Far from Heaven*, in its feeling of being "Sirk with the gloves off" (Naremore 61), *Mad Men* itself is far from being pastiche. Pastiche is marked by the knowing copying of generic forms. Haynes' film makes a great example of pastiche without comedy, in that it not only borrows plot elements from classic Sirk melodramas like *All That Heaven Allows*, but it also recreates the style and feel of Sirk's mode of expression — from framing to costumes to visual motifs like the autumnal foliage or the scarf blowing away in the wind (the former drawn from *All That Heaven Allows*, the latter from *Written on the Wind*), as Richard Dyer points in *Pastiche* (175). Dyer's take on *Far from Heaven* is that it is pastiche that does not get in the way of emotional engagement, as is so often assumed (174). He does, however, describe the experience of watching *Far from Heaven* in ways that will sound very familiar to any viewer of *Mad Men:*

> The mixture described above specifically in relation to the 1950s [as experienced watching the film]— of sympathetic imagining and registering of difference — also embodies the dialectic of our relationship to the past more generally. It suggests that we can enter into the feelings of our forebears through immersion in their art but also reminds us that this is a highly limited and circumscribed activity. This itself is a variation at the level of affect on the perennial ambiguity of our relationship to the past, in that irresolvable tension between a sense that people in the past were like ourselves, with desires, dreams, hopes and fears like us, and yet we cannot know that for sure, and moreover that much of what they felt seems strange, opaque, other. Pastiche can embody that tension at the level of how we feel about people in the past [178].

While his description of watching the 1950s through *Far from Heaven* does not exactly match the way that we watch the 1960s through *Mad Men,* Dyer's ideas about the past are useful in unpacking the way that *Mad Men* presents the past with such fascination, drawing us close to the characters as people but constantly keeping us at arm's length with reminders of pastness. It is especially true in light of the conclusion Dyer reaches about the point of pastiche. In realizing that our only understanding comes from cultural artifacts like films, we may also be able to reflect on the idea that our own feelings are "framed by the traditions of feeling we inherit, mobilise and hand on. In other words, the pastiche of *Far from Heaven* not only makes the historicity of its own affect evident but can also allow us to realise the historicity of our own feelings" (178). This tendency towards self-historicity is similar to the way *Mad Men* causes viewers to reflect on their own historical time.

Obviously, it is impossible to read *Mad Men* as pastiche in this sense. The acting styles, the language, the *Sopranos*-esque exploration of a likable but clearly morally flawed protagonist, all ground the show within its generic context as twenty-first century cable television drama. Pastiche's knowing reuse of generic elements allow for an awareness of the historically-bound nature of the viewer's own structures of feeling. *Mad Men* avoids the question of forms, opting for a formal approach that feels relatively "neutral" in twenty-first century television terms. The historical self-awareness the show produces through the various techniques discussed above creates a very similar effect to that of *Far from Heaven*'s pastiche — with the exception that *Mad Men* produces self-awareness in the sense of one's worldview, one's frames of reference. *Far from Heaven* takes this to the extreme of using melodrama to help understand the historical contingency of narrative form (as a structure of feeling), but *Mad Men* tells a 1960s story in a twenty-first-century way. This ultimately does not seem to be pretending that the thoughts and feelings of people in the 1960s are just as accessible as those in the twenty-first-century. One could argue that people are *not* necessarily more accessible in the twenty-first-century, but a kind of unprecedented psychological access to a morally and emotionally complex character is a hallmark of "quality" television like *The Sopranos* or *Dexter*, which at least give the *impression* that the viewer understands everything there is to know about a character. However, the gap between the contemporary mode of expression and the strangeness of the daily realities of the characters in the show — the way they dress, the technologies they use, even the basic standards of socially acceptable behavior — only makes the past seem more foreign. This no doubt varies geographically and with age across North America, but even so. This description of the relationship of the 1960s as "other" more clearly applies to viewers under forty, who cannot remember the period being portrayed on the show. However, I would argue that the strategies used in *Mad Men* serve to emphasize the strangeness of this bygone era strongly enough so that any viewer would feel alienated from the period.

Mad Men has a diegetic relationship with the past that is worth exploring as well; it ties into the complex way that our relationship to the past is dealt with on the show. "The Wheel" (1:13) brings to a head the various images of family photos that the show used throughout the first season. In "Marriage of Figaro" (1:3), Don remains on the outside of his daughter's birthday party with a video camera. Later, the box of Whitman family photos Adam sends Don before he hangs himself becomes first a threat in Pete's hands, and then, in "The Wheel," a draw to reconnect with Adam. After looking at an old photo of the two of them together, he picks up the phone, only to find out that Adam has killed himself. Harry's reaction to the final slideshow ties the scene to his earlier late-night conversation with Don. He ruefully talks about how he used take pretentious photographs, explaining his fascination with the cave paintings at Lascaux, especially the handprints with paint blown around them. As Don knows, there is a line to be drawn between the "I was here" of the cave paintings, the "I was here" of Adam's last act of sending a box of photographs to his brother, and the "I was here" of Don's wedding photos — all of them have an indexicality that allows their existence to be a trace of the existence of their makers. These traces are, as Dyer points out, how we experience the past. However, they are only traces. The images of Don and Betty's family life that Don uses in his pitch tell one story, but the viewers (and Don) know that the version of family togetherness he presents is a false one. If nostalgia is, as Don says, "Pain from an old wound," then it is not the pain of knowing it too well, but rather the pain of not knowing it enough, of never being able to experience it fully.

The experience of not being able to experience life fully, in the way that society's narratives tell us it is supposed to be lived, is central to the modern (and especially the postmodern) condition. Melodrama is supposed to represent "grandiose and moral entities put within reach of the people, a moral universe made available" (Brooks 43). It is meant to dramatize these grandiose questions by bringing them to light on everyday life. *Mad Men* is about advertising; it is about men and women contending with the repressive social attitudes of 1960s America; it is about sex; it is mostly about the quest for meaning. Don's story — his shifting identities and shifting between women — is a quest for something "more." In the very first episode, Rachel Menken, a few hours after being the only woman in the boardroom, tells Don that he seems to understand what it feels like to be an outsider, too. At this point, the viewer does not really know much about Don, besides the sounds of bombs that haunt his sleep, hinting that he is a war veteran. However, it is clear from Don's uncomfortable expression that there is some unspoken reason she is right. The rest of the series will see him try identities on: his relationship with Midge allows him to rub shoulders with beatniks without really being one; his relationship with Rachel allows him to feel that someone understands him; his attempt to be a family man at the beginning of the second season shows him trying to live up to the image of himself he sold at the end of "The Wheel," and failing, hiding out at foreign films (the one he sees in "The Benefactor" [2:3] notably shows a shadowy image of a hand pressed up to glass) in an attempt to escape and to generally *feel* something authentic.

Another character who longs for meaning but is unable to achieve it is Pete Campbell. In the first season, after he is married, Pete seems truly to feel that marriage has somehow changed him. He tells his office friends that marriage was an almost-spiritual revelation. This feeling, however, does not last. In "Red in the Face" (1:7) he spends a humiliating lunch hour returning a product called a "chip-and-dip," a vaguely fallopian item used to hold both chips and dip when one is entertaining, explaining this to everyone who sees it. Feeling thoroughly emasculated by his experience at the woman-centered return counter, Pete exchanges his chip-and-dip for an obviously phallic hunting rifle. The next day — after a brief low-angle shot of Pete that moves in on his anguished face — Pete recites to Peggy an elaborate, richly detailed fantasy about hunting, and having a woman cook him up the freshly caught meat. Pete's ideal of old-fashioned, unanxious masculinity makes sense given his position in life — though a contemporary viewer's distance the fantasy feels even more ridiculous than it would have sounded then. Peggy's belief that this moment would be wonderful is more surprising given her frustration with being treated like a piece of meat at the office. Melodramatically speaking, it is clear that the gun, for Pete, represents a return to the sort of uncomplicated world that melodrama speaks to so powerfully — there is something a bit sublime in the simplicity of this dream. However, despite perhaps sharing Pete's emotional reactions at the various humiliations he faced throughout the day, it is clear to the viewer that the dream Pete confesses to Peggy is driven by ideology. However, after spending the day with Pete, the distance of historical knowledge becomes mixed with pity — while a contemporary viewer most likely cannot relate to Pete's desire to go hunting (or Peggy's desire to cook his meat), they can sympathize with both of their desires for a sense of clarity, of simplicity, and of clear meanings. This longing, that sense of desire for something that cannot quite be put into words — and Peggy's breathless response, followed by her impulsive trip to the snack cart show the depth of her feelings for Pete.

Mad Men occasionally has forays into "art film" stylistic touches — like the aforementioned scene with Don coming home twice — but stylistically, it does not stray far from classical continuity editing. One touch that is particular to the show is a tendency to track in on the faces of the actor (or actors) in emotional moments. Because *Mad Men* operates with such a minimal score —

music, of course, being one of melodrama's best-known tools to express emotion ("melodrama" literally means "play with music")— it requires cinematographic flourishes to exaggerate the emotion. In the context of the show, it makes sense, as it literalizes the interplay between historical distance and emotional engagement *Mad Men* plays at. A scene will begin at an "appropriate" distance — a standard medium close-up — and then track in closer to the performers than the scene would really demand. The influence of this wordless close-up is because in melodrama, a strong degree of emphasis is placed on the unspoken, on the unspeakable. In melodrama, pure physical signs are taken to hold a deeper truth than that of language: "Words, however unrepressed and pure, however transparent as vehicles for the expression of basic relations and verities, appear to be not wholly adequate to the representation of meanings, and the melodramatic message must be formulated through other registers of the sign" (Brooks 56).

As much as it is driven by the political and social differences between the past and the present, *Mad Men* is still driven by affective response, not that emotion should be considered separate from politics, but more that melodrama—especially American melodrama related to the American Dream — has tended towards an idealized past or at least one with more open possibilities. *Mad Men* is exciting because it completely explodes that temporal structure. *Mad Men* has a strange, contradictory relationship to the past. On the one hand, it highlights aspects of 1960s society over which the current decade presents an undeniable improvement. However, on the other hand, the problems of the characters are linked just as much to more (seemingly) timeless problems, at least as old as capitalism. The appeal of *Mad Men* is that it shows our heritage of commercial emptiness is not a recent development. This makes it sound as though *Mad Men* is unrelentingly bleak, but watching the show is still a pleasurable experience. Despite the fact that it is occupied primarily with the despair that comes from capitalism's unfulfilled promises, through its emphasis on historical difference, it also makes it abundantly clear that things *can* change, by contrasting the sense of post-sacred emptiness with ample demonstrations of how much things have changed. The excitement of knowing this, of seeing how different our possibilities are from Don's and Pete's and Peggy's, there is a spark of hope that—even if Don cannot ever achieve the fullness of experience he longs for —*we* might. Though *Mad Men* does not present a detailed road map to a more uncomplicated emotional experience, and certainly does not begin to imagine an alternative to capitalist consumerism, it still holds the promise that things can and will be different.

In *Mad Men's* splitting the difference between political distancing and melodramatic emotional engagement, it allows viewers to conceive of the possibilities of change in the future. After the scene in "Babylon" I discussed at the outset of this chapter, so charged with possibility, Don and Rachel have an affair, break it off, and then Rachel, once so strong and independent, reappears in Season Two married and dressed in ill-suited pale pink. The utopia that their romance once represented has proved to be false. Yet even as Don continues to fruitlessly seek fulfillment from art films and affairs, there remains an unspoken promise that the future does not need to be like the past, that no matter how impossible it seems we could someday arrive at "the place that cannot be."

Works Cited

Brooks, Peter. *The Melodramatic Imagination.* New Haven, CT: Yale University Press, 1995.

Dyer, Richard. "Entertainment and Utopia." *Only Entertainment.* 2nd ed. Routledge: New York, 1992. 19–35.

_____. *Pastiche.* London: Routledge, 2007.

Gledhill, Christine. "The Melodramatic Field: An Investigation." *Home Is Where the Heart Is.* Ed. Gledhill. London: BFI, 1987. 5–42.

Greif, Mark. "You'll Love the Way It Makes You Feel." *London Review of Books*, 23 October 2008. 14 January 2009. < http://www.lrb.co.uk/v30/n20/grei01_.html>.

Williams, Linda. "Melodrama Revised." *Refiguring American Film Genres.* Ed. Nick Browne. Berkeley: University of California, 1998. 42–88.

4. Unleashing a Flow of Desire: Sterling Cooper, Desiring-Production, and the Tenets of Late Capitalism

David P. Pierson

Mad Men and Late Capitalism

Frederic Jameson explains in *Postmodernism* (1991) that late capitalism or the third stage of capitalism is a purer moment of capitalism than any form that has preceded it (3). He maintains that aesthetic production, for the most part, became integrated with commodity production; "the frantic economic urgency of producing fresh waves of ever more novel-seeming goods (from clothing to airplanes), at ever greater rates of turnover, now assigns an increasingly essential structural function and position to aesthetic innovation and experimentation" (4–5). Jameson also argues that the 1960s can be seen as a key transitional period in this third stage of capitalism not only because of new technologies (telecommunication, computerization), which drastically compress the time and space of business and financial transactions, but because of the formation of new cultural and economic sensibilities — "new types of consumption"; "an ever more rapid rhythm of fashion and styling changes; the penetration of advertising, television and the media" into an unparalleled degree in society (3, 19–20).

American Movie Classics' popular *Mad Men* series, which highlights the fictional Sterling Cooper as one of the leading national advertising agencies on Madison Avenue, rests on the temporal nexus of these dramatic economic and cultural changes in American society in the 1960s. The advertising agency, an economic and cultural catalyst of late capitalism, serves as a perfect example of Gilles Deleuze and Felix Guattari's (1983) "desiring machine" in that its primary function is to re-imagine and re-code their client's products to associate them with particular desires that link to wider social networks of desires, which comprise modern society (1–6). At the helm of these ad campaigns is Don Draper, the agency's enigmatic, creative director. Perhaps because of his deprived childhood and self-invented status, Draper is a master in fostering his creative team to connect various mundane consumer goods and services with seemingly innate desires that lurk deeply in the hearts and psyches of middle-class American men and women.

This chapter, relying on the works of Deleuze and Guattari, Jameson, and others, examines how *Mad Men* represents the pinnacle of the modern American corporation and pre–1970s capitalism. It argues that Freudian psychoanalysis, especially the Oedipal complex, functions to regulate desire and serves as a kind of social cement for the forces of late capitalism. While Sterling Cooper's employees are at the center of "desiring-production," they are not exempt from contending with the ongoing deterritorialization and reterritorialization concomitant with living in a capitalist society. The chapter also explores how the series serves as a nostalgic vision of pre–1970s capitalism for contemporary viewers, presenting a time period when working for a corporation was the aspiration of many middle-class professionals. As the series' central character, Draper is well-suited for the changing demands and opportunities attendant to corporate capitalism. He is also the type of person who is likely to survive in today's unstable, corporate environment. In many ways, Draper represents a crucial transitional figure for both pre–1970s corporate and post–Fordist, flexible capitalism.

Desiring-Production, Capitalism and Oedipalization

In *Anti-Oedipus*, Deleuze and Guattari argue that the Oedipal family structure is one of the primary modes of restricting desire in late capitalist societies and psychoanalysis helps to reinforce that restriction (262–271). The main goal in their study is to reveal the repressive and even fascistic nature of the ingrained relationship between psychoanalysis and capitalism in contemporary societies (Foucault xi–xiv). Deleuze and Guattari hope to liberate schizoid flows[1] of desire before they are arrested and constrained by language and other representational forms. Capitalism has a tendency of condensing all social relations to the same universal equivalency. In the process, it "deterritorializes" desire by destabilizing existing social codes and customs that serve to limit and control social relations and production, such as religious beliefs, folk traditions, family affiliations, and social classes. As it destabilizes these social structures it also reterritorializes them into the constricted boundaries of the market-driven commodity form (Bogue 88).

The Oedipus complex functions to make sure that all human desire is circumscribed to the individual and the traditional, nuclear family, and that only a small amount of residual and commodified desire is allowed to be invested in the social domain, which is regulated by the economic relations of capital. When capitalism deterritorializes existing social traditions it "sets adrift schizophrenic fluxes of bits and scraps of things, people, words, customs, and beliefs, which it then reterritorializes in the neurotic Oedipal triangle of father-mother-me" (Bogue 88–89). The process of Oedipalization serves as the social cement of late capitalism because it functions to hold together the social structure by making sure that the family or Oedipal triangle is the primary organizing principle in modern societies.

While psychoanalysis limits desire to imaginary fantasies, Deleuze and Guattari define desire as a real, productive force, which exists prior to the formation of language, representation, or subjectivities. They claim that desire is production or "desiring-production" not loss or lack. They oppose Jacques Lacan's notion of desire as emerging from individual "lack." They insist that desire is an unbound, energetic force which is close to Freud's conception of libido. Deleuze and Guattari stress the collective nature and the limitless range of desire, and that it cannot be condensed to the level of the individual. Desire is pre-representational and pre-individual, and is not internal to any subject. Desire is essentially unconscious and is indifferent to negation, personal identities and subjectivities, and is independent of linguistic expressions, which are central to Lacan's Symbolic order and theories (Bogue 89). The primary goal of advertising is to tap into the perceived collective desires of consumers in order to construct an effective ad campaign.

Deleuze and Guattari describe the productive nature of desire as a kind of "desiring-machine" that functions to produce a flow of desire as it is connected to other machines in a larger network of desiring machines. Every desiring-machine is connected to another desiring-machine that interrupts or breaks off part of the flow. They stress the inescapable interconnection between desiring-machines and social bodies or machines. No desiring-machines can exist outside of the larger social machines that form them and no social machines can exist outside of the multitude of desiring-machines that form them at the micro-level (Deleuze and Guattari 5–11). An ad campaign is essentially a desiring-machine, which functions to connect an object or commodity to a flow of desires, connected to a large web of other desiring-machines (media outlets, retailers, consumers).

The impersonal force of desire is repressively codified through Oedipalization. The Oedipus complex works to personalize and individualize desire, submitting all unconscious production to the social and sexual realm of the family unit. Similar to Foucault's conception of the panopticon, Oedipalization operates as an internalized, disciplinary energy repressing and attempting to regulate all desires to the domains of the individual and family. Deleuze and Guattari argue that psychoanalysis in modern societies serves as a repressive force which projects desire into the personalized, Oedipal triangle of mother-father-child (Elliot 146–147). The Oedipal triangle is further projected and replicated in other social realms from the state (father-mother) and its citizens (children), the corporation (Father) and its workers (children), and in the world of *Mad Men*, Draper (Father) and his creative team of account executives, copywriters, and illustrators (children) (Verhuldonck 2).

The discourses of Oedipalization are readily apparent in popular cultural forms, including novels, music, movies, and television series. Early network television was characterized by popular family situation comedy series, including *The Adventures of Ozzie and Harriet, The Donna Reed Show, Father Knows Best*, and *Leave It to Beaver*, which were centered on the family as the primary source of psychic solace and meaning for its members. These Oedipal replications also serve to reproduce social and power relations crucial to the maintenance and reproduction of social forms in societies.

Deleuze and Guattari assert that psychoanalysis, in its emphasis on the Oedipal, has created a Lacanian "ideology of lack" in that it constantly stresses the possibility of a unified human subjectivity in a world filled with partial human subjects and subjectivities. Because psychoanalysis conceives of human subjects as partial subjects and objects, humans continuously seek to fill this lack with a surplus of objects and commodities (Elliot 147–148). The capitalist production process functions to transfer human desire on to objects or commodities. Since the lack or loss can never really be filled, fulfillment is constantly deferred, which in turn unleashes a new flow of desire (Verhuldonck 3).

Since people rely on objects to replace the loss, they are also interpellated by consumer society. Also, because consumer culture and advertising repeatedly reminds us of this loss, we constantly seek objects to refill this loss with something new and exciting (clothes, car, relationship, social status) (Verhulsdonck 4). In supplanting this loss through commodities, people are repeatedly investing in their desires and thereby, establishing an economy of desire or a "libidinal economy" (Deleuze and Guattari 344–347). Deleuze and Guattari libidinalize Marx asserting that "lack is created, planned, and organized in and through social production.... The deliberate creation of lack as a function of market economy is the art of the dominant class. This involves deliberately organizing wants and needs amid an abundance of production; making all of desire teeter and fall victim to the great fear of not having one's needs satisfied" (28). Jean Baudrillard argues that modern advertising and multimedia have produced a system that leaves the individual in a constant state of ecstasy and schizophrenia, where he or she is unable to escape or disengage from the overpowering pull of television and mass media. Baudrillard maintains that mass media "touches, invests, and penetrates without resistance, with no halo of private protection" for the individual (132–133).

The process of how Oedipalization supports late capitalism is exemplified in several Sterling Cooper ad campaigns featured on *Mad Men.* In the pilot episode, "Smoke Gets in Your Eyes" (1:1), for example, Draper and his creative team must contend with creating a new ad campaign for Lucky Strikes cigarettes against dire public health warnings about smoking. Draper rejects an in-house research report, which shows that people continue to smoke because they harbor a Freudian death drive, an unconscious desire to experience death. Draper determines that the best strategy is to just ignore the ethical health concerns and focus on what advertising does best — remind people that everything is fine and by implication, it is acceptable to smoke Lucky Strikes. Since consumer culture and psychoanalysis constantly inform people that they are partial and unsatisfied subjects, a commercial message of mutual reassurance would be welcomed and effective for most consumers. Draper's suggestion associates with Harvey's assertion that late capitalism is characterized by the triumph of aesthetics over ethics and that aesthetics not morality becomes the primary social and intellectual concern (327–328). Ultimately, Draper's ad campaign decides to highlight an inane, insignificant feature of Lucky Strikes, namely, that its tobacco leaves are toasted.

Also, in "Ladies Room" (1:2) Draper and his creative team are assigned to produce an ad campaign for Right Guard, a men's antiperspirant. The team proposes a campaign that ties together the product's new aerosol design with the technological image of the space-age astronaut. Draper, however, surmises that Right Guard is actually purchased by women, who are the product's true consumers. With the product's appeal shifted, Draper asks his team and himself to consider the enigmatic question of what women want. He speculates that women used to want a rugged individualistic hero, like a cowboy, but was not sure about their current desires for a man. The common advertising and marketing practice of gendering the majority of commodities implicitly standardizes heterosexual gender identities, which in turn reinforce the Oedipal complex.

Throughout "Ladies Room," Draper poses his peculiar and patriarchal centered question to a number of close friends and colleagues. Roger Sterling, Draper's boss, responds to his question with a dispassionate, "Who cares?" Midge Daniels, Draper's bohemian mistress, responds bluntly by exclaiming that what women really want is to stop being asked that question. Draper finally theorizes that women ultimately want an excuse to get close or more intimate with a man who they care about. Apparently, a man who uses Right

Guard will be positioned better for this physical and emotional intimacy. While women as human subjects and desiring-machines certainly have an infinite range of desires, Draper confines and personalizes his theory of their core desire (to be closer to a man) within the Oedipal, socially normalized realm of heterosexual relationships with men. His theorization also functions to commodify this desire and to associate it with the product (Right Guard) in the ad campaign.

Sometimes the image of the traditional American family is used to market products and thereby, associate them to the Oedipal triangle. For instance, in the episode "The Wheel" (1:13), Draper and his creative team are given the assignment of producing a campaign concept for Kodak's revolving 35mm slide projector. Draper, deeply affected by the secret suicide of his stepbrother, makes a sales presentation focused on how the projector serves as a nostalgic "time machine" providing us with images of the past and near-present. He also asserts that the projector is like a carousel in that it enables one to travel here and there and then back to a place we are loved, like home. The lack or loss to be replenished by this commodity is a nostalgic yearning for the Oedipal family — father-mother-me. As Raymond Williams notes, advertising is a system where material objects (clothes, cars, perfume) are magically endowed with non-material sentiments, like social acceptance, sexual intimacy, and nostalgia. Ironically, these same sentiments have been displaced by capitalism, a system predicated on the universal equivalency of capital (Williams 170–195).

For his presentation, Draper projects images of his own family life with the projector. With his beautiful, blonde wife, two healthy-looking children, and his own stoic, handsome appearance, Don's family is the idealized version of the classic, middle-class American family in the early 1960s. Of course, the Drapers' family image belies its darker side, which includes Betty's discontent, Don's shadowy past and marital infidelities. Draper's presentation not only highlights the projector's nostalgic properties, but also supports the centrality of the family network to social life and public memory. Because people must contend with the continuous deterritorialization and reterritorialization associated with capitalism, nostalgia can provide them with a sense of continuity with the past.

The productive nature of desire as a desiring machine enables it to make connections with bodies (social, human) and to exploit them to its own ends. As Marx notes, the historical trajectory of early capitalism involved breaking the feudal arrangements of the peasant worker with the soil and the guild in order that it could "free" the worker's labor for its factories and other businesses. Capitalism also involves harnessing the laborer's organs (physical and mental energies) to tie it to the capitalist machine and to subordinate its

movements to its rhythms. Deleuze and Guattari claim that desiring-
attempt to make us productive, organic beings by rearranging our or
a design of their own making. From their perspective, any organ nom tne
body (social or human) is capable of performing labor and producing a flow
of desire, which connects to other desiring machines. The ability of laboring
organs to produce surplus labor and value not only enabled the shift from
primitive accumulation to capitalism, but also the creation of the capitalist
class (Buchanan 58–59).

Several Sterling Cooper ad campaigns associate the client's product with
the human body and thereby, reinscribe and rearrange its organs to produce
a flow of desires which will connect to other desiring machines (consumers).
In "Babylon" (1:6), Draper's creative team places a group of female office workers in a room with a one-way mirror so they can witness which Belle Jolie
lipstick colors they choose. Afterwards, Peggy Olson, Draper's secretary, comments that she did not try any of the lipsticks because another woman took
her color and that she wants to be more than "one of a hundred colors in a
box." Her comment provides the copywriters with a new creative idea, namely,
that Belle Jolie and its wide array of colors enables a woman to "individualize"
her appearance. Despite the contradictory notion that any "mass" marketed
product has the capacity to individualize anyone, nonetheless, the creative
idea works to transform and promote a woman's lips into a primary organ for
the flow of feminine desire and individuation. Of course, this desire for individuation coupled with the product serves capitalist purposes. The final campaign for Belle Jolie features images of several women puckering their lips
with the associated copy headline, "Mark Your Man." The campaign essentially makes a woman's lips the nexus for producing a flow of heterosexual,
feminine desire directed at men. The fact that the copy explicitly asks women
to mark their "man" rather than "men" reinforces the Oedipal triangle and
the family network.

Despite the repressive and restrictive nature of Oedipalization and late
capitalism, Deleuze and Guattari argue that a flow of desires frequently escape
the confines of these social bodies (244–245). In "Indian Summer" (1:11), for
example, Olson is assigned to develop creative copy for an electronic weight
reduction belt designed for women. When Olson takes it home and tries it,
she discovers that its vibrations produce the unintended effect of satisfying
some women's sexual desires. Although the weight loss product certainly can
be associated with a flow of sexual desires, Olson and the creative team are
careful about how much they can suggest these benefits in the campaign,
probably because they do not conform to accepted social norms of women's
sexuality in the early 1960s. They ultimately decide that they can only hint
about it with words like "stimulating" and "refreshing." Also, in this same

episode, Betty Draper discovers that the vibrating motion of a washing machine can be used to satisfy some of her sexual desires. The episode suggests that commodities can serve as partial objects in a release of desires which have escaped well-planned capitalist production and distribution.

Deterritorialization and Reterritorialization

One of the things that differentiates capitalism from primitive and despotic societies is that it operates internally rather than through external social codes. Deleuze and Guattari assert that primitive and despotic machines share a "dread of decoded flows — flows of production, but also mercantile flows of exchange and commerce that might escape the State monopoly, with its tight restrictions and its plugging of flows" (197). The capitalist machine has the tendency of replacing social customs and relations with a universal axiomatic which allows the open exchange and substitution of everything for everything. This universal axiomatic not only enables the free exchange of goods and services in an open market, but also bodies, ideas, knowledge, fantasies, and images (Bogue 100). For example, in "5G" (1:5), Draper's creative team arrests the flow of desire of some husbands to have a hidden, discretionary fund "outside" of their marriages to create a new investment instrument called the "Executive Account" for Liberty Savings Bank. The team's actions recode the flow of desire and transform it into a commodity (bank account) freely exchangeable in the market. Because capitalism is an abstract unit of equivalency, it is not reducible to a social code or set of codes as with primitive and despotic societies.

Deleuze and Guattari have compared the capitalist machine to the schizophrenic because it escapes dominant coding and continuously scrambles existing codes. The capitalist machine has the ability to insert itself into any culture, decodes schizo-flows of desire and old codes, and re-territorializes them through an axiomatic equivalency for the benefit of the capitalist system. At the same time that capitalism tends to undermine existing customs and social relations through decoding or deterritorializing, it tries to create or recreate artificial or residual territorialities to contradict its decoding tendencies. These territorialities can take the form of repressive institutions or units, like the State, church, family, or corporation, which seek to repress and control the flow of desires for the betterment of the system. Deleuze and Guattari point out that capitalism is not a monolithic unity and that flows frequently escape both its domain and the domains of the repressive institutions (244–250).

Sterling Cooper as a leading advertising firm serves as both a social body within the capitalist machine and a repressive institution territorializing and exchanging its employees' labor and bodies[2] for compensation. The company as a complex system within capitalist society is marked by simultaneous movements of territorialization (maintenance of existing relations) and deterritorialization (dissolution of existing relations). As with other companies, Sterling Cooper is affected by market pressures to increase work efficiencies and to expand into new markets. Because of the increasing need for the company to create effective ad campaigns for an expanding range of consumer products designed for women, Sterling Cooper eventually hires its first female copywriter — Peggy Olson. Since the company's creative team is an all boys club, Olson's hiring creates disruptive, deterritorializing tensions for the male as well as the female office workers. Draper attempts to maintain existing social relations by having Olson prove herself worthy of the position through a series of trial advertising accounts. While we may see Olson as an icon of deterritorialization, Deleuze and Guattari remind us that deterritorialization can only be grasped through "the indices of desiring-machines, which take a variety of forms — an airplane, a train, a bicycle, sewing machine, or whatever" (316). Machines are at the heart of dreams and industry serving as objects of flight and escape, and as production and circulation. In this vein, the arrival of the office's first photocopying machine at the beginning of the series' second season exemplifies deterritorialization because it will alter work habits (no more carbon copying) and will increase the flow of information both within and outside the company.

One of the features of late capitalism is the incessant expansion into, and linkage with, global markets and cultures. This feature is made possible in the 1960s because of new technological developments in telecommunications and airline jet travel. At the end of the series' second season,[3] Sterling Cooper experiences deterritorialization that will affect its corporate structure when they are taken over by Putnam, Powell and Lowe, a British advertising company. The merger between Sterling Cooper and the British firm will not only provide global reach for its advertising clients but will give them the resources to compete in the television arena. Although Don and the other Sterling Cooper partners will profit from the planned merger, nonetheless, the merger creates great tension among his creative team who are concerned about possible lay-offs and new management changes.

Nostalgia and *Mad Men*

Jameson asserts that the one of the central aesthetic features of postmodernism is pastiche or the imitation of styles and mannerisms from previous time periods in contemporary cultural forms (architecture, painting, films). The so-called "nostalgia film" uses pastiche and projects it into a collective, social level in order to recapture a "perceived" missing past that is now known primarily through a collection of fashion styles and images. He points to George Lucas's *American Graffiti* (1973) as the initial film of this new aesthetic discourse, which set out to evoke the perceived "lost innocence and reality of the Eisenhower era" before the unsettling arrival of anti-war and countercultural movements. For many filmmakers it seems that the 1950s remain "the privileged lost object of desire," not only because it was perceived as a period of social stability and prosperity but also it revealed "the first naïve innocence of the countercultural impulses of early rock and roll and youth gangs"[4] (18–19). Jameson highlights other nostalgia films, like Polanski's *Chinatown* (1974) and Bertolucci's *The Conformist* (1970), which colonized period styles to open up other generational epochs, namely, post-war America in the 1940s through to the Eisenhower era, and the rise of fascist Italy in the 1930s, respectively. He maintains that these films do not provide a genuine historicity, rather they appropriate the historical past for its stylistic features, conveying a past through the aesthetic attributes of the cinematic image and fashion sensibilities (19).

Similar to Jameson's description of nostalgia films, the *Mad Men* series colonizes the generational style and mannerism of America in the early 1960s. Indeed, one of the pleasures of *Mad Men* is relishing the style and fashions (clothes, home and office furnishings, music) which were part of the period. The series, which begins in 1960, is situated at the end of the Eisenhower era and the beginning of the Kennedy era. As such, it recaptures the conformity, prosperity, and hopeful optimism of this transitional period before the momentous events and political unrest (Civil Rights, anti–Vietnam War and countercultural movements) that would quickly overtake the nation. During the series' first two seasons, the only evident social dissenters are the urban bohemians and the early rumblings of the emerging Civil Rights Movement. As with *American Graffiti*, *Mad Men* represents a culturally perceived period of lost American innocence and reality prior to the social and political turbulence that would soon follow.

The series also offers an unsentimental yet nostalgic vision of a time when white males clearly dominated and controlled the domains of American business. While the traditional WASP males and their image became an easy target in the mid-to-late fifties with sociological works from David Reisman, C. Wright Mills, and William Whyte cataloging the anxieties, fears, and emptiness of their successful business lives, nevertheless, they continued to dominate the "popular cultural landscape" and the corporate world. By the early sixties, only a few groups, notably Jews and Catholics, made significant social gains in the academy and business realms (Clecak 13–20). Women and minorities were generally excluded from these domains.

Since *Mad Men* takes place at a time that is arguably the pinnacle of the American modern corporation, it recaptures a moment for the middle-class professional when working for a large company was the dominant career aspiration. This moment occurs in the environment of pre–1970s corporate capitalism when the majority of large corporations provided workers with a sense of stability, a clear pathway to career advancement, and a personal identity closely aligned with the company's goals. Richard Sennett claims that older-style companies and organizations provided an established setting where employees could garner a sense of self-worth and satisfaction in their job (1–2). Indeed, Charles Heckscher argues that most large American corporations followed "the ethic of paternalism" whereby the organization offered middle managers protection and security in exchange for undivided loyalty. This paternalistic ethic was central to the development and expansion of large bureaucracies that came to dominate the corporate world (Heckscher 6). In Draper's promotion to firm partner, Draper's nurturing and promotion of Olson from secretary to junior copywriter, and the approval of Harry Crane's idea to create a television department, Sterling Cooper follows the basic attributes of a paternalistic organization.[5]

Since the 1970s, the corporation, once the nerve center of modern capitalism, has become "dominated by fickle shareholders governed by short-term speculation, risk adverse mindset where destabilizing the organization sends a positive, rather than negative message to investors" (Sennett 37–42). The corporation often appears to be a shuttlecock batted back and forth by global capital markets, along with being prey to recent boom-and-bust economic cycles. Sennett argues that this organizational instability is unnerving and disturbing for workers. The company that downsizes, gets taken over, or has to constantly reinvent itself is no longer a secure place for workers (Sennett 48–52). Although on-demand production, flexible labor, and new communication technologies have provided workers with more freedom within and outside the workplace, nonetheless, these changes have also led to increased volatility and insecurity for American workers. Bennett Harrison asserts that as fast as large firms are going "flexible" with lean production, downsizing and labor outsourcing, the number of safe, stable and secure occupations seem to be declining. The workforce of this "new economy is systematically divided into insiders and outsiders" (Harrison 38). Some workers are employed full-time with year-round schedules and complete job benefits. But a growing number of Americans are conditional workers employed part-time or part-year with low wages and few benefits (Harrison 38–44). Ehrenreich quotes an observation made by David Noer, a management consultant, about today's corporate world: "Organizations that used to see people as long-term assets to be nurtured and developed now see people as short-term costs to be reduced.... [T]hey view people as "things" that are but one variable in the production equation, 'things' that can be discarded when the profit and loss numbers do not come out as desired" (225). *Mad Men*, however, does not view the corporation through rose-colored glasses. Sterling Cooper, as an exemplar, is rigidly hierarchal, numbingly conformist, and generally resistant to change. Social critics Reisman, Mills, and Whyte in the 1950s expressed grave concerns over social conformity in post-war America, especially within the confines of corporate and institutional bureaucracies.[6] These criticisms would have been seen as still relevant to the corporate business culture of the early 1960s.

Although there is a linear career tract, the corporation is also an intensely competitive environment for its workers. In the pilot episode, for example, Draper, frustrated with coming up with a new creative idea for Lucky Strike cigarettes, jokingly confesses to Daniels, his mistress, that he is finally finished as an ad man and his company will soon know it. He elaborates that the next time she sees him a group of young executives will be "picking meat off my ribs." Later, in the episode, we meet the type of young businessman that Draper must contend with on a daily basis — Pete Campbell, a pushy, ambitious account executive. In this same episode, Draper discovers that Campbell had taken a research report from his (Draper's) office and has used some of the information from it to promote his own ideas at a sales presentation for the Lucky Strike executives. Subsequent episodes feature Campbell unethically pitching copy to one of the Draper's clients and threatening to blackmail Draper into promoting him up the corporate ladder.

The pre–1970s corporation was not always a hospitable place for female workers. Women frequently faced sexual harassment and inappropriate conduct from both male co-workers and bosses. In *Mad Men*, the male workers, who hold the dominant positions of power and influence at Sterling Cooper, repeatedly and openly make sexual comments and gestures about the company's female workers, who are primarily employed as secretaries. In the corporate world, women's work was often not as valued as a man's, especially in terms of compensation and promotion within the company. When Olson, a secretary, accidently reveals to the men that she excels at creative brainstorming, Freddie Rumsen, a copywriter, both praises and demeans her at the same time. Throughout the first two seasons of the series, Olson must continuously struggle to be accepted as a fellow copywriter, to gain access to clients, all without alienating the other women who work at Sterling Cooper. Despite the intensely competitive nature and rampant sexism in the workplace, nevertheless, contemporary audiences, weary of the instability and job insecurity of what Sennett calls, "the culture of new capitalism," may perceive the series as a nostalgic expression of an earlier time when companies provided workers with some sense of stability and personal identity.

Draper as Transitional Figure

Draper is a crucial transitional figure for both pre–1970s capitalism and the new, flexible capitalism. He is not so much the traditional Horatio Alger or self-made, capitalist hero, rather he is a self-invented man capable of transforming himself to any given business situation to further his personal desires. Draper is well-suited for the changing demands and opportunities attendant to corporate capitalism in the 1960s. In "The Hobo Code" (1:8), we learn he was the illegitimate offspring of a brief encounter between his father and a prostitute. He was raised by his father, a stern, dishonest and callous man, and his step-mother, a kind-hearted, religious woman, on a small farm. Perhaps because of his unyielding father and impoverished childhood, Draper knows about the darker side of Oedipalization. He knows well the social demands placed on people, especially in the 1950s and early 1960s, of being seen to come from and to have a happy, traditional family. Because of his shame of his childhood and of being a bastard child, he keeps his family history a closely guarded secret from his wife, children, and co-workers.

While Draper has created the ideal suburban, middle-class family with his marriage to the lovely Betty and their two children to assuage the pains of his own childhood, nevertheless, he realizes, at some deeper level, that his near-perfect family and their image are actually a fragile social façade and a trap. He frequently escapes the conformity of his suburban life through sexual encounters with a host of uncommon women from the bohemian Midge Daniels to the urbane, Jewish department store heiress Rachel Menken, and the aggressive Bobbie Barrett, the wife-manager of comedian Jimmy Barrett. Draper instinctively knows that most people live their lives in quiet, lonely desperation struggling to achieve and maintain the traditional family and a satisfied personal identity. He understands that a certain gap or lack exists in the hearts of most Americans. This knowledge enables him to produce advertising that connects to this inner disparity.

Draper's realization that the world is actually comprised of superficial surfaces provides him with the confidence and the ability to assume a variety of social roles (husband, lover, salesman, boss), each of them demanded by a particular social situation without even a hint of contradiction. This attribute makes him a nimble and successful player in the rapidly changing corporate environment of the 1960s. The only social role which he is resistant in performing is the Oedipal role of father as disciplinarian or the Lacanian law, probably because it is too close to his own childhood experiences under his stern father.[7]

Draper is also the type of person who is likely to succeed in today's unstable and volatile corporate world under the domain of flexible capitalism. Sennett asserts that the new capitalism is often blind to a worker's past experience. He claims that an employee's past accomplishments are often perceived as useless in a corporate world which requires continuous retraining and reskilling. The worker who is proud of his or her work or who considers it a learned craft is often perceived as too prideful and therefore, resistant to retraining (Sennett 4). Barbara Ehrenreich claims that "likability," which includes being eternally optimistic and cheerful, is valued more by corporations than actual achievement and experience (37–39). In today's office climate, employees frequently find themselves placed in unusual business terrain where their bosses expect them to know new things and perform unfamiliar tasks. New workers admit that they often have to "fake it" when they begin a new position. Sennett argues that the only particular kind of person who can succeed in the new capitalist culture is a person with no true sense of self and "who doesn't need a sustaining life narrative" (4–5). This type of person is able to take advantage of new opportunities and to reinvent him or herself to meet the shifting needs of markets and management.

Besides his denial of his family background, we learn that Don Draper is really Dick Whitman. In "Nixon vs. Kennedy" (1:12), the audience discovers through flashbacks that, during the Korean War, an enlisted Whitman assumes the dog tags and identity of a Donald Draper, an officer killed by a gasoline explosion caused by an enemy mortar attack. A later episode ("The Mountain King" [2:12]) reveals that Whitman had formed an unusual social and financial arrangement with Draper's widow, which has worked to keep her confidence over the public deception. Because of his duplicitous character and lack of a consistent life narrative, Draper/Whitman has the necessary character dexterity and confidence to assume new roles and positions in new capitalism.

Unlike the anxious, approval-hungry, "outer-directed type" described by Reisman (19–25), Draper is coolly self-confident in his demeanor with his colleagues and often arrogant with Sterling, his boss, and with clients.[8] Draper is a model of the postmodern nomadic subject capable of skirting across cultural surfaces and able to easily move from one occupation and lifestyle to another. For instance, in "The Mountain King," he introduces himself as "Dick" to a group of blue-collar men working on a hot rod and tells them that he is looking for work. Draper's three week escape from Sterling Cooper and his troubled home life provide him with an opportunity to fantasize about a new life in California. Also, in "Meditations in an Emergency" (2:13), he learns that Herman "Duck" Phillips will be the new president of the newly merged Sterling Cooper and that he plans to de-emphasize the role of Creative in the company. Draper coolly responds that he will not be part of the new company and that he will be fine because he "sells products, not advertising." One can easily imagine Draper landing another position in a new career field. Despite *Mad Men*'s 1960s corporate settings, Draper's subjective flexibility make him a recognizable business character-type for present-day audiences.

Mad Men offers current audiences, jaded by the insecurity of flexible capitalism, a nostalgic vision of the modern American corporation as a dominant stable institution in pre–1970s capitalism situated in the early 1960s, a period of perceived cultural and political innocence. Sterling Cooper is a leading advertising agency at the center of rapidly emerging cultural and political changes taking place in American society. As a vehicle of capitalism and desiring-production, the agency arrests schizoid flows of desires, associates them with consumer products, and recodes them into exchangeable commodities. The Oedipal complex and psychoanalysis function to create an ideology of lack which personalizes and individualizes desire. At the same time that Oedipalization helps to produce a culture of consumption, it also tries to repress and restrict desire to the traditional family. The series presents audiences with an unique opportunity to contemplate the differences and similarities of corporate life under pre–1970s capitalism and contemporary, flexible capitalism.

NOTES

1. Deleuze and Guattari use the term "schizoid" to describe the schizophrenic qualities of flows of desire which tend to resist dominant social coding and easily scramble existing codes. Flows of desire are pre-language and pre-individual and have the capacity to insert themselves into all social realms within society.

2. Ronald Bogue maintains that Deleuze and Guattari's concept of desire shares similarities with Foucault's theorization of power. As with power, desire permeates all social relations, penetrates the body at the micro-individual level, and politically invests the body within the wider social networks of power and production. This political investment of the body may or may not serve the interests of existing social institutions. Bogue argues that Foucault and Deleuze and Guattari's ideas explain how relations of power function in "heterogeneous arrangements of body parts, texts, machines, goods and institutions" (106).

3. The episodes which address Sterling Cooper's merger and acquisition by Putnam, Powell and Lowe are "The Mountain King" (2:12) and "Mediations in an Emergency" (2:13).

4. For instance, 1970s feature films set in 1950s America include *American Hot Wax* (1978), *Badlands* (1973), *The Buddy Holly Story* (1978), *Grease* (1978), *The Last Picture Show* (1971), and *The Lords of Flatbush* (1974).

5. Of course, employees who do not fit into the company's self-image or please the management are fired. For instance, in the episode, "Six Month Leave" (2:9), Freddie Rumsen's bout of alcoholism causes him to urinate in his pants at the office. As a result, Rumsen is forced to take a six month leave without pay, which is an implicit way of firing him.

6. Here, I'm referring to Reisman's book-length, 1950 sociological study, *The Lonely Crowd*, Mill's *White Collar: The American Middle Classes* (1951), and Whyte's *The Organization Man* (1956).

7. In the episode, "Three Sundays" (2:4) Betty Draper presses Don to discipline his son Bobby. Don steadfastly refuses to punish him. Don reluctantly confesses to Betty that his father constantly beat him and all it did was lead him to fantasize about killing his father.

8. In the episode, "The Hobo Code" (1:8), for example, Draper berates the Belle Jolie representatives when they express reservations about the agency's ad campaign concept. Draper tersely tells them, "You've tried your plan, and you're number four." The representatives reluctantly agree to go with the agency's concept.

WORKS CITED

Baudrillard, Jean. "The Ecstasy of Communication." Trans. John Johnson. In *The Anti-Aesthetic: Essays on Postmodern Culture*. Ed. Hal Foster. Port Townsend, WA: Bay Press, 1983. 126–134.

Bogue, Ronald. *Deleuze and Guattari*. New York: Routledge, 1989.

Buchanan, Ian. *Deleuze and Guattari's Anti-Oedipus*. New York: Continuum, 2008.

Clecak, Peter. *America's Quest for the Ideal Self, Dissent and Fulfillment in the 60s and 70s*. New York: Oxford University Press, 1983.

Deleuze, Gilles and Felix Guattari. *Anti-Oedipus, Capitalism and Schizophrenia*. Vol. 1. Trans. Robert Hurley, Mark Seem and Helen R. Lane. Minneapolis: University of Minnesota Press, 1983.

Ehrenreich, Barbara. *Bait and Switch: The (Futile) Pursuit of the American Dream*. New York: Metropolitan Books, 2005.

Elliot, Anthony. *Psychoanalytical Theory, An Introduction*. Cambridge, MA: Blackwell, 1994.

Foucault, Michel. "Preface." *Anti-Oedipus, Capitalism and Schizophrenia*. Vol. 1. Gilles Deleuze and Felix Guattari. Trans. Robert Hurley, Mark Seem and Helen R. Lane. Minneapolis: University of Minnesota Press, 1983. xi–xiv.

Harrison, Bennett. "The Dark Side of Flexible Production." *Technology Review* 97.4. (May/June 1994): 38–46.

Heckscher, Charles C. *White-Collar Blues: Management Loyalties in an Age of Corporate Restructuring*. New York: BasicBooks, 1995.

Jameson, Frederic. *The Cultural Turn, Selected Writings on the Postmodern, 1983–1998*. New York: Verso, 1998.

_____. *Postmodernism, or, The Cultural Logic of Late Capitalism*. Durham, NC.: Duke University Press, 1991.

Mills, C. Wright. *White Collar: American Middle Classes*. Oxford UK: Oxford University Press, 1951.

Reisman, David, Nathan Grazer and Reuel Denney. *The Lonely Crowd: A Study of the Changing American Character*. New Haven, CT: Yale University Press, 1950.

Sennett, Richard. *The Culture of the New Capitalism*. New Haven, CT: Yale University Press, 2007.

Verhulsdonck, Gustav. *Late Capitalism in Deleuze and Guattari's Anti-Oedipus*. 2001. 5 February 2009. <http://web.nmsu.edu/~gustav/deleuze.pdf>. 1–7.

Whyte, William H. *The Organization Man*. New York: Simon and Schuster, 1956.

Williams, Raymond. "Advertising: The Magic System." In *Problems in Materialism and Culture: Selected Essays*. Raymond Williams. London: Verso, 1980. 170–195.

5. Kodak, Jack, and Coke: Advertising and *Mad*-vertising

Jennifer Gillan

Through its ten years of sponsorship of *The Adventures of Ozzie and Harriet*, Kodak indelibly linked picture-taking and home movie-making with contented family togetherness. Proclaiming before each broadcast, "Eastman Kodak Company is happy to bring you America's Favorite Family," Kodak outfitted the Nelsons in each variation of the opening credits sequence with Kodak cameras and products and declared, "They enjoy happy times together. Like most of us they know that *good times are picture times.*" This sentiment has a parallel in the narrative that *Mad Men*'s Don Draper offers to accompany his pitch to Kodak executives that the Carousel slide projector is not a spaceship but a time machine. Don renames the Kodak slide wheel "the Carousel" he says, because it allows us to travel around and then back home (1:13). Don understands his role in manufacturing and perpetuating the picture-perfect American family myth, and yet it still has the power to draw him in, as is evidenced both by the personal family slides he chooses for the presentation and by the effect the pitch has on him. Afterwards he is inspired to imagine a Kodak-moment Thanksgiving trip with his family, even though earlier he told them to visit relatives without him. Their biographies make apparent that the Nelsons also measured their lives by their correspondence to an ideal they actively worked to manufacture and maintain. While Don Draper and Ozzie Nelson might seem like an odd pairing, they have more in common than is immediately apparent, as both are trying to take up residence in an idealized representation of their lives that they know has little to do with actuality.

Embracing Kodak's brand emphasis on picture-perfect American families, Don and Ozzie act as if their real home lives and represented home lives captured on film are equivalent. *Mad Men* pivots on the actuality that a giant gulf exists between the images of the characters' contented family togetherness and their actual discontent and separation. Despite the fact that in popular memory the Nelsons along with the Andersons of *Father Knows Best*, and the Douglases of *My Three Sons* are remembered as contented and conflict-free families, the actual episodes that aired during the years that *Mad Men* fictionalizes do not completely contain their tensions and anxieties.

Sponsors were very much a part of the circulation of this idea of TV family contentment, a link made most explicit by George Burns and Gracie Allen as spokespersons for Carnation — a dairy company that offered "Milk from contented cows." To illustrate the point many shots were offered of Gracie serving up Carnation to family and friends seated in her TV set kitchen. Such shots were also predominant in the early 1952–1956 seasons of *Ozzie and Harriet*, which like *Burns & Allen* (CBS, 1950–1958) was a TV series conceptualized by a showbiz family offering a fictionalized middle-class, leisure-oriented version of its home life that must have been at odds with the actualities of the lives of always-working, wealthy Hollywood celebrities. When Kodak signed on as sponsors in 1956, the Nelsons moved outside to take pictures and movies of all the leisure activities in which they were engaging. Within a few years, they would be refreshing themselves with soft drinks from cosponsor Coca-Cola.

Over the lifetime of this series (ABC, 1952–1966) television advertising becomes more central to advertising agency business, with many changes occurring in the early 1960s depicted on *Mad Men* (e.g., Coca-Cola dumps the Nelsons and comes up with a new tagline to counter Pepsi's "For those who think young," the title of *Mad Men* episode 2:1) (Pendergrast 272; Samuel 153). Harry Crane is right that Sterling Cooper should have a separate television division. By 1963 Coca-Cola was spending 80 percent of its $33 million ad budget on television. The airlines turned to TV when color commercials started to become standard, signaling an address to an upscale demographic of color television owners (at first only 2 percent of the population), and encouraging airlines to up their TV advertising spending from $2.2 million to $8.5 million in 1963 (Samuels 189–93). Even more changes occurred in television and advertising before the series finale of *My Three Sons* (1960–1972). The effectiveness of *Mad Men* can be attributed to the care Matt Weiner and his production team take in knowing exactly what American culture and its advertising look like in 1963 and beyond so that they can construct storylines and Sterling Cooper campaigns that make for intriguing parallels.

Using the advertising that *Mad Men* has in common with family shows that coincided with the years its narrative covers (e.g., Kodak, Coca-Cola, and *Ozzie and Harriet*), this essay offers an historical perspective both on television advertising and American TV's representation of idealized suburban family life. It also addresses the family-unfriendly products (i.e., cigarettes and alcohol) with which *Mad Men* is associated, particularly through its branded entertainment deal with Jack Daniel's and the seemingly ever-present cigarettes and tumblers of amber liquor in the characters' hands. The essay gives an overview of some early TV parallels to this advertising, looking not only at the prevalence of tobacco company sponsorship of TV families, including the Andersons of *Father Knows Best* and the Ricardos of *I Love Lucy*, but also at how the coexistence of these sponsors and their messages with more family-friendly sponsorship and product integration is part of the ambivalence at the heart of American advertising, of *Mad Men*, and of the as-seen-on-TV, suburban family ideal.

A comparison of *Mad Men*'s Draper family with their midcentury TV counterparts reveals a long history of surprisingly ambivalent representations of gender-polarized, consumerist, suburban family life. In popular memory the late 1950s and early 1960s is characterized as providing a stark contrast to the critically aware contemporary era in which *Mad Men* has been produced. Reviewers suggest that the AMC series has at its center all of the ambivalence and anxieties that are left out of the TV programming of the period. Too much emphasis on the idea that the domesticom was the dominant form in the 1950s obscures the fact that there were various other kinds of programming, and that all of it was less uniform and conflict-free than we imagine. Even the domesticom showed variations in family forms, which indicate that they did not reflect an achieved heteronormative and nuclear family-oriented society, but rather an aspirational ideal, one toward which not everyone aspired. The ambivalence about men giving up bachelor lives and embracing the suburban ideal, for instance, is evident in the single "dad" TV shows, with uncles able to play fathers, while remaining playboys (e.g., *The Bob Cummings Show/Love That Bob* and *Bachelor Father*). More often than one would expect, anxieties about a rigidly gender separatist culture structured by bourgeois values manifest themselves in TV programming, particularly in elements of plot and characterization that are in conflict with the consolidation of consumer, middle class, and heteronormative orientation in early Cold War era American television.

Star Couples and Cigarette Advertising on 1950s Television

Far from being an imposition of twenty-first-century sensibility on an earlier era, *Mad Men* is an attempt to recalibrate the contemporary impression of our cherished memories of the 1950s and 1960s (Witchel). Too often assumptions about the era come from general impressions of 1950s family TV. Most people have never even seen an episode and those who have too often base their assessments on a few random episodes seen outside of their original network and cultural contexts, thereby missing the cultural commentary often embedded within them. Lumped together with *Father Knows Best* style domesticoms, reality star sitcoms, for example, re-work the problematic actuality of the family life of media business entertainers who, like Danny Thomas, play some version of themselves. A few rework their celebrity lives into a persona of someone working behind the scenes in media business, as is the case of Bob Cummings, who on his self-titled show (1955–1959) plays Bob Collins, the celebrity photographer who invites his widowed sister and her teenage son to share his house. Beneath all the collisions of suburban morality and bachelor dissipation, this bachelor uncle star sitcom stands out from the regular ones. Margo Miller claims it is because Cummings's show uses his theatrical mannerisms and his two not-very-feminine female sidekicks to call normative gender into question and perhaps even the actor's own idealized, magazine spread reputation as a contented heterosexual family man (a parallel to *Mad Men*'s Salvatore Romano). More typical are the star sitcoms that feature dual-earner husband and wife entertainers; while Howard Duff and Ida Lupino are movie stars playing a caricature of movie stars on *Mr. Adams and Eve*, most shows modified the star couple so that they experienced more typical breadwinner and homemaker troubles. Lucille Ball and Desi Arnaz had separate careers prior to *I Love Lucy*, but the TV show transformed Lucy into a funny housewife wanting to play sophisticated or glamorous parts in her husband's nightclub acts or his movies. While playing Ricky Ricardo allowed Desi to maintain his real life role as bandleader, bandleader Ozzie Nelson turned his TV persona into a man with no concrete occupation. Although set in a replica of the Nelsons' home, the show made no mention of Hollywood or the kind of life the Nelson family must have actually led. Whereas in real life his wife Harriet was a singer who met him on the road, later married him, had baby David, and then promptly relocated without them both to Manhattan to pursue an acting career for a year; once converted to TV housewife on *The Adventures of Ozzie and Harriet* all traces of whatever her adventures together with and separated from Ozzie were erased. Instead, it is staid suburban life that is depicted as an adventure (Nelson 241–2).

For these dual-earner star couples working together on television was as close to settling down as they were going to get given that it allowed them to both have careers without having to spend most of their time apart. Their representation of themselves as a couple becomes their job. Much like it became Don's and Betty's. As one commentator put it, "Betty wants to play the part of Don Draper's wife so she needs Don to play the part of himself." That recalls the announcement at the start of Ozzie and Harriet *Playing the part of Ozzie: Ozzie Nelson.*

As Season One makes clear Don thought his performance as Don Draper, successful advertising executive, would be confirmed by marrying Betty, the model he meets on a shoot for a fur account. Don convinces the company to give him the fur and then presents it to Betty and convinces her to marry him. She accepts and seven years later seems to have achieved her dream of being the wife of a dashing and successful man. Continuing to maintain and eventually upgrade that lifestyle requires Don to work long hours and he becomes more estranged from her and the children. Given the emphasis on the tension Don's separation from his family causes, the Drapers' situation shares some commonalities with Danny Thomas's as his star sitcom *Make Room for Daddy* (ABS, 1953–1957) was about the impact an often-absent husband has on his family both when he is on the road and when he returns. The TV show's title was suggested by Thomas's actual wife who used to tell her children they could sleep in her bed when daddy was away, but when he returned they had to go to their own beds to "make room for daddy" (Jones 106–7; Castleman and Podrazik 83–4).

Afraid Desi was making room for too many people in his bed when the two had to spend time apart on their separate careers, Lucille Ball was motivated by her real concerns about the impact of separation on her marriage to create her TV show *I Love Lucy* (Jones 65, 69). She and her Cuban bandleader husband met in 1939 while filming *Too Many Girls* and eloped in 1940. They tried to maintain a dual-career marriage, which led to plenty of separations, especially because of Desi's stint of military service. The stress on the relationship led them to divorce in 1944, but they reconciled and even had a second wedding ceremony in 1949. Lucy conceived of the sitcom as a way to keep them together and perhaps to keep Desi's notorious womanizing in check (Kanfer 115–26; Sanders and Gilbert 39). Soon they became "America's Favorite Couple," who directly addressed viewers to recommend Philip Morris in a credits sequence integrated commercial for the cigarette sponsor (Baughman 130; Desjardin 56–74; Murray 154, 172).

Given the anxiety level that must have existed in the actual Ball-Arnaz and Thomas households, it is only fitting that their star sitcoms were sponsored by a cigarette company. Cigarette advertising had a central place in 1950s TV, with several companies opting for a single sponsorship or alternating sponsorship of programs (Boddy 157). While cigarettes are the perfect accessory for the skirt-chasing bachelor uncle in *The Bob Cummings Show*, Winston also had *The Flintstones* puffing away. Of course, the first adult animated TV show debuting in 1960 was not intended to be read as a children's show or even as a domesticom (Samuel 174). As it was actually a throwback to the double couple, battle-of-the-sexes sitcom of early television (e.g., *The Honeymooners* and *I Love Lucy*), the cigarette sponsorship makes more sense, especially given its famous predecessor's Philip Morris sponsorship. Also a series featuring a mix of showbiz and domestic settings and offering an integrated cigarette commercial, *Make Room for Daddy* ended with Danny Thomas and Jean Hagen pitching American Tobacco Company's Pall Mall and Herbert Tareyton from the living room they shared as fictional husband and wife. Thomas' Desilu-produced sitcom, now called *The Danny Thomas Show*, moved to CBS (1957–1964), and increasingly changed from situations related to an entertainer father unable to contain the anxieties that his showbiz life and lengthy absences produced for his family to a more domesticated sitcom that downplayed the showbiz element in favor of more typical domestic situations after widower Danny remarries and sets up housekeeping with his new wife, albeit still in a Manhattan apartment. New sponsor General Foods was the maker of Jell-O, Maxwell House, and Post Cereals (Jones 104–7).

Such a small-ticket sponsor seems perfect for the prototypical suburban domesticom *Father Knows Best*, but it was a cigarette company that sponsored its initial 1954–1955 CBS season. Lorillard, the makers of the Kent Cigarettes which the Drapers' divorcee neighbor has in her bathroom vanity, owned a 10 P.M. Sunday time franchise into which it slotted *Father Knows Best* (Leibman 59). Such time franchises would soon give way to participating sponsorship featuring the multiple spot "magazine" style that would become the norm in American TV (Boddy 160–2). When Lorillard and CBS dropped the underperforming *Father Knows Best*, it moved to NBC for 1955. New sponsors Scott Paper and Lipton could be integrated into scenes in the Andersons' kitchen, just as we see Ritz Crackers and Ragu in the Drapers' (1:4). As Nina Leibman points out, "For the five years during which the program was sponsored by Scott Paper the Anderson home contained two paper-towel dispensers readily visible" from any kitchen shot (Leibman 111–12).

The integrated commercials for Philip Morris, Pall Mall, and Winston represent a 1950s style informational appeal (stressing the benefits of a product over others) as opposed to emotional appeal advertising that would replace it. They also represent the "recommended to you" approach, with the stars addressing viewers directly as "friends," implicitly in the case of Lucy and Desi, who reminded viewers that Philip Morris "Tastes good like a cigarette should," before the iconic cigarette boy would intone the tagline, "Call for Philip Morris."

It is this informational approach that Don takes in his American Tobacco Company Lucky Strike campaign. When he asks a waiter why he smokes rival brand Old Gold, he guesses it is because of the low tar or new filters, indicating that these are the selling points that Don would typically emphasize. The waiter says no, recalling he began smoking in the service, when cigarettes were part of each man's kit. He's not convinced when Don proposes that smoking the brand is just habit and he protests, claiming he simply loves to smoke even though *Reader's Digest* says it is dangerous (1:1). That magazine article and the trade commission cracking down on health claims are exactly Don's problem as he has been selling Lucky Strike by making informational claims via doctors' testimonials about Lucky's filtered tips making them safer cigarettes that soothe the "T-zone." Although in a panic because he can no longer make those claims, Don mulls over the waiter's implication that the love smokers have for brands is just a residual effect of loving smoking. As all the brands are really exactly the same, Don reasons, he can make any claim he wants about Lucky Strike as long as it no longer links smoking and health, which would be a mistake anyhow as it now would create a negative association to the lung disease reports. Don asks the client for information about the manufacturing process and stops him when he says that they toast the tobacco. He suggests that Lucky Strike lay claim to that toasting as the product's distinguishing feature, which will prevent anyone else from doing so. Lucky Strike, in turn, will stand out from the other brands in the minds of consumers just looking for a reason to continue doing what they love: smoking.

The informational appeal for a product stresses how it is made ("it's toasted") and why someone would recommend it to you ("Doctors recommend them to patients who smoke"). As junior account executive Pete Campbell implies, the straight information-based appeal is giving way to a more emotional appeal, which emphasizes how the product will make you feel ("Remember how great cigarettes used to taste? Luckies still do") and why it *is* you (Marlboro Man and "Lucky Strikes separate the men from the boys, but not from the girls"). The change is also apparent in the difference between *Ozzie and Harriet*'s information-based Hotpoint integrated commercials and the image-based Kodak ones. Information is what Ozzie and Harriet provide in the Hotpoint integration scenes in the early years of their series, telling viewers how appliances actually work and indicating that viewers who do not yet have these appliances should visit their local retailer. In contrast, Kodak cameras were wordlessly associated with the family, shown in their hands and hanging around their necks as they walked out of their sitcom house prior to the credits sequence. People who wanted to be the Nelsons would deduce that to do so they should acquire Kodak cameras and turn an ordinary occasion into "picture time."

While the Nelsons continue their Kodak relationship into the 1960s, neither *I Love Lucy* (1951–1957) nor Lucy and Desi made it into the new decade. After their sitcom ended its run at the top of the ratings in 1957, "America's

Favorite Couple" continued offering special episodes under other titles until 1960. As the 1960 marked the year of the dissolution of the famous showbiz marriage, the next time Lucy (along with Vivian Vance) showed up on TV for *The Lucy Show* (CBS, 1962–1968), she was no longer partnered with Desi or Philip Morris. By then, single sponsorships as well as sponsor-owned time franchises and corporate image sponsorships (e.g., *The U.S. Steel Hour*) had been replaced by "a participating sponsorship, with three, four, or as many as ten sponsors for a single series" (Boddy 158, 162). That's why Roger Sterling can suggest to Rachel Menken, the company president of her father's Fifth Avenue department store, that she start running spots during *The Danny Thomas Show* (1.1). It may be a subtle dig though by the anti–Semitic creative team, who later call Rachel "Molly Goldberg." It is a reference to the TV show *The Goldbergs*, which is one of the early 1950s ethnic sitcoms. Thomas' series was the only ethnic sitcoms to survive into the 1960s (Lipsitz). Given that by this point Thomas's character had a much more housewifely wife and a dutiful stepdaughter dubbed "America's Little Darling" in place of his sassy eldest daughter from the early seasons, sophisticated and quick-witted Rachel is unlikely to want to affiliate herself with the a series (Jones 107).

Although Sterling Cooper doesn't realize it, Rachel Menken is emblematic of a new world in which Pepsi would soon be challenging Coke through a demographic emphasis on "The Pepsi Generation." Coca-Cola stuck with "America's Favorite Family" as spokespersons and tried, "Zing! What a feeling with Coke," but Pepsi's demographic appeal to "Those Who Think Young" better represented the changing times (Pendergrast 272). Other things were changing as well. When networks began to sell timed-increments in between story segments to sponsors, many companies took the opportunity to get into television advertising and sell small-ticket items (as Sterling Cooper client Vicks Chemical would have with Clearasil and Hunts did with its ketchup on *My Three Sons*). Pepsi's challenge to Coca-Cola, in other words, was part of a new targeted strategy in which smaller companies took on the number one brands. Avoiding head-to-head competition, the smaller brands targeted segments of the potential audience to which the market leader might not be directly appealing. Before it settled on its successful "Things go better with Coke" tagline "Coca-Cola advertising floundered, searching for a unifying theme," Mark Pendergrast notes, whereas "Pepsi's efforts to identify with the dynamic youth market appeared more effective" (272).

Before ending its sponsorship of *Ozzie and Harriet* in 1961, Coca-Cola tried to appeal to Ricky Nelson's teen fans. In one spot, as the radio in the malt shop plays the new jingle, "Only Coca-Cola gives you that refreshing new feeling," Ricky sips a Coke and says, "Isn't that new song for Coca-Cola great?" His just-arrived brother David concurs, "Yeah, it's great" and tries to order his own Coke from the counterman who is too busy singing along to serve him. In another spot, there is just a close-up of Ricky enjoying a Coke as the announcer says, "For that refreshing new feeling, do as Ricky Nelson does," and the teen heartthrob says into the camera, "Have a Coke." As Kodak also increasingly put their cameras in David's and Ricky's hands, Ozzie adapted to the change just as he and Harriet had arranged their lives for the TV cameras so as to conform to the sponsor-friendly breadwinner / homemaker suburban norm. He had already been putting some of the focus on Ricky as a pop idol, but he eventually committed a good deal of story time to David and Rick as newlyweds to try a more demographic appeal (Leibman 66). By orchestrating this performance as creator, producer, and actor, Ozzie kept the life of the fictional Nelsons on-air for record time, so that even as their actual lives moved forward — David got married, Rickie became a recording artist, teen idol, and later newlywed — he sanitized the complexity of those real changes in lifestyle and incorporated them into the TV show. In contrast to the messy complexity of the Nelsons' actual lives, the Kodak-moment Ozzie and Harriet that are remembered today are the parents in a nuclear family that stands in as a snapshot of an America that once existed.

Grand Central Kodak Colorama Exhibit

Looking at the giant Coloramas (18 × 60 foot color display transparencies) exhibited by Kodak on the East Balcony of Grand Central Terminal starting in 1950 and continuing, with some changes, for forty years, one might also mistake them for snapshots of an America that once existed (Kodak). Diane Hope marvels that between 1950 and 1970 "no indication of the sociocultural changes occurring through those decades found reflection in Kodak portrayals" (314). Like the Drapers' family photographs, so much more complexity lies behind those captured and posed moments. Without any of the audience's insider access to their lives, Don's clients (1:1; 1:6), Betty's neighbors (1:7), and probably most people that meet the Drapers assume that they embody the Kodak ideal of the contented and successful suburban family headed by a WASP breadwinner who would pass by that Grand Central exhibit on the way to and from his commuter train. "Each day half a million people, mostly New York commuters, moved past the Colorama display," Hope remarks (314). With each year separating viewers from the original date of display came layers of nostalgia about the way we Americans were living in the 1950s and 1960s and how much our lives were characterized by family togetherness. As we know from the circumstances surrounding the Drapers' formal family photograph and from Betty's account of Don's reluctant trips to her family summer house, a place at which he feels unwelcome despite his seeming nostalgia for a box of Cape May slides (1:5), photographs capture more about the way we present ourselves to the world, or moments in which we come together, than they reflect any daily state of affairs or consistency of feeling. The timeline of the series is structured by holiday and special moments — Mother's Day, Labor Day, Thanksgiving, and Valentine's Day — that turn out to be anything but scrapbook or slide-projector worthy. While in advertising these holidays and special occasions are ones at which pictures are taken that emphasize togetherness no matter what the actual state of the relationships, the corresponding *Mad Men* episodes detail the actual separation and distance between family members, lovers, and colleagues.

Despite it all, it is clear that Don likes to think of his life as composed of the moments represented in his slide cases because those images are preferable to the more ambivalent reality that he and Betty both know more accurately characterizes their supposedly ideal suburban existence. *Mad Men*'s story arcs reveal that the era touted as one of nuclear family togetherness was often one of family separation with wives ensconced in suburbs and men in cities, often staying there over night and on holidays. One of the appealing, but ultimately misleading Kodak Grand Central Coloramas, "Family Romp in the Living Room" (1959), depicts the breadwinner horsing around with his children after work as his wife snaps their picture, something which *Mad Men* rightly characterizes as more rare than commonplace. Don often returns home after everyone else is in bed. One night Betty asks him if he wants to go look in on the kids, and he flatly refuses (1:5). After Don comes home late another night and barely acknowledges that a neighbor is sitting in the living room with his wife, Betty apologizes, realizing her man works too hard for all they have (1:4). When Sally comes in to greet him the morning after he and Betty have a late night out at an awards banquet, he tells her to go downstairs and eat her breakfast with the hired help. Another time (1.9) we see him rushing out the door as Betty serves breakfast to the kids. It is not clear whether even that bit of contact is the norm, especially as George Lois, the advertising executive who created the game-changing 1960s Volkswagen campaigns, recalls getting to the office by 5:30 A.M., a start time that would make it unlikely that he'd participate in his children's morning routine (Jaffee; Witchel). However much time he actually spends at home, it is clear that Don's success depends upon a good deal of time away from his family, not just long hours, but overnights and holidays (1:1; 1.9; 1:10). Given that commuter fathers only visited summer places on weekends, at most, the 1957 Kodak Colorama "Closing a Summer Cottage, Quogue, New York" is misleading as well. In it, a father is packing the car as one of his daughters is saying a reluctant goodbye to her summer crush and his son is taking a keepsake picture of his summer friends. Dad is loading the car, but it is unlikely he has spent as much time in the house as have his wife and children.

While a family beach outing is preserved in one of Don's slides, it clearly captures something that is again more rare than typical of the Drapers. Don and Betty discuss how she and the kids will be spending a good deal of August at her father's Cape May house, while Don is working three hours away in Manhattan (1:5). In "Long Weekend" he plans to come and join them on Saturday of Labor Day weekend, but he never makes it. While Labor Day is represented as a family holiday, Sterling Cooper partner Roger Sterling describes the holiday as an opportunity for men to work and frolic back in the city. Business trips present another such opportunity, which is exactly what the infamous 1971 National Airlines advertisements made clear with the slogan accompanying a picture of a sexy stewardess: "I'm Cheryl. Fly Me" or the alternate "I'm going to fly you like you've never been flown before" (*Time*). Only slightly more subtle was the 1965 American Airlines ad that uses a picture of a businessman carrying off a stewardess and the tagline, "People keep stealing our stewardesses." The copy continues in small print, "within two years most of our stewardesses will leave us for other men." The rest stresses that her service training makes the stewardess an ideal wife, although it plays on the doubleness of the reference to domestic and sexual services (Jackall and Hirota 86–7).

For a business executive, airline travel represents a separation from family, one that is often associated with a fantasy of sexual opportunity. Roger Sterling captures that idea when he praises the Pan Am account by imagining acknowledging its effect: making him imagine he is in London in a hotel with three stewardesses each time he sees it (1:9). When Don says in a later airline campaign brainstorming meeting that you get on a plane to be rejuvenated by the sense of adventure and to catch a glimpse of a woman's thigh because she is wearing her skirts just a little too short, he sounds as if he is agreeing with Roger (2:1). He reminds the junior copywriters, it's not about sex, but about "feeling something." It is only Peggy Olson who really understands what he means. Knowing full well that Don is unfaithful to his wife and often disappoints his children, Peggy still uses Don's life as a model for her "What did you bring me, daddy" airline campaign, featuring a gift-bearing executive being greeted by his daughter upon returning from a business trip. When she was still Don's secretary, Peggy learns that Don has trysts with a woman in the Village around the same time that she has to stall his wife and children for quite awhile when Don disappears during the day. Betty, Sally, and Bobby have shown up at the office all dressed up to get their annual family photo taken and sit around anxiously waiting for Don to return. The day must be burned in Peggy's memory as she assumes Don is off with his mistress at the time and doesn't quite know what to do or how to face Betty (1:5) . Flash forward to 1962 and Peggy, now a junior copywriter pitching for the airline account, is inspired when she looks at the Valentine's card that Sally has made for her father (2:1). She realizes that executives like Don would be attracted to a fantasy image of themselves as family men who think about their children even when they are away on business. The "What did you bring me" campaign also could work more cynically if the same executives are positioned as sugar daddies who are well-aware that they need to keep the women in their lives — daughters, wives, and even mistresses — happy by bringing them presents whenever they see them after an absence. To make up for not giving their time, they give gifts. As Joan Holloway, the recent recipient of a pearl necklace, says, male executives know what they want because they are willing to pay for it (1:10). Peggy emphasizes instead how doting fathers make up for unavoidable absences by providing children with tokens of affection as she knows that's what Don would do no matter what the actualities of airline travel might offer in terms of "friendly skies" companionship.

The Coke Side of Betty's Life

Betty is just as committed to maintaining the Drapers' image as the picture-perfect family, as is evident in her composure when she comes to the office prepared to take the family portrait and tries not to acknowledge that Don is out for suspiciously long time in the middle of the day. Only the viewer knows that at that moment he is dealing with the resurfacing of a past life that would have no place in his preferred family album. Jon Hamm, the actor who portrays him explains that Don "wanted the image of the perfect family, so he married the beautiful model. He takes his cues from advertising. The Coke commercial with the two kids and the dog. And there's no there there" (Witchel). Hamm is referring to "Shoot" (1:9) in which Betty is trying to climb back into her magazine-spread life by posing as the mother in a family picnic tableau that McCann is doing for Coca-Cola. She is hoping she can reanimate the model she was when she met Don (1:9). Unfortunately, the agency is just using her as leverage to convince Don to defect. When Don rejects their job offer, they drop Betty, forcing her to realize that, unlike Don, she is dispensable. She also has to face the fact that she can never again be that carefree single girl who so casually traded in an exciting lifestyle for a husband and a house in the suburbs. While the episode hints at the futility of trying to live within the advertisement's parameters, it becomes clear in the contrast between the magazine-spread version of the family picnic and the garbage-strewn reality offered in 2:7 that Betty and Don still want to try.

The tension that Betty feels between the desires for an exciting, but unpredictable single life of adventure and for a predictable, but stable suburban life is one that is central to American advertising more generally. It surfaces again in a Heineken campaign in which Don promotes Heineken as beer for the upscale hostess. The campaign exemplifies emotional-appeal advertising. Betty sees a display at the supermarket and decides it would make a great addition to her plan for a trip-around-the-world themed dinner party (2:8). Betty's purchase and Don's theory about supermarket placement sounds similar to the way Coca-Cola adviser Charlotte Montgomery describes how Mrs. Consumer of 1956 "would be wooed away by a more convenient package, a big promotion, and a slightly more interesting presentation." She would be a woman who thought of herself in the supermarket as a "completely independent agent," but was subtly being lured by advertising (quoted in Pendergrast 263). Betty is prompted to purchase because of her growing dissatisfaction with suburban life and her aspiration to worldliness. When Betty realizes that she fell for Don's sales pitch, she worries that his marriage proposal and the promise of an idealized suburban life might have just been a sales pitch, too. Betty is realizing that women are disposable and replaceable with new models, a lesson she learns as much from her husband as her father, who after his supposedly beloved wife dies immediately replaces her with another woman (1:10). Having a harder time being the look-the-other-way wife, Betty becomes increasingly frustrated, which is sometimes expressed in consumer terms. Finding one of her formal dining room chairs wobbles as she is polishing it with Pride, she violently breaks it into pieces as her children watch in shock (2:8). With the act she is starting to reject the advertising message that for a suburban housewife a squeaky clean home is a badge of honor. Her home is becoming less a source of pride, and more of shame, in part because Don belittles her attempts to be a sophisticated hostess and because she feels belittled by the fact that he carries on a sophisticated Manhattan life in which other women take her place beside him.

Don still wants Betty beside him as well, if only to complete the tableau, and Betty obliges. When Don arrives home with a new Cadillac Coupe de Ville, he puts Betty in the driver's seat and has her take them for a spin (2:7). They both seem to be heeding Betty's mother's advice, who told her to "hide the brushstrokes" in the masterpiece of her life (1:7). Cadillac might be selling to breadwinners, but it had their trophy wives in mind as its automobiles were designed to appeal to women with their in-dash vanity case, lipstick and tissue box holders, and their female-friendly powder puff color selection (Marling 141). As one Ford executive put it, "Beauty is what sells the American car. And the person we're designing it for is the American woman.... It's the women who like colors" (quoted in Marling 136). While *Mad Men* represents

Don buying a Cadillac to broadcast that he has "arrived," such a car is also one of the luxuries that is supposed to compensate wives for their often otherwise-engaged husbands. They take the car to an event in the city at which Betty is forced by the husband of one of Don's lovers to address the costs of ignoring the ugly realities of her lifestyle. On the drive home when she can no longer suppress her understanding that the Cadillac and other luxuries are payoffs for her tolerance of and silence about Don's infidelities, she gets sick all over the floor mat, which is ironic given the Ford executive's claim that it is designed for women like Betty: "We've spent millions to make the floor covering like the carpet in their living rooms" (quoted in Marling 136). Also ironic is that things come to a head when the TV commercial through which Don met the woman is broadcast into her living room, which becomes the catalyst that prompts Betty to kick Don out of the house (2:8). He seems mystified that she would do such a thing, but also tempted to take the opportunity to break away from the settled life for good. Given that he has twice asked women to run away with him, it is not surprising that when he goes on a business trip to California, he extends his stay to the point that it seems as if he plans never to return.

The crisis feels temporary as viewers know that Don is subject to bouts of nostalgia for the family in which he fantasizes that he lives. He seems to fall in love again and again with the advertising tableau, taken in by the fiction of family togetherness he helped construct and maintain. He is not alone as Peggy and many other Sterling Cooper employees not only sell fantasies for a living, but also choose to take up residence within them. Don acknowledges early on in the series that he is jaded enough to know that advertisers create desire, inventing our conceptions of romantic love, the bolt of lightning and the inability to eat and concentrate. He tells Rachel Menken that what she calls love was an invention of a guy like him to sell nylons (1:1). That his cynicism is a frustrated romanticism is hinted at when she questions his cynicism. That he's actually entirely not sure is confirmed in a scene in which his self-assessment is repeated by a beatnik named Roger, who believes advertising is nothing more than evil. Don has just taken a Polaroid of his downtown lover Midge lounging next to Roger and claims that the instant photo reveals that the two are in love. When they deny it Don reveals how much he understands the sentiment because he makes pictures each day to illustrate love. When Midge takes a second look at the photograph, she acknowledges its artificial quality as it appears to convey real emotion (1:8).

His knowledge of the manufacture of desire does not make Don immune to it, as is evident in the scene in which he purchases the Cadillac. Don buys the car to prove that he is no longer the small-time car salesman he was. A Cadillac is indeed a status symbol with extras such as "a set of four gold-

finished drinking cups" along with the standard luxury of "deep-pile uphol-
stery, padded interiors, coil springs," and the like (Marling 141). As the Cadillac
salesman makes an emotional appeal to Don as he looks at the Coupe de
Ville, one can sense that he feels the car is not a product he needs or even
particularly wants, but then he realizes that the car *is* Don Draper and by
buying it he will be better playing that role. Of course, there's irony for Don
and Betty in the salesman's pitch that they will feel as comfortable in the car
as they do in their own skin (2:7). As the name on the building, it's not surprising that it is Roger Sterling who tells Don he deserves a new car as a
reward. Roger's mistress tells him that he has the same attitude toward women
and will soon want to turn her in for a new model; in addition to her own
sexy hips, she is referencing the constant annual changing of the tail fins on
1950s and early 1960s automobiles and the planned obsolescence on which
the American auto industry depends (1:6). Alfred P. Sloan of General Motors
remarks that the rollout of new models is intended "to create demand for new
value and, so to speak, create a certain amount of dissatisfaction with past
models as compared to the new one" (quoted in Marling 136).

Mad-Vertising and Branded Entertainment

Dissatisfaction seems to be a primary motivator for drinking for many
at Sterling Cooper. Almost every character is associated with drinking and
often drunkenness leads to irresponsible behavior. Jack Daniel's, which
arranged a branded entertainment deal with *Mad Men*, probably preferred
the association of liquor with celebrating one's first account in episode 1:8,
offering a bottle as an upscale token of appreciation in 1:9, or ordering a round
of drinks for the table in 1:6. It probably didn't even mind the comments by
World War II vet Roger Sterling as he lounges on Don's office sofa and relishes
a glass of amber liquor, while cheerfully chiding Don for his Korean War generation's shortcomings because they drink for the wrong reasons: Roger's generation drinks because it feels good — because it is "what men do." It's a pitch
almost as full of emotional appeal as Don's for Kodak and Peggy's for Popsicles
(2:12). Since it is liquor and not Popsicles being celebrated, however, in a
show that also features drunk drivers, alcohol-related car accidents, and countless alcohol-fueled sexual encounters, it is hardly surprising that the *Mad Men*
Jack Daniel's link causes controversy. Critiques were especially concerned with
the "entwinement" of drinking and irresponsible behavior (Jaffee). Matt
Weiner countered that as *Mad Men* is "a period piece where people have consequences for their alcohol consumption," the entwinement is sometimes necessary for the story arc. Brown-Forman agreed and had little complaint about

the use of their Jack Daniel's brand, adding the all the codes are "self-regulation" anyhow (Jaffee). There were still restrictions associated with the representation of the brand, some of which Weiner found humorous. He joked, "You're sort of like, 'What is the purpose of Jack Daniel's if there's no sex after it and there's no fighting after it?'" (*Advertising Age*). Maybe that alcohol results both in a career-ending misstep and a character's heart attack is a form of internal critique. Smoking gets a more definite slap on the wrist by founding partner Bertram Cooper who says to Roger Sterling in "Red in the Face" (1:7), that it is actually a sign of weakness. He must be even less pleased with Roger after an alcohol-induced embarrassment in front of some important clients. The public service announcement feel of parts of this episode are counterbalanced by the sophisticated smoking and drinking of later episodes.

The Jack Daniel's deal is just one of a variety of AMC's and Lionsgate's strategies for *Mad Men*. It also had some magazine style TV sponsorship, notably by drug companies, but it made them more memorable with its *Mad*-vertising, which paired advertising for pharmaceuticals such as Viagra with interstitials offering factoids about the drug. For example one title card read: "Prescription drugs could not be advertised on television in the United States until 1997" and preceded a commercial for Caduet, anti-hypertension medication that Don might have benefited from taking (Flaherty). Creator Matt Weiner opined that it would have been easier to have a single sponsor "during the whole show and tie them into the show." He applauds the *Mad*-vertising concept, however, saying "It looks like something Don Draper would have thought of" (Benton). It is doubtful that Weiner would actually want to enter into a traditional single sponsorship deal given his comments about the restrictions associated with the multi-episode presence of Jack Daniel's. The biggest complaint about single sponsorship in the 1950s was loss of creative control (Boddy 160–63). After interviewing 1950s and 1960s TV producers, Nina Liebman concluded: "The constant and vocal presence of the sponsor's or the agency's representative on the set steered programs toward the sponsor's perspective. The look of a program was often altered after a script was written as the sponsor and producer cooperated to portray the product (nameless but visible) in the best possible light" (Liebman 110). In contrast, Weiner wants to use products to create texture to his story, not to sell the products. That worked fine when he was a production worker on premium subscription cable, but it is not completely practical on AMC as it is a basic cable channel, that is, at least in part, advertiser-supported. Whether he likes it or not, Weiner is in the advertising business as well as the business of entertainment (Jaffee).

An executive from Universal McCann that helped set up the Jack Daniel's underwriting explains that *Mad Men's* branded entertainment and its coordination of its commercial spots is representative of a new kind of television sponsorship "one that capitalizes on subject matter," by calibrating the flow between story segments to reflect it (Jaffee). In addition to sponsoring the season two finale episode, Heineken participated in season one's experiments in TiVo-proofing the flow of the Heineken campaign episode. After a story segment ended, a title card factoid, "Heineken was the first imported beer in America after the repeal of Prohibition in 1933" appeared prior to Heineken's commercial spot (Flaherty). Also a *Mad*-vertising participant, Jack Daniel's underwrote the interstitial spots featuring "legendary advertising execs who share their stories of what it was like to work in the business at that time." A particularly effective tie-in to the show was that one was about George Lois, the self-described "Greek big mouth" Korean War vet who branded Xerox and created Doyle Dane Bernbach's "Think Small" and "Lemon" Volkswagen print ads on which the WASPy Sterling Cooper creative team comment in "The Marriage of Figaro" (1:3) (Witchel). Unlike Sterling Cooper, which is resistant to adapting its strategy to a changing media landscape, often underestimating the impact of new media (e.g., television), new products (e.g., imported small cars) and demographics (e.g., youth culture) on the advertising industry, AMC took a risk when it acquired its first original drama series from Lionsgate, newly launched as an independent willing to embrace new media approaches to content distribution and advertising and offering a features approach to marketing its TV productions. Together they opted for multiplatform advertising, incorporated a social networking presence (e.g., Facebook and Twitter accounts), created a content-immersive faux *Advertising Age* insert, hired flash mobs to attract attention in Grand Central Terminal, where *Mad Men* billboards had a large presence near subway entrances, and developed the unique *Mad*-vertising interstitial and commercial pod pairings obviously designed to discourage the fast-forwarding through commercials that is made possible by DVR viewing.

In addition to on-air buys, *Mad Men* offers companies the opportunity to split time buys between television and alternate content delivery platforms (such as Jack Daniel's sponsorship of the series' Web site and the Zippo lighter collaboration on the Zippo-style DVD case) (Elliot 2007). A company could distribute its purchase time across multiple media platforms or it could be the single sponsor of one off-air platform or some aspect of special content on offer there. Of course, any kind of deal can be tailored to whatever is the company's desired percentage of branded entertainment sponsorship or spot-oriented magazine sponsorship. Such variety, advertising executive Benjamin Palmer notes, is indicative of how today's producers and advertisers are not that different from those in the *Mad Men* era: "Even before the internet, advertising has always had to come up with a point of view that would work well in a magazine, on a sign, along the side of a bus, or on TV, all at the same time" (Hitt). Don Draper is adept at such flexibility.

Recall Don Draper's statement that America is a country without a past but with a "new frontier." Let's pretend we know what 1963 looks like." It is played for the sincerity in the Kennedy era in which it is spoken, albeit by Nixon men who fail to appreciate the Volkswagen campaign. Matt Weiner and his production team pick up on these ironies in the years in which subsequent seasons are set. It is clear that the Drapers and Sterling Cooper cannot even imagine what the later years of the 1960s will look like. Since Weiner's team has a very clear idea, especially given their commitment to period research and authenticity, they can always create intriguing tie-ins to events in American advertising and cultural history. My bet is on the Draper kids to inspire advertising campaigns and bedevil Don and Betty into the 1970s. After all, they are part of the born-into-television generation whose consumer habits have shaped much of what we have taken to be standard in print and television advertising. It will be the latest consumer behavior of the Millennials, the television generation's "born digital" children, who will continue to shape how *Mad Men* and the original dramas that follow in its wake are marketed in the coming years. Let's pretend we know what 2020 will look like.

For access to the tapes of the 1950s/1960s sitcom broadcasts, I am indebted to Mark Quigley and the University of California, Los Angeles Film and Television Archive.

WORKS CITED

Baughman, James L. *Same Time, Same Station: Creating American Television, 1948–1961.* Baltimore, MD: Johns Hopkins University Press, 2007.

Benton, Joshua. "'*Mad Men*' Ads Keep You on Your Couch." Nieman Journalism Lab at Harvard. Blogs. 23 Oct. 2008. <http://www.niemanlab.org/2008/10/mad-men-ads-keep-you-on-your-couch/ >.

Boddy, William. *Fifties Television: The Industry and Its Critics.* Urbana and Chicago, IL: University of Illinois Press, 1993.

Castleman, Harry and Walter J. Podrazik. *Watching TV: Six Decades of American Television.* Syracuse, NY: Syracuse University Press, 2003.

Desjardin, Mary. "Lucy and Desi: Sexuality, Ethnicity, and TV's First Family." *Television, History, and American Culture.* Ed. Mary Beth Haralovich and Lauren Rabinowitz. Durham, NC: Duke University Press, 1999. 56–74.

Elliot, Stuart. "What Was Old Is New as TV Revisits Branding." *New York Times,* 13 June 2007. http://query.nytimes.com/gst/fullpage.html?res=9B01E1D6173FF930A25755 C0A9619C8B63&sec=&spon=&pagewanted=all.

_____. "Madison Avenue Likes What It Sees in the Mirror." *New York Times,* 23 June 2008. http://www.nytimes.com/2008/06/23/business/media/23adcol.html.

Flaherty, Mike. "AMC introduces 'Mad-vertising': Blurbs reference products and theme of 'Men'" Variety, 22 August 2008. <http://www.variety.com/index.asp?layout=print_ story&articleid=VR1117991021&categoryid=2526>.

"Fly Me." *Time* 15 November 1971. <http://www.time.com/time/magazine/article/0,9171, 903213,00.html>.

"Fly Me Again." *Time* 24 June 1974. <http://www.time.com/time/magazine/article/0,9171, 944906,00.html>.

Hitt, Jack, moderator. "Multiscreen Mad Men." *New York Times Magazine*, 23 November 2008. http://www.nytimes.com/2008/11/23/magazine/23roundtable-t.html.

Hope, Diane S. "Memorializing Affluence in the Post War Family: Kodak's Colorama in Grand Central Terminal (1950–1990)." *Visual Rhetoric: A Reader in Communication and American Culture.* Ed. Lester C. Olsen, Karen A. Finnegan, Diane S. Hope. Thousand Oaks, CA: Sage, 2008. 313–325.

Jackall, Robert and Janice M. Hirota. *Image Makers: Advertising, Public Relations and the Ethos of Advocacy.* Chicago, IL: University of Chicago Press, 2003.

Jaffee, Larry. "All the Mad Men." *Promo Magazine*, 1 Aug. 2007. http://promomagazine. com/entertainmentmarketing/mad_men_080107/.

Jones, Gerard. *Honey: I'm Home: Selling the American Dream.* New York: Grove, 1992.

Kamp, David. "Rethinking the American Dream." *Vanity Fair*, April 2009. 118–123; 177–180.

Kanfer, Stefan. *Ball of Fire: The Tumultuous Life and Comic Art of Lucille Ball.* New York: Alfred A. Knopf, 2003.

Kodak. "The Kodak Colorama." *Kodak e-Magazine.* http://www.kodak.com/US/en/corp/ features/coloramas/colorama.html.

Liebman, Nina. *Living Room Lectures: The Fifties Family in Film & Television.* Austin: University of Texas Press, 1995.

Lipsitz, George. "The Meaning of Family, Class and Ethnicity in Early Network Television Programs." *Camera Obscura*, January 1988: 79–118.

Marling, Karal Ann. *As Seen on TV: The Visual Culture of Everyday Life in the 1950s.* Cambridge, MA; Harvard University Press, 1994.

Miller, Margo. "The Bob Cummings Show's 'Artist's at Work': Gender Transitive Programming and Counterpublicity." *Spectator*, Spring 2008.

Murray, Susan. *Hitch Your Antenna to the Stars: Early Television and Broadcast Stardom.* New York: Routledge, 2005.

Nelson, Ozzie. *Ozzie.* Englewood Cliffs, NJ: Prentice Hall, 1973.

Pendergrast, Mark. *For God, Country and Coca-Cola.* New York: Basic Books 2000.

Samuel, Lawrence R. *Brought to You By: Postwar Television Advertising and the American Dream.* Austin: University of Texas Press, 2001.

Sanders, Coyne S. and Tom Gilbert. *Desilu: The Story of Lucille Ball and Desi Arnaz.* New York: William and Morrow, 1993.

Witchel, Alex "'Mad Men' Has Its Moment." *New York Times Magazine*, 22 June 2008. http://www.nytimes.com/2008/06/22/magazine/22madmen-t.html?partner=permal-ink&exprod=permalink.

THE WOMEN OF
MAD MEN

Elisabeth Moss as Peggy Olson in "Babylon" (1:6) of Mad Men *(2007) (AMC/Kobal Collection).*

6. *Mad Men* and Career Women: *The Best of Everything?*

Tamar Jeffers McDonald

The Fifties were hypocritical and secretive ... on the surface it was such a happy, lovely time, but it wasn't like that at all, it was what we pretended, and underneath was exactly what's happening today: the broken hearts, the looking for love, the lies, the fears... [Jaffe cited in Montagne, 2005].

While author Rona Jaffe is here recalling the historical context for her first novel, *The Best of Everything*, published in 1958, her words have resonance for viewers of Matthew Weiner's hit television show, *Mad Men*, despite the show's storyline beginning in 1960. "The Fifties" lasted longer than the decade from 1950 to 1959, and are not bound by those end-dates. As Wini Breines has noted, "...eras do not commence and close in neat, round decade numbers; the fifties as a cohering cultural entity is an intellectual construct" (xii). Similarly, W. T. Lhamon, Jr., in his examination of cultural changes wrought by and in the year 1955, defends his decision to treat the year inclusively:

I imagined my mid-decadal year more like a sieve than a bucket because I wanted to catch a particular tangle. My 1955 would include *Invisible Man*, for instance, even though Ralph Ellison began his novel in the late Forties and published it in 1952. My 1955 would also expand to welcome Thomas Pynchon's novel *V* (1963) ... [which] wore its fifties dependence on its sleeve [xvi].

Fifties fashions, jokes, novels, movies, automobiles, advertising slogans, music, did not all change on 1 January 1960, and indeed it is the fifties fashions, jokes, novels, movies, automobiles, advertising slogans and music — the cultural ephemera we rely on to date a specific period — that play such a large part in creating the feeling of authenticity in *Mad Men*, a show which, as Lhamon comments of Pynchon's novel, wears "its fifties dependence on its sleeve," sometimes literally.

Jaffe's quotation about surface and depths evokes the duality at the heart of *Mad Men*. The tension between attractive appearances and disillusioning realities is present not just within the narratives unfolding within the show, but is also inherent in the series' own makeup. The program operates a curious attraction/repulsion mechanism: the glossy surfaces, adorable outfits, fabulous furnishings and glamorous everyday objects draw viewers in, yet the characters' sexism, racism, selfishness and snobbery, as casual as it is endemic, repel. This push/pull response is part of what makes the show so fascinating, and it relies very much on the perceived authenticity, as well as the allure, of the artifacts displayed.

Mad Men can be celebrated for its acute conjuring of mid-century zeitgeist: from costumes to cars, catchphrases to cocktails, the show meticulously evokes the sights and sounds of its historical period, summoning up scenes of conformist suburbia and *populuxe* Manhattan familiar from Richard Yates' novels and Doris Day movies. Like the central characters of *Revolutionary Road* (1962), *Mad Men* has its philandering husband working in New York City in an advertising job, while the wife tends house and children, brooding over lost chances, in an upstate suburb. Like, too, the second Day-Hudson outing, *Lover Come Back* (1961), the advertisers' control over the everyday decisions of thousands of Americans is the source of mocking glee for the execs at *Mad Men's* Sterling Cooper. Embedding the show within the historical contexts vouched for by well-known contemporaneous texts lends the series a kind of verisimilitude, but also an insubstantiality. Riffing off famous contemporary films and books, *Mad Men* is the copy of a copy, a media text based not only on history but on other media texts. Shimmering with self-reflexivity and allusion, it can, however, also elevate some of its time capsule souvenirs to a position beyond that of merely providing authenticity as period objects or topical references.

This chapter proposes to discuss one such example of the well-chosen artifact which reveals a deeper interest than just displaying the show's pop culture awareness. Rona Jaffe's bestselling novel *The Best of Everything* and the 1959 film version are referenced in one episode of *Mad Men*. This text acts here as a physical artifact — a garish paperback — invoking a particular era; it also functions symbolically in its specific episode, since musing about the aging Joan Crawford's role in the film betrays Betty Draper's anxieties about herself. Beyond this, however, the text acts as a key to wider issues central to the series as a whole: ideas about female agency and desire, not only sexual desire and the search for fulfillment, but also — and equally transgressively for the time — the desire for intellectual and career satisfaction. *The Best of Everything* thus provides *Mad Men* with a touchstone for exploring assumptions about women's relations with sex and career, especially through the character of Peggy Olson.

The Best in "Babylon"

Jaffe's book and the Jean Negulesco–directed film based upon it are both referenced in "Babylon" (1:6). Don Draper is in bed looking at the book, which his wife, Betty, has presumably been reading. When she comes into the room, they discuss the book and the film, Don finding the former — seemingly with approval —"dirtier" than the movie. Betty says she likes the book more than the film. *The Best of Everything* seems to be included here as zeitgeist: the film was released in October 1959 and this scene takes place on Mother's Day, May 8, the following year. However, although no other mention is made of either book or film, *The Best of Everything* can also be seen furthering various themes developing throughout the show. For example, countering Betty's feelings that Joan Crawford is too old to be on screen, Don notes that Salvatore Romano, Sterling Cooper's art director, is obsessed with her. For the modern viewer who knows about the movie star's gay following, this serves as a sly hint about Sal's closeted homosexuality, regularly intimated across the show's episodes. Beyond this, musing on how Crawford was once, but is no longer, a great beauty, Betty is prompted to think about her own inevitable aging and this, in turn, brings her to muse about her mother's death, a subject Don is anxious to avoid as he believes it is making Betty "melancholy." As the couple cuddles up in bed and Betty tells Don how aroused she is by thoughts of him during the day when he is at work, the text which initiated the couple's conversation seems forgotten. But Betty's confession of strong desires actually links back to the novel and its film rendering.

Betty tells Don about her everyday routine at home: every mundane task seems both undertaken in order to dissipate, and yet shot through with, an all-pervasive sexual longing. Betty confesses that "I never let my hands idle"; as performed, the line seems to suggest that were Betty not occupied in busy-work she would be masturbating. She *dare* not let herself stop working, or her desires will overwhelm her. Don seems amenable to hearing his wife's fantasies about his homecoming, moving in to take advantage of her erotic mood. But he has missed the point: as she insists that she *wants* him, he assures her, blandly, that she *has* him. But it is not Don *per se* that Betty desires so much as his recognition that she has strong sexual feelings demanding fulfillment. Betty is not telling him she is aroused and ready for sex now, so much as insisting he see her as a sexual being with equal needs and frustrations. And this is both a transgressive notion for a 1960s housewife and the very point that leads us back to *The Best of Everything*.

Again, as the scene shifts to the agency and a normal Monday at work, the Jaffe text may seem to have been forgotten, or at best, meant to resonate slightly in the memory again when Don is presented by prospective clients with another topical best-seller to read: *Exodus* by Leon Uris. The two books existed both side-by-side on the popular book lists, and at opposite extremes of a spectrum built round quality and "taste," with Jaffe's lurid pot-boiler at one end and Uris' worthy, weighty tome at the other.[1] But although the more worthy read can be seen to prompt Don to contact Rachel Mencken again, in order to probe her about Israel, thus leading the story on to Don's next romantic entanglement, it yet remains that the sensationalist text carries the most significance within both the episode and the series as a whole.

This is because the "Babylon" episode turns out to be a key one in the first season. Positioned almost exactly halfway through the first series, it provides the moment where Peggy distinguishes herself from the mass of secretaries, at the Belle Jolie lipstick trials, and takes her first step across the line from secretary to copywriter. We also learn that Joan and Roger Sterling are sexually involved, thus fulfilling our assumption of Joan's toying with the men in the office. Her mature sophistication about sex has been hinted at in her costume, dialogue and in Christina Hendricks' sensual performance, but is now confirmed by the program as Joan and Roger are seen after sex in a hotel room.

As regards Don, this episode shows him realizing that his sometime-lover Midge has friends and a lifestyle outside his ken. As noted, he is positioned moving towards Rachel instead; when he meets her for a drink she allows him to hold her hand briefly, thus hinting at their future intimacy, and, in helping him with his task of selling Israel as travel destination, talks about the idea of "utopia." Rachel insists that while she sees herself as an American, the idea of establishing a nation-state for the Jewish people is important to her. Having been in exile for so long, the Jews are entitled to a home at last. Don comments dryly that this sounds like "utopia" but the educated Rachel is not put off by his put-down. Instead, she one-ups his show of learning by demonstrating she knows the linguistic roots of the word: Utopia had two meanings to the Greeks — both "the good place" and "the place that cannot be."

Within the context of the scene, Rachel's comment seems to imply that her being with Don — which both desire — must be classed as the second form of utopia. In the program as a whole, however, it has wider significance, as well as suggesting why the episode's title is "Babylon," the first place of Jewish exile. Many of the characters can be seen to be in exile, remote from the place or people they would like to be with, or just be, including obviously Don Draper himself.

For the women in the episode, however, being in exile, and yearning for "the good place," is presented in different ways. The series does not assume they all want the same thing, contrary to the notions of women all yearning for a house, husband and children perpetuated throughout traditional fifties media. As the episode shows, Betty wants sex; Peggy wants career fulfillment; Joan wants freedom and a life of her own outside of her sexual affairs; Rachel wants Don as her lover.

Foregrounding the females' desires, in all their variety, the show thus links back to *The Best of Everything* since that text too is all about what women want. Before we can more closely tie the text into *Mad Men*'s characters and narratives, an examination of the text itself proves necessary.

The Best as Text

Jaffe's novel tapped into a well-established trope of both literature and film: "*take three girls...*" Multiple heroines give authors and film-makers a range of career and romance options for their female characters, allowing creators to diversify their fates: as Laura Jacobs describes the formula, "one girl wins, one draws, one dies" (204). *The Best of Everything*'s three protagonists largely conform to this pattern, although it might be difficult to tell who "wins"; there are divergences between the book and film which complicate this issue, making the film, perhaps unusually, the less conservative text. As such it will be the master narrative described here.[2]

Caroline Bender (Hope Lange) arrives for a job interview at Fabian Publications in New York City. She re-reads the advert that brought her there:

> SECRETARIES! You Deserve The Best of Everything!
> The Best Job — The Best Surroundings
> The Best Money — The Best Contacts!!

Promptly at nine a stampede of secretaries arrives in the office. Caroline attracts the attention of office manager Mary Agnes (Sue Carson), who sets her a typing test while talking about her impending wedding. As Caroline is typing, a hung-over man comes in and stares at her. He is Mike Rice (Stephen Boyd), head of a teen magazine which Mary Agnes says keeps the whole company going.

Caroline is hired, getting a desk and a boss to serve for the day: Amanda Farrow (Joan Crawford), head of Derby books, and scourge of secretaries. Caroline reviews her reasons for being in the job: she is no careerist, but whiling away time until her fiancé Eddie returns from a scholarship abroad. Caroline's reverie prevents her hearing Farrow calling her. Farrow issues conflicting orders and patronizing remarks, but Caroline endures their first meeting and escapes back to the typing pool, where she meets April Morrison

(Diane Baker)—it is her first day too. At lunch Caroline meets Farrow's usual secretary, Gregg Adams (Suzy Parker) who has been playing sick to attend an acting audition.

After lunch Caroline has more run-ins with Farrow, while April spends the afternoon taking dictation from Mr. Shalimar (Brian Aherne), one of the top bosses, who makes it clear he would be happy to give her more *physical* work. After his pass is rebuffed, he gives the tearful April sandwiches and some taxi money, considering the matter closed. April runs out of the office, but on reflection is impressed by Shalimar's nerve. The final scene of the first day shows Caroline sitting up all night to read an unsolicited manuscript.

After this carefully worked out beginning, establishing key characters and hinting at future intersections between them, *The Best of Everything* speeds up. Gregg auditions for Broadway director David Wilder Savage (Louis Jordan), but is unsuccessful; after they meet again, an affair begins, netting Gregg a role in one of Savage's plays. Caroline submits her ideas about manuscripts to an encouraging Shalimar. One evening she is at work late when Eddie rings: he is back in the States but has married an heiress. Caroline is heartbroken; Mike Rice happily helps her get drunk and takes her home with him, but when she passes out while he is kissing her, honorably leaves her unmolested. The next day at work Mr. Shalimar makes Caroline a Reader, despite Amanda Farrow's disapproval.

During the Fabian annual picnic, with Caroline enjoying her new job and Gregg enjoying her affair, April meets Dexter Key (Robert Evans) who entrances her with his spontaneity, willingness to break rules, and good looks. Mike accuses Caroline of becoming too career-minded.

At Mary Agnes' wedding, April, who has caught the bride's bouquet, almost faints; she tells Mike and Caroline she is pregnant, and leaves to inform Dexter. All this femininity gets to Caroline: she takes Mike home and cooks him dinner. As they kiss, the phone rings: it is Eddie. Mike realizes she is still hooked on her former beau and leaves.

Dexter, arriving to take April "to get married," is perturbed she has told Caroline. The reason for his annoyance becomes clear when, in his car, Dexter admits he is really driving her to an abortionist. April is horrified, jumps out of the car, and miscarries.

Amanda Farrow leaves Fabian's. She had been having a relationship with "a certain married Vice President" of the company; breaking with him, she goes off to marry a widower with two children and a farm, and Caroline is promoted:

> CAROLINE: Isn't it wonderful, Mike?
>
> MIKE: You have everything you want now, haven't you? Miss Farrow's job,

Miss Farrow's office, and in another month or so you'll have the rest of Miss Farrow's life.

CAROLINE: What do you mean?

MIKE: Isn't that when your married boyfriend comes to town?

Gregg is sacked from the play, dumped by Savage, and goes slowly insane at the dual rejection. Caroline and Eddie meet: he confesses he still loves her. After a few days — and nights — together, however, he offers to make Caroline his mistress, rather than get a divorce. She refuses. Amanda Farrow returns, having found business has ruined her for marriage. Caroline happily gives back her office and clients, although she retains her editor status.

Gregg, snooping outside Savage's apartment, backs out a window and falls to her death. Caroline, April and her new boyfriend — the doctor who attended her after the accident — rush to the scene. The film concludes, as it began, at Fabian's. It is the end of the working day: Caroline gives some tasks to her own secretary to complete before close of business, but then relents. April has plans with her new beau, so Caroline leaves the office alone. But Mike Rice is waiting; the two exchange smiles and walk off together.

I have related this narrative in some detail both because *The Best of Everything* is not particularly well-known, and since so many of the incidents and details seem to me fruitful for discussion in connection with *Mad Men*. Before I explore the character and story strands from the Fifties text which seem to resonate with the recent one, I want to open up a few more of the film's specific points to greater scrutiny.

The film follows its source novel by providing Caroline with a reason to be in the Fabian offices: in neither is she looking to become a career woman, but is simply passing the time productively. Thus she is not to blame for her career success, or indeed having a *career*— as opposed to a job, a wage-generating occupation — at all. The idea that blame could be attached to a woman seeking success at work is a particularly pertinent one for *Mad Men*, and is fully supported by a mass of media material from the late forties onwards in America. Hollywood took a full part in this suspicion of the professional woman; whenever possible from mid-century onwards, films took pains to show that while many "business girls" on the loose in the city were not really looking to better their career prospects, just their marriage ones, those who *were* genuinely intent on a career ultimately became unhappy with this choice.

A young woman was generally shown as a "scheming ingénue," in Brandon French's phrase (81), that character often played by Debbie Reynolds and Maggie MacNamara, who attempts to parlay her way to a husband without bestowing her physical favors, using a job as a means of passing the time until *He* wanders into her trap. Similarly, the tagline for *Ask Any Girl* (1959) suggests Shirley MacLaine's character is on "the jobhunt that is really a manhunt," and Helen Gurley Brown, in her 1962 best-seller *Sex and the Single Girl*, confirms women's ulterior motives in seeking employment: "What you do from nine to five has everything to do with [men].... A job is one way of getting *to* them. It also provides the money with which to dress for them and dress up your apartment for them" (80). Brown contends that most working females choose a job both to meet men and to cover their living expenses, clearly dividing the workforce, as do the films of the time, into those with jobs and those with *ambitions*: "Many companies do not allow dating among co-workers and clearly they are not with it! Why else do they suppose you are working except to cover a few items like food, rent, car payments, bank loans and other trivia? (Bona fide career girls notwithstanding)" (30).

These contemporaneous media texts tie in closely with the image seen within the first few moments of *The Best of Everything*, when Caroline contemplates the job advert for Fabian's. The advertisement claims that, amongst other things, the job will give her "the Best Contacts!!" But why should a secretary need contacts? An advertising executive would need contacts because she would need to build her links within the industry — often, as *Mad Men* shows, through bibulous expense account lunches. But what would a *secretary* need contacts for? The work she needs to do is handed to her by her existing bosses.

"Contacts" makes sense if it actually means, in this context: "males." While Mary Agnes may have found her fiancé outside the office, many of the women in the typing pool at Fabian's might be hoping for "contact" with one of the male executives which they can convert into marriage. This is perhaps why the office workers all assume Caroline is out to get Mike Rice. Uninterested in maneuvring Mike into marriage, Caroline runs the risk of becoming, in Gurley Brown's evocative if perhaps sneering phrase, a "bona fide career girl." Partly *The Best of Everything* sees this fate, as other mid-century texts did, as the road to ruin. For example, a 1962 *Cosmopolitan* piece damns "The Non-Woman: A Manhattan Enigma" as "Sexy but sexless, ravishing but ruthless," adding that this monster "is female but about as feminine as the steel and glass skyscrapers" (149). The "Non-Woman" is a career woman, an unnatural urban creature criticized by the (female) author of the piece for pleasing herself rather than men: "[New York] offers most single women the greatest opportunity for glory. Not with men, but with positions of power in a variety of businesses" (Battelle 62). The phrase "Not with men" indicates the author's assumption that men are the appropriate sphere for female opportunities, the hunt for the right man and marriage to him forming the whole gamut of women's proper endeavors. Battelle assigns the misleading of these unnatural, de-sexed creatures to the allure of the trappings of success: "So undoubtedly [they] ... are the products of the age. They are the college graduates, the middle-class women with smart wardrobes and attractive homes or apartments, who have fallen victim to what might be termed the emotional fallout resulting from the great emancipation explosion" (63). *The Best of Everything* is ambivalent, however, about Caroline's particular successes in the business world. It is careful to show that she does not enter Fabian's in order to become an editor; rather her natural curiosity about books leads her to read manuscripts Farrow has rejected. Shalimar also comments that she "has a gift" for finding gold in the slush pile, which reinforces that it is not graft but *instinct* that propels her upwards at work.

Furthermore, although the film implies a connection between Caroline's romantic disappointment and career success, the latter incident follows the former so rapidly that no causality can be assumed. Caroline is dumped by Eddie, passes out at Mike's apartment and then comes into work the next morning to be told she has been promoted. Her status elevation thus seems more like life dealing her a good hand straight after a bad one than the result of her own ambitions.

However, the film does seem to try to join the mass of mid-century anti–Career Woman propaganda, condemning Caroline for forgetting her femininity and being taken over by ambition when, at the picnic, Mike denounces her new changed persona. Although she utters protests throughout his entire speech, his condemnation is louder on the soundtrack and remains a coherent sentence despite her interruptions:

> Caroline, do you know why you're doing all this? ...It's because the man you thought loved you, loved someone else.... When you tried to forget with the first guy, you passed out instead ... and now you've closed the door, being a woman is too painful so you're not going to be one ... men aren't lovers, they're competition, so let's not join 'em, let's lick 'em!

Despite the virulence of this attack, the film undermines its support for the view of Caroline as misguided career woman in two main ways. First, this is by allowing *Mike*, an embittered alcoholic, to be the one to chastise Caroline. Second, the narrative has shown no signs of her having "closed the door" to her femininity. The breakneck pace of the story has not left time for Caroline and Mike to have become estranged by her new career commitment; by not showing an incremental waning of their friendship and concomitant waxing of her career interest, the film undermines Mike's comments so that, instead of acting as the cool voice of reason, he comes across as a disappointed lover. Because all the criticism of Caroline as career woman exists in Mike's perceptions rather than screen-time, the film renders its own potential condemnation of the woman's inappropriate ambition rather nebulous.

The figure of Amanda Farrow is a similarly ambiguous one. Although she appears to be a stark warning of the dangers of ignoring feminine concerns and promoting career ones, the film actually makes her an example of a woman happy and fulfilled once she realizes her proper place is in the *office*, rather than the home. Farrow differs here from other fifties and sixties representations of the career woman; they are generally shown regretting the time wasted in headlong pursuit of the attention and glamour attending a good job, as this defeated speech from Sylvia (Celeste Holm) in *The Tender Trap* (1955) shows, as she muses over what brought her to the big city:

> A career! Glamour! Excitement! And this is the place to find it. So we come to New York. And we do pretty well. Not great, but pretty well. We make a career. We find the excitement and the glamour. We go to first nights. We buy little mink stoles. Headwaiters call us by name. It's fun. Wonderful. Till one day we look around and we're thirty-three years old, we haven't got a man....

While Sylvia is regretting not finding a husband, *The Best of Everything* allows Farrow to get one, and then to realize that being a wife and mother is not for her. When she reappears in the film, after trying family life, she is softened, but any expectation that it is marriage which made her happier is overthrown: it was a disaster. Her new calmness comes instead from being allowed back into her career, from realizing she was not missing anything in not being with a man. The film shows Amanda to be happier in her job than toiling for the husband and adopted family: the only thing that has changed (since she comes back to same job, even the same office) is her realization that she can have more fun with her career than housework. The borderline hysteria of Farrow before her exit from the office — visually matched by the fussy, oversized jewelry which insists on her femininity even as her masculine-cut suits and high powered job unsettle it — is replaced in Crawford's performance by a new relaxed persona when she returns to Fabian's. Her anger *and* her big costume jewelry have disappeared — replaced by calmness, and understated pearls. Above all, her permanently closed office door which stood as a sign of her alienation from societal pleasures — and, as Mike Rice had warned Caroline, of her own closed-off femininity — now remains firmly open, so that she can greet her colleagues.

While the film seems to hint at its end, therefore, that Caroline might follow in Farrow's footsteps, it also removes the sting from this possible fate by closing with Amanda both careerist *and* kindly. Caroline walking off with Mike Rice into Friday evening Manhattan offers a way of confirming the woman's commitment to her job without ruling out the possibility of romance too; while the voice of Johnny Mathis on the soundtrack urgently pleads that "*romance* is the best of everything," the film has not, as he sings, "proven" this fact, but surely the reverse. The women lost whenever they dedicated themselves to love — April lost Dexter and her baby, Caroline lost Eddie, Gregg lost Savage and her life. Amanda and Caroline emerge as winners however by keeping their eyes on their jobs. Whether or not Mike and Caroline spend the weekend together, the office will be waiting on Monday morning — but the film makes this seem a triumph.

"Are you putting me up for your club, Miss Farrow?" *Mad Men* and Career Women

While *Mad Men* can be seen making similar use of several of the themes and characters present in *The Best of Everything*, the series (so far, at least) has adroitly sidestepped the more lurid aspects of Jaffe's plot, although borrowing its narrative template and main characters.

It is easy to see Joan Holloway as a version of Gregg, another sexy redhead who thinks she is using her sexuality to get what she wants, but often finds herself being used instead. Comments indicate she formerly had a relationship with Paul Kinsey but ended this when he gossiped about her. Joan, as a sexually active but unmarried young woman, requires discretion in her lovers, and hence perhaps prefers married men who have as much to lose, reputation-wise, as she does. Gregg too is obviously no virgin, prepared instead to use her sexuality to secure dramatic roles; she is certainly not insulted or surprised when David Wilder Savage proposes sex. Gregg seeks to be smart, to parlay this one-night stand into a dramatic role, and a future career. But she loses her part for over-acting, and is soon replaced as Savage's lover.

While Joan seems to play her games more skillfully, there are hints throughout the series that she too is subject to disappointments, in both career and romance. Joan may conduct her love affairs more calmly, without the dip into melodramatic posturing which marks Gregg's behavior, but there are hints in her relationship with her doctor fiancé that she too has chosen unwisely. Dr. Greg Harris seems a perfect catch: handsome, well-to-do, professional and caring, he is summed up by Peggy as "a keeper." But this word has a more sinister edge to it which the show also suffers Joan to experience and us to witness: while a "keeper" may be someone worth holding onto, the word also implies a possessive and controlling persona. After he insists they have sex in Don's office, violently forcing Joan against her will, Greg's handsome features seem just a facade hiding an ugly nature. Although she regains her pose of pride in the man, boasting about him to Peggy, the long thoughtful pauses Joan enacts also intimate she is now worried about being trapped in a marriage with a violent and unpredictable man.

Joan also has her share of career slights. While she seems scornful of Peggy's attempts to rise out of the typing pool, Joan too experiences the thrill attending a job well done in "A Night to Remember" (2.8). Asked by the head of the new television department to help out by reading scripts, she gladly takes the work home with her and finds herself swiftly adept. Although she is skilled and on site, however, Joan's sexualized image prevents her being taken seriously by the male executives and she is passed over for the full-time position in favor of a man. Joan's fortunes here slightly echo those of Caroline, as she is prepared to put in unpaid hours at a task she finds interesting. Unlike the central woman of *The Best of Everything*, and unlike Peggy, however, she cannot transfer across the line between secretary and executive.

While Joan thus seems a fairly straightforward rendering of Gregg, the series' most interesting move is not simply to reproduce the characters of Caroline and April within the show, but to *amalgamate* them in Peggy. In *The Best of Everything*, Caroline loses her fiancé but gains a career, moving from secretary to editor by virtue of hard work and single-mindedness. Peggy inherits Caroline's shrewdness and career trajectory, just as she takes over April's sexual naïveté. Blending Caroline and April in the single person of Peggy fleshes out the latter: instead of acting as Joan's prudish opposite, reducing both women to stark polarizations, Peggy's absorption of characteristics from both women makes her a more rounded character, and thus a more interesting one: sexually both innocent and desirous, career-wise both eager and ruthless.

In her April-aspect, sexually innocent Peggy is similarly seduced by a suave playboy who never intends to commit to her. She too becomes pregnant while unmarried. But in its handling of her pregnancy the television series ups the ante of the film's use of this plot device and, significantly, its mode of representing it.

At the time the film version was made, the disgrace of unmarried pregnancy was still so great that even mentioning it in a movie seemed risqué. Although the Production Code, which had held sway throughout Hollywood since its rigid imposition in 1934, had undergone a recent partial relaxing around the mid-fifties, now permitting the use of such terms such as "virgin" and "mistress" (Leff and Simmons 225), these words and their sexualized storylines were still regarded as highly inflammatory. In keeping with this, April's seduction by Dexter and her announcement of the resultant pregnancy are both performed off-screen. While this would be normal practice for the former event, not permitting April even to announce her impending motherhood seems extremely squeamish.

The consummation scene between Dexter and April directly follows one of sexual harassment at the office, when Mr. Shalimar accosts divorcée Mrs. Lamont (Martha Hyer). As he is led drunkenly away, the sounds of mocking laughter ring out from the party-goers, so that the scene which brings about the end of April's sexual innocence begins with a sound bridge of this laughter:

this audio hangover colors the seduction, picking up the party moment's sense of prurience, sexuality and unwanted physicality. At first it seems that Dexter's attentions to April are, by contrast, only too welcome, as the scene fades in with the pair kissing passionately on a heap of cushions. However, April pulls away, telling Dexter they must stop. He demolishes April's argument that physical consummation would ruin their relationship, insisting that she is ruining it by *not* yielding. April indicates her conventional ambitions when she asks the man she loves, haltingly, "Would you ... ever marry a girl ... who wasn't ... pure?" Dexter's equivocating response — he would *if he really loved her*— should not, but does, satisfy April and she sinks back on the cushions, her arguments and her virginity equally vanquished. The seduction fades out with another sound bridge: this time the sound bleeding in is applause. Although the viewer quickly catches up and realizes that the clapping attends a performance of the play Gregg is in, it seems at first as if the film is sardonically applauding Dexter's smooth manipulation of April, the artful way in which he switches expertly between a variety of roles — skilled sensualist, importuning lover, angry suitor — in order to assure her compliance.

April's loss of virginity thus occurs in the interstices between two visible scenes, an invisibility which serves to underline its illicit nature. Her acknowledgement, to Caroline and Mike, of her pregnancy, is similarly elided, occurring also within time represented — or indeed *un*represented — in a cut. April catches Mary Agnes' wedding bouquet. She is thrilled as she wants to marry Dexter, but then becomes faint. Mike and Caroline see her distress and escort her outside; after the cut, the next moment has Caroline asking "Does Dexter know?" and April, confirming he does not yet, determining to go to him at once.

What we can presume is Peggy's loss of virginity is accomplished in a similarly invisible and swiftly accomplished scene, in the very first episode of *Mad Men*. Pete Campbell appears drunk at her apartment door, on the eve of his marriage. Peggy calls out to her roommate that she is going to bed, and takes Pete with her. Their second sexual encounter, however, when they conceive their child, *is* screened for the viewer.

While the sex is shown, the announcement of pregnancy in *Mad Men* is not, since Peggy refuses to deal with the real reason for her very noticeable weight gain. Elisabeth Moss, who plays Peggy, noted in an interview that she felt sure the young woman knew in some part of her mind what was happening to her body, but managed to compartmentalize and ignore this knowledge (Nussbaum). *Mad Men* thus follows *The Best of Everything* in having its innocent character become pregnant, but increases the drama of this plot development by having her deny it, even to herself. While the announcement of April's baby is accomplished silently and invisibly in the cut between two

scenes, Peggy's baby is entirely elided for and by its future mother. This escalation of denial — not just on the part of the text but the woman involved —
dramatically indicates the stigma attendant on unmarried motherhood in this
period.

While Peggy can be, therefore, seen as a version of the innocent April,
one factor points out that her character is actually more hard-willed and practical than her filmic forebearer. Peggy does not go to Pete with her pregnancy
or, after its arrival, the resultant baby. She does not need a version of Dexter
to tell her what to do. Although it is possible that she agonizes about what
to do with the child, the fact that we do not see this, but rejoin her, at the
start of the second series, with her life seemingly unaltered, indicates that
whatever her suffering over giving the baby up for adoption, it is not for us
to witness. Though she has not kept her secret from her sister or Don, Peggy
has successfully managed to move forward without letting the baby impact
on her career, and it is this aspect of her persona — the iron in her soul being
necessary for work success — that demonstrates the show has modeled her after
The Best of Everything's Caroline, as well as April.

The parallels between Caroline and Peggy are from the start numerous,
and come in both overt and more subtle forms. Obviously, both young women
arrive for their first day at the new job in the office at the start of the respective
narratives, both are secretaries, and both eventually elevate themselves from
this position through a combination of natural talent and hard work. We have
already seen how Caroline becomes a reader for Fabian's, based on her willingness to read manuscripts from the slush pile. Peggy's first step towards creative duties occurs in the "Babylon" episode under consideration. Unwilling
to contemplate the arcana of color on which Belle Jolie seem to be basing
their current campaign, the male execs under the leadership of Freddy Rumsen
decide to consult their on-site lipstick experts, and get Joan to organize a
"brainstorming" session using the office women. When Freddy collects the
lipstick-smudged tissues later, he gets into conversation with Peggy, who
passes him the waste-bin, calling it a "basket of kisses." Freddy immediately
reveals his inherent disdain for the female brain: he asks her who told her
that.

Perceiving the aptness of her comments on the lipstick, Freddy Rumsen
later muses to Don that it resembled a dog playing the piano. This echoes —
although no doubt unconsciously on Freddy's part — Samuel Johnson's *bon
mot* about seeing women in the pulpit: "A woman's preaching is like a dog's
walking on his hind legs. It is not done well; but you are surprised to find it
done at all" (Boswell 235). The series frequently highlights the sexist beliefs
of the period in which *Mad Men* is set; comparing Peggy to a trick animal is
a concise yet devastating way to evoke the advertising men's astonishment

that women could have enough creativity to invent potential ad slogans, while the echo of eighteenth-century scorn also shows both how archaic and how ingrained such prejudices are.

The equivalent patronizing moment in *The Best of Everything* occurs at the Fabian picnic, just before Mike and Caroline begin to quarrel. Mike finds Caroline playing croquet and talking business with Shalimar and another boss, animatedly conveying ideas, confidently quoting figures and percentages. Although she is engrossed in the conversation, Mike grabs her arm and hauls her away, just giving her time to call back to the other men, "Your costs would be less and your profits greater!" Shalimar chuckles at the display of he-man tactics on Mike's part before noting meditatively, "You know, there just *might* be something to what she says...."

Although Mike is soon to attack Caroline for indulging her "hot-eyed ambition," she has behaved respectfully to her business superiors here, suggesting ways to improve turnover and couching her ideas in a style which, while confident, does not imply that she herself has anything to gain: she does not say "*our* costs and *our* profits," but is careful to maintain a respectful distance in her language. Nevertheless, Mike ignores the fact that she may have an important idea, and Shalimar dismisses her by his condescending attitude. Peggy too has to face such behavior at work, even once she makes it into the executive ranks, asking Roger Sterling if she may inherit Freddy's old office in "The Mountain King" (2.12); Peggy apologizes if she has been impolite — even aggressive; however, Roger interprets her request as simply "cute." This combination of being belittled even as she is granted what she wants is the price Peggy pays as a career woman in the business world of 1962.

Mad Men further pursues the parallels between its characters and those of *The Best of Everything* in allowing Peggy to become, not just like Caroline, but also like Caroline's own eventual role model, Amanda Farrow. And as *The Best of Everything* does at the end, it shows that Peggy in Farrow-mode is happy and fulfilled being at work. In the same episode where Peggy makes a successful bid for Freddy's office, she is earlier seen exploring the open-plan secretarial floor late one night. A close-up reveals Peggy searching through someone's desk drawer; she filches a cigarette, lights it and exhales happily. Then a longer shot shows her stretch luxuriously and sensuously, before wandering off across the office space, usually public, but at night her own private playground.

When she inherits Freddy's former office, Peggy's pleasure is even greater. She enjoys moving in, having an office boy carry her things, having the other male creatives envy her. She also inherits Freddy's bar, and is found later by Pete enjoying a solo whiskey. She asks Joan about getting the name on the door changed too; the door exactly recreates Caroline's too — same dusky pink shade, same silver lettering — reminding us that Caroline too earned her own nameplate. Pete also prompts us to remember the aspects of Caroline's success when he asks Peggy if she is now getting her own secretary with the new office. When she supposes so, his immediate response is that "*she's* in for it." Pete's insinuation is, presumably, that Peggy will be an even harder task mistress than an executive who had not risen from secretary status, a shared background not being sufficient to breach the gap between boss and secretary now, and the former with every reason to ensure the latter never forgets the differences and distances between them. But if Peggy showed that she could be ruthless — as with her dismissal of a woman chosen to voice an advertisement in one episode (1:8) — Caroline did not, when she relented and let her secretary leave without finishing on a Friday evening, thus perhaps offering hope for Peggy's adjustment to her newly exalted position.

It is Gregg who voices the sneer used as the title for this section; Farrow has warned that her relationship with Savage will finish, and she too will end up alone. While Gregg does not want to be inducted into "Farrow's club" of single, maturing business ladies, the film gradually, and almost despite itself, removes the sting from this slur, and ends by showing Caroline a full member. She has the responsibility as well as the trappings: office, secretary, suit, hat and pearls; but she also has Mike Rice and the promise of a weekend of non-work excitement to come. Thus despite its own intention to damn Farrow with the successful professional/failed woman pairing familiar from other mid-century media texts, *The Best of Everything* shows that Caroline could do worse than become just like Amanda. Perhaps *Mad Men* is similarly endorsing Peggy's ability to become a female executive without "closing the door" on romance and femininity. Peggy's willingness to leave her office door *open* symbolically suggests that she may be an exec in the mold of the fulfilled Amanda Farrow of the film's conclusion.

The Best of Everything?

While *Mad Men* borrows and then complicates Jaffe's characters, its co-option of the office as key locus of action justifies the writer's emphasis on the women's career ambitions, her insistence that these are as significant as their romantic ones. *The Best of Everything* can thus be seen to provide the television series with a contemporary cultural artifact which can act as both window and, perhaps, as mirror: while it can offer a glimpse through to a former time, it can also offer reflections of our current one.

The mirror was an image which attained specific cultural currency regarding advertising in the period under discussion. A lead article in *Time* from

1962 defended the profession from various charges of amorality and manipulation, insisting that it did not drag down, but merely reflected, as a neutral looking glass, the morals and mores of its society: "Allowing for occasional flaws in the glass, advertising is simply a mammoth mirror of the world around it" ("The Mammoth Mirror"). A further reference to mirrors within the article proves even more pertinent to *Mad Men*, however:

> Admen overreact to any criticism of their industry — however casual, ill-informed or unimportant. This has caused John Crichton, president of the American Association of Advertising Agencies, to tartly and correctly chide his fellows for spending too much time "staring into the mirror to count the pimples, broken veins and wattles on the serene, handsome and competent face we hope to present to the public." ["The Mammoth Mirror"].

On the one hand it is easy to see that Don Draper's "handsome and competent face," one which viewers of *Mad Men* know may not be marked with visible blemishes, is actually a mask. On the other hand, this duality returns us to the central theme of appearances/reality with which this chapter began, and which the series seems to find so fruitful to explore, that attraction/repulsion which reels viewers in with the gorgeous facades and then appalls at the cruelties and prejudices seemingly permissible on the cusp of the 1960s. Here however is the crucial point: the show does not merely mirror the times in which it is set but our own contemporary moment. *Mad Men* prompts us to be repelled by the careless institutionalized sexism it shows and then ask ourselves if our times are so different. Is it easier now for women to get ahead in business? Would Peggy Olson or Caroline Bender receive better treatment today?

While Jaffe's scandalous text does not overtly ascribe blame for its women's career failures and disappointments to "the glass ceiling," *Mad Men*'s adoption, co-option and enlargement of *The Best of Everything*'s themes can be seen to offer a commentary on contemporary employment practices — perhaps even within its own arena, the entertainment industry. It was noticeable, for example, that when *Mad Men* was nominated for 16 Emmy Awards on 16 July 2009, this included four out of the five nominations for "Outstanding Writing for a Drama Series" — and that two from the team of five nominated writers were women. As Melissa Silverstein, blogger of *Women and Hollywood*, pointed out, *30 Rock*, which secured the same number of nominations for "Outstanding Writing for a Comedy Series" has *no* women writers on its team (Silverstein).

While the text from "the Fifties" therefore seems at first used by the current television show as a period artifact, to authenticate its historical setting, *Mad Men* actually employs *The Best of Everything* to and for greater effect. It borrows the template of the narrative, revisiting key events as well as the book/film's archetypal characters. But by combining and complicating them, it moves beyond simply utilizing a garish paperback as set dressing, to operating the text as a prism, refracting its more lurid colors and using it to shed a clear light on practices and assumptions not only from the past, but in today's workplaces.

   This essay is dedicated to Stelianos Christodoulou, Jan Langbein and Paul McDonald in gratitude for their kind assistance in its preparation.

NOTES

   1. *The Best of Everything* spent a respectable total of 31 weeks on the combined book best seller lists, but *Exodus* remained there for an astonishing 151 weeks (Justice 276, 441).
   2. While there is not room to go into all the differences between source and filmic adaptation at this point, one significant detail in particular should be noted: the fate of Caroline, arguably the main central figure. The book has her suddenly and rather uncharacteristically give up her job and morals to become the very public mistress of an entertainer; the film maintains the novel's predominant bittersweet tone and finishes with the woman possessing success at work and holding the promise of imminent romance too.

WORKS CITED

Advertisement for forthcoming April issue. *Cosmopolitan* February 1962: 149.
Ask Any Girl. Dir. Charles Walters. Metro Goldwyn Meyer, 1959.
Battelle, Phyllis. "The Non-Woman: A Manhattan Enigma." *Cosmopolitan* April 1962: 61–63.
The Best of Everything. Dir. Jean Negulesco. 20th Century Fox, 1959.
Boswell, James. *The Life of Samuel Johnson.* Ware, Hertfordshire: Wordsworth Editions, 2008.
Breines, Wini. *Young, White, and Miserable: Growing Up Female in the Fifties.* 2nd ed. Chicago: University of Chicago Press. 2002.
French, Brandon. *On the Verge of Revolt: Women in American Films of the Fifties.* New York: Frederick Ungar Publishing, 1978.
Gurley Brown, Helen. *Sex and the Single Girl.* New York: Bernard Geis. 1962.
Jacobs, Laura. "The Lipstick Jungle." *Vanity Fair* March 2004: 405–415.
Jaffe, Rona. *The Best of Everything.* New York: Simon and Schuster, 1958.
Justice, Keith. *Bestseller Index: All Books, by Author, on the Lists of Publishers Weekly and the New York Times Through 1990.* Jefferson, NC: McFarland, 1989.
Leff, Leonard J., and Jerold L. Simmonds. *The Dame in the Kimono: Hollywood, Censorship and the Production Code.* Revised ed. Lexington: University of Kentucky Press, 2001.
Lhamon, W. T., Jr. *Deliberate Speed: The Origins of a Cultural Style in the American 1950s.* Cambridge, MA: Harvard University Press, 2020.
Lover Come Back. Dir. by Delbert Mann, Universal Studios. 1961.
"The Mammoth Mirror." *Time* 12 October 1962. <http://www.time.com/time/magazine/article/0,9171,829287–1,00.html>.
Montagne, Renee. "Jaffe's 'Best of Everything' Stands the Test of Time." 27 July 2005. NPR. <http://www.npr.org/templates/story/story.php?storyId=4763874>.
Nussbaum, Emily. "On *Mad Men,* Elisabeth Moss plays one of TV's newest nerd girls — but with an unsettling twist." *New York Magazine* <http://nymag.com/arts/tv/profiles/48663/>.

Silverstein, Melissa. "Emmy nominations...." *Women and Hollywood* blog, Friday 17 July 2009. <http://womenandhollywood.com/2009/07/17/emmy-nominations-30-rock-breaks-record-but-not-so-great-for-women-creatives/#more-3168>.

Uris, Leon. *Exodus.* New York: Doubleday, 1959.

Yates, Richard. *Revolutionary Road.* Boston: Little, Brown, 1961.

7. "A Mother Like You": Pregnancy, the Maternal, and Nostalgia

Diana Davidson

In "Shoot" (1:9), Don Draper takes his wife's manicured hand across their candle-lit dining room table and assures Betty that as a mother to their children, she does indeed have a job and continues by telling her that she is the greatest mother in the world. The camera cuts between the faces of husband and wife. It is endearing moment: the suave war hero-cum-ad exec loves his Grace Kelly-esque wife because she embodies his maternal ideal. The beautiful white couple seems to share a tender and sincere moment as their preschool-age son and daughter sleep soundly in the upstairs of their ostentatious suburban home. On the surface, the Drapers have achieved the postwar American Dream of the early 1960s.

But in this moment, we as viewers know that Don is serially unfaithful and Betty is seeing a psychiatrist for her "nerves," "sadness," and "melancholy" over having just lost her own mother. The catalyst for this conversation is Betty's dismissal from a modeling job as an all-American blonde selling Coca-Cola; and, although she is beautiful and has worked as a model, we know she was offered the campaign by a rival firm trying to persuade Don to leave Sterling Cooper. Just to keep us guessing, writers Chris Provenzano and Matthew Weiner end the episode, called "Shoot," not with this image of domestic bliss but with Betty standing in her yard at 1 P.M., in a cream-colored chiffon nightgown and robe, cigarette in her mouth and rifle in her hands. Her pink nails repeatedly pull the trigger to shoot her neighbor's pigeons as the radio broadcasts Bobby Helms singing "Special Angel." She shoots at the pigeons because her neighbor threatened to harm her children's dog if the golden retriever harmed his birds. Whether the scene is Betty's reality or fantasy is not clarified; but, nevertheless, it signals her competing desires to rupture her role as a fragile "Birdie"/angel-in-the-house and to protect her children from the disappointment and loss of the world outside their home.

Mad Men simultaneously presents us with a nostalgic look at post-war, pre-second wave feminist motherhood and ruptures that identity as a construction, as if it were a campaign created by Don Draper's team at Sterling Cooper in Manhattan. *Mad Men* shows us motherhood through a historical lens: Weiner and his team give us a show that enables both a remembering of certain kinds of motherhood and/or a relief that these experiences of motherhood are in the past. Both Season One and Season Two end with unhappy and unplanned pregnancies, signaling the biological determinism of women's roles as mothers four decades ago. We are also shown motherhood through nostalgia — something Draper defines in "The Wheel (1:13) as "pain from an old wound." By reading the characters Betty Draper, Joan Holloway, Peggy Olson and Anna Draper through their relationships to pregnancy, children, and the maternal, this chapter contends that representations of motherhood in *Mad Men* are as much about a contemporary audience's ambivalence around motherhood as they are about representing an authentic 1960s American identity.

I.

Mad Men's first season takes place in 1960: the development of affordable automobiles enables suburbia to flourish, the civil rights movement is gaining legislative and cultural momentum, and the United States is the most prosperous nation in the world. It is also three years before Betty Friedan's *The Feminine Mystique* is published; six years before Friedan helps found NOW (National Organization of Women); seven years before President Lyndon Johnson signs an executive order banning sex discrimination in federal employment; a decade before the first women's studies department is formed at San Diego State University; thirteen years before *Roe vs. Wade* ensures women the right to have legal and safe medical abortions. Friedan's book opens with the following oft-quoted paragraph:

> The problem lay buried, unspoken for many years in the minds of American women. It was a strange stirring, a sense of dissatisfaction, a yearning that women suffered in the middle of the twentieth century in the United States. Each suburban wife struggled with it alone. As she made the beds, shopped for groceries, matched slip-cover material, ate peanut butter sandwiches with her children, chauffeured Cub Scouts and Brownies, lay beside her husband at night — she was afraid to ask even of herself the silent question —"Is this all?" [1].

Betty Draper's character could have been created from Betty Friedan's opening passage — name and all. Actress January Jones portrays a beautiful wife and mother in post-war, pre-feminist America who appears to have it all. She fulfills the role of wife and mother and, in return, Don's salary provides her with a large house in suburbia and a car: two material signs of reaching post-war success. As a model, Betty was an individual whose beauty was used to sell products. As a wife and mother, Betty has become a product of her time, the prosperous post-war/pre-feminist era, where a middle-class woman's worth was in her ability to produce children, raise children, keep house, and entertain. Betty starts to challenge this identity and her role within her marriage to Don. In Season One, Betty struggles to understand what it all means which, by Season Two, metamorphoses into Friedan's revolutionary question: "Is this all?"

Betty is intertwined with the objects of the house and the car throughout the series' first two seasons. Women's associations with houses and the domestic realm is a well-established literary and cultural trope that represents a historical reality of women's space. Throughout *Mad Men*, the Drapers' house becomes synonymous and entwined with Betty: the domestic realm is where Betty is both safe and entrapped. She is shown watching the kitchen clock, chain-smoking as the children eat fish sticks and fries, counting the minutes until Don returns from his Manhattan office. When Betty leaves her house, the outside world is configured as a dangerous place where she does not know how to behave. She is humiliated when she goes to Sterling Cooper with the children to meet Don for a photography appointment and he forgets; she tells her neighbor Francine Hanson that it is like visiting a foreign country without knowing the language ("5G" 1:5). She is tempted and made uncomfortable by Arthur's sexual advances at the equestrian stables throughout Season Two. She responds inappropriately to young Glen Bishop's request for a lock of her hair when she leaves her house to babysit him. Betty's identity is determined by the boundaries of the domestic space.

Betty's association with the family car is also historically and symbolically fertile. The advent of affordable automobiles after World War II changed the landscape of American cities; it enabled upwardly-mobile middle class people like the Drapers to live in big homes in growing suburbs away from "the nightmare" of raising children in Manhattan as Betty describes it to Francine ("5G"). Vehicles were signs of having arrived, as a Cadillac salesman tells Don ("The Gold Violin" 2:7). In "Ladies Room" (1:2), both Don and Betty talk about her body as a car when she is having medical problems: Don advises Betty to get a second medical opinion and suggests she "open the hood and poke around." During her first visit to psychiatrist Dr. Wayne, Betty herself says that it is like when your car has a problem, you take it to a mechanic, and the problem disappears. Betty is as much Don's prize as is his silver Coupe de Ville.

The men in Weiner's series sometimes view their wives, and other people's wives, as possessions. This is evident when Don's boss Roger Sterling has dinner at the Drapers' home, drinks too much, and comes onto Betty at the kitchen sink while Don is in the garage fetching more alcohol ("Red in the Face" 1:7). In this episode, Betty's attractiveness functions against her identity as a mother. While Don idealizes her beauty, along with her maternal kindness, his boss Roger Sterling sees her maternal identity as separate from her beauty/sexual desirability: he drunkenly grabs her around the waist at her kitchen sink and insults her. Don is not aware of exactly what has transpired between his boss and his wife. Regardless, he blames her and violently grabs Betty's arm. The next day, at the office, Roger apologizes to Don for coming onto Betty with a story about getting drunk and wandering into the wrong apartment building and with the appalling penetrative analogy that everyone has "parked in the wrong garage." Betty is wife, mother, house, car, and garage all in one; she is seen as a role and as property—not as an individual person.

In Season One, Betty nearly drives the car, with her children in the backseat, into a nearby house after coming home from an errand. The two symbols of her limited agency come crashing together. Betty's hands shake and she blames her nerves which is an important plot development, as it leads her to see a psychiatrist; it is a moment that foreshadows how she reconfigures her relationship to the home and her role within it.

Betty's associations with the house and the car come to symbolize her resistance to her role of wife-and-mother that begins at the end of Season One and dominates Season Two: she takes control of the house and car and, in doing so, changes the boundaries of her identity. In "Indian Summer" (1:11), Betty and a post-partum Francine sit in a baby nursery. Betty tells Francine that she let an air conditioner salesman into the house, noting Don's anger at her admission. When Francine admits her husband would break her arm for such an act, Betty tells her Don lost his temper because he is so "very protective." Betty relishes telling her friend about her transgression and later fantasizes about letting the air conditioner salesman not only in her house, but up to her bedroom, and into her body. She imagines this encounter as she presses her pelvis up against the vibrating washing machine (another commodity indicating the Drapers' wealth and an appliance designed to ease the work of running a household). In "For Those Who Think Young" (2:1), Betty uses her physical beauty to convince a roadside mechanic to fix her car for three dollars (the money she has in her purse) as opposed to the nine dollars he quotes her. She stands on the side of the road, in the dark, with the literal and metaphorical car hood open and smoking. Unlike her interaction with the air conditioner salesman she invites into the house, asks to leave, and later fantasizes about, Betty's moment with the mechanic is very real. Betty's sexual desire for these two men is as much about transgressing the boundaries of her house (letting a stranger in, having sex in her car on a dark roadside) as they are about transgressing the boundaries of her wifely body.

Betty takes full control of the house in Season Two after being told by comedian Jimmy Barrett that Don has been sleeping with Bobbie, his wife. This proof of Don's infidelity is the catalyst Betty needs to redraw the terms of her marriage. After a small breakdown where Betty spends a day chain-smoking and drinking in last-night's dress, she decides to control Don's presence in the house. Initially, she makes Don leave their bedroom and sleep on the couch and eventually, she asks him to leave the home. In "The Inheritance" (2:10), the estranged couple has sex while keeping up appearances during a visit to Betty's ailing father. Don believes they have reconciled, but upon entering their house, Betty coldly tells him that nothing has changed between them. Just as Betty is losing her paternal figure, Don loses his paternal power as his wife determines how, when, and if he will see their children. He is no longer the head of the house or the father who knows best. Part of the reason that Betty resists reconciliation is that, in his confused state recovering from a series of strokes, Betty's father Gene mistakes her for her dead mother during their visit. She literally becomes her mother when her father touches her arm and asks her to attend to their guests and, sadly, when he grabs her breast and suggests they head upstairs to the bedroom. Betty's rejection of Don when they return to their home is an assertion that she will no longer be her mother—the wife and caretaker who serves both in the dining room and in the bedroom.

There is one person in Betty's life who serves as a maternal figure and model but their relationship is defined by the racial and class boundaries of women's labor in post-war America. When Betty goes to her childhood home to see her father, we meet Viola, a middle-aged African American woman who has worked in the house since Betty was a child. Viola is the only person who tells Betty the truth when she says Gene is getting worse; she advises Betty that she needs to focus on her own family. This is in contrast to the advice Betty's mother once gave her about life that she is "painting a master-piece" and she should be careful to "hide the brushstrokes" ("Red in the Face" 1:7). In a tender moment, Viola lets Betty rest her head on her breast and comforts her as if the grown woman were a child. However, Viola and Betty's relationship is, of course, defined by race and class differences; while Viola comforts her, Betty admonishes her for letting her father's girlfriend and her brother ransack the house after her mother's death. This servitude relationship reflects a reality of American history that middle-to-upper class white children were raised by black women for multiple generations. It is a dynamic Betty replicates towards the end of the second season by making her African American housekeeper Carla responsible for an increasing number of the Draper children's needs. Clara becomes Bobby and Sally's primary caretaker: she takes them to school and the park, feeds them, and puts them to bed. We are also shown that Carla and Sally have conversations and a bond; these interactions serve as a mirror to Betty and Viola's relationship ("A Night to Remember" 2:8).

In Season Two, the series starts to reveal not only Betty's unhappiness as Don's wife but also Betty's ambivalence about being a mother. From the beginning of the series, Betty is shown as a young mother who cares for her two young children in a detached and obligatory way. In Season Two, Betty starts sending Sally and Bobby to bed earlier, she forgets to feed them supper, and she spends less time with them as she asserts her independence by riding horses. Betty is not the kind and loving mother Don idealizes her to be. And her children notice. For instance, when she catches Sally smoking her cigarettes, Betty locks her eight-year old daughter in a closet. The little girl tells her mother that Don has left because she is "mean and stupid" ("The Jet Set" 2:11).

In her chapter "Anger and Tenderness" in *Of Woman Born*, Adrienne Rich reproduces an "entry from my journal, November 1960." Like the passage from Friedan's book, Weiner and company. could have taken this as inspiration for Betty's character. Rich writes,

> My children cause me the most exquisite suffering of which I have any experience. It is the suffering of ambivalence: the murderous alternation between bitter resentment and raw-edged nerves, and blissful gratification and tenderness.... Their voices wear away at my nerves, their constant needs, above all their need for simplicity and patience, fill me with despair at my own failures, despair too at my fate, which is to serve a function for which I was not fitted [11].

We can imagine that if the anxiety-ridden Betty kept a diary, she may write something similar to Rich's testimony about motherhood as a "function for which I was not fitted." *Mad Men* shows us that Betty Draper is unhappy for many reasons: she feels entrapped in her role of wife and mother, she desires to know her secretive husband on a deeper level, she suspects (and then has confirmation of) her husband's infidelity, and because she has just lost her own mother when Season One begins. While she has friends in her neighborhood who are also stay-at-home mothers, apart from Francine, Betty does not have anyone she confides in; and, her relationship with Francine is limited by the social conventions expected by her role as an upwardly mobile mother and wife. For example, Francine comes to Betty when she discovers her husband has been cheating because Betty will know what to do, signifying that Betty's friends suspect Don's infidelity. Betty pretends that she has never expe-

rienced what Francine is going through. Even Betty's therapy sessions are iso-
lating: she talks and Dr. Wayne silently makes notes. With her mother dead
and Viola bound by her position in service, Betty has no maternal model and
has little community in which to confide or find support. She does not even
have books such as Rich's (published in 1973) or even Friedan's (published in
1963) to read. Instead, she reads *The Agony and the Ecstasy*—and even though
we know she might enjoy the biography of Michelangelo because she has fond
memories of visiting Italy before she married Don, Irving Stone's title is a
fitting contradiction which describes Betty's state of mind.

The choice to end Season Two with Betty's pregnancy and her shocking
decision to have sex with a stranger in a bar (while the children stay with Don
in his hotel room) signifies the limited agency a middle class wife and mother
has in pre-feminist America. The episode is titled "Meditations in an Emergency" (2:13) in homage to Frank O'Hara's 1957 volume of poetry introduced
in Season Two's first episode. The first line of O'Hara's title poem can be read
alongside Betty's character in this season-ender. But even to viewers unfamiliar
with O'Hara's work, the title signals both the emergency of the Cuban Missile
Crisis, and the crisis Betty faces with this unplanned, and unwanted, pregnancy. Upon being told by her paternalistic physician that she is going to
have a baby (she is not simply "pregnant"), Betty inquires about the possibility
of abortion without saying the actual word. Dr. Aldridge also speaks about
abortion without saying the word, claiming it an option only for young girls,
not for women of means. Likewise, she reminds Francine, at the beauty parlor,
that it is not a good time to have a baby. Francine assures Betty that everything
will be okay, that her own infant daughter was an accident, with tears in her
eyes. Betty's decision, at the episode's end, to let Don back into the role of
husband and back into the home is one of necessity, something Don seemingly
realizes as he remains silent when she tells him she is pregnant. In this scene,
the couple sits across the kitchen table (as opposed to the formal dining table
as in "Shoot" 1:9) and Don again grabs his wife's hand. The artifice of "all
this" has eroded and the episode leaves us in doubt as to whether it can be
repaired. Betty's pregnancy, in 1963, necessitates reconciliation within her
marriage; however, instead of feeling that this plot development offers a potential for rebirth and a new life for the couple, we are left feeling that this
unwanted pregnancy primarily signifies loss.

II.

It may seem odd to write about Joan Holloway in relation to motherhood
in *Mad Men*. As Sterling Cooper's office manager, an unmarried working

woman (until Season 3), she has little in common with Betty Draper, Betty's confidante and neighbor Francine, the divorcée mother Helen Bishop, or Trudy Campbell the young wife of an ad exec who desires to become pregnant but cannot. However, it is Joan's initial difference from other women in the series that makes her, I contend, as central to the show's representations of motherhood as are these other characters. Sex and motherhood are separated in interesting ways throughout the series and Joan is firmly associated with the former.

Joan has the power not to become a mother: in the first episode, she makes an appointment for new girl Peggy Olson to see her personal doctor and get a prescription for the birth control pill (implying that contraception is a job requirement for Sterling Cooper's secretarial staff). In Season One, Joan is in control of the cerebral and corporeal aspects of her past and present sexual relationships. She reads the men of the ad agency with the same savvy and critical distance she uses to dissect D. H. Lawrence's *Lady Chatterley's Lover* in the lunch room. Joan does her best to reject the bird-in-the-cage that her married lover and boss Roger Sterling presents her with while they tryst at lunch hour in a Manhattan hotel room; she does not want to be a "Birdie" Draper. Joan refuses Roger's offer of an apartment but, reluctantly, takes the symbolic bird home (1:6).

The series gives us an explicit cultural reference through which to see Joan: Marilyn Monroe. The '50s screen star functions as both a historical figure (i.e., a real person in the real time of the show) and as a cultural text. Monroe is written about by the most celebrated American writers of the twentieth century: Norman Mailer, Joyce Carol Oates, Gloria Steinem, and Marilyn's second husband Arthur Miller. Her platinum blonde bombshell look and vulnerable sexuality is also emulated and replicated by contemporary female entertainers: Lindsay Lohan, Madonna, Jessica Simpson, Anna Nicole Smith, and Britney Spears. Monroe is also read as a failure of the "American Dream": the woman who rose from rags-to-riches but died alone at thirty-six from a drug overdose. She was a woman who had her own production company, worldwide fame, and wealth, but she was never able to realize her desire to have children and become a mother, adding to her struggles with depression. Gloria Steinem writes in her biography *Marilyn/Norma Jean*: "She personified many of the secret hopes of men and many secret fears of women" (22). In the episodes "Maidenform" and "Six Month Leave" (2:6; 2:9), Joan is read by men as a Marilyn-figure and associates herself with the '50's screen star and, now, cultural icon.

In "Maidenform," Paul Kinsey pitches an idea to Don on marketing Playtex bras, pleading a case that all women are either a "Jackie" Kennedy or a "Marilyn" Monroe. To illustrate his point, Kinsey opens Draper's office door and points to the secretaries at work. He points at Don's new secretary Jane Siegel standing at a file cabinet, wearing her brunette hair in a chignon, and says, "Jackie." He then points at an unnamed secretary with a platinum blonde bob and says, "Marilyn." When red-headed Joan saunters by, her tight-fitting wool dress accentuating and exaggerating her hourglass figure, Kinsey lets the "M" sound linger on his tongue, "Marilyn." He says that Marilyn is "really a Joan." The men laugh. Joan asserts her sexuality, and power, within a socially acceptable framework of identity for women in pre-feminist 1960s.

We see the limited dichotomy of identity for women in the "Maidenform" episode when Don pitches Kinsey's idea to the Playtex executives. He unveils Sal Romano's poster featuring a split image of two photographs of two women. One is dressed in a black wig, black bra and panties, white pearls and black evening gloves, and holds a china tea cup. The other wears a platinum wig, white bra and panties, feather boa, and holds a champagne glass. The "Jackie" model is turned to the side and gazes demurely at the camera while the "Marilyn" model grins head-on into and the diamond pattern on her girdle is placed strategically over her pubis. Don calls the product "The Harlequin" because it will be made in black and white for the two different sides of each woman. He then tells them that the girls in the mock-up are actually the same woman — one made up as both a blonde and as a brunette. The tagline for the campaign is pitched as "Nothing fits both sides of a woman better than Playtex." Don tells the executives that the idea is a flattering mirror. Indeed, the campaign mirrors the dichotomy of female identity that dominates the series: women can take on the identity of happy homemaker and mother (like the First Lady) or a sexy seductress without children (like the blonde bombshell). Ironically, of course, the historical fact of President Kennedy's affair with Monroe is known to contemporary viewers which makes Don's comment that "we want both" more relevant.

If Joan is Marilyn, then Betty can be read as a "Jackie": the wife-and-mother who looks after the house and the children. In the same episode he pitches the Playtex campaign Don tells Betty that he doesn't like her new bright yellow bikini. Betty's swim gear covers as much if not more than the underwear the Playtex model poses in for the campaign's image, but Don tells her that the bikini makes her appear desperate. Don firmly separates motherhood and sexual desirability in his own life — going outside his marriage to fulfill his sexual needs. So, while the men at Sterling Cooper may say they want both a "Jackie" and a "Marilyn" we are shown that they want them in different women, not as two sides of the same, as the Playtex campaign implies.

"Six Month Leave" (2:9) positions Joan with Marilyn Monroe, and specifically, with Monroe's tragic death. The episode opens with Don opening up his hotel room door (as Betty has kicked him out) to read about the actress's death through the headline "Accident or Suicide?" on the front page of the waiting newspaper. Monroe's death is the topic of elevator conversation between Don, Peggy and Hollis and in one of the early scenes, the office pool of secretaries is shown in collective devastation as girls dry tears and talk about the star's death with incredulity. Joan is specifically linked with Marilyn when, after thinking Roger would be gone for the day, she sneaks into his office to lie down on a couch. Roger walks in and discovers her crying and they talk about Monroe's death as they talk about the way he treated her during their love affair. Roger is characteristically glib about Monroe's death, but Joan is genuinely moved: "This world destroyed her." While Monroe's death can be read as a significant moment in American culture, as symbolizing the death of a certain construction of femininity, the death of a rags-to-riches success story who married and divorced both the greatest baseball player and greatest playwright of her day, and the birth of a certain kind of relationship between celebrity and the American public. In *Mad Men*, Marilyn is a text through which Joan can speak to Roger about the pain he caused her during their affair and how both of their constructed identities shaped the outcome. Of course, Joan's association with Marilyn also heightens us to the possibility that Joan is more vulnerable, fragile, and "alone" than her sexy bravado reveals, foreshadowing the trauma she experiences at the end of the second season.

In Season One, Joan works within the dichotomy of being a Jackie or a Marilyn in pre-feminist American culture and seems comfortable and confident asserting her power as "a Marilyn." She understands how the office works, as Peggy says and seemingly enjoys the perks and fluidity of being a mistress as opposed to being "caged in" by a lover or spouse. However, in Season Two, Joan starts to try and move within this dichotomy: she tries to become a "Jackie"—i.e. a respectable wife—by becoming engaged to a doctor. Three events precipitate this change. First, her lover Roger has two heart attacks and Joan realizes how much she cares for him; however, she can do nothing but wait for second-hand information from people in the office who can go visit him without raising suspicion of an inappropriate relationship. Roger breaks off their affair shortly after his attack, callously telling her she was "the best piece of ass" he ever had. Second, in retaliation for her comment that his relationship with his African-American girlfriend Sheila is all for show, Kinsey takes Joan's driver's license from her purse, photocopies it, circles her birth date, and posts it on a bulletin board for all the Xerox machine users—the women she manages—to see she is over thirty. Third, new girl Jane Siegel (a "Jackie") replaces Joan as the beauty of the office, and as the object of Roger's affections. Joan asserts her power as office manager and reprimands Jane for being deemed unprofessional ("The New Girl" 2:5). When Joan discovers that Jane snuck into the eccentric Mr. Cooper's office after hours, along with

most of Draper's team, Joan fires her ("The Gold Violin" 2:7). Jane manipulates Roger into letting her stay at Sterling Cooper and relishes taking her
post at Draper's desk the next workday morning. She tells her supervisor that
Roger said Joan was impetuous and was not serious about dismissing her.
Jane then says to Joan that she does not need a mother ("The Gold Violin"
2:7). Jane's comment about being a mother is a slight at Joan's age and a slight
against the possibility that Joan could offer her any useful advice or guidance.
We can imagine that Joan realizes her days as a "Marilyn" have an expiration
date and she decides to become a "Jackie." She becomes engaged to handsome
Greg Harris, who, she tells Peggy, spends his free time in Harlem tending to
Negro children ("The Mountain King" 2:12).

  Mad Men historicizes that in 1960s America, once a woman is seen and/or
constructs herself as "a Marilyn," it is hard to become "a Jackie." Ironically,
it is Joan's fiancé, the person who should love her most, who punishes Joan
for her desire and her power by raping her on the floor of Don's office ("The
Mountain King" 2:12). In a shocking and fan-debated scene, Greg forces himself on Joan, despite her clear refusal and her protests that "this isn't fun." Her
fiancé asserts his presumed right to Joan's body and sexual power: he humiliates
and violates her to feel he has control within their relationship. After the rape,
Joan is visibly shaken but goes out for dinner with Greg nonetheless. The
next day, at work, she tells Peggy that her wedding is the following December.
The tension of "Jackie" vs. "Marilyn" is firmly entrenched within cultural
attitudes about marriage, work, and morality represented in *Mad Men*: for
both the men and women who enforce it, and for the (mostly) women who
challenge it. As Weiner told interviewer Logan Hill, for *New York Magazine*,
"Joan is a story of a generation.... Our moms had friends like her — very confident and sexy and they got punished for it." In Season Two, Joan loses control
over her body and sexuality in order to gain the possibility of becoming wife-
and-mother.

III.

  Of course, no character in *Mad Men* knows more about motherhood
and loss than Peggy Olson. Peggy is a young, earnest Catholic girl from Brooklyn who begins her career at Sterling Cooper as Don Draper's secretary in
Mad Men's first episode. By the middle of the second season, Peggy is the not
only the first female copywriter at Sterling Cooper but also the first woman
to have her own office. Peggy is different from the other working women at
the ad agency. During Kinsey's Playtex pitch, she asks where she fits into the
mix. While Ken Cosgrove dismissively says "Gertrude Stein," Don answers,

"Irene Dunne." Peggy does not fit the fantasy dichotomy of "woman" in postwar/pre-feminist America. Peggy is different not only in how Sterling Cooper's men see her, but in her views of the world: for example, her response to Marilyn Monroe's death is as practical as it is empathetic. While she seems sympathetic in telling Hollis and Don in the elevator that it is hard to imagine Marilyn could ever have been lonely, she appears calloused as she tells Don they should feel lucky Playtex rejected the campaign because "We would have had to pull it indefinitely." Don sees her for the advertising exec she is becoming. Peggy works hard to separate the spheres of work and home; and, like Joan, she suffers unspeakable trauma and loss.

In Season One's final episode, Peggy and *Mad Men's* audience discover the reason behind her progressive weight gain. On the same day Draper promotes her from secretary to the firm's first female copywriter, Peggy goes to the hospital with what she thinks is food poisoning. Her "bad sandwich" turns out to be a baby boy. After giving birth, she is silent and turns her head away when a matronly nurse cradles the newborn and asks her to hold him. The young woman who succeeds where no woman has at Sterling Cooper, who shows her savvy for understanding women's desires and uses that understanding to market products ranging from lipstick to vibrators, who negotiates and tolerates the sexism of the 1960s advertising world, does not realize she is pregnant or about to give birth. Sterling Cooper, and Don Draper specifically, deem her as exceptional enough to make it in a man's world; the state of New York deems her incompetent to care for her infant and the baby is put up for adoption. Throughout Season Two, Weiner shows this apparent contradiction as a symbiotic relationship as a commentary on women, careers, and motherhood in early 1960s.

There is a deafening silence around Peggy's pregnancy: she herself does not speak about it until the final episode of Season Two. Even when the men on Don's creative team remark that Don sent her to a fat farm, this is positioned as a crude joke and the issue is not brought up again. Both at Sterling Cooper and within the dynamics of her family (namely her devoutly Catholic mother and jealous sister), Peggy works hard to forget the fact that she is a mother and gave up an infant. Peggy has to move on with her life, reflecting a reality for women in a time when adoptions were handled by the state and were "closed."

Peggy experiences the trauma of an unplanned and unrealized pregnancy, unexpected birth, loss of her child, and her sister and Father Gill's judgment associated with the terrible sin of having a child outside marriage. Peggy chooses to keep her pregnancy, birth, and the child's adoption silent and secret from the infant's father while in the hospital and when she returns to work. Like a campaign pitch, Peggy creates an artifice through which to see herself and her child cannot be a part of that—until she decides, in the final episode of Season Two, to tell Pete about their baby.

The father of Peggy's son is account executive Pete Campbell. Ironically, Pete and his wife Trudy consult a fertility specialist because they are having trouble conceiving and a seemingly insurmountable rift forms in their relationship because she wants to adopt and he does not. Pete's mother Dorothy Dyckman, an upper-class woman from an old New York family, tells her son that she will write him out of his inheritance if he and Trudy choose a child from "the discard pile" ("The Inheritance" 2:10). By contrast, Trudy's father is self-made and wealthy; he pulls his Clearasil account from Pete's portfolio when Pete refuses to give his daughter the baby she wants to adopt. Property, wives, children are all part of the same paternal lineage and a deeply entrenched value in Western society that a successful man needs all three to carry on his "line." So it is a tragedy—for all three people in this love triangle—as Peggy provides Pete with a son he does not know exists.

Pete and Peggy only have two sexual encounters in Season One: they have sex once before Pete marries Trudy and once after. In contrast to Trudy, Peggy is so fertile she gets pregnant the first time she and Pete have sex (and perhaps the first time she ever has sex) even though she is on the birth control pill (courtesy of an earlier visit to Joan's doctor). The sad truth is revealed at the conclusion of Season Two when, during the Cuban missile crisis, Peggy and Pete are two of the only people left at Sterling Cooper. They sit and have a drink on the couch in Pete's office pondering the onset of nuclear war. Pete tells Peggy she is perfect—even wishing he might have married her instead of Trudy. Peggy decides to break her silence and tell him the truth he appears to seek, telling him of the baby and leaving Pete speechless, sitting alone on the office couch where the two once had early-morning sex (2:13).

Peggy's experience with the medical community during the birth of her son, and the absence of it afterwards, shows a particular medicalization of pregnancy and childbirth that existed throughout most of the twentieth-century (and is recently being renegotiated). Peggy is hospitalized, institutionalized, for a psycho-neurotic disorder which would now be called post-partum depression. Ironically, she is confined to St. Mary's, which, because of her Catholic background, would have particular meanings around motherhood, sacrifice, and a "virgin" birth. In the episode "The New Girl" (2:5), we are shown in a series of flashbacks that she is heavily medicated and confined to a bed in a ward with other women. Her child is absent. Peggy's response to both her mother and a psychiatrist who approaches her bedside is silence. However, when Don visits Peggy in the hospital she responds to his simple declaration that she move on. He says that she will be shocked "you how much it never happened." Peggy meets Don's eyes and nods. Of course, we know from Don's own experiences in adopting a new identity, that the past cannot be forgotten. Peggy's choice to be silent, to seemingly forget, is a survival mechanism. After all, she does not have the money to attend expensive psychotherapy session as Betty Draper does, and she has to face Pete every day in the office if she wants to continue working at Sterling Cooper (and as the firm's first woman copywriter, the risk of moving to another firm and having to work her way up from secretary again is too great).

Peggy wants a career specifically, a career in advertising. Through Peggy's complex character, *Mad Men* presents the reality that women could choose to be a wife and mother or, enter the male-dominated world of work. Of course, this choice is bound to class and race issues as women who were (are) not middle or upper-class have long had to balance working outside the home, raising other people's children, while also raising their own. Ironically, Peggy excels at creating and tapping into representations of femininity, "woman," and motherhood that contribute to the gender division, sexism, and parental roles of post-war/pre-feminist America. Peggy comes up with Belle Jolie's slogan to "Mark Your Man" with their lipstick ("The Hobo Code" 1:8), she shows how ruthless she can be when she fires a voice actress for not sounding confident enough to sell a vibrating belt being marketed as a weight loss device ("The Wheel" 1:13), and she lands the Popsicle account by creating an image of a Jackie Kennedy-esque mother standing in her kitchen splitting a frozen treat for her two children ("The Mountain King" 2:12). In the social dynamic of 1960s America, Peggy's career success is not something she could achieve if she had kept the child as a single woman or shamed Pete into being with her (as then she would be at home like Betty Draper). But Peggy represents a woman who gives up her child to break the glass ceiling; sadly she is, in the first two seasons, assigned campaigns where she is asked to replicate the norms that make it difficult for women to work and mother.

IV.

Although she has only appeared in a few episodes, Anna Draper is an important character to consider when reading motherhood in *Mad Men* as she offers symbolic agency for maternal identity. Anna is the wife of the "real" Don Draper, the engineer who dies in Korea and whose identity and dog tags Dick Whitman rips off Draper's burned corpse to become our Don Draper ("Nixon vs. Kennedy" 1:12). When she confronts Dick/Don ("The Gold Violin" 2:7) Anna tracks Dick/Don to a used car dealership and confronts him. Dick offers up Don's dog tags and Purple Heart and claims to not know Draper had a wife. Surprisingly, Anna is angrier that her husband failed to mention her on the battlefield than she is at Dick for subsuming her dead husband's identity. Anna lets go of her own identity as the real Don Draper's wife and literally gives Dick Whitman a new life.

Not only does Anna give Dick/Don the chance at a new life, but she becomes a maternal figure for him. In "The Mountain King" (2:12), we are shown flashbacks of Anna and Dick/Don's relationship after they discovered one another and before he married Betty or started working at Sterling Cooper. It is maternal and non-sexual. Even though they seem to be a similar age, Anna takes care of Don, worries about him, and gives him permission to propose to Betty. In return, Don sends her money to help pay for her house; he takes care of her, but not in a spousal way; he is more like a son sending money to his widowed mother.

Don's maternal relationship with Anna is significant because we know that he did not have a loving maternal figure when he was a child. Don confides to his lover Rachel Menken that his mother was a prostitute who died giving birth to him ("Long Weekend" 1:10). He tells Rachel that he was raised by his father (his mother's client) and his father's wife who told him, when he was a little boy, that he was a "whore-child" ("The Hobo Code" 1:8). We can speculate that Don tells the heiress-cum-department store developer because she tells him that her mother died giving birth to her. This interaction works on multiple levels. On one, it represents a reality of maternal morbidity, infant health and medical care pre–World War II. The conversation also gives Don someone to relate to in terms of maternal loss and the abandonment he works hard to forget (and that he has never shared with his wife Betty). We can speculate that Don's tragic childhood shapes his ideals of motherhood that he thrusts upon his wife Betty and makes him receptive to a maternal connection with Anna.

Anna's decision to grant Don the chance at a new life can be read symbolically as a move to recover agency in the identity of motherhood: Anna is caring and compassionate but she is not tied to the conventions of motherhood or the biological realities of it as the other women characters are in *Mad Men*. She connects motherhood to larger concepts such as the soul, the world, and creation itself. Anna maintains agency while assuming a maternal role. Of course, Anna's role exists outside the day-to-day realities of becoming pregnant and the decision about working or not working while raising children; we do not know if Anna has any children or has ever been pregnant but the show leaves both questions unaddressed. At the end of Season Two, when Don feels lost and believes he has damaged his marriage to Betty beyond repair, he leaves an LA business conference and goes to see Anna in southern California. He seeks out her maternal guidance that has comforted him in the past.

In the present-time of "The Mountain King," Anna uses tarot cards to advise Don and tells him a card with a nude woman on it represents the world's soul and she resides in a very important spot in his life She tells him that the only reason he is not happy is that he believes he is alone. As Joan Holloway is associated with Marilyn Monroe, Anna becomes associated with this tarot card earth mother figure who assures Don he can change. Don mulls over Anna's advice and then walks into the Pacific Ocean to be baptized and reborn before he returns home to New York to try and reconcile things with Betty.

In "The Wheel" (1:13), Don uses slides of Betty, Sally and Bobby in a pitch presentation to Kodak. He tells the camera company executives that nostalgia is a "deeper bond" with a product. He shows photos of his children in a little red wagon, Betty cradling a newborn Sally (in pink blanket) in her arms, and their wedding. He believes nostalgia takes humanity to places where we can relive experience, explaining that he has named the product "the carousel" because it lets people travel "round and round," like a child. It is a moving and evocative scene both in and outside the text: Harry Crane is moved to tears and has to leave the boardroom. But as viewers we know just enough about Draper, and the nature of his job at Sterling Cooper, to question if this seemingly sincere meditation on his family is slick artifice being employed to secure a big corporate client. *Mad Men* itself warns us to be careful about nostalgia: indeed, when Don returns home that evening to an empty house, Betty and the kids having gone to her father's for Thanksgiving, we are left feeling that not only his presentation, but his whole family life is an artifice.

We watch *Mad Men*'s representation of motherhood knowing the show is portraying an America on the cusp of second-wave feminism: we watch it with a sense of nostalgia, "the pain from an old wound." As audience, we can sit back and feel triumphant that things are much better for women now. In many ways, things are better: present-day motherhood is different than it was in 1960's America. Female birth control availability and options, sex education in public schools, legalized abortion, and men's increased willingness to use condoms in the advent of the AIDS epidemic, have given women more choice in preventing and terminating pregnancy. Reproductive technologies such as in vitro fertilization and drugs that stimulate ovulation give women more control and choice over when to become pregnant. Reproductive technologies also make motherhood a possibility at later ages than previously thought "safe," or socially acceptable, and lead to multiple pregnancies. Women's increased control over reproduction means more opportunities for different kinds of careers: women can establish themselves in professions, work in dangerous jobs previously limited to men, travel the world and even go into space. In terms of childcare, corporate and community daycares exist where children receive education and socialization according to latest pedagogical and developmental research. However, this is not to say that equality exists either in the bedroom or the boardroom. While things are better for women in the workforce, the stereotype of the "Mommy track" within professions and the illegal dismissal of women who need time to care for infants and children in non-unionized jobs is still an all too common reality. Many middle class mothers juggle work and family out of economic necessity rather than because of an ideological individually-driven choice to work outside the home. Childcare is often hard to find and expensive: too many women work to pay for daycare. Class and race still determine who makes up a workforce of nannies and housekeepers; and, in the age of globalization, American women increasingly hire women from developing nations, creating new levels of inequality between women based on nationality. Contemporary motherhood contains more choices than motherhood in the early 1960s, but it is still a difficult identity to negotiate on personal and political levels.

In *The Mask of Motherhood: How Becoming a Mother Changes Our Lives and Why We Never Talk About It*, Susan Maushart writes that North America is "a culture that glorifies the ideal of motherhood but takes for granted the work of motherhood, and ignores the experience of motherhood" (461). Smart, complex and engaging representations of motherhood in popular culture, and on television in particular, are rare at the moment. We have the tabloid extremes of Brangelina and Britney and reality show voyeurism through *Jon and Kate Plus Eight* and *Nanny 911*. Chicklit fluff, such as *Shopaholic & Baby*, represents children as designer accessories and reaches bestseller lists. Like Betty, contemporary women have few cultural role models when it comes to mothering. Perhaps this is why *Mad Men's* complex representations of motherhood, through its central women characters, resonate with viewers: we are looking to our collective past to fill a gap, an absence, a loss.

Betty, Joan and Peggy are deeply entrenched in limited roles and suffer the sexism and violence that inspired the feminist movement to begin at the end of the 1960s. However, things have not changed so much that viewers cannot relate to Betty, Joan, and Peggy either through our own experiences, situations of friends and family, or, through memories of our own mothers. I do not want to put forth an argument that only women (as opposed to men) can explore problems or write authentically about motherhood-as-identity, obviously women's relationship to motherhood is not solely mitigated through other people as is men's. It is significant that the majority of writers on Weiner's team are women. In an article to promote the start of Season Three, published in *The Wall Street Journal*, Amy Chozick writes,

> Behind the smooth-talking, chain-smoking, misogynist advertising executives on "Mad Men" is a group of women writers, a rarity in Hollywood television. Seven

of the nine members of the writing team are women. Women directed five of the 13 episodes in the third season. The writers, led by the show's creator Matthew Weiner, are drawing on their experiences and perspectives to create the show's heady mix: a world where the men are in control and the women are more complex than they seem, or than the male characters realize.

Weiner's team tells Chozick that they use their own life experiences — such as financial inequity in a marriage and infertility — to inform the plot and characters of *Mad Men*. The working women who write *Mad Men*, regardless of their biological status as mothers, have faced tough decisions about motherhood. This is also why the show's portrayal of 1960s motherhood in all its messiness resonates for us as contemporary viewers. *Mad Men* breaks silences around Betty's ambivalent mothering, Joan's punishment for trying to move within a Jackie/Marilyn dichotomy, and Peggy's necessary forgetting of her loss and sacrifice. *Mad Men* looks to the past to gives us a reality we know — one that is complex and difficult and still needs to be challenged, reconstructed, and negotiated.

Thank you to Stan Bissell, Heather Davidson, and Joanne Muzak for watching Mad Men *with me and reading this essay at various stages.*

NOTES

1. In his chapter "Surprises," in the important *A People's History of the United States*, Howard Zinn discusses these events (and many others) as important in understanding post-war feminism. Zinn contextualizes feminism alongside other events of the sixties and seventies: the civil rights' movement, the Vietnam War, prison reform, and the Native Renaissance.

2. On 10 August 2008 Liesl Bradner reported in the *LA Times* that "A book of poems featured prominently in AMC's widely lauded *Mad Men* sent viewers scrambling to find copies of Frank O'Hara's *Meditations in an Emergency* after the second-season premiere July 27. Google reports the book of verse shot to No. 1 on its "Hot Trends" list for that day and is out of stock on Amazon.com."

3. In the 2 August 2009 edition of *New York Magazine*, actress Christina Hendricks tells journalist Logan Hill: "What's astounding is when people say things like, 'Well, you know that episode where Joan *sort of* got raped?' Or they say *rape* and use quotation marks with their fingers," says Hendricks. "I'm like, 'What is that you are doing? Joan got raped!' It illustrates how similar people are today, because we're still questioning whether it's a rape. It's almost like, 'Why didn't you just say *bad date*?'"

WORKS CITED

Bradner, Liesl. "*Mad Men* using Frank O'Hara's *Meditations in an Emergency* boosts sales." *Los Angeles Times* 10 Aug. 2008. http://articles.latimes.com/2008/aug/10/entertainment/ca-amazon10.

Chozick, Amy. "The Women Behind Mad Men." *Wall Street Journal* 7 Aug. 2009. <http://online.wsj.com/article/SB10001424052970204908604574332284143366134.html>.

Friedan, Betty. *The Feminine Mystique*. 1963. London and New York: W.W. Norton, 1997.

Hill, Logan. "Dangerous Curves: Christina Hendricks, TV's retro-sexy secretary, on living in a *Mad Men's* world." *New York Magazine*. 2 Aug. 2009. <http://nymag.com/arts/tv/profiles/58170/>.

Kinsella, Sophie. *Shopaholic & Baby*. New York: Dial Press/Random House, 2007.

Lawrence, D. H. *Lady Chatterly's Lover*. 1928. New York: Dover Publications, 1996.

Maushart, Susan. "Faking Motherhood: The Mask Revealed." *The Mask of Motherhood: How Becoming a Mother Changes Our Lives and Why We Never Talk About It* in *Maternal Theory: Essential Readings*. Ed. Andrea O'Reilly. Toronto: Demeter Press, 2007. 460–482.

O'Hara, Frank. "Meditations on an Emergency." *Meditations on an Emergency*. 1957. New York: Grove/Atlantic, 1996.

Rich, Adrienne. *Of Woman Born: Motherhood as Experience and Institution*. 1973. London and New York: W.W. Norton, 1986.

Steinem, Gloria. *Marilyn/Norma Jeane*. New York: Henry Holt/Signet, 1986.

Stone, Irving. *The Agony and the Ecstasy*. New York: Doubleday, 1961.

Zinn, Howard. "Surprises." *A People's History of the United States: 1492 to the Present*. 2005 ed. New York: Harper Perennial Modern Classics. 503–541.

8. Mad Men/Mad Women: Autonomous Images of Women

Sara Rogers

Peggy Olson assures her new boss Donald Draper that she is "not that kind of girl" in the series premiere of AMC's *Mad Men in* July 2007. This is the second time in that first episode titled "Smoke Gets in Your Eyes" that Peggy makes this assertion. Thrown into the glamorous and hyper-sexualized advertising workplace Peggy sticks out like a sore thumb. A plain dressed, plain looking, and very serious girl, Peggy immediately stands in contrast to the stunning, well-dressed, and womanly Joan Holloway. Joan, who is clearly the head secretary, quickly shows Peggy the ropes of the office and quickly sends her to the doctor's office for birth control. All of this happens in the first episode in between takes of men in three piece suits smoking, drinking, and trying to score more than just advertising accounts.

Mad Men centers on the 1960s advertising men of Madison Avenue, specifically the fictional Sterling Cooper agency. They drink copiously, smoke, and cheat on their suburban wives. The show is accredited with boosting the AMC network, increasing advertising revenue for the network by 50 percent and helping recruit new viewers a third of whom make more than $100,000 a year (Lowry 34). The upper-middle class viewers aside, the show offers more than a nostalgic view of the 1960s. Though the leading male, Donald Draper, may seem to take most of the limelight of the show as he deals with a false identity, a double life in the city and the suburbs, and other illustrious affairs, it is the women of *Mad Men* that make the show interesting. While Joan Holloway and Peggy Olson may seem to be perpetuating the stereotypes of both the hyper-sexualized secretary and the female nerd, they are in fact representing autonomous women who are in charge of their own lives and know how to gain power — and how to use it for their advancement in the workplace. Therefore Joan and Peggy are both assertive representations of women in television.

Despite the fact that the show takes place nearly fifty years ago it speaks to an audience today. As evidenced by the numerous articles written about *Mad Men* since its initial airing in 2007: from *Time* magazine, to *Newsweek, Business Week, New York Magazine, Advertising Age,* and even feminist magazine *Bust,* people are talking about the show, and they're not just talking about its accurate representation of a decade.[1] One such article in *Time* ascertains the show's "wider sense of history," and a description of Don Draper as an "American Archetype" (Poniewozik 73–4). Despite the 1960s context, the show speaks to a larger sense of time: though the age of smoking indoors and drinking at ten in the morning during a business meeting may have passed, the overall themes of *Mad Men* still ring true today. Those themes being, I believe, the American Dream, patriarchy and the struggle against it, and general conflicts that face all of our daily lives of family and work and the balance between the two. Furthermore, Don is not the only "American Archetype" of the show; Joan and Peggy are both representing familiar female characters that relate to women today.

Joan represents the stereotypical, hyper-sexualized secretary who struggles with more than one inter-office affair while longing for a man who can handle her independent spirit permanently: a man who can respect her knowledge in the workplace at the same time that he respects her power in the bedroom. Peggy, on the other hand, fulfills the stereotype of the intelligent, mousy girl trying to make it in the big city. Peggy manages to climb out of the secretarial pool to make it as the first female copywriter at Sterling Cooper.

Yet, *Mad Men* should not be mistaken as a show that fulfills stereotypes, but rather seen as one that presents an implicit critique to enlighten viewers. Horace Newcomb and Paul Hirsch discuss how television can be used to discuss and reflect the culture that it is representing in their article "Television as a Cultural Forum." They begin by discussing the "cultural basis for the analysis and criticism of television [as] the bridge between a concern for television as a communications medium, central to contemporary society, and television as aesthetic object, the expressive medium that, through its storytelling functions unites and examines culture" (503). In this sense, television is not only a source of entertainment, but also an examination of the popular culture of a society at any given time. This means that a society can look to television for an understanding of multiple aspects of culture. Perhaps the most important point made by Newcomb and Hirsch is: "We suggest that in popular culture generally, in television specifically, the raising of questions is as important as the answering of them" (507). This means then, that television does not need to consciously offer solutions to society's problems, and that simply bringing up issues such as race, gender, and homosexuality promotes discussion and raises questions for the audience allowing new issues to be explored without offering iron clad answers. For *Mad Men's* Peggy and Joan this means raising questions of women's experience in corporate America, to get an audience thinking about how far women in corporate American culture have come over the past four decades.

Television has often been more progressive then society itself. Thinking about how far American culture has come since the times when real women like Joan and Peggy wandered the halls of corporations in the 1960s it is hard to think if society has "fixed" all of the problems of women in the workforce. Douglas Kellner discusses the changing images of women and minorities in television by the late 1960s and 1970s as "relatively progressive in contrast to the racism and sexism that prevailed, and still prevails in large parts of the country" (120). Kellner continues, "Indeed it was precisely this tendency of the television networks to go for a mass audience and to mediate among conflicting social groups that rendered the medium an instrument of integration and inclusion rather than one of exclusion." Here Kellner is discussing how television, at times, has been more progressive than society itself, but by being an instrument of inclusion, television becomes a symbol of progress that culture can perhaps emulate.

Statistically speaking, images of women in television have progressed greatly since the 1960s as David Gauntlett discusses in *Media, Gender and Identity: An Introduction*. Gauntlett states, "In the 1950s, 1960s, and 1970s, only 20 to 35 per cent of characters were female. By the mid–1980s, there were more women in leading roles, but still there were twice as many men on screen" (47). Broken down by genre, Gauntlett reports that by 1987 nearly half of the characters in comedy programs were women while only a third were women in dramas and action-adventure shows. These statistics demonstrate the inequality of representations of women in television in the past. More disturbing than the numbers, however, are the characters the women were playing — most of whom, Gauntlett states, were "married housewives," while male characters "were more likely to be assertive (or aggressive)," and female characters "were more likely to be passive." Throughout the majority of the 1950s, 1960s, and 1970s, the images of women on television were one-dimensional with very few representations of autonomous women.

In comparison, for the 2004–05 season Gauntlett reports on a study conducted of all the major networks, a total of 129 programs, in which "every person that appeared on-screen and spoke at least one line," 39 percent of characters were female (64). Though this study does not break down the numbers specifically by genre the numbers are strikingly similar to the numbers from the mid-twentieth century. However, the depth and range of female characters portrayed has grown significantly. As Gauntlett states, "Men and women are seen working side by side, as equals, in the hospitals, schools and police stations" (62). The numbers of how many women are in television roles may not have changed much, but the roles they are playing have. But does this mean that female characters are now the equals of male characters?

Gauntlett cites television shows such as *Friends* and *Ugly Betty* as showing progressive male/female relationships and new ideas of female beauty in popular culture (70). Susan Douglas also discusses positive female images in television in her article "Signs of Intelligent Life on TV." Douglas looks at the female stars of *ER, NYPD Blue,* and *Chicago Hope*—shows that attract the same type of audience as *Mad Men*—upper-middle class (272). Furthermore, these shows also discuss some of the same issues that the women of *Mad Men* face — namely the struggle between being successful in career or successful in relationships. Douglas states, "The overall message in the three shows is that, yes, women can be as competent as men, but their entrance into the workforce has wrecked the family and made women so independent and hard-hearted that dealing with them and understanding them is impossible" (272). Another feminine struggle that Douglas points out is that of being seen and not heard, or heard and not respected. Douglas calls this "The Ariel Syndrome" named after the Disney character Ariel "who traded her voice for a pair of legs so that she could be with a human prince she'd seen from afar for all of ten seconds" (272). She continues by describing "The Ariel Syndrome" as a voice problem that "grips many women;" she says, "Watch out female characters who 'don't want to talk about it,' who can't say no, who don't speak up. They make it even harder for the women who do speak their minds, who are of course depicted as 'bitches.'"

I think *Mad Men* offers a shift in "The Ariel Syndrome." Peggy does not give voice to her personal life — indeed, denying personal realities to the extent that she ignores an unexpected pregnancy throughout the first season. By the end of the second season, however, Peggy establishes her voice in both personal and career realms. Peggy truly journeys throughout the first two seasons. She begins as a secretary trying to fulfill the duties of a sexualized secretary that Joan models so well, and ends as a self reflective copy writer with her own office. Though Peggy does struggle, at first, with her voice in her personal life, she eventually finds a way to marry her professional and personal lives, and truly become an assertive image of an independent woman.

From the very first episode Peggy resists all the stereotypical demands of her job. As Joan struggles with attempts to "train her" on the sexual demands of being a secretary in the glamorous Sterling Cooper offices, Peggy may seem to represent the stereotypical "smart girl" who has no sex life, in fact no life at all outside of work; this, however is simply not the case for Peggy. Sherrie

Inness discusses the female geek in *Geek Chic: Smart Women in Popular Culture*. Peggy, like the many geeks that have gone before her, does not fit the mold of the "stereotypical dumb blondes," that Inness believes, "American popular culture cannot seem to get enough of" (2). She's smart, she dresses poorly, and she continually asserts that she's just not "that type of girl." What makes Peggy different from the other geeks that have gone before her is that she still has the ability to attract men. Inness says, "No matter how brilliant Sabrina, Velma, or their sisters were, they were shown as lacking the sexual allure of their 'airhead' female cohorts" (2).

Peggy from the first episode, however, has the love of Pete Campbell, or at least the physical attraction. In the series' premiere Pete immediately is intrigued by Peggy and defeated when Peggy ignores the sexual harassment that he throws at her. Upon meeting Peggy, Pete tells her she should dress more like a city girl now that she works in Manhattan. When Peggy ignores his critique, Pete is intrigued so much that, after his bachelor party, he shows up at her apartment and seduces her. Though to the audience Pete seems to see Peggy only as fresh meat, their relationship continues to develop throughout *Mad Men* even as Pete goes forward with his marriage to another woman. Furthermore though Peggy lets him in her apartment — into her life outside of work, she does not let their interlude affect her in the office; in fact her personality at work is positively a-sexual, except for her initial induction into the office.

When Peggy first arrives she has to take in the big city atmosphere, the birth control, the men in suits, and Joan's instructions to put a paper bag with some eye holes over her head, get undressed, and really assess her assets, Peggy's response is that she is always honest, but she doesn't seem to really understand what Joan is asking her to do since she does not see her body as a tool for power the way Joan does (1:1). Peggy sees her brain as the only power tool she needs. Taking all of Joan's instruction in, Peggy tries to fulfill her given role by putting her hand on top of her boss's (Don) at the end of the episode. Don rebuffs her, but Peggy is clearly more appalled with herself than with his dismissal of her sexual advance. Peggy chooses instead to fulfill her own dreams and desires and not the desires of the men around her, or the expectations of a society that demanded women to keep their mouths shut and do as they were told. For this reason Peggy becomes a symbol of autonomy as she struggles to maintain belief in herself and to enact her own choices despite contrary pressure from her peers and her male superiors.

For example as the first season progresses, the audience sees Peggy alienate herself from the rest of the girls in the office, often eating lunch alone in the office, ignoring the fashions that the other women wear and refusing to participate in the constant office gossip. As a woman, in the 1960s however, she cannot exactly be one of the boys and therefore she cannot relate to the men either. Instead she becomes a bit of a loner, developing an asexual relationship with her boss Don who — as the creative genius of Sterling Cooper — also is a brilliant loner in the show. Peggy is in limbo in the show's representation of strict gender lines; she is not exactly one of the men in suits, but she certainly is not one the secretaries either (Nussbaum 67).

Peggy's storyline really starts to take off in the mid-season episode "Babylon" (1:6) when Peggy gets her first big break as a copywriter. When all of the secretaries of Sterling Cooper are asked to "brainstorm" for a new lipstick campaign one secretary says to Joan as she hands out lipstick that brainstorming "sounds intimidating." Also, as the other girls look to Joan for answers to the lipstick company representative's questions, Peggy simply observes. She does not try on any lipstick herself but watches the other girls try them on, and listens to what they say about them. In the end as Fred Rumsen, the man in charge of the account comes into the room from the two-way glass that the men were using to secretly observe the women, Peggy hands him the trash bin filled with lip blotted tissues and cleverly calls them a "basket of kisses." When pressed about what she thinks, she claims she never wanted to be "one of a hundred colors in a box" (1.6). This ends up being the angle the ad executives go with for the campaign and lands Peggy the copywriting job, though at first only on top of her secretarial work. Peggy is calculating in her observation of what is going on around her and uses it to her advantage to get ahead. Furthermore her observation of the women trying on lipstick is representative of how she views herself. She is not like the other women; she cannot be categorized as just another secretary, as just one of a hundred colors in a box.

As Season Two begins, Peggy is seen in a state of personal limbo. She has given up a baby that she kept a secret from everyone, including the father Pete, and even her own self. Peggy is shown in church quite a bit during the season, because of Father John's interest in her that Peggy begins to confront what has happened to her personal life, and whether or not she will face the truth. In "A Night to Remember" (2:8) Father John Gill confronts Peggy about her clear discomfort in church. Peggy denies being uncomfortable, but in her interactions with Father Gill throughout the season she becomes increasingly uncomfortable eventually telling him that he wouldn't understand what she has been through and that perhaps he actually has it easier because he does not have to live like a woman.

Peggy's personal struggles continue through Season Two. Fred Rumsen is fired for drinking too much on the job, and Peggy again puts her observational skills to good use to see that no one was asking for Fred's office. Professionally, at this point in the show Peggy has moved from part time copywriter/full time secretary to full time copywriter and has her own office that she shares with the copy machine and files. In "The Mountain King" (2:12) Peggy bravely approaches Roger Sterling, the man whose company bears his name, and she tells him that with her new promotion and account, she needs her own office, separate from the Xerox machine. Sterling is surprised but impressed and gives her the office, commenting on the aggressiveness of younger women and how there were "thirty young men out there who didn't have the balls to ask me." So, when Peggy gets her own office and the promise of her very own secretary, not only is she seen to be breaking barriers for women of the 1960s, but her hard work begins to earn visible respect, and her intelligence is a positive image for women today. Peggy defies "The Ariel Syndrome": she lets her voice be heard and because of this she passes several other men by to get one of the largest offices on the floor and gains the respect of a partner of the company.

Beth Berila discusses women in positions of power in traditionally all male jobs in her article "Savvy Women, Old Boys' School Politics, and *The West Wing*. Berila states, "Women in these professions need to be strong enough to go head-to-head with powerful male opponents and colleagues who consider women 'aggressive' and 'bitchy' if they are too assertive. If they are not direct enough, they are too 'soft' and weak'" (153). Despite this general idea of how women in professional jobs are viewed Peggy is still successful. Many of her colleagues are angry with her for getting her own office, but it is clear they are angrier for not having the gumption to go after the empty office.

By the end of the second season Peggy seems to have achieved the impossible; she has her own office, a promise of her own secretary, and has permanently left the life of a secretary behind. Furthermore in the Season Two finale, "Meditations in an Emergency" (2:13), Peggy confronts her personal life when she confesses having had Pete's child.[2] Pete confesses his love for Peggy, and that he believes that she is perfect, and Peggy finally confronts her past by telling Pete that she could have trapped him into marriage, but she chose not to do so. Peggy repeats herself in this exchange, I believe, to reaffirm her choice to give the baby away; to remind herself of the decisions that she has made, and where that has left her. She explains that she has her own dreams and goals and that marriage is not one of them as yet. With this revelation, Peggy finally recognizes the loss she has endured in giving away a child, but also she realizes what she has gained. Most importantly, she never lost herself, and though she feels like part of her is gone forever she has reconciled her professional and personal life. Furthermore, Peggy has reconfirmed that the choices she made were her choices, not society's or Pete's, but hers. In the Season Two finale Peggy maintains her autonomy and herself. As Season Three progresses, Peggy is yet again in crisis. It is yet to be seen how she will handle a new job offer, a new affair, and a beginning struggle with Don. However, I do still believe that Peggy will maintain her autonomy despite her new personal troubles.

Commenting on different types of female images, Beth Berila states that women who are "attractive and see themselves as sexual beings ... are viewed as 'using their sexuality to get ahead'" (153). This aptly describes Joan, but only on the surface. Berila suggests that using sexuality to get ahead is negative, though this is not necessarily true. Joan owns and uses her sexuality in much the same way Peggy owns and uses her brain. This is not to say that Joan is lacking in intelligence; she simply uses it in a different way. She is aware of the power that her sexuality wields and she uses it intelligently to gain power over the other women in the office (with the exception of Peggy) and even to control and use the men in the office to her benefit. A woman owning her sexuality can be an empowering sign of autonomy within a patriarchal society.

Joan is assuredly autonomous in choosing to use her sexuality to gain control within the offices of Sterling Cooper. When Joan walks into the first episode of the show she is immediately noticeable. She wears formfitting clothes, has bright red hair and swaggers seductively when she walks. Even her voice exudes sexuality as she tells Peggy that the men of Sterling Cooper may act like they want a secretary but most of the time they desire a woman somewhere between "a mother and a waitress" (1:1). When Joan tells Peggy to go home and examine her body in the mirror to figure out what her best assets are, Peggy thinks the advice ridiculous, but to Joan it is an absolute necessity to know how to use your body as well as your mind to succeed. Joan is the secretary that all the other secretaries look to, she knows how the office works and she instructs Peggy on which girls to "make nice with" (the telephone operators) and how the girls are judged based on who their bosses are. It is Joan who is quick to send Peggy to her "friend" the doctor to get birth control to protect her. Simply put, Joan knows what she wants, knows how to get it, and attempts to take a mentoring role toward Peggy.

In his essay "Gendered Television: Femininity," critic John Fiske states, "The ability to understand, facilitate, and control relationships is often shown as a source of women's power.... Men are often shown as deficient in these abilities," Fiske continues by saying this "can serve as a source of self-esteem for the fans and as an assertion of women's values against the place assigned to them in patriarchy" (183). Fiske's assertion applies to Joan's ability to understand, facilitate, and control relationships, which she uses to keep her position of respect and power within the office. Joan's assertion of self and her palpable confidence is also a source of self-esteem for women.

In "Babylon" (1:6) the audience gets a glimpse at the affair that has been going on between Joan and the married Roger Sterling. It is clear that Roger is in love with Joan; he begs her to let him buy her a place so they can stop meeting in hotels. He claims that she has given him the best year of his life, and wants nothing more than to keep Joan easily accessible in an apartment that he would keep for her. Joan, on the other hand, falls for none of this. She is happy to have an affair with Roger, but is not ready to give up her happy single life for a married man. Roger gives Joan a bird so that she will not have to be alone in the apartment he wants to buy for her, but Joan wants nothing to do with the pet. What she sees is herself caged along with the bird; Joan refuses to sacrifice her independence for a married man who cannot see past her sexuality.

However, this does not keep Joan from teasing Roger sexually every chance she gets. When testing the lipsticks for the new ad campaign, Joan is keenly aware of the two-way mirror and she knows Roger is behind it watching with the other men of the office. She walks up confidently to the window, turns around to say something to another girl and bends down to reach for something exposing her curvaceous figure for all the men to see, and of course making Roger salivate. At the end of the episode Joan is sent to let Peggy know that she is being given the opportunity to write copy. Peggy is ecstatic and it is clear that Joan is uncomfortable giving news to a girl that she sees as below her that she now has more responsibility. However, when Peggy wants to go and thank the men Joan says no; they were very specific that they wanted her to tell Peggy — asserting, once more, that the men still view her as the woman in charge even if they are letting Peggy take on more work.

As the second season of *Mad Men* begins Joan's skills as an expert secretary are put to the test when she is asked to help in the television division of Sterling Cooper in "A Night to Remember" (2:8). When Joan is sent to help Harry Crane read scripts, she embraces the new responsibility, even helping Harry to land more ad space from Maytag. At home, however, Joan's new fiancé, Dr. Greg Harris, does not seemed pleased with Joan's new distraction. When he comes home from picking up dinner Joan has not set the table, something that Greg immediately points out. He then comments on the amount of reading she has been doing, Joan responds that it is part of her job. Greg, however, does not understand how important Joan's job is to her; he believes her job consisted of being looked at. Greg clearly wants Joan to be nothing more than a housewife, and throughout the conversation, Joan seems to be ignoring what he is saying, and becomes increasingly uncomfortable. It is clear that Greg is not comfortable with the work that Joan does, whether or not it is simply being started at by the men at work, or helping land accounts. Greg is intimidated by the power that Joan wields with her work and with her sexuality.

At the end of "The Mountain King" (2:12), Joan brings Greg to Sterling Cooper to show him around the office. Greg is clearly uncomfortable with Joan's ease while in the office, and of the respect she receives from the men who clearly know her better than he does. A previous scene shows Joan in bed with Greg and as Joan tries to take control, Greg is disgusted, pushing her off of him and interrogating her on where she gained such experience. In the next scene the couple is at Sterling Copper while most of the office has left and Greg asks Joan to pretend like he's her boss pulling her in to her actual boss's office and tries to seduce her. She resists him because it is her boss's office and she thinks it is inappropriate, but he insists that this must be what she wants and effectively rapes her on the floor. This scene is indicative of Greg's fear of her sexuality. To him, she is so powerful that the only way he can assert his masculinity and power over her is to force sexual dominance. Joan does not shed a tear and they go to dinner as if nothing happened. At the start of Season Three, Joan is still with Greg, but their relationship is clearly strained. Joan remains more successful personally and professionally than Greg, and whether or not they will remain together is yet to be seen.

Joan and Peggy both grow significantly throughout the first two seasons of *Mad Men*. From the first episode, when Joan instructs Peggy on how to use her sexuality to get ahead, to later, when Peggy's realization that her intelligence is all she needs, both women achieve a personal growth that makes them exciting to watch. "A Night to Remember" ends with Joan rubbing her shoulders where her bra strap has dug in, symbolizing the weight she carries on her shoulders as a woman in a patriarchal society. It is in this episode that she has the discussion with Greg of looking for houses instead of reading scripts. It is also in this episode where the audience begins to see Joan's discomfort with her relationship with Greg, and perhaps the beginning of a realization that she will not lose herself for Greg. The same episode ends with Peggy in the bathtub clearly contemplating her current situation as a woman who has given up a child, and how that challenges her faith as Father Gill pesters her regarding her discomfort in church. By the end of the season, however Joan leaves the flowers Greg has brought her behind after their interlude in Don's office, symbolizing that perhaps she is ready to leave Greg behind as well. Furthermore, Peggy is shown confidently telling Pete of the child and the life they lost together, reclaiming her personal life, and moving forward trusting and owning her decisions.

Joan and Peggy are two very different representations of women, but I believe they send similar messages. Both Peggy and Joan are autonomous; they make their own decisions, run their own lives without measured evaluation or the input of others, and use their individual skills in the office to gain power and climb the corporate ladder. Though Joan's job title does not change in the first two seasons of *Mad Men* she is clearly the woman in charge, as all the other women look to her, and the men respect her at the same time that they want her sexually. Set in the past, *Mad Men* offers a glimpse at a time when corporate cocktail hour was twenty-four hours a day, but it speaks to a modern audience with resonance. When considered in contrast to other representations of women on television today and specifically in context to other representations of women in *Mad Men* itself—such as Don's wife Betty as the lonely housewife, devoid of any self identity—what Joan and Peggy offer the audience are two women who know what they want, and it shows their attempts at realistically balancing their personal and professional identities. The complicated characterizations of Joan and Peggy raise questions about the experiences of women in America that I believe can generate real-life answers.

NOTE

1. See following pages for citations from *Time, Business Week, and New York Magazine*. See also: Natalie Zmuda. "'Mad Men' as Fashion Muse." *Advertising Age* 79, no. 30 (August 4, 2008): 6–6, Jennie Yabroff, and Susan Elgin. "A Word From Our Sponsor." *Newsweek* 152, no. 5 (August 4, 2008): 58–59, and Erin DeJesus. "Mad Women." *Bust* (Dec/Jan, 2009): 50–55.

WORKS CITED

Berila, Beth. "Savvy Women, Old Boys' School Politics and The West Wing." *Geek Chic: Smart Women in Popular Culture*. New York: Palgrave MacMillan, 2007. 153–169.
Douglas, Susan. "Signs of Intelligent Life on TV." *Signs of Life in the USA: Readings on Popular Culture for Writers*. Eds. Sonia Maasik and Jack Solomon. Boston: Bedford/St. Martin's, 2006. 242–253.
Fiske, John. *Television Culture*. London: Routledge, 1997.
Gauntlett, David. *Media, Gender and Identity*. New York: Routledge, 2002.
Hirsch, Paul M. and Newcomb, Horace. "Television as a Cultural Form." *Television: The Critical View*. 5th Ed. Ed. Horace Newcomb. New York: Oxford University Press, 1994. 561–574.
Inness, Sherrie A. "Who Remembers Sabrina? Intelligence, Gender, and the Media." *Geek Chic: Smart Women in Popular Culture*. Ed. Sherrie A. Inness. New York: Palgrave MacMillan, 2007. 2.
Kellner, Douglas. *Television and the Crisis of Democracy*. Boulder, CO: Perseus, 1990.
Lowry, Tom. "How Mad Men Glammed up AMC." *Business Week* 4 August 2008: 34.
Nussbaum, Emily. "Square Peggy," *New York Magazine*. July 2008: 67–68.
Poniewozik, James. "The New New Frontier." *Time*. 4 August 2008: 73–74.

9. Maidenform: Temporalities of Fashion, Femininity, and Feminism

Meenasarani Linde Murugan

In the summer of 2007 television promos started appearing for *Mad Men*. Though this was the first original drama series to appear on AMC, a cable network that had been devoted to "American Movie Classics," the ads offered enough critical endorsements for the pilot to viewers so that it was immediately granted membership to the elite club of "quality" television programs, even if it was not on HBO. Matthew Weiner, executive producer of *The Sopranos* (HBO 1999–2007), created the show, and the ads featured scenes of men and women glancing at each other, somewhat flirtatiously, as they walked through an office. Immediately from these 30-second promos, high production values could be noted, as the colors were intensely vibrant, such as the deep mahogany wood of the desks, Peggy Olson's coral lipstick, Joan Holloway's moss green fitted sheath dress, and the deep grays of the mad men's suits. The details transported us to a time that was definitely retro and chic in the impeccable styling of the clothing, hair, makeup, and interiors.

Though the exact year was difficult to discern, there was a "1950s" element to the images. Amy Winehouse's "You Know I'm No Good" (2007) added to the retro "feel" of these images. Even though this was a contemporary hit song, it used a retro soul sound to add a new twist to her melancholy lyrics about relationship troubles. The choice of this song was not only appropriate as the beat matches the somewhat feline walk of the women through the halls of Sterling Cooper, but the lyrics are contrapuntal to the melody and beat of the song. Though it sounds seductive as the Dap-Kings' instrumentals lure us into a retro world with jazzy riffs while Winehouse croons like Sarah Vaughan, in the end she reminds us that she is, as we should already know, "no good."

Similarly, though *Mad Men* seduces us, primarily with visuals, but also with "classic" vocal standards, as the pilot ends with Vic Damone's "On the Street Where You Live" (1956), we soon learn that this is not such an inviting or enticing environment for women to be in as they have to usually bare the burden for the playboy lifestyle that many of the mad men enjoy. Rather than keep the pain of these (white) women hidden, minute, or laughable in the narrative, as corporate dramas from television's past may have, such as the episode *Patterns* from NBC's *Kraft Television Theater* (1955), the women — specifically Betty Draper, Peggy Olson, and Joan Holloway — are made into full and complex characters that experience pain and pleasure, despite the oppressive gender politics of the early 1960s. The rendering of these women as full characters is not only indicative of talented writers, producers, and actors, but also demonstrates how the show, in transporting us to a time period, is trying to fight the impulse to essentialize when recreating historical narratives. This refusal to essentialize (white) women of the period occurs on two fronts in the characterizations of Betty, Peggy, and Joan. On one front, these women do not occupy similar ages or classes, which in turn affect their actions, or the way they may behave, as the limitations of the sexist culture affect them. On the other, these women are all visually differentiated through body type, hair, makeup, and fashion, demonstrating that even in an oppressive misogynistic culture there were multiple ways to visually display and express one's self. This resists the June Cleaver television stereotype we have of pre-feminist women, showing multiple ways of negotiating femininity and proto-feminism.

This is not to say that the visual aspects of a character do not affect their behavior, as in many ways these two fronts work in tandem. Though a character can be written before an actor is even cast, especially in a television series, that actor will instill a new life into that part, and have the time to evolve in that character. Furthermore, in a period piece, costume is incredibly important in putting the actor in a different, in this case period, mindset, as it not only modifies the actor's appearance but also modifies the way in which one comports one's body. Of particular relevance to this discussion is Janie Bryant's costuming for Betty, Peggy, and Joan, not only as it adds to the complexity of their characterizations, demonstrating different negotiations with femininity, but also because the vast research and immaculate execution of these garments illustrate the variety of dress styles that were present in the early 1960s. By displaying a variety of styles, *Mad Men* resists essentializing a time period, which, despite the seductive visuals, complicates the show's relationship to nostalgia.

The post-war/Kennedy era extends from 1945 to 1963, the end of World War II with the armistice on August 14, 1945, to the assassination of John F.

Kennedy on November 22, 1963. This period has often been a site of nostalgic return in films such as *American Graffiti* (1973), *Back to the Future* (1985), and *Far from Heaven* (2002). Though the latter does not specify the year of the film's setting, *American Graffiti*'s version of 1962 and *Back to the Future*'s version of 1955 both share strong visual similarities with one another as with *Far from Heaven*'s revision of 1950s domestic melodramas and women's pictures. Among featuring common cultural staples, such as automobiles, popular songs, and/or television shows from the period, these films all feature similar women's fashions, epitomized by "the extravagantly feminized hourglass shape ... which became the dominant body image during the 1950s" (Cook 207). This hourglass shape was adorned with dresses with full skirts and stiff petticoats underneath. Generally this dress style emphasized softness and curves, dependent on a corseted waist and uplift bra.

Mad Men resists the nostalgic tendency to compound the late 1940s, 1950s, and early 1960s by displaying a variety of female fashion silhouettes that illustrate changes from the 1950s to the early 1960s. Though the typical hourglass shape with a full skirt is presented on the show, usually worn by housewives like Betty, other silhouettes are presented, indicative of how women had roles outside the domestic sphere. Furthermore, even as a housewife, Betty is not like 1950s sitcom mothers Donna Stone and June Cleaver, who are only shown in dresses with full skirts, as Betty also wears pants, shorts, bikinis, and has skirts and dresses of different silhouettes.

The variety of clothing displayed demonstrates how the program seeks to create a more realistic view of the time period and its characters. Throughout the series, if the women are primarily shown in one environment, the home or office, we will soon get to see them in another environment, that is decidedly different, whether it be a housewife at the stables or a working girl at home. The full and varied wardrobe demonstrates how these female characters are not wholly defined by their roles, as working girl or housewife, and that accompanying "uniform." The variety of fashion on the show then serves to complicate our preconceptions of women during this time period, most of which were perpetuated by family sitcoms featuring the stereotypical happy housewife.

The exaggerated hourglass shape and full skirt is the bare essential of what came to be known as the New Look style. Though the New Look is not in any way entirely "new," it was launched as such by Christian Dior in 1947. This look was influenced by a Victorian style that employed a full skirt with a petticoat, crinoline, and corset. Maureen Turim notes in "Designing Women: The Emergence of the New Sweetheart Line," that this reversion by Dior to the Victorian age might also have been aided by the success of costume dramas such as *Gone with the Wind* (1939), which though based in the U.S., had a similar model of fashioning femininity (215). Dior posited his style as a return to femininity in reaction to the more uniform-like suits women wore during World War II. The war strongly influenced the fashion of the 1940s, not simply in a vaguely aesthetic sense, but because of rationing, expensive fabrics had to be used frugally. Furthermore, limits on the use of rubber for consumer goods made lingerie, corsets, waist cinchers, and girdles excessive. What resulted for many was a style that was much more "masculine," with boxier cuts. Though the everyday women's fashions stressed simplicity and utility in the silhouette, even in Hollywood fashions, such as the oeuvre of Adrian during the 1940s for stars such as Joan Crawford, suits and dresses with broad shoulders and slim hips were the standard, though the fabrics were richer or more embellished than what was available in stores.

Dior's New Look then not only introduced a more "feminine" look to the world of *haute couture*, trickling down to ready-made dresses, but also to women on screen. In Turim's essay, she discusses how the "trickling down" of the New Look to ready-made brands was greatly aided by film costume designers, such as Edith Head, specifically the dresses that Elizabeth Taylor's character, Angela Vickers wore in *A Place in the Sun* (1951): "The four gowns, three white and one black, do not simply signify Angela Vickers's wealth; rather, the appearance is almost magical, ethereal. Embroidered flowers or lace perfectly outline and adorn Taylor's breasts, representing both her sexuality and her maiden innocence" (221). Because of the film's popularity and the high profiling of Head's designs in not only *Variety* but also *Life* and *Seventeen*, the New Look, or its American adaptation in the form of a "sweetheart" dress, "helped bring the style to mass audiences and mass manufacture for such middle-class social events as high school proms and sorority balls" (222). The sweetheart style could also be adapted for more casual occasions, as it was a popular silhouette for summer dresses. Head's adaptation of the New Look in *A Place in the Sun* put Dior's look in an American context, where it no longer simply signified high fashion but also Hollywood stardom. Specifically, here was a version of Hollywood stardom that was not only glamorous but also youthful.

Though the sweetheart style of dress with the corseted waist and tight bodice could be seen on mostly younger women, this style's adaptation of the New Look silhouette was modified to be palatable for older women, specifically women who were in the domestic sphere. Though these women wore dresses that had a similar hourglass silhouette, likewise carrying connotations of novelty departing from wartime fashion and redefining femininity, the shirtwaist dress they wore was slightly loose.[1] "The dress itself was a fancy ornamental variation on the shirtwaist, the relaxed, suburban edition of the New Look.... It was a 'lady look': neat, coherent, feminine, and yet ... one which permitted a freedom of movement in keeping with car pools, servantless homes, and the other conventions of modern housewifery" (Marling 25). Karal Ann Marling in *As Seen on TV: The Visual Culture of Everyday Life in the 1950s*, focuses on first lady Mamie Eisenhower's appreciation of the New Look, specifically as it was adapted by U.S. designers like Mollie Parnis. "Mamie's New Look," as the chapter is titled, is a version of the New Look that is fashionable and youthful, yet is still "womanly" "Unlike high fashion clothes, the Parnis shirt-waist made a woman look well turned out but normal" (26). Parnis, gushing about Mamie, said, "She's proving that a grandmother needn't be an old lady. She's making maturity glamorous" (Parnis in David and David 211–212; Marling 26). The alignment of the New Look shirtwaist dress with maturity marks Betty as a mother, meaning more maternal than sexy. Though she is still styl-ish, the New Look silhouette is sometimes at odds with her incredibly youthful face and body, as yards of voluminous crinolines surround and dwarf her slim figure. If Betty's day clothes age her, her eveningwear marks her as an incred-ibly glamorous and enchanting woman. Though she rarely wears fitted sheath dresses, like the working girls, Joan and Peggy, her evening gowns are rich, embellished, have floor-length hemlines, but have slimmer, more A-Line skirts.[2] The gowns' elegance mark her as a lady, akin to Grace Kelly, as she is told by Jim Hobarth, who wants her to model for his company ("Shoot" 1:9).

When Betty goes to the modeling call, the camera tracks left showing all the women waiting to have their photos taken. We see women in cropped fitted pants and blouses or fitted sheath dresses that end at the knee. They all recline in the modern populuxe futuristic furniture, nonchalantly crossing their legs as they smoke cigarettes. After we see four women, we finally see Betty in a medium length shot, in a prototypical "sweetheart" dress, that is strapless, with vertical pleats in alternating colors of pink, black, and white, rendering her into a festive cupcake. She waits like a patient schoolgirl with her hands in her lap, holding her black clutch. She remarks to the photogra-pher that she feels over dressed, but that she has been out of the modeling business for a while. The contrast in dress, between Betty and the other women demonstrate how style has changed from the 1950s to the early 1960s, from the "sweetheart" look to the more modern "slim-line." The cultural shifts are so noticeable that adults ranging from people in their late-twenties to fifties feel "out of touch' with the changes that have already happened by 1960 or that soon will happen especially between Season One, set in 1960, and the following seasons, set in 1962 and 1963. Furthermore, the changes in style demonstrate how this new model of femininity is less "frilly," as the women are in fitted sheath dresses or pants. There is more practicality in their clothing, an emphasis on the body itself as being on display as opposed to the pretty packaging of the dress.

Though styles had changed from the 1950s to the early 1960s, both the full and fitted skirts were still widely available and seen on many women in the 1950s and early 1960s, as well as on screen. "In *How to Marry a Millionaire* (1953), Marilyn Monroe, Lauren Bacall, and Betty Grable supposedly refused to wear the full skirts of the sweetheart line, possibly fearful of the effect Cinemascope might have in distorting the already wide proportions of such skirts" (Turim 225). This desire by the actresses for slimmer skirts demonstrated how even though New Look style dresses were popular through the 1950s in the stores, "films in the mid–1950s began to display a very different prototype for audiences to follow. The slim skirt, either as tight and sexy, or looser and chic, began to replace the full skirt" (225). This coexistence of two skirt styles, in the stores and on screen was also supported by different skirt styles in high fashion during the 1950s. "By the 1950s high fashion showed a straight and full skirt simultaneously (something rare in the history of fashion)" (216). The different skirt styles were not just indicative of the diversity in taste at the time, but in the cinema these two skirt shapes could be utilized to differentiate female characters in the narrative. "In *Gentlemen Prefer Blondes* (1953), tight skirts represent women as sexual warriors and gold diggers and the sweetheart bridal gowns establish their legitimization as wives" (225). Despite the cinematic portrayal of these different dress styles, ready-made dress stores still marketed both styles of dresses "According to the Sears catalogue at this time real-life fashions had no such rigid divide: while the woman in her twenties could choose to adopt either outline for any outfit, even younger girls were being offered both the bouffant [New Look] skirts and the sheath [slim-line] look too" (Shih, ed. 1997: 115 in Jeffers 2005: 51). The cinema then, with films like *Gentlemen Prefer Blondes*, provided a short hand for what different outfits in the store could connote, even if both styles were being advertised for all.

Another movie star that wore the slim-line style was Doris Day, who revitalized her image in *Pillow Talk* (1959), by having her Jean Louis costumes signify a new sex appeal and modernity, in contrast to the girl-next-door/tomboy image of her previous films, such as *Calamity Jane* (1953). In Tamar Jeffers's "*Pillow Talk*'s Repackaging of Doris Day: 'Under all those dirndls...,'" she notes how Day's character in the film, an interior designer, wears slim-line clothes, relaying that she is sexually experienced, "following the generic film rule that sexually experienced women showed off their bodies [aligning] her with cinematic gold-diggers and career girls, rather than sweethearts and wives" (51). It is also important to note in Jeffers's analysis, that the slim-line fashion of Day's character, Jan, is not only appropriate because it conveys sex appeal but also is indicative of a certain type of working woman, that is very much feminine, but not "frilly" like the "sweetheart." This departure from a "frilly" femininity aligned with the young girl and/or housewife demonstrates how the slim-line reformulated femininity as something that could be compatible with work outside of the home and could connote a certain amount of sexual agency, such as in the characters of Peggy and Joan, or the other women who wait with Betty at the modeling call ("Shoot" 1:9).

The mobility and practicality associated with these fitted dresses can be seen in their adoption by working women. They suggested a more proactive, albeit feminine, woman as it was still a dress albeit not one limited by layers and layers of skirts. The dress was incredibly body conscious, thus emphasizing curvaceous womanly figures, like Joan's zaftig silhouette. Though Turim notes, "how ribbons placed on the sweetheart style can render its wearers as gift-wrapped presents offered up to the male," the slim-line, despite its connotation with the workplace, also presents woman as spectacle (226). The dresses are snug over the bust, tapered at the waist, fitted through the hips and thighs, end at the knees if not slightly higher, allowing for a dress that is extremely body conscious, carrying connotations of modernity, in not only its sleek form but also as it informs women's work, femininity, and sexual mores.

Though the sheath dress ironically carried more connotations of modernity than the New Look, the undergarments were the same regardless of dress shape. Girdles, corsets, and waist-cinchers were necessary to perfect the "natural" hourglass shape of a feminine woman. Undergarments are particularly highlighted on *Mad Men*, as we see Betty, Joan, and Peggy get ready for their days at the beginning of "Maidenform" (2:6). Interestingly, though the show uses pre-recorded music from the period throughout the series, The Decemberists's "The Infanta" (2005), a contemporary indie rock song, accompanies the montage of the women getting dressed. The contemporary music in the sequence interestingly aligns these women of the early 1960s with women today and the routines we all take to put ourselves together for the day, even though these women wear considerably more layers than we do, as they all have slips over their bras, panties, and girdles.

This use of contemporary music is much like the use of Winehouse's song in the first season promos. Here though, it is even more striking because it is used in the narrative of the show as opposed to the advertisements or opening credits. The style of "The Infanta" is much more aggressive and fast than the lounge or folk songs we usually hear. "The Infanta" owes much to the music of the later 1960s with the growth of folk, psychedelic, and acid rock. This aural discontinuity creates a momentary temporal collapse, which allows us to perhaps see our contemporary selves in these women as well as perhaps envision how these women will change in the coming years with the cultural shifts. Importantly, the music ends as soon as we cut to Don Draper throwing the Maidenform magazine ad on his desk. The contemporary music is for the women alone, as the lyrics detail the arrival of a daughter of Spanish royalty.

Though *Mad Men* seems incredibly distant from the reality many women face today, as the abundance of sexual harassment in the office demonstrates why second wave feminism needed to happen, we still live in a world where women do not receive equal pay as men. This fact allows for a painful contemporary resonance with Peggy's pleading to Don for a raise ("The Fog" 3:5). Though in many ways the current state of gender relations is deeply indebted to second wave feminism for structural changes that have allowed for some women to have successful professional lives, culturally there has been a shift away from the feminist legacy. Susan Faludi argues in *Backlash: The Undeclared War Against American Women* (1991) that beginning in the early 1980s, the conservative media has worked to defuse the momentum of the feminist movement. This reactionary stance of the media has significantly molded "the way people [...] think and talk about the feminist legacy" (McCabe and Akass 9, 76, 77). Angela McRobbie in "Postfeminism and Popular Culture: Bridget Jones and the New Gender Regime" complicates Faludi's thesis, noting how "postfeminism actively draws on and invokes feminism as that which can be taken into account in order to suggest that equality is achieved, in order to install a whole repertoire of meanings which emphasize that it is no longer needed, a spent force" (28). What we are left with are social anxieties since the movement destabilized gender roles of masculinity and femininity, or emotional isolation as a consequence of female independence (Tasker and Negra 4).

One way to quell the anxieties of loneliness and an insecure femininity is the post-feminist reconsideration and re-appreciation of feminine consumption, wherein "dressing up equals fun, and fun equals empowerment" (König 140). Charlotte Brundson in *Screen Tastes* remarks on the apparent similarity of the post-feminist woman's relation to fashion and beauty culture as that of the pre-feminist woman, yet she maintains that unlike the pre-feminist woman "who manipulates her appearance to get her man, the post-feminist woman also has ideas about her life and being in control, which clearly come from feminism" (Moseley 86, 199). Though much of feminine fashion and beauty culture before the feminist movement was concerned with capturing male attention, the intended end was not always "landing a husband," or conforming to old stereotypes of the happy housewife.

In many ways there is an infantilization of pre-feminist women in their usually perfunctory participation in feminine beauty culture. The nuanced characters of Betty, Joan, and Peggy on *Mad Men* demonstrate how these women want more than just a husband. Furthermore in constructing their appearance, for especially Betty and Joan, there is knowledge and owning of the male gaze. They know how to comport themselves to get what they want, which is something Peggy figures out as she plays with her femininity throughout the series. Though there are limitations to how fulfilled these women can be, because of sexist institutional and cultural structures, these women are not wholly ignorant sheep to the slaughter of feminine beauty culture.

In *Fresh Lipstick: Redressing Fashion and Feminism*, Linda M. Scott suggests that the "working girl" is a type of woman that is absent from a reductive understanding of how feminism and the women's movement changed women's lives, with the importance of Betty Friedan's *The Feminine Mystique* (1963), emphasized as largely influential for "freeing" women from their domestic traps. Though the character of Betty on *Mad Men* offers a vantage point from which the show could possibly engage that discourse, Joan and Peggy, since they are already working, will most likely engage with feminism in a different way. But beyond speculation, Joan and Peggy experience a more tangible freedom than Betty because they are working women that have their own homes, allowing them the freedom to choose how they spend their time.

In preparing for her role as Joan, Christina Hendricks was told by Weiner to read Helen Gurley Brown's *Sex and the Single Girl* (1962). Joan was loosely based on the book so for Hendricks the book "did help as far as the mentality of what a secretary or what a woman at the time would accept or what was expected of her" (Newman M02). Brown's book in the early 1960s challenged a reductive view of women's roles as posed in *The Feminine Mystique*. The book was incredibly successful earning "about $2 million today. In less than two years, the book 'went paperback' with an unheard-of first run of 1 million copies" (Scott 245). As indicated by its success, the book found an audience, in the abundance of single working woman who were interested in learning more about not necessarily "how to get married but how to stay single — in superlative style" (Brown 11). Despite the book's success, the critical response was negative. Though many may have disagreed with Friedan's argument, the text was treated with respect, as opposed to Brown's book, which was derided because of its casual writing style in the form of a how-to-guide and its significant market impact. But at the heart of these negative responses, despite the gender, prejudice and/or politics of the reviewer, was a scathing critique of the fact that Brown "openly encouraged working girls to have affairs with married men" (Scott 245). Brown upset the upholding of the institution of marriage and the role of the housewife. Still, her looking at married men as "fair game" did not mean she condoned being a "home wrecker" or stealing someone else's husband, nor did she condone sleeping your way up the company ladder or being a "gold digger." Above all Brown charged single women to "do your own work. Don't live off of anyone else, don't be a parasite, make your own money, use your own talent, live up to your potential" (Brown in

Scott 246). This prioritizing of professionalism and independence over opportunism demonstrates Brown's envisioning of the single girl or "working girl"
as someone who does not have to be de-sexualized or un-feminine in order
to be serious about their job.[3] This is in strong contrast to Friedan's assertion
"that working women of the 1950s were seen as masculine" (Scott 246).

This combination of sexuality, femininity, and professionalism as put
forth by Brown can not only be seen in the working girls on *Mad Men*, who
would have most-likely read this guide book in the 1960s, but also post-feminist single girls, such as the women of the book (1997, reprinted 2001, 2006,
2008), TV series (1998–2004, HBO), and movie (2008) under the *Sex and
the City* name. This resonance between women then and women now is further
capitalized upon in the 2004 reprint of *Sex and the Single Girl*, where the back
cover of the book reads: "Before *Sex and the City*'s Carrie Bradshaw, Samantha
Jones, Miranda Hobbes, and Charlotte York tore up the town, there was Helen
Gurley Brown.... It's been over 40 years since Helen Gurley Brown's *Sex and
the Single Girl* sent shockwaves through American culture. How times have
changed, or have they?" (Brown back cover). Though the question is a
provocative one, it is not one that should cause panic as the cover is in an
eye-popping fuchsia-pink, with a cartoon girl on the front, effervescently
flirting with us as she tips back her martini glass.

Even contemporary post-feminist journalists, such as Maureen Dowd,
op-ed columnist at *The New York Times*, who describes herself as "more of a
fun-loving (if chaste) Carrie Bradshaw type" (Dowd 6), has some uneasiness
about the ways femininity in its abandonment of feminism has caused a regression to pre-feminist ideals. She remarks with some dismay that contemporary
dating manuals, such as *The Rules* by Fein and Schneider, "encourage women
to return to pre-feminist mind games by playing hard to get" (18). Furthermore, she states that even though when she was younger she felt that she
"didn't fit in with the brazen new world of hard-charging feminists" (6), that
some things were obviously changing "because a succession of my single girlfriends had called, sounding sheepish, to ask if they could borrow my out-
of-print copy of *How to Catch and Hold a Man*" (18). This book from 1967,
by Yvonne Antelle, even for Dowd seemed anachronistic when she received
it from her mother since the feminist movement was in full momentum at
the time (17). Still Dowd's recollections and critiques on the current, yet
simultaneously "past," state of gender relations, demonstrate how feminism,
as McRobbie argues is "taken into account," yet glaringly absent from post-
feminist culture, as there seems to be a return to a pre-feminist ideal of femininity signified through marriage.

Marriage and the family have become increasingly prominent concerns
for women in post-feminist television as evidenced by programs like *Desperate*

Housewives (ABC 2004–present), an instantly popular show which captured a large amount of the predominantly female audience from *Sex and the City*, which ended its HBO broadcast in 2004. Though this show does puncture the image of the happy housewife, much as Betty's character does on *Mad Men*, these women are contemporary yet still share her anxieties born of the early 1960s, such as dealing with a spouse's infidelity, disobedient children, the desire to work but the inability to find time, and sexual fulfillment. The show blatantly plays with the aesthetics of 1950s suburbs and family sitcoms, borrowing from *The Stepford Wives* (1974), David Lynch's *Blue Velvet* (1986) and *Twin Peaks* (ABC 1990–1991), all of which dismantle, make melodramatic and/or horrific the supposedly "idyllic" world of 1950s. Though the program plays with pastiche, these contemporary characters have real concerns that are at times melodramatic but are identifiable for viewers and seek to resonate with contemporary audiences.

In "Still Desperate: Popular Television and the Female Zeitgeist," Rosalind Coward argues that the juxtaposition of contemporary women's problems on *Desperate Housewives* with the retro look of Wisteria Lane, the setting of the show, demonstrate a strong critique of post-feminism and its adopting of pre-feminist movement culture in an attempt to re-appropriate whatever oppressive connotations the objects may have had, such as a Wonderbra (Moseley 199). For Coward, though post-feminism offers women the option to choose how they want to live or present themselves through re-appropriation, what many women run the risk of is "forcing emotional life to reflect ideals" (40). Rather than having these women's contemporary desires fulfilled, as they chose to live and work at home, "the retro exteriors link the modern wives of Wisteria Lane with 1950s suburbia. What is being articulated is continuity of disappointment" (40). While 1950s housewives tried to break free of the limitations of domesticity, the women of Wisteria Lane, with feminism "taken into account," chose these roles, though both the housewives of the past and present are if not desperate, then at the very least are similarly dissatisfied with their lives.

"Continuity of disappointment" is an operative phrase here because it not only links the pre-feminist movement women of *Mad Men* and their anxieties to post-feminist women and their concerns as seen on *Sex and the City* or *Desperate Housewives*, but among the women on *Mad Men*, it serves as a way to connect Betty, Joan, and Peggy despite that they are not a cooperative unit. Though *Mad Men* is not only about its female characters, there is a quality that strongly resonates with today's women and post-feminist pop culture, leading *Huffington Post* writer Lauren Cahn to claim, "*Mad Men* Is the New *Sex and the City*" (2008). Yet unlike *Sex and the City*'s quartet of female friends or *Desperate Housewives'* quintet of four friends and one "frenemy," *Mad Men* instead shows three women who are not that good of friends, or even cognizant of one another, since Betty is disconnected from Joan and Peggy because she is a housewife. Though Peggy and Joan work together, they have different priorities informed by their different displays of femininity, causing them to butt heads at times. Despite the different roles these women play, they are linked, not only because they are the main female protagonists, but also because they share a similar dissatisfaction with their lives. Similar to the montage that opens "Maidenform" (2:6), the end of "A Night to Remember" (2:8) cuts from a frustrated Betty calling Don, refusing him permission to come home because she is angered and feels betrayed by his infidelity, to Joan getting ready for bed and rubbing the a red bruise on her shoulder from her bra, and then to Peggy in her bathtub deeply sighing as she splashes water on her face. Though these women are not friends nor do they have Carrie Bradshaw's voiceover over their vignettes musing over what it means to come to terms with the truth about being a woman, in its heartbreaks (romantic and professional), or facing the truth about yourself and your own past, they are linked through a collective frustration and despair with the limitations of being a woman in a sexist world where the men cannot even begin to empathize with them. Though this is one of the more downbeat moments in the narrative, moments of hope and gratification exist for some of the female characters as the show progresses. Just as *Sex and the City* was able to give a more nuanced view of what it is like to be a single woman, albeit white, urban, and extremely privileged, in a post-feminist time, *Mad Men*, in playing with nostalgia, gives us a more colorful and varied view of women, albeit all white, in a pre-feminist moment.

Another similarity between the two programs is that *Mad Men* has captured viewers' attention not only for the resonance that the female characters have with contemporary women but also because many viewers covet the show's vintage fashion. Even fashion designers Thom Browne and Michael Kors have cited the show as an inspiration for their fall 2009 and fall 2008 collections, respectively (Slaves 2009). The fashion press, as they did with *Sex and the City*, also latched onto the popularity of *Mad Men*, and featured articles on how to get the look, as it championed the program for its "classic" style (Mohney).

The use of the word "classic" is noteworthy as it carries with it connotations of not only the past and "timelessness," but also class in a socio-economic and cultural sense. Though viewers may covet the garments of the women on *Mad Men* as they did for the women on *Sex and the City*, there is nothing exceptional about the way the women dress on *Mad Men*. They are beautiful women in their own right and wear well-made garments, but the extras are just as well dressed. Everyone of that time period was expected to dress in a manner that appears very polished by today's standards. Quite differently, the women of *Sex and the City* are exceptional as New Yorkers, because they are styled in such a way that is spectacular in the clothes' use of loud colors and liberal mixing and matching of cheap, vintage, and designer garments and accessories. Their outfits reference different time periods in the history of style. Furthermore the spectacle is aided by having the women be at times inappropriately dressed for the weather or occasion. Though they are stylish, and in many ways, especially with Carrie's outfits, fashion forward, their clothes stand out in relation to the other wealthy and most-often stylish New Yorkers that coexist with them. Their swanky extras are chic but understated, rendering them as sufficient background allowing for the spectacular quartet to pop! (Bruzzi and Gibson 123–129). The spectacle of their clothing is also enhanced by the knowledge of how expensive the clothing is, especially Carrie's Manolo Blahnik heels that usually start at $500 a pair.

On *Mad Men*, all the women, leads and extras, have to conform their dress to one period. Though there is variation in silhouettes, demonstrating different feminine styles, there is a uniformity of polish to all their garments. The craftsmanship that goes into the extras' clothing is the same as that which goes into the lead characters' outfits. The desire for the look of *Mad Men* then is the desire for the fashion, and the undergarments that make those silhouettes possible, of a past era. The look is not only "classic" because it is a past look, but it also carries the association of "timelessness," which "suggests something that seems to transcend the specificities of historical period" (Moseley 196).

In Rachel Moseley's study of fan reception of Audrey Hepburn, she discusses many fans' appreciation of Hepburn's "classic" style, because it "is inherently rooted in the late 1950s and early 1960s, and equally structured by precisely that which it effaces — the signs of class," since "the term 'classic' usually refers to a hegemonic style of dress which is acceptably neutral — inoffensive because free of the signs of working-class femininity or other unacceptable forms — a little black dress, for instance" (196). A similar desire for an effacement of class through a "classic" look can be seen in the appreciation of the *Mad Men* costumes. On the show the only way clothing noticeably demarcates class are situations in which people, usually in the service industry, must wear uniforms, such as janitors, elevator operators, or domestics. Furthermore this visual difference in clothing is usually accompanied by a racial difference, meaning most people we see in the service industry are black, such as Hollis and Carla, as opposed to the all-white lead cast of characters.

The clothes' "classic" aesthetic, removed from an understanding of fashion history and how styles "trickle down" from designers to available dress patterns at stores or dresses and ready-made shops, equates this style with a polished appearance that is accessible for many regardless of socio-economic class. Furthermore, the elegant look of the clothes, in how they are tailored as well as dependent on highly structured undergarments that perhaps create good posture at the expense of bruises, also aligns "classic" with being "well bred." As opposed to expensive fashion today that is incredibly label conscious, loudly displaying their brand name, such as Ed Hardy or Louis Vuitton, this "classic" look is compromised of well made garments, that look expensive because they fit individual bodies well.

The "classic" look then, whether it is emulating the women on *Mad Men* or a screen idol, like Audrey Hepburn, offers an opportunity for today's woman to "dress up," and participate in a "coolness" or glamour" that has somehow been lost, implied in the term "classic" and its relation to the past. Though post-feminism, as Brundson suggests, can mobilize "dressing up" and beauty products toward empowering ends, I am somewhat apprehensive to label this as wholly progressive. Arguably, Hendricks' portrayal of Joan is incredibly refreshing to see on television, since there are few women on the big or small screen that are curvy and sexy, yet even she remarks on the importance of structured undergarments. Though her voluptuous figure is not supplemented by padding, she notes, "My girdle has boning, and I wear those bullet bras, as you know. It's a lot underneath and it's all authentic. I have two scars from the rubber where I attach my garters. I would complain more, but it makes me look good" (Corocan). Though, as Hendricks notes in interviews that the girdle changed her posture and forced her to walk with more confidence in her stride, making her feel good about how she looks, the undergarments as seen on the show and off-screen take a toll on the body ("A Night to Remember" 2:8), and ultimately privilege aesthetics over practicality or comfort. No matter how these aesthetics from a ubiquitously sexist period can be re-mobilized, there is still some physical toll that is taken on the body, which is difficult to see as wholly libratory for women.

I do not mean to be puritanical, as many third-wave feminists of *Bust* and *Bitch* magazine don garters and seamed stockings and participate in burlesque shows. There is not a purely hermetic relationship between 1950s and 1960s fashion and oppressive politics, without room for re-appropriation. Furthermore, different women privilege aesthetics over comfort or practicality. Just because one adopts a pinup style or participates in beauty culture does not necessarily mean one is against feminism or no longer sees the use for it. Still, this loving aesthetic return to the Camelot era gives me some pause, even if the "classic" look is what one chooses to wear. Somehow this "choice" of the "classic" look seems pre-determined, as women today, who have had the benefit of growing up in a time of and after the women's movement, are still being disciplined into style types with shows like *How Do I Look?* (Style Network 2004–present) and *What Not to Wear* (UK: BBC Two 2001–2003;

BBC One 2004–2007; U.S.: TLC 2003–present) among other prescriptive style makeover reality shows. In many ways the choices we have now, whether they be "classic," trendy, bohemian, or preppy, seem only slightly more liberating than the Jackie or Marilyn roles that the ad men try to pigeonhole the women of the office into ("Maidenform" 2:6), since they all hinge on preserving some form of heterosexually defined femininity.

Still, we do have more options in the ways we want to present ourselves, and perhaps now more women of different races, ethnicities, and classes can participate in this feminine post-feminist culture as seen in fashion and women's magazines, but still only marginally in popular television and film. Furthermore, like Don's bohemian mistress Midge Daniels, women now relish in the ability to change their look every day, even if they are being disciplined by TV programs to streamline their look to give one succinct message about their identity. Though having the freedom to choose is incredibly important, having the freedom and the fearlessness to create new options or redefine the decision making process is also an equally significant freedom that needs to be seized. This not only includes creating different kinds of styles or fashion, perhaps creating as opposed to solely consuming, but also means not being solely defined by or having to choose between romantic relationships, family, sexual fulfillment, beauty, and professional success, among other factors in one's life. The persistence of these concerns from the pre-feminist moment seen in *Mad Men* to post-feminist works of pop culture demonstrate not only how these are important concerns for women in their persistence but also how perhaps the backlash against or the effacement of the feminist movement today has undone some of its cultural advancements, allowing women to be portrayed in limiting and reactionary terms.

Mad Men's perspective on the women of the early 1960s is deeply informed by the post-feminist pop culture today as well as third wave feminism. Just as Brundson exalts the value of dressing up because it re-mobilizes what was seen as oppressive, *Mad Men* looks back on a blatantly oppressive time period for women, but tries to instill the show with the moments of rupture from the grand narrative of (infantilized) women needing to be liberated from patriarchy. The narratives show moments where women exercise agency by breaking away from the norm or at times find an odd solace in their femininity, though constricting. The show displays how women have very conflicted feelings about their relationship to femininity and proto-feminism. Though these conflicting desires belong to women before the feminist movement, these unresolved tensions hold true today, creating an odd circularity of time as it relates to femininity and feminism.

Postfeminism, as laid out in Yvonne Tasker and Diane Negra's introduction to *Interrogating Postfeminism: Gender and the Politics of Popular Culture*, "broadly encompasses a set of assumptions widely disseminated within popular media forms, having to do with the 'pastness of feminism,' whether that supposed pastness in merely noted, mourned, or celebrated" (1). Accompanying this "pastness of feminism" is post-feminism's "distinct preoccupation with the temporal. Women's lives are regularly conceived of as time starved; women themselves are overworked, rushed, harassed, subject to their 'biological clocks,' and so on to such a degree that female adulthood is defined as a state of chronic temporal crisis" (10). This emphasis on temporality is analyzed by Jane Elliott in *Popular Feminist Fiction as American Allegory: Representing National Time*, in which she concludes her book with a discussion of contemporary post-feminist fiction, or "chick lit," like *The Devil Wears Prada* (2003), and marks them as "Hurried Woman Tales." Ultimately these "tales," she suggests, are not simply about a temporal crisis in which there is too much for the modern woman to do, but importantly indicate "that there can be no future for feminism, no way forward from the realization of its utter powerlessness before time" (167). Though feminism is and was instrumental in allowing women these hurried (working) lives, these tales show the ideology's inability and failure to be applicable to these women's lives, as they now have to juggle simply too much.

One solution for the hurried woman who cannot find enough time comes in the form of various surgeries and beauty products that forestall aging. Another way that narratives deal with the temporal crisis of post-feminist pop cultures involves a forestalling of aging by retreat, regression, or a prolonging of girlhood or adolescence. Diane Negra argues that the ideal femininity that is produced in post-feminist "chick flicks" is "tilting away from the professional path," resulting in narratives of retreatism, "in which a heroine gives up her life in the city to take up again the role of daughter, sister, wife or sweetheart in a hometown setting" (Negra 5). She singles out the films *Practical Magic* (1998), *Hope Floats* (1998), *One True Thing* (1998), and *Sweet Home Alabama* (2002). Similarly another post-feminist "chick flick," *13 Going on 30* (2004) manages a similar type of retreatism by transporting the adolescent girl and sweetheart into the body of a thirty-something akin to the women of *Sex and the City*. Here an ideal femininity is found through a behavioral regression as opposed to a geographic retreat. I see *Mad Men* alongside these post-feminist narratives, as trying to find a femininity that resonates with today, by temporally returning to a moment before feminism came and "hurried" women's lives. The fact that these "un-hurried" women are shown as complex characters, demonstrate how there was something of value in that model of femininity, whether it was simply aesthetic presentation. Still, the overt sexism of the men demonstrates why the feminist movement needed to happen.

Mad Men is in no way as simplistic or prescriptive as the retreatist narratives found in these post-feminist "chick flicks." This program is much like *Sex and the City*, in that the openness of this "quality" television text offers scenarios in which endings or female identities are not so fixed. Rather than romantic comedies that emphasize women downshifting their careers or completely renouncing the professional world and re-embracing the domestic, *Sex and the City* presents women who embrace girlhood while still keeping professional jobs. Still, even the quartet eventually veers toward committed long-term relationships, with hints of pleasure found in domestic life, especially in the character of Charlotte. These multifaceted character identities are made possible in both programs, as their narratives offer opportunities for ambivalent endings to episodes, allowing characters more time and space to develop and work through different roles.

This temporal crisis, then, of the post-feminist "hurried" woman narratives is an interesting one in the world of television since from the beginning of the medium there has been in an interest in the structuring of woman's time, particularly in the home (Spigel 73–98). This can be seen in instructional programming from the early 1960s, such as Julia Child's *The French Chef* (WGBH 1963–1973) but is also seen today with all the programming on Food Network as well as shows on other networks devoted to teaching one how to entertain, re-decorate a room in a weekend, or look *10 Years Younger* (UK: Channel 4 2004–Present; U.S.: TLC 2004–2005, 2008–present). Television can then simultaneously be seen as an aid in the managing of women's responsibilities but also a perpetrator in exacerbating the temporal concerns in post-feminist pop culture. *Mad Men* and *Sex and the City*, being "quality" television texts, allow their female characters time to work through different parts of their identities, relishing in the process as opposed to the instantaneous "Before meets After," slogan of the cable channel, Style Network. Though the "quality" television format allows for more televisual time for the characters to go through their processes, the narratives still demonstrate a concern for the temporal as all the women on *Sex and the City*, though not retreating in time or space, have anxiety about ageing, manifesting in a celebration and prolongation of girlhood. Even on *Mad Men*, Betty, who is approaching her thirties, and Joan, who is already in her thirties, display frustration not only in their loss of youth and the single girl life, but also because they are unfulfilled with their adult lives, though they both are married, or soon will be.

AMC advertises itself as the "Future of Classic." Here the circularity of time and the desire to reformulate the "classic" for the future by returning to the past parallels the desire to reformulate femininity today by returning to a moment of femininity that existed before the feminist movement. If this is the case then is the world of *Mad Men* the future for women? Though I ask this question provocatively, I am concerned with how feminism will factor into the future for women, especially as it is mediated by pop culture. If we are caught in these narratives concerned with the circularity of time and gender roles, it is suspect whether there can be a future for feminism if it is a structured absence from this past-present relationship. Feminism then becomes like a forgone clothing fad, an aberration in the trajectory of femininity, a "braless blip" on the line connecting the fitted sheath dress then to the "future of classic" look of today. McRobbie notes how in this post-feminist age, that is concerned with the temporal, "the category of 'young women,'" is fixated upon, leaving feminism as "decisively 'aged' and made to seem redundant. Feminism is cast into the shadows." (McRobbie 27). Rather than being deemed "classic" or the "future of classic," feminism will, unfortunately, have to settle for, at best, being simply old, if post-feminist pop culture has not completely erased the movement from cultural memory.

NOTES

1. Despite the influence of Dior on the 1950s shirtwaist dress, it is important to note that the shirtwaist dress already existed prior to 1947. "They had been worn as early as the 1900s and were based on the design of a man's shirt.... In their pattern book of dresses from 1916, The Woman's Institute of Domestic Arts and Sciences notes that a shirtwaist dress is 'a simple, practical dress' and that 'even for the classroom or for business, because of its trim simplicity and graceful dignity, it has its advantages.'" See Mary Brooks Picken, *Dresses, Part 2*. (Scranton, PA: Women's Institute of Domestic Arts and Sciences, Inc., 1916), 55, in Heather Vaughan, "Icon: Tracing the path of the 1950s Shirtwaist Dress," *Clothesline: The Online Journal of Costume and Dress* (http://www.clotheslinejournal.com/shirtwaist.htm). Just as Dior looked to Victorian style to re-envision a new look, he also simply applied this Victorian style to an already practical and commonly made dress pattern. In this way, though Dior's New Look trickled down to ready-made brands, it was a look that was already partly appropriated from street fashion.

2. In the first two seasons Betty is never in fitted sheath dresses, but after her third pregnancy in the third season we see her out with Harry Francis and Don in slim silhouettes. See "Seven Twenty Three" (3:7) and "Souvenir" (3:8).

3. It is important to note that even though Brown champions the single girl lifestyle and individual enterprise, much of the success she was able to achieve as a writer of books such as *Sex and the Single Girl* and *Sex and the Office* (1965), as well as her later role as editor-in-chief of *Cosmopolitan* (1965–1997) was due to her "landing" of her film producer husband, David Brown, who suggested to her that she become writer in the first place. In many ways though the single life is celebrated, it is an ephemeral state, that though fun will most likely lead to marriage. For a more detailed critique of Brown's guide and personal narrative see Moya Luckett, "A Moral Crisis in Prime Time: *Peyton Place* and the Rise of the Single Girl," *Television, History, and American Culture: Feminist Critical Essays*. Ed. Mary Beth Haralovich and Lauren Rabinovitz (Durham: Duke University Press, 1999), 75–97.

WORKS CITED

Antelle, Yvonne. *How to Catch and Hold a Man*. New York: Essandess Special Editions, 1967.

Brown, Helen Gurley. *Sex and the Office*. 1965. New York: Barricade Books, 2004.

_____. *Sex and the Single Girl*, 1962. New York: Barricade Books, 2004.

Brundson, Charlotte. *Screen Tastes: Soap Opera to Satellite Dishes*. London: Routledge, 1997.

Bruzzi, Stella and Pamela Church Gibson. "'Fashion is the Fifth Character': Fashion, Costume and Character in *Sex and the City*." *Reading Sex and the City*. Ed. Kim Akass and Janet McCabe. 2004. London: I. B. Tauris, 2008.

Bushnell, Candace. *Sex and the City*. New York: Warner Books, 1997.

Cahn, Lauren. "*Mad Men* is the New *Sex and the City*." *The Huffington Post*. 18 August 2008 <http://www.huffingtonpost.com/lauren-cahn/emmad-menem-is-the-new-em_b_119379.html>.

Cook, Pam. *Screening the Past: Memory and Nostalgia in Cinema*. London: Routledge, 2005.

Corocan, Monica. "*Mad Men*'s Christina Hendricks Is a Vintage Soul." *Los Angeles Times*. 2 November 2008 <http://www.latimes.com/features/lifestyle/la-ig-christina2-2008nov 02,0,63413.story>.

Coward, Rosalind. "Still desperate: Popular television and the female Zeitgeist." *Reading Desperate Housewives: Beyond the White Picket Fence*. Ed. Janet McCabe and Kim Akass. London: I. B. Tauris, 2006.

David, Lester and Irene David. *Ike and Mamie: The Story of the General and His Lady*. New York: G. P. Putnam, 1981.

Dowd, Maureen. *Are Men Necessary?: When Sexes Collide*. New York: Berkley Books, 2005.

Elliott, Jane. *Popular Feminist Fiction as American Allegory: Representing National Time*. New York: Palgrave Macmillan, 2008.

Faludi, Susan. *Backlash: The Undeclared War Against American Women*. 1991. London: Vintage, 1992.

Fein, Ellen and Sherrie Schneider. *The Rules: Time-tested Secrets for Capturing the Heart of Mr. Right*. New York: Warner Books, 1995.

Fielding, Helen. *Bridget Jones's Diary*. London: Picador, 1996.

_____. *Bridget Jones's Guide to Life*. London: Macmillan, 2001.

_____. *Bridget Jones: The Edge of Reason*. London: Picador, 2000.

Friedan, Betty. *The Feminine Mystique*. New York: Dell, 1963.

Jeffers, Tamar "*Pillow Talk*'s Repackaging of Doris Day: 'Under all those dirndls....'"*Fashioning Film Stars: Dress, Culture, Identity*. Ed. Rachel Moseley. London: BFI, 2005.

König, Anna. "*Sex and the City*: a Fashion Editor's Dream?" *Reading Sex and the City*. Ed. Kim Akass and Janet McCabe. 2004. London: I. B. Tauris, 2008.

Luckett, Moya. "A Moral Crisis in Prime Time: *Peyton Place* and the Rise of the Single Girl." *Television, History, and American Culture: Feminist Critical Essays*. Eds. Mary Beth Haralovich and Lauren Rabinovitz. Durham: Duke University Press, 1999.

Marling, Karal Ann. *As Seen on TV: The Visual Culture of Everyday Life in the 1950s*. Cambridge: Harvard University Press, 1994.

McCabe, Janet, and Kim Akass, eds. *Reading Desperate Housewives: Beyond the White Picket Fence*. London: I. B. Tauris, 2006.

McRobbie, Angela. "Postfeminism and Popular Culture: Bridget Jones and the New Gender Regime." *Interrogating Postfeminism: Gender and the Politics of Popular Culture*. Ed. Yvonne Tasker and Diane Negra. Durham: Duke University Press, 2007.

Mohney, Chris. "'Mad Men' Fashion: Then & Now." *BlackBook* 2 September 2008 <http://www.blackbookmag.com/article/mad-men-fashion-then-now/3952>.

Moseley, Rachel. *Growing Up with Audrey Hepburn: Text, Audience, Resonance.* Manchester: Manchester University Press, 2002.

Negra, Diane. ""Quality Postfeminism?": Sex and the Single Girl on HBO." *Genders* 39 (2004). <http://www.genders.org/g39/g39_negra.html>.

Newman, Melinda. "'Some of us have curves.... Should we be trying to hide them?': Christina Hendricks Is Making a Name (And a Figure) for Herself in 'Mad Men.'" *Washington Post* 20 July 2008: M2.

Picken, Mary Brooks. *Dresses, Part 2.* Scranton, PA: Women's Institute of Domestic Arts and Sciences, Inc., 1916.

Scott, Linda M. *Fresh Lipstick: Redressing Fashion and Feminism.* New York: Palgrave Macmillan, 2005.

Shih, Joy, ed. *Fashionable Clothing from the Sears Catalogs, Late 1950's.* Atglen: Schiffer Publishing, 1997.

Slaves to Fashion, "12 Questions For 'Mad Men' Costume Designer Janie Bryant." *Glamour: Fashion, Daily Style Blog.* 26 January 2009 <http://www.glamour.com/fashion/blogs/slaves-to-fashion/2009/01/tk-questions-for-mad-men-costu.html>.

Spigel, Lynn. *Make Room for TV: Television and the Family Ideal in Postwar America.* Chicago: The University of Chicago Press, 1992.

Tasker, Yvonne and Diane Negra, eds. *Interrogating Postfeminism: Gender and the Politics of Popular Culture.* Durham, NC: Duke University Press, 2007.

Turim, Maureen. "Designing Women: The Emergence of the New Sweetheart Line." *Fabrications: Costume and the Female Body.* Ed. Jane Gaines and Charlotte Herzog. New York: Routledge, 1990.

Vaughan, Heather. "Icon: Tracing the path of the 1950s Shirtwaist Dress." *Clothesline: The Online Journal of Costume and Dress* July 2005. <http://www.clotheslinejournal.com/shirtwaist.htm>.

Weisberger, Lauren. *The Devil Wears Prada.* New York: Broadway Books, 2003.

10. Every Woman Is a Jackie or a Marilyn: The Problematics of Nostalgia

Tonya Krouse

It is the early 1960s. The location is Manhattan, or, more specifically, the offices of Sterling Cooper, a Madison Avenue advertising agency. The opening credits, accompanied by a sample of RJD2's retro-sounding "Beautiful Mine," appear over a slick graphic background that depicts cartoon skyscrapers and a suited man in silhouette. Viewers watch the man plunge through the sky, not knowing whether he fell, jumped, or was pushed, past the skyscrapers, past sexy images of women's body parts — both distinct from and superimposed onto the animated buildings — past advertising slogans like, "Enjoy the best America has to offer." Immediately following this opening sequence, the pilot episode offers the following copy in large, white block letters on a black background:

MAD MEN.
 A term coined in the late 1950's to describe the advertising executives of Madison Avenue.
 They coined it.

These images and lines provide viewers with a glossy first impression that draws them in to AMC's critically acclaimed series, *Mad Men.*

The premise of the series is sophisticated, but the narrative structure of most episodes is quite straightforward. The central figure of each episode's plot is typically the show's protagonist, the suave and mysterious creative director of the advertising agency, Don Draper. Various subplots circulate around Don and amplify his complexity, subplots which focus on the people with whom Don interacts on a daily basis: his colleagues at Sterling Cooper, the women office staff who work for the agency, his mistresses, and finally his family.

In terms of format, most episodes have an advertising campaign at their center. Whether the product is Right Guard, a mid-century version of a vibrator called "The Rejuvenator," or Playtex Bras, the themes that emerge in the creative development of the ad campaign expose the primary preoccupations of the episode for the viewer, and the characters' individual storylines provide sophisticated and personal explorations of the themes that the ad campaign first introduces. This allows viewers to drop into a particular episode and understand at least some of the action, even if he or she has not followed the series from the beginning.

Nevertheless, the structure of the series as a whole is novelistic, with each individual episode working like a chapter in a longer and more involved narrative in which characters grow and change from episode to episode. This makes the series "appointment television," which "is designed to appeal to affluent, highly educated consumers who value the literary qualities" of a television series and which networks use "to hook this valuable cohort of viewers into their schedules" (Jancovich and Lyons 3). The series' meticulous attention to period detail in its costuming, set design, and staging, as well as its emphasis on tight, sophisticated writing have pulled viewers in, putting AMC on the map as the most recent cable network to attempt to attract viewers away from the big three networks.[1]

In this regard, *Mad Men* succeeds. After a somewhat slow start when the first season of the series appeared, by the end of Season Two *Mad Men* emerged as the cornerstone of AMC's programming. Across its three airings, the Season Two finale "pulled in 2.9 million viewers," and 49 percent of adult viewers between ages 25 and 54 who watched *Mad Men*'s second season "have household incomes above $100,000, giving the show the strongest concentration of upscale viewers ... of all original scripted series on basic cable" (Nordyke). Clearly, this series taps into what television's most sought-after viewers desire in a series. Not as clear, however, remains the precise nature of what drives the desires of *Mad Men*'s audience of educated, affluent viewers.

The series not only transports its viewers to a world in which the clothes are glamorous, the liquor flows freely, and the characters smoke cigarettes without fear for their health or that they will be socially ostracized but also to a world in which characters do not blink at racist, sexist, or antisemitic behavior, and the men philander with bad-girl mistresses while their good-girl wives keep the home fires burning. Viewers can follow Don's affairs as if they are watching a soap opera, but at the same time viewers must reckon with his wife Betty's downward spiral, Don's secretary Peggy's unplanned pregnancy, breakdown, and decision to give the child up for adoption, and the office manager Joan's rape.[2] The glossy production values, the attention to historical authenticity and accuracy, and the fascinating characters of the show inspire a kind of nostalgic longing in the viewers that the series captivates. Nevertheless, that identification is — for viewers and critics of the show as well as for the show's creators, cast, and crew — potentially problematic.

The gender roles and sexual double-standard that govern the universe of *Mad Men* cause discomfort, and this discomfort reflects the paradox at the heart of the show. On the one hand, in the first decade of the twenty-first century, we would like to believe that we have left the misogynistic gender and sexual politics of 1960 Madison Avenue behind. On the other hand, the historical specificity of the show gives us permission to take pleasure in a world in which those gender and sexual politics are front and center. This chapter aims to explore this paradox. Matthew Weiner claims that "*Mad Men* is about the conflicting desires in the American male and the people who pay the price for that, who are women" ("Establishing *Mad Men*"). The central question for the show's audience becomes whether their own desires, particularly as they relate to gender and sexuality, desires which ostensibly attract them to this show, mirror the desires that the show represents, whether they resist them, or some combination of these two possibilities.

Careful analysis of two episodes of the series, "Ladies Room" (1:2) and "Maidenform" (2:6), allows viewers to interrogate the ways in which gender and sexuality circulate in *Mad Men* and to consider specifically how the show's period representations of female gender and sexuality shape the series as a whole. Examining these two episodes, viewers realize that the universe of the series offers only two primary roles for women to embody: chaste housewife (Jacqueline Kennedy) or promiscuous mistress (Marilyn Monroe). The ingénue Peggy, who still lives in Brooklyn, has yet to choose one of these roles, though the series makes it clear from the outset that sooner or later, she will have to choose.[3] As Joan advises her in the pilot episode, she will be living in the city in a year or two if she is a success, or if she is truly successful she will live in the country and not have to work. By the second season's end, Peggy, the up-and-coming copywriter, still hasn't fallen into line, but viewers note that the "independent" women on the series — the office manager Joan, the bohemian Midge, the department store owner Rachel, the manager Bobbie — tend to fall into the promiscuous mistress category. Really making the right moves, for women in the world of *Mad Men*, involves relinquishing independence.[4]

In "Ladies Room," the client for the week is Right Guard aerosol deodorant. The creative team initially comes up with a pitch that features an astronaut, with the tag line "It works in my suit ... or yours." Don rejects the pitch saying it will remind people of the future, and this scares them. He says show them a rocket and they will begin building bomb shelters. After Paul Kinsey, who was late to the meeting because a person had committed suicide by jumping in front of the subway, challenges him, he says it is understandable that we are searching for other planets because the Earth will eventually end. Don's dismissal of the ad responds to the anxieties of the atomic age, but more significantly, it directly alludes to problems with his wife at home. Don knows that women are the consumers for Right Guard even though it is a product for men to use. Additionally, if his wife is any indication, women — if we exclude those females whom Don counts as mistresses — feel anxiety both about the future and about the stresses of the present day.

All of this relates to a recurring problem that Betty has been experiencing, in which her hands go numb and she can't perform simple tasks. Indeed, the episode opens with a scene in which she experiences this sudden numbness while in the ladies' room with Mona Sterling, the wife of her husband's boss Roger, who helps Betty reapply her lipstick. On the day preceding the pitch, the numbness in Betty's hands recurs while she is driving in the car with her children, precipitating an accident. Viewers learn that Betty has already visited her regular physician to investigate this problem, and the doctor indicated that there was no evidence of a physical cause: he recommended that she see a psychiatrist. Don says to Betty that he believed only unhappy people went to psychiatrists and wondered if she was unhappy, even though they have each other, the house, and the children. Betty responds that of course she is happy. Don, however, perceives his wife's underlying anxiety. The future, Don knows, might cause anxiety, and moreover it might inspire people to regress into a "safe" space that alienates them from other people, and from products as well, a pre-advertising past, the bomb shelter.[5] For this reason, Don seeks a pitch that evokes not hope or optimism for an unforeseeable future, which would drive consumers to a static nostalgia for a time before new products, but rather a pitch that evokes "the real" of the present moment.

Indeed, this impulse helps to explain why Don's chosen profession is advertising. In the advertisements that Don creates, he avoids the anxieties of the "real" world and simulates comfort and stability. According to Jean Baudrillard, "All original cultural forms, all determined languages are absorbed in advertising because it has no depth, it is instantaneous and instantaneously forgotten" (*Simulacra* 87). The allure of advertising depends on the fact that it exists only in the present moment, and Don understands this. For this reason, a pitch that appeals to a longing for the future makes no sense. Such appeals to the future won't make consumers buy, for consumers fear the future, fear the unknown. Appeals to "the real," even if— maybe especially if—"the real" no longer exists, will make a successful ad campaign.

Don redirects his team to consider who will buy brass tacks. His conclusion, "some woman,' leads Don to say that they should instead ask, what women want. In this assertion, Don alludes to Freud's famous question, and this question guides each of the subplots of the episode. Don wonders whether they are ignoring "some mysterious wish" that women have and he sends his team off to come up with a new pitch. All the while, we know that he wonders what his own wife wants, indeed what she lacks, that produces the periodic numbness in her hands; he consults with his boss, Roger, to determine what Roger thinks women want; he wonders what his beatnik mistress Midge wants.

After the pitch meeting and after lunch, Don meets with Roger, who had mentioned at the dinner in the episode's opening that his daughter was seeing a psychiatrist. Don asks him what he thinks women want. Roger answers, glibly, "Who cares?" and he gulps down his drink. As the conversation continues, Don more explicitly asks about the fact that he had mentioned his daughter is seeing a psychiatrist, and after Roger evades the direct question, Don finally asks, sincerely, how someone could be unhappy with all the things they have. Roger responds what women want: "Everything," Roger reduces women's unhappiness to competitiveness with other women. Unable to acknowledge that his daughter may be unhappy, he reduces her therapy to a product that he might advertise — "this year's candy pink stove." Further, he equates that which the consumer can buy with happiness. Happiness is, for Roger, itself a commodity. Don, taking Roger's comments to heart, does two things: he buys Betty a white gold watch, something shiny and pretty that he hopes will take her mind off her anxieties, a "candy pink stove" for a grown woman. When this doesn't alleviate her anxiety, and after Betty confesses her horror at the thought that their daughter Sally might have gotten a scar on her face in the car accident — and how much worse such a scar would be for her than for their son Bobby — he agrees that she can see a psychiatrist if she would like to do so.

On the day that Don brings Betty into the city to see the psychiatrist, he calls in sick to work in order to spend the day in bed with his mistress, the bohemian Midge. We see Don waiting in the hallway outside Midge's apartment. It is morning, Don should be at the office, and Midge, in a red wig, is only just getting home. Don begins telling her about the fact that Betty is seeing a psychiatrist, and Midge reprimands Don for doing so, telling him that when he talks about Betty, it makes her feel "cruel." Don says to Midge that he is unsure if she has "everything or nothing." Midge responds that she lives in the present and then, after kissing Don passionately, "Nothing is everything." Don responds that it sounds like she lives in the Village," dismissing Midge's assertion of her values. He does not seem to understand that her point of view results not from where she lives but from her beliefs about how a woman might productively live a life outside of marriage. Notably, her emphasis on living in the present moment mirrors Don's beliefs about what good advertising should do.

At the end of the day, Midge, in a brunette wig and about to leave the apartment, tells Don that he should shower before he goes home because he stinks. He, smoking a post-coital cigarette, asks her what women want. She answers that one of the things is not to be asked that question. Her answer inspires Don, who responds that you should "know better than to ask" what women want. He asks Midge for a pen and translates their interchange again, presumably into the new and improved copy for the Right Guard campaign that women want. "Any excuse to get closer." In Don's translation, viewers realize that Don objectifies Midge, in spite of her own values and in spite of her performed autonomy, and he uses her perspective as a way to forward his own ambitions.

Don's interactions with Midge illustrate both the power of the woman who takes on the mistress role as well as her impotence. On the one hand, Midge determines the shape of her own life, just as she determines what wig to wear on a given day. Unlike Betty, she does not experience anxiety so deep that she loses the use of her hands; she chooses where she goes, whom she sees, and when she comes home. Nevertheless, Midge's autonomy is undermined by Don's perception of her. Viewers see in their interactions that Don does not engage with Midge on her own terms: he mines her for inspiration, and he twists what she says into his next great campaign. He ignores her when she says that what women want least is to be asked what they want, first translating that contradiction into the sexy command that you should "know better than to ask," and then further translating it, when he writes it down, "Any excuse to get closer," which in fact directly contradicts the implied meaning of Midge's initial response to Don's question. Midge may be an independent, beatnik, career girl who lives in Greenwich Village, but while Don may find her sexy for those qualities, he also dismisses her for them. Ultimately, he reduces her perspective to the fact that she lives "in the Village."

Don sets Midge up as the free-living antithesis of his conservative, chaste wife. That signifies her appeal, while it at the same time renders her challenges to Don ineffectual. Ultimately, Midge is an object, property, a product — just as Betty is. The only difference lies in the fact that Don values Midge as a product that promises to be sexy and available, whereas he values his wife as a product that promises to be nurturing and respectable. The narrative underscores this with the fact that Don leaves Midge to take Betty out to a fancy dinner in the city. When they arrive home, she goes up to bed, while Don phones the psychiatrist that she saw earlier in the day to get a report about what is wrong with her, compromising doctor-patient confidentiality, and letting viewers know that Don, with the aid of the psychiatrist, aims to figure out "what women want," in order to appease his wife. He wants her problems to disappear, but he doesn't believe that his behavior relates to those problems, nor does he acknowledge that to check up on her with her psychiatrist constitutes a breach of trust, much as his affairs do.

Betty and Midge exemplify the virgin/whore dichotomy that rules the universe of *Mad Men*. Put another way, women in the series invoke the figures of the angel and the monster that Sandra Gilbert and Susan Gubar interrogate in their seminal work of literary criticism, *The Madwoman in the Attic: The Woman Writer and the Nineteenth Century*. According to Gilbert and Gubar, "The ideal woman that male authors dream of generating is always an angel" (20). Becoming this angel requires "the surrender of her self — of her personal comfort, her personal desires, or both — that is the beautiful angel-woman's key act, while it is precisely this sacrifice which dooms her both to death and to heaven" (25). In contrast, the antithesis for Gilbert and Gubar is the monster, "a striking illustration of Simone de Beauvoir's thesis that woman has been made to represent all of man's ambivalent feelings about his own inability to control his own physical existence, his own birth and death" (34). The angel is the mother who renounces her autonomy in order to raise children and to keep the home fires burning, and this is the role that Betty so perfectly performs, even as it causes her mental and emotional distress. In contrast, the monster, the mistress, possesses sexual autonomy, and she challenges the patriarchal privilege to which her lovers feel entitled. As a woman who does not become pregnant even as she enjoys sex, she calls to question not only her status as the "property" of one man but also her lovers' ability "to control his own physical existence, his own birth and death."[6]

In this episode, Betty operates as Don's angel, Midge as his monster. In Betty, he has a wife who has sacrificed her own identity to perform the roles of wife and mother. A cosseted and coddled figure in the private sphere, she keeps the home fires burning while Don goes off into the big wide world to provide. Betty should signify security, but the problem with her hands makes Don anxious about whether the role that she embodies has stability. In contrast, Midge, the monstrous mistress, challenges Don through her autonomy, and compromises his security in the patriarchal order. Nevertheless, Midge as monster is a figure of Don's own creation, and through his construction of her as such, he has the power to nullify the danger that she represents. He twists her words, he mines her for inspiration, and at the end of the day, he can return to the sanctity of his home that his angel protects. Don's relationship with Midge will not last, just as it does not last with his other mistresses, for when he realizes that he cannot control her, he will find a replacement. In the world of *Mad Men*, these are the roles available for women.

One character stands in between these roles: Peggy. In this episode, we see little of Peggy, who pines for Pete, with whom she had sex after his bachelor party in the pilot episode, and who now is on his honeymoon with his new wife Trudy. She does, however, have lunch with Paul, who regular viewers know once had an affair with Joan. After giving her a tour of the office and explaining how the agency works, Paul says to Peggy that there are women copywriters. Peggy asks if any of them are good, and Paul replies that they are. He says that while it is obvious when copy has been written by a woman, she sometimes could be "the right man for the job." This conversation plants the seed of ambition in Peggy's mind, and it foreshadows the development of her character. Later in the episode, however, Paul tries to seduce Peggy. When she resists, he asks if she "belongs to someone else." This subsequent encounter, with a person whom Peggy had thought she could count as a friend, jars her. She consults with Joan about it, and Joan nastily replies that Peggy should enjoy it while it lasts. For all of Joan's power within the office, her power depends on her complicity with the office's patriarchal structures. Joan reinforces the sexist culture of the office, and she refuses to be a friend or ally to Peggy.

Thus, what we see in the characterization of Peggy is a girl who has limited options. She can "belong to someone else," she can enjoy it while it lasts, or finally, she can become a woman copywriter, which may involve taking on a mistress identity or it may involve taking on an even more monstrous role: mannish careerist. To become a successful woman copywriter closes off the option of becoming the angelic wife, and if she achieves greater success than the men around her, it may also close off the option of becoming the monstrous mistress. This episode positions Peggy as the one female character who has the power to choose what she becomes, but the episode severely limits her possible choices. This dearth of choices — not only for Peggy but also for all of *Mad Men*'s female characters — becomes even more pronounced as the series moves forward into its second season.

The "Maidenform" episode reveals its themes in the pitch that the creative team must develop that week. Playtex, a Sterling Cooper client that had been happy with their campaign, has just seen new ads from their competitor, Maidenform, ads which are sexier and edgier. Playtex has asked the agency to come up with a campaign that will rival the Maidenform campaign.

Don brings the creative team into the office and asks them to offer up their ideas. Paul, who got the other men on the account's approval over drinks after work the night before, presents his idea to Don that all single women are either a Jackie Kennedy or Marilyn Monroe. He then opens Don's office door so that the men can look at the female staff in the central office, and demonstrates his theory by pointing out Jackie and Marilyn figures among the typists and secretaries. Peggy, whom the men on the account had not invited for their cocktail-hour brainstorming session, challenges Paul's idea and says that maybe this is just how men see women. Paul replies, "Bras are for men. Women want to see themselves the way men see them." Paul's reply nullifies Peggy's challenge, and the men begin speculating about what Peggy "is" according to the theory of the campaign. Kenny offers, significantly, "Gertrude Stein."

Peggy, who has ascended into the ranks of the copywriters in the agency, the lone woman who does not serve as office support staff, resembles neither fetish — neither the virgin/angel (Jackie) nor the mistress/monster (Marilyn). Rather, Kenny equates her with the mannish lesbian, Gertrude Stein — sexless, masculine, aberrant. In this, Kenny targets Peggy's failure to perform "womanliness" appropriately, "both to hide the possession of masculinity and to avert the reprisals expected if she was found to possess it" (Riviere 38), as she advances in her career. Don attempts to rescue Peggy by comparing her to Irene Dunne, a film actress of the 1930's and 1940's, but Peggy's male peers in her age range respond to his suggestion blankly. Only Freddy, the older drunk, acknowledges Irene Dunne as a sex symbol. Don, finally, signs off on the Jackie/Marilyn idea as the one that Sterling Cooper will pitch to Playtex, and plans move forward for auditioning models and for developing the campaign, in spite of Peggy's objection.

Once again, the client for the week, and the campaign that the client requires, illuminates Don's personal situation. The episode opens with a seductive montage of the show's female characters pulling on control-top pantyhose, donning panties, brassieres, girdles, and slips — those trappings of feminine fashion of a time gone by. Accompanying this montage is the pleasingly retro song "The Infanta" by the indie rock darlings The Decemberists,[7] and when the montage is complete, the scene shifts to Don and Betty, guests of "the Pattersons" at a country club barbecue for Memorial Day. Don chats with a man at the club who is in public relations, and just after Don has become distracted by watching Betty, across the room, interacting with a younger man — Arthur, whom she met at the stables and who, unbeknownst to Don, made a pass at her there — the public relations man regains his attention when he says about the new president, John F. Kennedy that while Jackie travels the world the president is chasing actresses. Don replies that everyone is happy. The man responds he is constructing a bomb shelter. Once again viewers see, as they did in Season One's "Ladies Room" episode, the juxtaposition of the veneer of perfection and hope for the future with the dark reality of the early 1960s, which includes a philandering president and fear of nuclear war.

As James Naremore asserts, "as we shift back and forth between office politics and domestic life, we become increasingly aware of the cultural anthropology of the period" (61), and of course, this comment early in the episode about the Kennedy White House and John F. Kennedy's extramarital affairs fore-shadows the Playtex campaign that Paul will create. Still, however, this cultural anthropology that the show displays is almost entirely focused on patriarchal power structures, and indeed, that cultural anthropology is filtered through the lens of nostalgia. Naremore continues, "The show's historical details are accurate and amusing ... and the production design creates a certain nostalgia for a world in which men chain-smoke, wear Brooks Brothers suits, and have three-martini lunches" (61). Naremore's continuation makes clear that the nostalgia for the period that the show invokes and upon which it relies ulti-mately leaves women out of the picture. When viewers examine the storyline that centers on Betty in the episode, this becomes most evident.

One traditional part of the Memorial Day barbecue at the Pattersons' country club is a swimsuit fashion show. As the models parade in their period perfect bikinis, pool cover-ups, and matching high-heeled sandals, Don excuses himself, telling Betty that he must go in to the office. In no surprise to the viewers, Don actually goes to a telephone booth to call his mistress, Bobbie Barrett, who reveals for the first time that she is a mother. This visibly jars Don, who likes to keep women in his life firmly placed in either the wife or the mistress role. Wives are Jackies and mistresses are Marilyns: wives can't be sexy, and mistresses can't be mothers.

Later in the episode, Don's reaction when he sees Betty in a swimsuit that she bought at the barbecue makes his ideas about how women should be categorized explicit. Telling her that he doesn't like the swimsuit, Don asks Betty if she wants to be ogled by "tennis pros" and "loafing millionaires." The swimsuit, a bright yellow bikini with matching sheer yellow jacket cover-up and high-heeled sandals, hardly seems scandalous to contemporary viewers. To Don, however, Betty's choice of swimwear, and the fact that she looks attractive and sexy in it, poses a threat. Betty in a sexy swimsuit threatens to upset the binary opposition between virgin and whore, angel and monster, with which Don and the other men on the series seem most comfortable. Betty, hurt, accepts Don's rebuke and agrees to change her clothes.

In contrast, of course, all Don wants from his mistress Bobbie Barrett is sexiness. Bobbie first appears in "The Benefactor" (2:3) as the manager-wife of the vulgar, insulting comedian, Jimmy Barrett. Like Don's mistresses in Season One, a large part of Bobbie's sex appeal involves her independence and the fact that she is making it in a man's world. In this episode, however, Don learns that Bobbie is the mother of two children, a boy of 18 and a girl in college. Just as Betty's choice of swimwear threatens the binary opposition between Jackie and Marilyn that Don and the men in the office endorse, so, too, does the fact of Bobbie's motherhood. This becomes most clear in Don and Bobbie's final encounter in "Maidenform." Bobbie says sexily to Don as the two begin their tryst that she is flattered to be able to keep him interested. Don replies, forcefully, "Stop talking." Unlike Betty, who does what she's told, Bobbie keeps talking, and she reveals that one part of her attraction to Don involves the gossip that she'd heard about his prowess as a lover. Ultimately, this is the last straw for Don. He ties Bobbie to the bed, and much to Bobbie's chagrin, he gathers his things and leaves. Bobbie, even more explicitly than Betty — who ultimately allows herself to be chastised by Don and follows his orders — refuses to play by the rules for how women should appear and behave. Nevertheless, the show insists that such women must be punished. In this case, Don leaves Bobbie humiliated and tied half-clothed to a bed. Later in Season Two, the voluptuous office vixen Joan gets raped by her doctor fiancé on the office floor ("The Mountain King" [1:12]). Ultimately, the masculine authority figures of the series police all women, and the efforts to control those monstrous Marilyns are all the more brutal.[8]

In "Maidenform," an episode all about what forms women take on and what forms are natural to them, just as in "Ladies Room" in the first season, Peggy stands out as the one character who has yet to choose to embody a Jackie or a Marilyn identity. Throughout the second season, however, Peggy does face more pressure. For example, when Peggy asks Joan why she has not been included in all of the memos for the Playtex account and why she has been excluded from important parts of the campaign like casting models, Joan dismisses her. She tells her if she wants to be taken seriously she should stop dressing like a little girl. Further, Peggy sits silently while Don makes the pitch to the Playtex executives.

As viewers know, this campaign works for Don because it allows women to see themselves through the male gaze, as objects of desire for their boyfriends or husbands. Men want to limit women to one of two roles — the virgin or the whore — and thus women want to characterize themselves as virgins or whores to appeal to men. Female consumers will respond to the campaign, thinks Don, because it is a "flattering mirror" in which to see themselves. The female consumer's imagination, in effect, is a product of male desire. Interestingly, however, particularly as we recall Peggy's response to the campaign, the client decided before seeing the pitch that this approach would not increase sales. Even though the Playtex executives comment, "I like the girl," and "very impressive," to the mock-up ad, they ultimately reject the new campaign. What matters to the client is what women will buy — and women buy based on claims about fit. The client believes that women want to buy a product — not a male fantasy of woman.

The client's view in many respects validates Peggy's perspective throughout the episode and, further, her refusal to embody one of these two stereotypes for femininity. Ultimately, Peggy's subjectivity, at least at this point in the series, does not depend upon choosing to become a Jackie or a Marilyn. Still, if Peggy wants to advance at work, she will have to attempt to negotiate these dominant stereotypes about femininity in a more sophisticated way than she has done to this point. As Joan Riviere asserts, "women who wish for masculinity may put on a mask of womanliness to avert anxiety and the retribution feared from men" (35). By the end of the pitch meeting with the Playtex executives, Peggy seems to realize this.

As the meeting concludes, Peggy overhears the men on the creative team make plans with the Playtex executives to meet after work at a strip club for drinks. Peggy, refusing to be left out once again, gives herself a makeover. She makes herself up and dresses herself up to look like the sort of woman who would comfortably go into a strip club to meet with a client — not like the "little girl" she has looked like throughout the series so far. Upon entering the club, Peggy agrees to sit on the client's lap. In this moment, Peggy has made a choice. This choice angers Pete, who wants to characterize Peggy as virginal and sweet. This choice compromises Peggy, to some extent, who when she first started at Sterling Cooper would have resisted interacting in this sort of a way in a work setting. Still, Peggy gets ahead. By the season's end, Peggy has gotten herself a private office, and she continues to excel in the workplace. What viewers wonder, however, is where Peggy can go from here. Is there room for a woman who is neither a Jackie nor a Marilyn?

"Are You a Jackie or a Marilyn? Or Someone Else?"

Almost immediately upon the airing of the "Maidenform" episode, a quiz surfaced on the Internet, "Are you a Jackie or a Marilyn? Or Someone Else? *Mad Men*-Era Female Icon Quiz." The quiz, available on the Web sites OkCupid and HelloQuizzy, was taken by many women, who posted the results on their blogs. Women could discover whether they were, indeed, Jackie or Marilyn, or whether they were Bette Davis or Grace Kelly, or a range of other popular culture icons of femininity. In addition, the blog *Jezebel* ("Celebrity, Sex, Fashion for Women"), which offers regular posts about the series with a focus on its female characters, commented on this episode. Tracie summarizes, "The boys club at the agency decided that women want to be what *men* want them to be, but even the men weren't sure exactly that was: Pete went on to cheat on his wife with a bra model and Don ended up getting pissed at his wife for buying a bikini. The whole virgin/whore thing? Not much has changed since 1962 in that respect." Commenters to the site, however, write things like the following in response to Tracie's post: "I really hope that this means we get to see some more rockin' clothes on Peggy"; "Marilyn here ... no question"; "Jackie all the way. I wear some Jackie inspired dresses to work quite often"; "And can I just add that the minute I saw this on *Mad Men*, I said to myself (possibly out loud) I can see it on *Jezebel*: Are you a Jackie or a Marilyn?"

As these responses show, a significant portion of viewers'— even female viewers'— pleasure in watching the series depends on a nostalgic identification with the desires, biases, and questionable — by today's standards — choices of the show's characters. Reviews of the show, however, seem to resist delving into this facet of the audience's reception of the show. Many reviews emphasize the show's "other-worldly" quality, as does Mary McNamara, writing for the *Los Angeles Times*: "For boomers, the series is a glimpse into the storied past; for anyone younger, it might as well be another world, in which everyone dresses like grown-ups and behaves like wayward children." Still others, like *USA Today*'s Robert Bianco, go one step further, noting the way that the show succeeds in transporting the viewer, while at the same time congratulating the viewer for seeing through the glamorous façade that the show presents:

> The beauty and joy of *Mad Men* is the way it immerses us in a shimmering view of the early '60s, a seemingly well-ordered world fueled by cigarettes and alcohol, where men and women wear their clothes and hair like suits of armor, and look darn good doing so. We know it's a façade, of course, and one that is about to shatter under an assault of drugs, sex, race, rock 'n' roll and Vietnam. The genius of the writing and the acting is the way it reveals what we may have missed at the time: The cracks are already there.

As Bianco's assertion makes clear, *Mad Men* works — or is supposed to work — because viewers are "too smart" to fall for the "shimmering view" that it provides.

If this is the case, though, then what are we to make of the throngs of women who ran out to take a quiz on the Internet to determine whether they are Jackies or Marilyns? What do we make of the nostalgic longing that the show produces for a world in which men were men and women wore girdles? Yes, the show is dark, and yes, especially as we move through the second and third seasons, viewers receive more and more information that indicates that perhaps this "other world" isn't so great after all. And yet, the *Entertainment Weekly* review by Ken Tucker perhaps gets the show's appeal more right than most other reviews of the series: "What gives *Mad Men* its zing is that play is part of work, sexual banter isn't yet harassment, and America is free of self-doubt, guilt, and countercultural confusion. It's the ripe fantasy before it turns rotten." *Mad Men* works as a twenty-first century guilty pleasure precisely because it encourages viewers to enjoy a world in which political correctness doesn't exist and in which today's rules — about behavior in both professional and personal spaces — do not apply.

"White people often find the truth very depressing at theme parties."

Indeed and in particular, the gender and sexual norms that *Mad Men* reproduces are all too real, and regardless of viewers' sophistication, the show implicates its audience in the "sins" of its mid-twentieth-century characters. The images and plotlines that the show offers exemplify what Baudrillard calls in *Simulations*

> *the satellization of the real*, the putting into orbit of an indefinable reality without common measure to the fantasies that once used to ornament it.... This is nothing else than the short-circuit of the response by the question in the test, instantaneous process of re-condition whereby reality is immediately contaminated by its simulacrum. (339)

As simulacrum of the opening years of the 1960s, *Mad Men* obsessively recreates a world that for most Americans never really existed, but at the same time the "accuracy" of the costumes, props and plot-lines of the show authorize a reading of the show as reality.

At the same time, viewers then feel the impulse to copy the show, whether through determining whether they are Jackies or Marilyns, or, as the satirical website *Stuff White People Like* jokes in a recent post, by hosting *Mad Men* parties:

> During the actual event you should constantly mention how much people used to smoke and drink back then. A few white people will lament the days when they could smoke anywhere, then another white person will say something about cancer and it will get awkward. At this point you should try to steer the conversation back to cocktails and how good everyone looks.
> The party should essentially run itself, however, you can severely curtail the amount of fun by saying: "I'm glad this isn't really 1960 or else I'd be serving all of you."
> White people often find truth to be very depressing at theme parties.

This passage illuminates the superficial nostalgia that drives some of the show's appeal, contradicting Tim Hunter's assertion that the show's creator Weiner "doesn't want to draw attention to the period. He wants to be in the period" ("Establishing *Mad Men*"). Rather, it corroborates producer Scott Hornbacher's insight that "There's an aspect of the show that's thrilling for people to watch that's about the hair, the clothes, the makeup, the sets, the set dressing, the props, all of that. Just because it's fascinating" ("Establishing *Mad Men*"). This fascination with the period seems directly to contradict the assertion that the show aims not to draw attention to the period; moreover, it calls to question an audience's ability to maintain ironic distance while at the same time the superficial trappings of the show's historical moment seduce the audience.

Ultimately, the allure of the clothes, the cocktails, and the chain-smoking provides an alibi for educated, affluent viewers who would rather not reckon with the less glamorous aspects of the period and show.

Similarly, *Saturday Night Live*'s parodic "Don Draper's Guide to Picking Up Women" gets to the heart of viewer's impulse to identify with this show and with these characters. As the spoof concludes, Jon Hamm, the host of that week's show, reprises his character Don Draper, and he asserts in rapid-fire his concluding step four:

> Look fantastic in a suit. Look fantastic in casual wear. Look fantastic in anything. Sound good. Smell good. Kiss good. Strut around with supreme confidence. Be uncannily successful at your job. Blow people away every time you say anything. Take six-hour lunches. Disappear for weeks at a time. Lie to everyone about everything. Drink and smoke *constantly*. Basically, be Don Draper.

The *SNL* parody succeeds in drawing attention to Don Draper's problematic allure. In contrast to the series itself, which appears to believe that viewers "know better" than to want to emulate these characters, the parodic appropriations of the show that *Stuff White People Like* and *Saturday Night Live* perform reveal the ways in which the show exploits viewers' fantastic identification with the show's characters and period.

The series, however, does not work as parody, nor does it have the critical force of parody. Instead, the show depends on pastiche as its primary mode, and, as Frederic Jameson writes about pastiche,

> it is at least compatible with addiction — with a whole historically original consumers' appetite for a world transformed into sheer images of itself and for pseudo-events and "spectacles" ... Appropriately enough, the culture of the simulacrum comes to lie in a society where exchange value has been generalized to the point at which the very memory of use value is effaced [18].

The culture of the simulacrum comes into being at the very historical moment that *Mad Men* depicts. That said, *Mad Men* itself embodies the nostalgia and lack of critique, at least in some respects, at which Jameson takes aim. Reserving particular ire for "nostalgia films" like *American Graffiti*, Jameson charges that these texts "restructure the whole issue of pastiche and project it onto a collective and social level, where the desperate attempt to appropriate a missing past is now refracted through the iron law of fashion change and the emergent ideology of the generation" (19).

What makes *Mad Men* of tremendous interest is that rather than trying to recapture "the privileged lost object of desire" that is the 1950s, which exemplifies "not merely the stability and prosperity of a Pax Americana but also the first naïve innocence of the countercultural impulses of early rock and roll and youth gangs" (19), it rather seeks to recapture that period after that naïve innocence is lost, the period of temptation and the fall. This is not "genuine historicity," but rather an appropriation of a past that never existed in order to work out the desires and anxieties of the present day. For this reason, particularly as we are interested in evaluating the gender and sexual norms that guide the characters and plotlines of *Mad Men,* viewers can usefully refuse to regard the show as merely a critique of a historical elsewhere, and instead acknowledge the ways in which the show puts on display the darker desires of its contemporary audience.

"A world that we kind of yearn to go back to."

In order to explore this, viewers must grapple with the problematic given that the show, in its representational precision related to the historical period, somehow avoids nostalgia. Matt Roush, a critic for *TV Guide,* claims that "what really makes *Mad Men* so special is that it presents a world that we kind of yearn to go back to, but it is not an idealized world of nostalgia" ("Establishing *Mad Men*"). Such a statement epitomizes the elusiveness of trying to pin down this show's relationship to history, for it is unclear how Roush would distinguish yearning for a historical past from nostalgia. Further, such a statement offers little insight into what it might mean that "we kind of yearn to go back to" that world of *Mad Men,* whether it is "an idealized world of nostalgia" or not, given its depiction of gender and sexuality.

In spite of *Mad Men's* commitment to historical accuracy, when viewers watch *Mad Men* they do not encounter a historical "real" but rather a simulated hyperreal. *Mad Men* is a twenty-first-century simulacrum of 1960s Manhattan: it potentially says much more about twenty-first century culture generally and twenty-first century gender and sexual roles in particular than it does about the historical period that it purports faithfully and obsessively to render for its audience. Further, as the show's audience identifies with its characters and storylines, it is not yet clear whether that identification might facilitate resistance. Patrice Petro suggests that there are two possibilities, when female viewers identify with seemingly stereotypical scripts for women. "While in some instances an empathetic mode of identification may very well put women's pleasures in the service of patriarchy," writes Petro, "in others it may in fact encourage an understanding that leads to strong emotional response, which, in turn, may lead to recognition and to action" (29). Early responses by critics and viewers seem to indicate the former rather than the latter, but it is possible that as the series continues in subsequent seasons, this will change.

In either case, however, nostalgia remains the dominant mode of aesthetic response to the series and the dominant mode through which the series approaches the representation of history. For Baudrillard, "When the real is no longer what it was, nostalgia assumes its full meaning" (*Simulacra* 6). *Mad Men* begins at the very moment that "the real is no longer what it was." Weiner asserts in the commentary to the pilot episode: "The irony in this episode is about the things we know now that we didn't know then," and indeed, this is the irony of the series as a whole. What viewers know, throughout the series, is that "reality" as it was understood in the immediate aftermath of World War II no longer exists. The show's characters, while they do not yet seem to recognize this consciously, often glimpse this shift as well. Setting the show in an advertising agency, which tries to create a "real" that will encourage consumers to buy products, underlines this point. Further, debonair Don Draper, the show's protagonist, lives under an assumed identity, and as he battles his demons from the past while negotiating his complicated personal and professional life of the present, he takes as his motto the advice that he gives to Peggy in "The New Girl": "Get out of here, and move forward. This never happened. It will shock you how much it never happened." For Don Draper, there is no real, but there is a longing for a past that never really existed. He simulates an identity, just as he fosters the simulation of various ad campaigns, and just as other characters simulate their lives. *Mad Men* takes as its subject the very moment that "nostalgia assumes its full meaning."

As we look at *Mad Men* as a historical representation, it makes sense to acknowledge that we as viewers are complicit in the simulation that the show creates. At its best, as Naremore contends, "For all its historical fetishism, *Mad Men* foregrounds its link with our own time. It brings ongoing American social tensions explicitly to the surface and expresses strong ambivalence about the past" (61). At its worst, however, the series invites readers to emulate ideologies of the past and to reproduce those ideologies uncritically. To borrow Baudrillard's language, *Mad Men*'s

> obsession with historical *fidelity*, with a perfect rendering ... , this negative and implacable fidelity to the materiality of the past, to a particular scene of the past or of the present, to the restitution of an absolute simulacrum of the past or the present, which was substituted for all other value — we are all complicitous in this, and this is irreversible [*Simulacra* 47–48].

In other words, the historicity of *Mad Men* provides no alibi for its gender and sexual politics, nor does it foreclose the possibility of nostalgic identification or desire. Indeed, the show's meticulous historicity might operate as the precondition of its viewers' nostalgia. Further, it might indict viewers who, through their "appointment" viewing of the show, glamorize in the present day *Mad Men*'s historically authentic misogyny.

NOTES

1. This trend can be traced to HBO's success with series like *The Sopranos* and *Sex and the City*, and more recently, networks like FX (*Nip Tuck* and *Rescue Me*) and TNT (*The Closer* and *Saving Grace*) have tapped into the hour-long drama format to boost ratings and to establish their networks as tough competitors against both network and subscription cable television channels.

2. In Season Three, viewers also get a clearer picture of Betty's dissatisfaction with her life, Peggy's difficulties in breaking through Sterling Cooper's glass ceiling, and Pete's rape of the au pair next store—the result of which is his neighbor's suggestion that he doesn't care what Pete does as long as Pete keeps it out of the building ("Roman Holiday").

3. As season three progresses, Peggy remains between these two roles, but she appears to be veering closer to the "promiscuous mistress" end of the spectrum. This seems most apparent in "Love among the Ruins," when Peggy picks up a strange man in a bar and goes home with him, and "My Old Kentucky Home," when Peggy gets high with Paul and Smith while they are supposed to be working on a campaign.

4. Joan's rape in "The Mountain King," which occurs only after she snags a doctor fiancé and gives up her sexual independence, drives this point home most forcefully. When readers encounter the married Joan in the third season, her trading power for marriage becomes even more evident.

5. The show provides a similar escape for viewers in a post–911 world in deep economic recession, keeping those viewers locked into contemporary consumer culture by sidestepping difficult issues about the future.

6. The show renders this most clearly in "Ladies Room" when Don jealously interrogates Midge about a new television that she has acquired. Ultimately, Midge soothes Don by dropping the television set out of the window, but Don's anxiety about the set's origins epitomizes his need to control the women in his live by assigning them a role.

7. The choice of the song by The Decemberists underscores *Mad Men's* drive to capture an affluent, hip, white, niche audience, for this band's fan base trends toward this audience as well. A funny coincidence worth noting is that the satirical website *Stuff White People Like* takes aim not only at *Mad Men,* which I discuss later in this essay, but also at "indie music" (http://stuffwhitepeoplelike.com/2008/01/30/40-indie-music/), which appears throughout the series' soundtrack. The juxtaposition of contemporary indie music with the retro appeal and meticulous attention to historical detail in the series itself draws attention to the constructedness of *Mad Men's* historicity.

8. After the episode with Joan's rape aired, *New York Magazine* writer Emily Nussbaum sensitively noted: "*Mad Men* has always acted as a vicarious time machine; in the first season, there was a definite ambiguity to the show's critiques, mixed as they were with nostalgia for a world of gimlets and clear gender roles.... But as the show has focused ever more tightly on its trinity of women—Betty the Wife, Peggy the Career Girl, Joan the Mistress—that nostalgia has warped. Betty was trapped; Peggy was thwarted. Only Joan still seemed somehow free, and that scene, so poignantly filmed, ending with her disassociated gaze under the coffee table, stamped that fantasy shut."

WORKS CITED

Baudrillard, Jean. "The Orders of Simulacra" Eds. Philip Rice and Patricia Waugh. *Modern Literary Theory: A Reader.* 4th Ed. New York: Hodder Arnold, 2001. 338–340.
_____. *Simulacra and Simulation.* Trans. Sheila Faria Glaser. Ann Arbor: University of Michigan Press. 1994.
Bianco, Robert. "Review: 'Mad Men' Will Persuade You to Stay Tuned." *USA Today,* 25 July 2008. Web. 30 June 2009.

Clander. "#123: *Mad Men.*" *Stuff White People Like: This Blog Is Devoted to Stuff White People Like* 11 Mar. 2009. 30 June 2009. <http://stuffwhitepeoplelike.com/2009/03/11/123-mad-men/>.

"Don Draper's Guide." *Saturday Night Live.* 25 Oct. 2008. *NBC.com* 30 June 2009. <http://www.nbc.com/Saturday_Night_Live/video/clips/don-drapers-guide/787241/>.

"Establishing Mad Men." *Mad Men: Season One.* DVD. Lionsgate, 2008.

Gilbert, Sandra M. and Susan Gubar. *The Madwoman in the Attic: The Woman Writer and the Nineteenth-Century Literary Imagination.* New Haven: Yale University Press, 1984.

Jameson, Frederic. *Postmodernism: Or, the Cultural Logic of Late Capitalism.* Durham, NC: Duke University Press, 1991.

Jancovich, Mark and James Lyons. Introduction. *Quality Popular Television: Cult TV, the Industry, and Fans.* London: BFI Publishing, 2003. 1–10.

McNamara, Mary. "TV THIS WEEK — THE BIG THING — It's a 'Mad' Ad World." *Los Angeles Times*, 15 July 2007. Web. 30 June 2009.

Naremore, James. "Films of the Year, 2007." *Film Quarterly.* 61:4 (2008): 48–61.

"The New Girl." *Mad Men.* Writ. Robin Veith. Dir. Jennifer Getzinger. AMC. 24 Aug. 2008.

Nordyke, Kimberly. "Viewers Go 'Mad' for Finale." *Hollywood Reporter* 28 Oct. 2008. *LexisNexis Academic* Web. 6 June 2009.

Nussbaum, Emily. "Nussbaum on 'Mad Men': How Joan's Rape Changed Everything." *New York Magazine*, 24 Oct. 2008. Web. 30 June 2008. <http://nymag.com/daily/entertainment/2008/10/nussbaum_on_mad_men_why_joans.html>.

Petro, Patrice. *Aftershocks of the New: Feminism and Film History.* New Brunswick: Rutgers University Press, 2002.

Riviere, Joan. "Womanliness as a Masquerade." 1929. Eds. Victor Burgin, James Donald, and Cora Kaplan. *Formations of Fantasy.* New York: Methuen, 1986: 35–44.

Tracie. "*Mad Men:* Are You a Marilyn or a Jackie?" *Jezebel: Celebrity, Sex, Fashion for Women.* 2 Sept. 2008. Gawker Media. 30 June 2009. <http://jezebel.com/5044527/mad-men-are-you-a-marilyn-or-a-jackie>.

Tucker, Ken. "Mad Men (2007)." *Entertainment Weekly*, July 2007. Web. 30 June 2009. <http://www.ew.com/ew/article/0,,20046314,00.html>.

Vintagegriffin. "Are you a Jackie or a Marilyn? Or Someone Else? Mad Men-Era Female Icon Quiz." *HelloQuizzy* 30 June 2009. <http://helloquizzy.okcupid.com/tests/are-you-a-jackie-or-a-marilyn-or-someone-else-mad-menera-female-icon-quiz/>.

_____. "Are you a Jackie or a Marilyn? Or Someone Else? Mad Men-Era Female Icon Quiz." *OkCupid* 30 June 2009. <http://www.okcupid.com/quizzy/take?id=3922607843063499456/>.

THE NOSTALGIA OF
MAD MEN

Rich Sommer, Aaron Staton, Christina Hendricks, Michael Gladis in Mad Men *(2007)* *(AMC/Kobal Collection).*

11. Camelot Regained

Scott F. Stoddart

I.

The Democratic candidate was thought to be inexperienced — a one-term senator who believed he could make a run for the presidency despite the country's economic prosperity; the Republican candidate was a twenty-year veteran, anointed by the incumbent party to carry on its popular conservative agenda. The Democratic candidate fought a formidable foe in the primaries, emerging victorious over the party's political machine because of a newly motivated youth movement; the Republican candidate ran, for the most part, unopposed, sealing his nomination well before the convention. The Democratic candidate was forced to articulate his personal ideology in a searing speech that proved intimate ideologies could become presidential assets; the Republican candidate was forced by the party to name a vice-presidential candidate who was not of his personal choosing. The Democratic candidate revolutionized his campaign using new technologies to wage the battle against an opponent who did not appear equipped to use them; the Republican candidate played catch-up by employing Madison Avenue to mold a softer, friendlier image for his candidacy, creating a nominee who appeared safe, rather than modern. The Democratic candidate, in a series of televised debates displayed vibrancy, polish, intelligence; the Republican candidate displayed intelligence, but appeared confused, tired, and old-fashioned.

Many readers may think that my homage to Theodore White's *Making of the President* series (1960–1972) refers to the 2008 presidential election between the Democrat Barack Obama and the Republican John McCain. However, as regular viewers of *Mad Men* know, the first season's climactic "Nixon vs. Kennedy" (1:12), reveals the wealth of similarities between the 1960 presidential election and the 2008 presidential election. Choosing to base

much of the first season on this infamous political battle, series creator
Matthew Weiner allows his audience to experience that drama as it unfolds
at Sterling Cooper. The struggle makes our world appear not so removed
from the past. The "Camelot" of 1960 melts into the "Camelot" of 2008.

In a *New York Times* op-ed piece, cultural critic Adam Cohen hypothesizes about the popularity of *Mad Men*:

> For many viewers, *Mad Men* is a window on their parents' world — an era of
> three-martini lunches, gas-guzzling domestic cars and boundless optimism about
> America's place in the world. John F. Kennedy was in the White House, and
> women were choosing between rival style icons Jacqueline Bouvier Kennedy and
> Marilyn Monroe.
>
> To a generation beaten down by sky-rocketing unemployment, plunging
> retirement savings and mounting home foreclosures, *Mad Men* offers the
> schadenfreude-filled message that their predecessors were equally unhappy — and
> that the bleakness meter in American life has always been set on high [A18].

Cohen hypothesizes that there really was no "golden age" of capitalism — that
the anxieties of the earlier period mirror many of our own. Therefore, *Mad
Men* works as a constant reminder that nostalgia (for those who remember
the era) and history (for those who cannot) are very closely linked within the
American psyche, one point that Matt Weiner wants the series to make: "I
started off writing the show as a scathing analysis of what happened to the
United States ... but the more I got into Don [Draper], the more I realized
this [time period] is an amazing place. Something really did change in those
years — the late '50s and early '60s. What would it be like to go to that place?"
(E21). The time period captured in the series thus far, 1960–1963, was a period
of intense change. The conservative agenda of the Eisenhower years, steeped
in the suburban complacency of conspicuous consumption, began to give way
after Kennedy's election, making way for a cultural and social dynamic that
shifted the American landscape. The parallel to the threshold where Americans
currently stand is uncanny.

It is this unsettling time that *Mad Men* seeks to reconsider. *Mad Men*
actively deconstructs the mythology that has surrounded the Camelot era for
the past fifty years. I disagree with Jaime J. Weinman, who believes that in
extolling this "fun visit to a time when drinking, smoking and sexual harassment were normal," the series promotes "the cool, sexist fun" of a by-gone
era — falling into the nostalgia trap. Instead, I agree with Fredric Jameson,
who suggests that a series like *Mad Men* is much more complex. When the
critic/spectator only focuses on the superficial fashions and glosses the "stylistic
connotation" that conveys "pastness," we miss the past as "referent" — a postmodern term that reveals how the ideology of the past can be understood as
a cautionary moment in an existential present (19). Ideological constructs

assist in making *Mad Men* a series that is more than its superficial gloss; what I want to argue is that *Mad Men*, immersed in a specific historical moment, strives to de-romanticize the central myths of this period of American culture that blind us from understanding how societal change can be both inspiring and paralyzing.

Weiner has always said that that the series is a tribute to his parents, his father a neuroscientist, his mother a law school graduate, married in 1959. The politically-charged home atmosphere he and his three siblings grew up in was one marked by the shifting times. "Theirs was an intellectual home steeped in academics, literature, classic movies, and 1950s-inflicted leftist politics, a home where Weiner was raised on heroic tales of blacklisted writers, where he was expected to know who Gene Tierney was, and where his dad packed *Swann's Way* for every vacation" (Handy 282). Weiner believes that Salinger's *Catcher in the Rye* led to his longtime obsession with the period, and the novel became the foundation for what his vision for the series would be:

> Maybe it's a kind of wised-up, at times even loathing nostalgia — precisely the kind of contradiction that drives the show creatively.... One thing he quite consciously set out to do with *Mad Men* was to reclaim the 1950s and early 1960s from the condescension of "baby-boomer propaganda," as he put it, the easy ironies with which the era has been caricatured in popular culture [Handy 283].

This propaganda revolves around two mythological constructs that infiltrate reflections of the era. The first myth involves Sloan Wilson's *The Man in the Gray Flannel Suit*, a popular novel and MGM film starring Gregory Peck that created the archetype of the suburban professional who returned from World War II an ideological contradiction. Wilson's Tom Rath is a white-collared executive who comes to represent the 1950s American Dream: a lovely home in the suburbs, an adoring family, and a solid job that requires him to use his stimulated brain rather than his brawn. Yet, even though the "gray flannel suit" became the uniform of the late 1950s — exemplified in Janie Bryant's design palette for the series[1]—*Mad Men* dismantles this icon to expose the trappings of a masculine ideal that pervaded the times — an ideal still very much with us today. As will be seen, almost every critic of *Mad Men* identifies Don Draper as the "man in the gray flannel suit," linking the series' protagonist with Wilson's original. However, this is not Weiner's intention:

> [The series] is NOT *The Man in the Gray Flannel Suit*. This is not *Patterns*. I love those things. Those are opera that people at the time watched. I am writing about the audience FOR those things. I'm writing about the husband and wife that are living in a world and they SEE *The Apartment*. What is it like to SEE the man in the gray flannel suit. And to be a veteran. What is it like to SEE *The*

Best of Everything—where this woman thinks she is going to get married and Robert Evans is taking her to get an abortion [McNamara].

Weiner plays off Wilson's archetype, proving that the critics actually misread both Wilson's original, who is a much more complex character, and Don Draper, whose traits actually embody what Barbara Ehrenreich terms "The Gray Flannel Dissident" (29).

The second mythic deconstruction involves Kennedy's Camelot. The presidency of John F. Kennedy lasted only 1,000 days, abruptly ending with his assassination. The legacy puts the youthful, charismatic intellectual at the center of a changing world: Allen Matusow observed, "So luminous was the image created by Kennedy [at his inauguration] that for countless of his countrymen no disaster of policy, no paucity of achievement, would ever dim it" (quoted in Reeves 1–2). During his brief presidency, many journalists and historians celebrated the vibrant character of the chief executive and as a result, the myth took root. After his death, the Camelot School celebrated his achievements in a variety of histories and memoirs—what Thomas C. Reeves has termed "a literature of adulation, the likes of which the nation had not experienced since the death of Lincoln" (4). Rather than simply celebrate the Kennedy legacy, *Mad Men* exposes Camelot, revealing it as an age of anxiety where everyday people fear the escalation of Communism, dread the threat of nuclear attack and panic at the shifting of gender and race roles.

These myths that pervade historical discussions and pop culture depictions of the late 1950s/early 1960s are at the heart of Weiner's attitude toward the era where he situates *Mad Men*. Weiner's love of the period stems from his personal connection to 1950s Madison Avenue (his grandfather was a Mad Man) and his meticulous research into the era. His method, however, is bent on correcting the way that historians and the entertainment world have used these myths to depict the period. In response to a viewer question: "What is the most challenging thing about recreating an entire era?" Weiner responds,

Not being distracted by the way history has interpreted it. It's really hard. You have to construct it out of what you think to be the truth based on the way human beings behave, and then you have the popular media, which often says something is very important and it turns out it wasn't. And then people's memories of when things happened and in what order is very unreliable. There are some things we get wrong, but more likely there are things we know are 100 percent right and people can't accept that. It was very hard for people to believe that the lifestyle in the Village in the '50s was very much what the Summer of Love was like. In fact, it was like that in the '30s. We feel so smart because we are here and we can look back and we know exactly what happened. We have a sense of superiority, but the truth is it keeps happening over and over again and we should get ready for it to happen to us instead of thinking that we're over it ["Matt Weiner Interview"].

Verisimilitude is key to Weiner's method — his characters need to reflect the realities of the era and the challenges they face, moving from the comfort of the Eisenhower age to the shifting tides of the Kennedy era; they need to resonate with the contemporary audience — an audience that, as noted by Adam Cohen, appears to be experiencing its own age of anxiety.

II.

The deconstruction of the first myth that involves "The Man in the Gray Flannel Suit"— the archetype devised by Sloan Wilson in his 1955 novel, and captured in Hollywood through the MGM film starring Gregory Peck and Jennifer Jones (1956)—culminates in "Six Month Leave" (2:8), when sleazy comedian Jimmy Barrett calls out to Don Draper in a crowded room, "Look, it's the man in the gray flannel suit!" It is a remark that causes Don to lose his cool for once.[2] His violent response is a result of the fact that "Don Draper" is the elaborate masquerade of lowly Dick Whitman, Don's real identity, who invented Draper as a "Mad Man," making him into one of the men in gray flannel who populate the collective mythic images of the late 1950s and early 1960s corporate America.[3] Because of the iconic stature of Wilson's Tom Rath, many of the early critics of the series labeled Don Draper as "the man," linking the myth of the "gray flannel suit" to the series, referring to actor Jon Hamm and Don Draper interchangeably as "The Man in the Gray Flannel Suit." The critics include: Bruce Kirkland, *Edmonton Sun*; Matthew Gilbert, *Boston Globe*; Michael Hainey, Men.Style.com; Robert Abele, *L. A. Weekly*; Paul Rudd, writing for *Interview*. Valerie Steele, in an interview for "The Fashion of *Mad Men*," on the Season Two DVD, speaks about Hamm's ability to convey the classic feel of "the man in the gray flannel suit" as a contemporary icon. While these cultural critics seek to read the series as a celebration of the "Gray Flannel" philosophy they believed Wilson espoused, they misread the original text and the series as a celebration of this American ideal. The image of the man in gray flannel has come to represent a "heroic" figure who maintained "a measured acceptance of the limits of one's private endeavors at a time when action on a broader political scale could only seem foolish — or suspect" (Ehrenreich 17). Instead, Wilson's novel criticizes America's corporate and social culture, revealing how it emasculated American men. The novel's protagonist, Tom Rath, fights against this corporate sterilization, seeking a balance between his individual desires and his familial obligations. Struggling against 1950s conformity is at the heart of Wilson's novel.

Mad Men embraces this decent and the series uses the pervasive myth of the 1950s to examine the era's supposedly solid foundation. *Mad Men* deconstructs the notion that the Man in Gray Flannel is an archetype to celebrate. Instead, he is a walking dichotomy, a renegade fighting to protect his stature in the community while asserting his individuality — the very thing that puts his social position in jeopardy.[4]

In actuality, Sloan Wilson's Tom Rath is more than his gray flannels, and he is the polar opposite of Don Draper in many ways. While Don appears happy as the creative mastermind at Sterling Cooper, impressing clients with his keen abilities in packaging Lucky Strike cigarettes, Right Guard spray deodorants, Maidenform brassieres and Kodak Carousel slide projectors, Tom is not happy being an "organization man" — he recognizes his misery while navigating the commuter trains dressed like all the other men. His gray flannel suit serves as a symbol of the corporate clone in "the uniform of today" (Wilson 8) — a job and a look he despises. Tom wrestles silently with the demands his wife Betsy puts on him as he travels to work, and the novel's first sentence reveals his frustration: "By the time they had lived seven years in the little house on Greentree Avenue in Westport, Connecticut, they both detested it" (1). Tom believes that going after a new position will help him to earn the money he needs to provide security and happiness for his family:

> Tom began hesitantly, and was suddenly impatient at the need for hypocrisy. The sole reason he wanted to work for United Broadcasting was that he thought he might be able to make a lot of money there fast, but he felt he couldn't say that ... people were supposed to work at advertising agencies and broadcasting companies for spiritual reasons [10].

Tom frankly admits that he needs money to stop Betsy from complaining, "to buy a more expensive house and a better brand of gin" (13). Tom feels alone in this post–World War II America, knowing that his responsibilities to his family have entrapped him in this corporate merry-go-round. He understands how competitive the job market has become, and he understands his family's frustrations with desiring more. He feels at a loss — the conquering hero returning from the war who should be welcomed with a job that will provide personal and monetary satisfaction. Instead, he believes that the only advantage he has is his ability to recognize the "hypocrisy" of this new corporate world.

Don Draper, conversely, appears to have no problem celebrating his position at the office and at home. When Roger Sterling tells him to go out and buy something that will signify his success and stature, Don purchases a new Cadillac — a status symbol of upward mobility (2:7). Don and Betty's home in Ossining is a testament to Don's success, a beautifully apportioned dream house that serves to underscore the dichotomy that is the Draper marriage — the façade obscuring ugliness, a result of Betty's growing frustration with Don's philandering. Season One finds Betty on the psychiatrist's couch, the only place she can articulate her frustrations; Season Two reveals Betty's emerging alcoholism as her silences become more lethal, throwing Don out of the house after Jimmy Barrett's revelation of Don's affair with Bobbie Barrett; Season Three finds Betty redecorating the home while contemplating an affair with a local politician — all before discovering the secret that is Don Draper and leaving on the train to Reno for a divorce (3:13). The Draper home obscures truth; the Rath home exposes reality.

Betsy, Tom's wife, greets him at the door with a myriad of complaints regarding the children's unruly nature, and he begins to confront her anguish as he addresses his job application at United Broadcasting the next morning:

> He tried to think of something to write, but all he could remember was Betsy and the drab little house and the need to buy a new washing machine, and the time he had thrown a vase that cost forty dollars against a wall.... He thought of [his daughter] Janey saying, "It isn't fair!" and the worn linoleum on the kitchen floor [12].

Tom's central problem differs dramatically from Don's: Tom does not like what he has done with his life, though he is equipped to do little else; Don enjoys the life he created from a chance encounter in Korea, when an accident he caused took the life of the real Donald Draper. Don's frustrations with life stem from his anxieties over the changing cultural landscape; Tom's come from his inability to do something he respects with his life that will provide for his family. Wilson uses this aspect to detail Tom's fragile psychology as he begins to reflect on the "probably irrelevant, but quite accurate fact that he had killed seventeen men" (12) during the war — a fact that allows him to question the futility of his suburban existence. Don Draper, born out of a cowardly mishap, refuses to release his troubled psyche, seeking to contain his emotions rather than face his truth.[5]

One aspect that Tom Rath and Don Draper share is their ability to use their personal pasts to gain some perspective on how suburbia restricts their desires. In Tom's case, his tour during World War II culminates in his fathering a son with an Italian girl. In an extended flashback, Wilson reveals the coupling through a slovenly romanticism — far from the harsh intensity of the novel's suburban drama. Tom and Maria live together in secluded harmony in the remnants of a shabby apartment on bread, wine, and passion — an idealized form of occupation, to say the least. A need for the simplicity of romantic shabbiness is reflected in Don's fascination with Midge and her beat generation cronies in Season One and in his affair with teacher Suzanne Farrell in Season Three. Yet the scenes staged in both apartments take on a sense of romantic shabbiness that never suits Don, whose gray flannel attire serves as a constant reminder that he does not belong in these milieus.

One other shared trait is how both men relate to the past. When Tom's tour of duty ended, he promised to remain in touch with Maria, but the pace of suburbia (and, assuredly, fear of Betsy's response) forces Tom to keep the memories to himself—again, similar to Don, who never speaks of "his people." In both men, the memories gradually fray their cool demeanors. In the novel, Tom admits to himself that these flashes of the past disrupt his moving forward: "The past is something best forgotten; only in theory is it the father of the present. In practice, it is only a widely unrelated dream, a chamber of horrors" (97)—an attitude that Don seemingly adopts as his mantra, passing it to his protégée Peggy Olson, in the hospital after she has Pete Campbell's baby that she will be surprised how easy it will be to forget it ever happened (2:5).

Contemplating the past, however, has different results for these men in gray flannel. Tom's reflections prompt him to embrace his new job at United Broadcasting, where he works for Ralph Hopkins, an industrialist with a particular interest in social justice. Hopkins' crusades, particularly in respect to mental health, inspire Tom to believe that he can make a difference in the world. While hearing from Maria, who requests his financial assistance, causes anguish in Tom and Betsy's marriage, the novel ends on a positive note: Tom's position in the corporate world brings him prosperity and spiritual fulfillment; the Rath marriage is stronger because the truth binds the family unit together, making the novel a showcase for Eisenhower-era prosperity and values.

Much to the contrary, the truth fragments the Draper marriage, and Don's constant philandering with Midge Daniels and Rachel Mencken (Season One), Bobbie Barrett (Season Two) and Suzanne Farrell (Season Three) makes a mockery of his suburban lifestyle. The historical changes highlighted on the show: Kennedy's election (1:12), the Cuban Missile Crisis (2:12), the escalation of the war in Vietnam (3:11), and Kennedy's assassination (3:12) destroy the world Don has created for himself, the continued secrecy separating him from both his friends and family. The "accident" of leaving his desk keys in his bathrobe pocket—an act that allows Betty access to Don's past, including Anna (3:11)—exposes the truth of his background, creating a parallel to Wilson's novel, where the truth gives the wife power to either maintain the family, or signal its demise. In Wilson's text, Betsy's forgiveness preserves the family; in *Mad Men*, the truth puts Betty on a train bound for Reno. The revelation of Don's secret toward the end of Season Three lifts the fog that surrounds the Drapers and pervades the series.[6]

Weiner's use of the Gray Flannel philosophy to impact his storytelling is a fascinating aspect of *Mad Men*. In respect to the novel, Catherine Jurca claims,

The Man in the Gray Flannel Suit insists that they [these men] can define themselves only by repudiating their middle-classness; other people belong in a development, not me, everyone else is happy as a corporate drone, except for me. And
their fundamental dissatisfaction with the suburb and the corporation proves an
engine of mobility that frees them from the constraints of each ... thinking of
oneself as a victim may be the necessary condition for not becoming one [87].

As we have seen, Don actually revels in his middle-classness; he sees his suburban home as a steady foundation; he has no patience for anyone who believes
themselves a victim. Most importantly, Draper basks in his place in the corporate world: in one of the final sequences of "Shut the Door, Have a Seat"
(3:13), Don comes out of the hotel bedroom after his last conversation with
Betty and sees the members of his corporate family rolling up their sleeves as
they laugh and grab for sandwiches — embarking on a new venture together.
His slight smile in close-up indicates that he would rather be here in the midst
of this corporate turmoil than anyplace else. Don is more certainly a "gray
flannel rebel," the opposite of Wilson's mature archetype:

He accomplished his major "developmental tasks" by his late twenties, found a
wife and made the appropriate adjustments to marriage, established himself in a
white-collar job that would lead, over the years, to larger offices and longer vaca-
tions, bought a house, and nestled into the "congenial social group" with whom
he would share highballs and the tribulations of lawn maintenance. He was
adjusted; he was mature; he was, by any reasonable standard, a success as an
adult male breadwinner. But (maybe because he was just a little smarter than
other men) he knew that something was wrong [Ehrenreich 29].

Tom Rath seeks a way to maintain his family and succeed in spite of his corporate surroundings; as Season Three closes, Don Draper has risked his family
and his corporate reputation by undermining the London firm, creating a
new corporate identity and a new family out the remnants of Sterling Cooper.

III.

The Camelot myth pervades *Mad Men*'s first three seasons; not only does
the political campaign provide a backdrop for its early episodes, but Marilyn
Monroe's death (2:9) and the Kennedy assassination (3:13) loom large as the
series progresses.[7] According to White, the Camelot myth and its association
with the Kennedy administration were born immediately upon the president's
assassination. On the evening of 23 November 1963, while planning the state
funeral (one she hoped to mirror the state funeral of Abraham Lincoln), Mrs.
Kennedy told the writer that she often listened to the cast album of *Camelot*
with the president in their private quarters at night, before bed (Maier 521).

White adapted the tale to suit his take on the slain president's administration and legacy, birthing the idea that Kennedy's tumultuous term was a mythic time of "a royal life style, gallant knights, and quests for truth and justice" (Felkins and Goldman 448).

Soon after the president's death, the realities of his administration gave way to "The Camelot School," a series of journalists, historians, family, and personal friends who wrote books and articles that "eulogized" the president's public image. "JFK became a sort of superman, a legendary figure who presided over Camelot, his administration one of unmatched wisdom, virtue, and style" (Reeves 4).[8] Subsequently, historians have wrestled with the actual impact of the successes attributed to Kennedy—a myth that his youthful idealism characterized the zeitgeist that ushered him into office. In reality, "the Kennedy luster profited not only from its own style but, to a considerable degree, from the relative drabness and inertia of the Eisenhower fifties" (Parmet 32). Dubbed "the royal family" by an exuberant press, excitement followed the young family into the White House. Kennedy's inaugural address, daring to "ask not what your country can do for you; ask what you can do for your country," proved that the intellectual new president had a way with words characterizing a youthful idealism that Americans had not experienced before. "A non-ideological nation succumbed to attractions that were more regal than philosophical" (Parmet 33). The changing tide that permitted the Democratic liberals to sweep out the old Republican conservatism is the very aspect that *Mad Men* seeks to underscore.

In actuality, while journalists and historians went on to transmit the Kennedy administration after his death through these myths, the Kennedy mythology had begun to take hold in the culture well before his assassination. Here are a few of the pervasive myths that complicate the American collective consciousness concerning Kennedy-era America:

- *Kennedy was a liberal politician.* Theodore Sorensen admits that Kennedy's liberalism was a concoction invented by historians (himself included) after his death. "Kennedy never identified himself as a liberal," he wrote in a *Newsweek* piece during Ronald Reagan's first term, "and on fiscal matters he was more conservative than any president we've had since." (72)
- *The Kennedy years were a time of social and economic transformation.* For the most part, the Kennedy years served as a bridge between the conservative, economic prosperity of the Eisenhower years and the liberal New Frontier agenda of Lyndon Johnson's 1964 campaign. Economic wealth and distribution—including the extremes between the classes and races—remained the same from 1956 through 1963. Edward R. Murrow's shocking documentary of his travels through America, *Harvest of Shame* (1960), reminds

us about the economic disparity that remained unchanged in America until Johnson's welfare reforms of 1965.

* *Kennedy's policies help to reform American education.* Because of his calling for volunteers to begin a "Peace Corps" during his inaugural address, Kennedy is often remembered as an innovator in education reform. However, according to recent reflections by Sorensen, Richard Goodwin and others, Kennedy's beliefs were not altruistic — he believed that committing to a broader education program was the only way for America to win the Cold War. Kennedy suffered a mighty defeat with his first education bill in 1961; his second attempt in early 1963 did pass, but it did not grant Americans the wider access to private schools that he hoped. The most far-reaching education reform, the Elementary and Secondary Education Act, was a plank in Lyndon Johnson's Great Frontier platform of 1964, and not made into law until 1965.
* *Kennedy would have prevented America's further involvement with Vietnam.* According to Herbert S. Parmet, "A Gallup survey in 1983 reported that 65 percent of those canvassed believed that the United States would have been much different if Kennedy had not been killed" (33). At the time of his assassination, Kennedy had no plans to remove troops from Vietnam; instead, he played a chief role in escalating American involvement in the civil war in Southeast Asia.[9]
* *Kennedy did not change attitudes toward the presidency; his assassination did.* The most pervasive myth is that Kennedy was not truly aware of the effect he was having on the image of the presidency; however, as Parnet states, "Not since FDR's time had the Executive Branch cast such an intimidating shadow" (37). Kennedy's successors have suffered by comparison, because he actively changed attitudes toward the presidency through his masterful understanding of how television could be used to make the public feel good about the White House. Kennedy's demeanor during the 1960 debates is famous, but few recall his keen abilities during his televised press conferences. He carefully orchestrated access to the First Family; with his First Lady by his side, they conveyed an elegant style right from the start. Mrs. Kennedy's famous televised tour of the White House (used beautifully in "For Those Who Think Young" [2:1]) was a public-relations coup devised to make Americans feel confident about the youthful family residing at 1600 Pennsylvania Avenue.

While misleading, certain mythologies that pervade a culture help it to make sense of a chaotic period. The shifting social climate and the youthful president were big changes for Americans to face at the time. The myths that demarcate the period obscure its anxieties — an aspect that Weiner seeks to expose through *Mad Men.*

Myth-making machinery built by 1960 election lore has complicated readings of the Kennedy administration, and rethinking these myths makes *Mad Men* historically interesting. According to White, the 1960 presidential election was fought in suburbia. For the first time, winning big urban centers would not be vital to winning an election; the terrain would shift to the more metropolitan centers established for the returning G.I.'s. By the time of the 1960 census, two-thirds of the population growth in America — some 28,000,000 people — had moved from urban centers to suburbs: "one had the impression of a strange new society being formed: a series of metropolitan centers growing and swelling in their suburban girdles until the girdles touched one another" (White 217). The shifting of the election turf was not the only difference. America had become progressively professionalized during the Eisenhower years: "for the first time in American history, the number of white-collar Americans (professional, managerial, clerical and sales people) had become greater than the number of those who held blue-collar jobs (productive or operative)" (White 221). The ground rules for how to win this election meant playing by a set of rules not familiar to the more seasoned politicos working for either political camp.

The high prosperity of the Eisenhower years altered the terrain as well. Not only did the average American enjoy a more luxurious lifestyle, but couples married earlier and took advantage of higher wages and the ease of credit. (One estimate claims that one dollar out of every nine was owed to some form of credit; before World War II, one dollar out of every fourteen was so pledged) (White 224). The fact is that this professional suburbanite was markedly more conservative than the more liberal city dweller, having prospered during the conservative Eisenhower years, having reaped the benefits of the G.I. Bill, and now working for a more established conglomerate, rather than striving in a smaller, localized business of the inner city. These factors posed a significant hurdle for the Kennedy machine; his very public wealth paired with his Catholic upbringing only added to the uphill struggle.

Television was to emerge as the new battleground and the great equalizer. While Richard Nixon employed Carroll Newton and Ted Rogers of Madison Avenue to help shape a friendlier image of himself (Black 417), Kennedy began taking voice lessons from a speech professor in Boston who taught him to use his diaphragm rather than his larynx (White 251). The candidates' images were introduced to a broader American electorate through the first gavel-to-gavel broadcast coverage of the nominating conventions. Nixon's acceptance speech to the GOP convention was well-received in Chicago, and his polling numbers jumped as a result. However, weeks later, Kennedy's televised speech from the Rice Hotel in Houston, where he denounced rumors that he would take marching orders from the pope if elected president, electrified his candidacy, showing Americans that the younger candidate could take an important issue and address it head-on: "Television networks were to broadcast his performance the next day in fragments around the nation. Kennedy volunteers were to use the filmed record over and over again in both Catholic and Protestant areas.... [N]o measure is available of how many millions saw the film played and replayed" (262). Other than the televised debates, this single speech made Kennedy appear presidential and helped him to overcome certain odds to succeed with the narrowest of wins over Richard Nixon.

The idea of the Kennedy White House as Camelot developed gradually throughout the thirty-five months of his administration, affectionately termed "The Thousand Days" by Arthur M. Schlesenger some months after the president's assassination. As an example of how the Kennedy myth was already in place before his death, we can turn to 1961's "President Kennedy," an essay in which Gore Vidal establishes much of the courtly discourse. In detailing Kennedy's differences from previous administrations, Vidal gets at the root of Kennedy's appeal: "The affection of the press for Kennedy is a phenomenon, unique in presidential politics.... [H]e is a bona fide intellectual (on the other hand, the working press is apt to be anti-intellectual); but finally, and perhaps more to the point, Kennedy is candid with the press in a highly personal way" (798). This "affection" is part of the myth-making transmission, praising Kennedy's unique manner with the press, who, ultimately, created the myth. In Vidal's words, Kennedy understands his advantage and uses it to help him gain popularity. "Kennedy," Vidal continues,

> is unique among recent Presidents in many ways. For one thing, he has ended (wistfully, one hopes forever) the idea that the presidency is a form of brevet rank to be given a man whose career has been distinguished in some profession other than politics or, if to a politician, one whose good years are past, the White House being merely a place to provide some old pol with a golden Indian summer [800].

Youth and social standing are key elements to the Kennedy myth, distinguishing the old guard—namely the retiring Eisenhowers—and Vidal illustrates how this quality could produce a new image for the presidency. His use of the term "brevet rank" drips with disdain as Vidal invokes not only Eisenhower but other presidents elected as a reward for military service (Ulysses S. Grant comes immediately to mind—often ranked as one of the worst presidents). Separating the youthful Kennedy from older, not necessarily wiser, presidents separates Kennedy from the other presidents—including those to come, helping to elevate his actions regardless of his administration's achievements.

Vidal goes on to praise Kennedy's youthful energy, never linked to the office before his rise.

Kennedy ... regards politics as an honorable, perhaps inevitable, profession in a democracy. Not only is he a master of politics, but he also takes a real pleasure in power. He is restless; he wants to know everything; he wanders into other people's offices at odd hours; he puts in a ten-hour office day; he reads continuously, even in the bathtub [802].

Vidal's assessment provides the foundation of what would become the Camelot myth as he praises the president for elevating the atmosphere of the presidency by soliciting the economic advice Kenneth Galbraith and the philosophical guidance of Robert Frost (798), adding a dash of elegance to the White House with his taste in art and culture. Vidal concludes with these thoughts — traits that epitomize the Kennedy myth: "He is a rare combination of intelligence, energy and opportunism.... He intends to be great" (803).

After Kennedy's death, a cottage industry emerged: a coterie of journalists, historians and acquaintances who came into contact with Kennedy during his brief 45-year life wrote books to capitalize on the nation's grief by mythologizing the fallen president further. For example, Joseph Campbell uses mythic tropes to underscore his impressions of Kennedy's funeral:

The symbolism of the gun carriage bearing the flag-draped coffin, drawn by seven clattering gray steeds with blackened hoofs, another horse prancing slowly at their side, bearing an empty saddle with stirrups reversed.... I saw before me, it seemed, the seven ghostly steeds of the gray Lord Death, here come to conduct the fallen hero youth on his celestial journey [quoted in Felkins and Goldman 53].

"Kennedy's assassination," Felkins and Goldman conclude, "is the tragic context in which archetypal images of life and death, the Promise and the loss of Promise, dramatically collide" (449); They appear to borrow their analogy from John Reston, who wrote that "what was killed in Dallas was not only the President, but the promise" (127).

The Gray Flannel and Camelot myths are fascinating elements of the Eisenhower and Kennedy eras because no other presidencies appear to have given rise to such pervasive legacies. As Freud says in "Creative Writers and Day-Dreaming," myths allow humanity to experience pleasure and release pain through their public dreams. In de-romanticizing this era, *Mad Men* plays historical fact against nostalgic recollection to create a central storyline that recalls a particular glamour in the culture while recognizing that anguish regarding a conservative mindset facing a youthful presidency, a growing Communist threat, a cultural revolution regarding race and gender relations, infiltrated the daily lives of the men and women who worked on Madison Avenue. *Mad Men* illustrates the effect of the changing tide on the average American.

IV

In the DVD commentary for *Mad Men*'s first season, Matt Weiner calls "Nixon vs. Kennedy" (1:12) the climax of the season because it brings together so many of the plot strands in anticipation for the cliff-hanging denouement of "The Wheel" (1:13). As mentioned earlier, the 1960 election serves as a backdrop for the action of Season One, but it also operates as an essential historical mirror for Weiner's deconstruction of the era's two presiding mythologies.

The approaching election surfaces right from the series's start in "Smoke Gets in Your Eyes" (1:1). Weiner builds on the historical fact that Nixon employed Madison Avenue to assist with marketing his image when Roger Sterling casually mentions that "Dick Nixon" is looking for help in combating "Jack Kennedy" during the fall election, using his verbal acumen to seduce Don into securing the account; noting that Kennedy is a young, handsome, navy hero and that it should not be very hard to persuade the country that "Dick Nixon is a winner." The challenge appeals to Don's desire to make the impossible work for him, but he remains loath to assist this cause. Roger's partner Bertram Cooper makes it known to Don and the entire staff that he wants the account because Eisenhower's eight years as president have been good for the company, but he knows it will be a difficult account to land, "like chasing a girl who doesn't want to get caught" (1:2). Don, true to his gray flannel conservatism, champions the Republican candidate's political acumen by recalling the brilliance of the "Checkers speech"; finding it "an admission of guilt wrapped in a distraction," Don acknowledges his preference for a politician who openly operates as an ad man — one who understands the commodity of image.

Establishing the election as the setting for Sterling Cooper's organization allows the series to acknowledge its historical background and use it, permitting the electoral battle of "Nixon vs. Kennedy" to be played out in the office. Don Draper, the creative genius, squares off with Peter Campbell, the young up-start account executive who becomes Don's nemesis. The dichotomy between Draper and Campbell plays out through the season in parallel to the national *battle royale* between Kennedy and Nixon. Although he resembles the handsome Kennedy in style and charisma, Don openly compares himself to Nixon, the more experienced, seasoned executive. By forcing Campbell, whose clumsy duplicity may remind the viewer of Nixon's future self, to take on the role of Kennedy, the young, untried junior, Weiner complicates the action of the series, dismantling the obvious to expose the mythology of Camelot.

As the series explores the inner-character life of Don Draper, the office politics begin to mirror the national political landscape. With Don's admission that he doesn't like being powerless (1:4), his past comes back to haunt him in "5G" (1:5) when Dick Whitman's younger brother, Adam, comes to Sterling Cooper, revealing the story that Don has hidden from everyone — that he is really Dick Whitman, born a "whore's son" whose mother died in childbirth, leaving him the unwelcome ward of his father, the young Dick the by-product of a poverty-stricken, deeply religious family[10] — an upbringing not so dissimilar to Richard Nixon's.[11] Don rebuffs Adam's attempt to reconnect, causing his back-story to appear like a "distraction" wrapped in "an admission of guilt," particularly when he ends the episode by bringing Adam $5,000 and a cold command to go back to thinking he was dead. Don leaves the fragile Adam shattered and the viewer eager to understand how Dick Whitman "draped" himself in the gray flannel cloak of the self-possessed Mad Man to become the man we know as Don Draper.

Pete Campbell's background is remarkably similar to John Kennedy's in that he was born the second son of a wealthy family dominated by a narrow-minded patriarch set on seeing his sons achieve power through added wealth. In "New Amsterdam" (1:4), we learn Pete's history when he is faced with realizing that his new wife Trudy has a desire for uptown real estate — something he cannot afford on his salary at Sterling Cooper. As the second son, Pete lives in the shadow of his highly successful brother, an attorney who is the pride and joy of the elder Campbell. On the eve of asking for assistance with a down payment, Pete learns of his father's disapproval, telling his younger son that advertising is "no work for a white man." Pete loathes his parents' conservative dilettantish streak — a quality the Campbells share with Trudy's parents, who drop Peter's mother's maiden name Dyckman, emblematic of Manhattan royalty, at the end of the episode to secure favor with the condo board.

One quality that Don and Pete share is their inability to remain faithful to their respective spouses. Don's affair with Midge Daniels takes place over the entire first season, along with his prolonged pursuit and ultimate conquest of Rachel Mencken, fracturing his image as the sanctified suburban conservative all the more. Of course, his wife Betty ultimately discovers Don's flagrant philandering, causing the Draper marriage to mirror the Sirkian melodramas popular in the late 1950s, where glossy surfaces mask ugly realities. Pete proves unfaithful to Trudy twice in Season One, bedding the office ingénue Peggy Olson in the first episode, and again in the office ("The Hobo Code" 1:8) after an emasculating experience with his wife. It is at this point that Don empowers Peggy as she composes her first copy for Belle Jolie lipstick, promoting her from secretary to junior copywriter, infuriating Pete when Don then places her on one of his chief accounts. Pete continues to take advantage of Peggy, desiring her to remain subserviently feminine; Don openly glows each time he assigns Peggy to a new account, taking an active interest in her developing confidence.[12]

Infidelity becomes the one trait that Don and Pete share with the Massachusetts senator who was known for his liaisons with beautiful women, despite being married to one of the world's renowned beauties, Jacqueline Bouvier. As repeatedly mentioned through the series, Kennedy's philandering appeared to be common knowledge despite the family's best efforts to keep these activities quiet.[13] Similarly, Don and Pete pursue and conquer women who defy their conservative ideology regarding female subservience. Midge, the West Village bohemian; Rachel, the department store mogul; and Peggy, the up-and-coming copywriter, each represent a facet of the changing role of women in Kennedy's America.[14] Don and Pete's philandering adds more credence to the notion that the election mirrors life at Sterling Cooper when we measure Betty Draper's growing depression and subsequent drinking against what we now know of Pat Nixon's misery in regard to her husband's ambition, and Trudy's passing resemblance to the young Jackie, with her bobbed hair, tailored suits and pillbox hats.[15] Betty and Trudy take on the roles of supportive political wives as their respective spouses compete at the office as the season plays out against the election.

The place of women in Camelot is the subject of "Shoot" (1:9), which shows Sterling Cooper creative team's response to Kennedy's campaign tactics, using actual footage of the campaign's advertisements and newsreels. While acknowledging that Nixon has an eight-point lead in the polls, Roger makes the team members watch a kinescope of Jackie Kennedy advocating her husband's candidacy in Spanish — a tactic that the Kennedy campaign team used to attract Spanish-speaking voters in the inner-cities. Startlingly, Jackie's image fills the screen in close-up, as she carefully speaks her "finishing school" Spanish advocating the difference her husband will make for immigrant Americans. Art director Sal Romano says that Jackie will not be popular with women because she will be too much like their prettier sister, resulting in a round of laughter. Weiner appears to rely on stereotype: the catty remark suggests that the closeted Sal understands all too well the idea of appearance in the political battle; while the others keep trying to expose the issues as a fundamental element of the approaching meeting with Nixon's campaign team, Sal alone sees that the election will be won on image.

The subtle genius of this particular episode is in the secondary plot, when Jim Hobart of McCann Erickson, a rival ad agency, solicits Don's attention by employing Betty as the new face of Coca-Cola. As Don gradually awakens to the ploy, Betty sees Hobart's attention as her opportunity to return to her glamorous roots as a fashion model, her profession when she met Don.

She tells Don how much fun it will be to relive that life, a nod to her more carefree existence, and her decision to audition for the campaign dressed in a pink, white and black "Giovanni" exemplifies her likeness to the political wife shown on the screen in the agency — using her image to bolster her husband's candidacy (although unwittingly). Hobart sends the photos of Betty to Don; the pictures exemplify a sense of elegance not necessarily associated with drinking Coke (just as Jackie brought a sense of elegance to her role as candidate's wife, and, ultimately, as first lady). Holding the photos, Don recognizes Hobart's bribe, but he seizes the moment to make his decision to stay with Sterling Cooper more lucrative — allowing him to reap a substantial raise with no binding contract. McCann drops Betty as a model, citing that the client wants to go with "more Audrey Hepburn" rather than with "Grace Kelly" and Betty is left to return to her career as a homemaker. Though she never reveals to Don that she was terminated from the project (choosing instead to say that it was her decision to remain at home with the kids), he knows that it was his decision that prevented her from returning to her former glory. The episode, showing Kennedy's use of Jackie to sell his candidacy and mirroring it against Don's use of Betty to sell his own candidacy back to Sterling Cooper, projects a political tone to the series as the 1960 election was a battle between presidential images.[16]

The Nixon campaign officially comes to Sterling Cooper in "Red in the Face" (1:7). Bert Cooper sets up a meeting with the Nixon "brain trust" in an effort to win the account. Alone for the evening, Roger invites himself to Don and Betty's, and, after a make-shift dinner fueled by lots of alcohol, makes a pass at Betty, which Don witnesses. Don chastises Betty for flirting with his boss, but he knows that Roger overstepped his boundaries, and Don plots to use the meeting with the Nixon strategists to stage his revenge.

The creative team meets to discuss the options in selling Nixon's image and the difficulty the team is having in making him appear a more likeable candidate. They attack the image of Kennedy that now appears iconic — that he does not wear a hat, Cooper exclaims. The one hold-out is Pete Campbell, who understands what drives Kennedy's popularity: "He is Elvis." Meanwhile, Don lunches with Roger on raw oysters and martinis before returning to the office where the elevator is out of order. Puffing cigarettes, Don and Roger mount the 23 flights of stairs drunkenly discussing the impending meeting with Nixon's team as they climb. Roger admits he may have drunk too much, but rests assured that the "GOP will never smell the booze over the Brylcream," a cautious admittance that he, himself, is not sold on pouring the company's resources into supporting Nixon's image *pro bono*. When they finally arrive at the meeting, noticeably inebriated and 45 minutes late, Roger greets the gentlemen by vomiting all over the foyer in front of the entire office.

As Don struts to take the meeting with a wry smile (to the strains of Rosemary Clooney's "Botch-a-Me"), an earlier scene makes sense: Don slipping money into the palm of Hollis, the elevator attendant, to fake mechanical difficulties, forcing Roger to take the stairs. Knowing that Roger's ulcer will flare with a combination of rich food and too much liquor, Don jeopardizes the Nixon account to get back at his unsuspecting boss. While not dealing directly with the details of the election, the episode uses the politics of the time as a colorful backdrop for the series' action.

"President as product" takes center stage in "Long Weekend" (1:9). At the continued request of Bert Cooper, the creative team — seeking ways to assist Nixon — screens a Kennedy advertisement currently running on television. The animated sequence does not feature the handsome Kennedy but cartoon characters waving Kennedy banners, singing an irritating jingle that sounds more "like a Maypo ad." The would-be campaigners follow this spot with one that Madison Avenue has created for Nixon: the vice president looks directly into the camera, speaking frankly to "my fellow Americans." Don winces, telling the cameraman to turn it off. He articulates the real difference between the two campaigns: Nixon is a "self-made man" and is the "Lincoln of California." Kennedy is privileged. If the real story was being told, the election would not be close. Don says that when he sees Nixon he sees himself.

The frank analysis by Don is the key to understanding how the election of 1960 shapes the series' first season. Don is the self-made man and he obviously hates being on the losing team, a fact that appears inevitable given Nixon's strategy. Don understands what the image of Nixon should have been for the campaign, and it is telling that he waits until now to articulate it. In essence, he knows that he could have won the campaign for the office, and possibly turned the election around, but he chose to remain above it. In turn, his attitudes become clear toward the end of the episode, when we see the famous "Eisenhower ad" that Kennedy adopted in the final weeks of the campaign. This use of Nixon's boss reveals Kennedy's innate television savvy, something Nixon did not have. The advertisement was a decisive weapon in the election, attacking Nixon by using Eisenhower who could not think of one contribution Nixon had made to the success of the presidency.[17] Don knows that image alone is not powerful enough to win; one needs to have a cool exterior and a clear vision — traits he would hesitate to admit he shares with the ultimate victor.

"Nixon vs. Kennedy" (1:12) is punctuated with actual Election Day footage, opening and closing the episode that puts Sterling Cooper on the losing side. The episode incorporates a dual plotline involving an office party on Election night, its aftermath, and the office politics of the following day, when Pete threatens Don with exposure, provoking an inevitable showdown. The episode creatively mirrors the anguish involved with the election, as the nervous anticipation of the late returns sets the stage for the anxieties that the conservative Mad Men will experience as the young, inexperienced Kennedy takes office.

The episode opens with news footage showing long lines at the polls. As mentioned earlier, over 69 million people voted in the election, which remained undecided until late the following day. The tension is palpable throughout the office as the boys' club — Harry Crane, Paul Kinsey and Ken Cosgrove — plan the festivities for an office party to watch the returns. The ensuing party, staged after Draper and Cooper leave for the day, is edited in a spirited manner as the staff gets drunk on *crème de menthe* — poured into the water cooler once the "good stuff" is gone. The episodic quality of the office party degenerates to a game of scuttle, actually played at office parties of the period.[18] Then, Ken finds a copy of a play written by Paul — a play about Don Draper and the agency — which the drunken office stages. The celebration takes another turn as the officemates dance a polka around the office when the newscasters announce that one battleground state, Ohio, finally goes to Nixon.

The frivolity in the office is important to this episode, because the spectator knows that Kennedy will win the election. The fun and games that characterize the day-to-day office culture of the first eleven episodes of the series mirror the light-hearted confidence of the Eisenhower years; this attitude will shift once Kennedy takes over and the troubles abroad with the Soviets and Cuba, and the racial tensions at home complicate America. When Peggy enters the next morning, the office looks like a disaster area, the camera following her in a complex tracking shot: all the workers are passed out, thrash strewn from one end of the swanky office to the other, Peggy's wastebasket filled with *vomit-de-menthe*. The scene reveals, metaphorically, that the party is over and that a new age is about to begin — displacing the myth that the Kennedy years were readily welcomed by a younger, urban generation ready to embrace change. The sight of Sal, Ken and Paul drinking a tomato-based hangover cure as Peggy washes out her wastebasket reveals the fragile condition of Sterling Cooper and the anxious nation.

The episode's second plot places Don and Pete's on-going feud center-screen, as Pete makes it clear that he knows Don's true identity. In a previous episode (1:5), Don's brother Adam sent a box of family memorabilia to the office that was inadvertently delivered to Pete. On the night of the election, Pete reveals his obsession with this private treasure trove of information, dressed in print pajamas eerily looking more childlike than adult. Pete sifts through the box during a bout of insomnia; Trudy interrupts him, letting us know that this has been going on for some time and that she considers it unhealthy. She says her father also had a box he kept in a closet: "I looked in it once, and I wish that I never had." She insists that Pete return the box to the rightful owner, knowing it belongs elsewhere.

Pete returns the box to Don the following morning under the pretense that it had been mis-delivered, and he uses the occasion to ask Don if he has reconsidered his qualifications for a big promotion at the office to senior account executive. When Don lets Pete know that he will always be supervised, Pete threatens Don by claiming to know his real name is Dick Whitman and he is a deserter. Don, standing tall in gray flannel from a low-angle shot tells Pete to leave, leading to a dissolve that reveals to the spectator how "Don Draper" was born during the Korean War when Dick assumes the identity of his fallen commander.

The struggle between Don, Sterling Cooper's creative genius, and Pete, the young account executive, mirrors the Nixon–Kennedy show-down, and it intensifies as the episode continues. Given the details of Don's upbringing — his alcoholic father, his over-zealous stepmother, and their being labeled "dishonest" by the community — Don rechristens himself as "Don Draper," allowing him to become an Horatio Alger figure. He will not be brought down by Pete's threat. Here, Don takes on the image of Richard Nixon, deciding that Pete's underhanded tactics will not add another complication to his life. Pete's attempt to thwart Don is a pathetic attempt to show how valuable he is to Sterling Cooper — a position that Don believes Pete maintains because of his familial connections, underscored in "New Amsterdam" when Don fires Pete, and Cooper reinstates him because Pete is a "Dyckman" who "once owned everything north of 125th Street." Pete reeks of his privileged upbringing and never attempts to disassociate himself from it at the office — another Kennedy trait.

The official election results are still not in by mid-afternoon, and the anxiety of this moment is reflected in the tension at Sterling Cooper. After meeting with Rachel Mencken — and being rebuffed by her inability to walk away from her life — Don returns to the office to find Peggy quietly sobbing in his office. Their short conversation, where Peggy reveals that her complaints about the previous evening's festivities resulted in two black workers being fired, appears to set Don off— her comment that while she follows the rules, bad people are free to act as they like obviously resonates with him. Don responds by marching in to Pete's office to bring the matter to a head, calling his bluff by going to Bert Cooper: "You have a deep lack of character," he tells his young colleague. As the two men strut across the office, Pete, true to his boyish nature, draws a childish analogy to westerns in his effort to halt Don: "This is not a cowboy movie where two old friends face each other with their guns drawn, and no one shoots. I will shoot you."

The next few moments are crucial as Don articulates all of his anger toward Pete in a quiet, pointed manner. Playing out in the doorway of Cooper's office, in front of a television broadcasting Kennedy's exuberant victory speech, Don chastises Pete, reminding him that he came from a rich family and never had to work for anything. Given the Kennedy's reliance on family money and connections in securing the election (and Bert Cooper's earlier statement about fraud in Chicago) Don appears to articulate Nixon's inner jealousy. Nixon campaigned against the Kennedy machine as "the common man from Whittier," but he reportedly saw the young senator as "a whimsical, pleasant, bright lazy man who had simplistic views, and had made no contribution to the Senate, and suffered severe withdrawal symptoms if his appetites of a rutting panther were unfulfilled even for a few hours" (Black 398, 402). In this confrontation, however, Kennedy does not win: in telling Cooper the truth, Pete looks childish—weak and foolish—while deceitful Don emerges triumphant as Cooper intones to the young Pete, "The Japanese have a saying: The only man in the room is the one standing in the room. I see Don Draper standing in this room. Now, I'd put your energy into bringing in accounts." After dismissing Campbell, Cooper gives Don his permission to fire him, but cautions against it: "One never knows how loyalty is born."

The final image of the episode brings us back to the election. As Don enters his house, exhausted from his encounter with Pete, he comes upon Betty asleep on the sofa, the television playing Nixon's "conditional" concession speech. The televised image closes on the out-going vice president embracing his wife, admitting that it looks as if Kennedy will be anointed. The camera gradually pulls back to show Don gazing at the set, paralyzed—the darkened room seeming to reflect the new era about to begin—not one filled with the confidence of Eisenhower's conspicuous capitalism, but with the anguish of darker, deeper anxieties of an uncertain future. Although he has won his battle against the young, rich upstart, we know that given the facts about Don Draper's past, he will not rest on these laurels for long.

V.

The time surrounding the 1960 presidential election is not the only time Matt Weiner's *Mad Men* dismantles the Gray Flannel and Camelot myths to reflect on his characters' lives. As the secretaries and copywriters at Sterling Cooper surround the office's single television set in Harry Crane's office on the afternoon of 22 November 1963, watching in horror the unfolding details regarding the assassinated Kennedy (3:12), Don Draper's personal life crumbles, his sturdy image convulsing in uncharacteristic sobs as Betty embraces the emotional chaos of the country and seizes the opportunity to end their marriage. The upheaval at home and throughout the country empowers Don to take some control of his destiny as he drops his guard to embrace Roger Sterling, Bert Cooper, Alan Price and even Pete Campbell in the founding of a new corporation (3:13)—a venture as daunting and uncertain at the time—and one that would appear similarly risky now. Don provides a singular image of Season Three finale, Don, in his gray flannel suit, seated on a sofa at a typewriter perched on a coffee table in a suite at the Pierre, the temporary locale for this new corporate entity, smiling as he types new copy for a client, embodies the perseverance of this American hero. He embraces chaos with a mixture of determination, hope, a little fear and a lot of moxie.

The parallels between the *Mad Men* era as suggested by Adam Cohen continue to haunt the psyches of those avid viewers who eagerly await each week's episode. As Maureen Dowd suggests,

> Some things have changed since the "'*Mad Men*' era" and others have not:
> The elevator operator isn't the only black face in the building. Executives no longer sip amber highballs and puff Lucky Strikes all day long.
> And other things have not changed.
> Some women still wriggle into girdles (now called Spandex). And some men still gravitate toward interns, nannies and secretaries (now called personal assistants).

What pervades cultural commentaries now is the acute possibility that the 2008 election ushered in our own Age of Anxiety, causing us to regain a sense of Camelot with the election of Barack Obama and his inheritance of the war in Afghanistan. As hypothesized by Matthew Bai,

> Since November 1963, through a succession of politicians who inspired and then dashed their hopes, boomer liberals have been pining for a leader who would reignite the spirit of their youthful idol. With Obama, they may yet end up closer to the reality of Kennedy, as opposed to the ideal, than they actually might have wished [12].

The idea that Barack Obama might be our new Kennedy is not original to Bai, but his notion that the desperate uncertainty felt by Americans, fueled by an unwinnable war, an unsure economy, and a shifting minority landscape, have caused images of Camelot to surface once more.

Returning to Adam Cohen's original thoughts, the success of *Mad Men* does not parallel the popularity of the movies during the Depression when throngs went to the theatre to escape the mundanities of life through Busby Berkeley musicals. "In tough economic times, the advertising-biz drama *Mad Men* is offering beleaguered Americans heaping helpings of other people's misery" (A18). As I have argued, Weiner's series does not simply extol the virtues of the era; instead, by actively redressing the mythologies of mid-century American culture, *Mad Men* offers us a window for looking at our own world objectively through the guise of history.

NOTES

1. In the DVD commentary for "Shoot" (1:9), costume designer and art director Janie Bryant speaks of her conscious decision to employ color in the series. "Gray is the dominant color of Sterling Cooper. The world of McCann Erickson is washed in light and gold-tones in contrast."

2. In an earlier episode (2:3), Jimmy meets Don and Betty at Lutesce to apologize for one of his hideous outbursts directed at Mrs. Schilling, the owner of Utz Potato Chips. He greets Don by saying, "I loved you in *Gentleman's Agreement*," openly comparing him to Gregory Peck, the star of *The Man in the Gray Flannel Suit*.

3. A secret past is one of the few traits Tom Rath and Don Draper share: Tom's obscuring to his wartime romance; Don's hiding his background as a poor, unwanted bastard.

4. In fact, cultural critics have tried to claim that Weiner was directly influenced by two other texts of the era: William H. Whyte's *Organization Man* (1956) and Richard Yates' *Revolutionary Road* (1961). He claims that he did not discover either text until after the first season aired and friends pointed him in the direction of these texts (Kaplan E3).

5. The second dimension of Don's actions are made clear during "The Jet Set" (2:11) when we meet the original Mrs. Draper, and we see the lengths he has gone to in order to maintain his image.

6. The image of fog permeates the series, particularly an episode titled "The Fog," (3:5) when Betty gives birth to the couple's third child, Eugene, named after her recently deceased father.

7. In "Love Among the Ruins" (3:3), Roger meets with his estranged wife, Mona and his daughter, Margaret, to discuss wedding plans. A copy of her wedding invitation reveals that Margaret's wedding will take place on November 23, 1963 — the day after the Kennedy assassination.

8. Some of these works include officially sanctioned celebrations of Kennedy's life, such as *Four Days: The Historical Record of the Death of President Kennedy* (1963) a joint venture of American Heritage and United Press International. Most were memoirs by Kennedy intimates, including Evelyn Lincoln's *My Twelve Years with John F. Kennedy* (1965); Theodore C. Sorensen's *Kennedy* (1965); Kenneth O'Donnell and David F. Powers' *Johnny We Hardly Knew Ye* (1972); Walt Rostow's *The Diffusion of Power* (1972); and Rose Kennedy's *Times to Remember* (1974). Arthur M. Schlesinger's *A Thousand Days: John F. Kennedy in the White House* (1966) won the Pulitzer Prize for History upon its release. It is important to note the Kennedys' role in perpetuating this myth. Jackie Kennedy tried to halt the publication of two books, William Manchester's *Death of a President* (1967) and Jim Bishop's *The Day Kennedy Was Shot* (1968). She urged JFK's friend and associate Paul B. Fay, Jr. to cut some 2,000 words of his memoir *The Pleasure of His Company* (1964), fearing that these books — even those written by close friends — would expose the dead president to some embarrassment.

9. This is the point of Koji Masutani's *Virtual JFK: Vietnam If Kennedy Had Lived* (2008) — a documentary that hypothesizes how different the Vietnam Conflict might have been had Kennedy not been assassinated.

10. "Out of Town" (3:1) opens with Don heating milk in the middle of the night for a pregnant Betty and interacting with memories he, obviously, cannot know much about: his mother giving birth to him, her dying after his delivery, and his subsequent delivery to his father via the midwife.

11. Richard Nixon's mother was a Quaker, and the real the religious force in his life. Nixon's father was a cruel, unloving businessman who ran a general store in Whittier, CA during the depression. Nixon's mother lived to see him elected president in 1968.

12. In "Six Month Leave," (2:9), Freddy Rumsen is fired for drinking on the job (and wetting his pants prior to pitching a new campaign for Samsonite). Don, angry at Roger for listening to Duck Philips and Pete Campbell, promotes Peggy, giving her all of Freddy's clients. When Peggy admits dismay at Freddy's firing, Don tells her: "Do not be upset because you are good at your job." A close-up of the slight smile on Don's face as Peggy leaves lets the viewer see his delight in knowing that his decision to promote Peggy will make Pete angrier.

13. This is very evident in two episodes of the second season. In "The Benefactor" (2:3) Jimmy Barrett remarks to Betty that she does not look like Mrs. Kennedy, "but you sure are his [JFK's] type." In "Maidenform" (2:6), the ad campaign conceived by Paul Kinsey revolves around Kennedy's favored feminine types: The "Jackie" and The "Marilyn."

That said, it is hard to not see this aspect of the series as revisionist. In *The Dark Side of Camelot*, journalist Seymour M. Hersh argues that "longtime friends and associates of Monroe and Kennedy acknowledged that the two stars, who both enjoyed living on the edge, shared a powerful, and high-risk attraction to each other" (103), but this was hardly common knowledge. John H. Summers concurs,

> When John F. Kennedy ascended to the presidency, reticence had become a fixed principle of American political exchange, according to the journalist Jules Witcover. The accepted attitude was that a political figure's private life was his own business unless it affected the performance of his public duties, and therefore reporters did not go out of their way to learn about the private life. Only if a senator fell down drunk on the floor of the Senate might that fact be reported. If another senator had a mistress on the side and continued to do his job, the press figured — so what?
> Kennedy, known in certain circles for his habitual womanizing, enjoyed protection both from the national press corps and from political rivals, who sometimes attempted to document his liaisons but who never organized a public campaign to discredit him — even though, as the Catholic husband of a widely esteemed First Lady, the president was doubly vulnerable to exposure. (838)

Given this evidence, it appears that Weiner's use of Marilyn Monroe in this context is anachronistic, at best.

14. These images of women continue throughout the series as we are introduced to Bobby Barrett, the ruthless agent of comedian Jimmy Barrett (Season Two) and with Suzanne Farrell (Season Three), Sally and Bobby's teacher who is a free-thinking civil rights activist who believes in discussing the legacy of Medgar Evers with her students and reading the speeches of Dr. Martin Luther King aloud in class.

15. Of course, Pat Nixon's drinking problem did not surface until much later in life when she admitted seeking assistance at the Betty Ford clinic, well after her husband's presidency. However, like much of the use of history in *Mad Men*, Weiner uses items like this to make his audience aware that he is aware.

16. In the DVD commentary of this episode, Matt Weiner and costume designer Jane Bryant state that this episode is about the "commercial value of beauty" and that the use of the kinescope was a tangible link between Betty Draper's beauty and Jackie Kennedy's.

17. According to Theodore White, Nixon's initial strategy was to "carry his message to the American people by the most imaginative use of television ever displayed in a national campaign" (312), which is why he hired Madison Avenue, much to the chagrin of his television advisors, who had been with Nixon's campaign from the start. Nixon's advisors wanted to employ the services of President Eisenhower, who they knew still had an incredible amount of good will with the public, but the Madison Avenue crowd opted to use

Nixon front and center, creating the kind of public service announcement that Don criticizes. Conrad Black surmises that this was one of the serious faults of the Nixon campaign, because the Madison Ave. executives did not take Kennedy's candidacy seriously, part of the reason Nixon came so ill-prepared for the first debate (400). Not using Eisenhower for Nixon led to Kennedy's use of the President in a negative campaign ad mentioned, edited by his strategists who manipulated a sound bite recorded in August 1960. In it, Eisenhower is asked to name one important policy or idea initiated by the Vice President Nixon during his eight years in office; Eisenhower pauses, shakes his head, and emphatically says, "Give me a week. I might think of one." Black believes that the power of this clip — played ubiquitously on television — cost Nixon many votes in the battleground states (401).

    18. In an interview with *Time*, Helen Gurley Brown detailed the need for "sexual chemistry" in the contemporary office (circa 1960), and extols the virtues of harmless gameplay — what she calls "a playful professional pastime" — such as scuttling, at the office. "Everyone enjoyed the pursuit and no scuttle was ever reported to the front office. Au contraire, the girls wore their prettiest panties to work." She admits, sadly, that she was never scuttled in her years at the office.

WORKS CITED

Abele, Robert. "*Mad Men*'s Gray Flannel Nightmare." *L. A. Weekly* 12 July 2007. 8 September 2009. <http://www.laweekly.com/content/printVersion/60544>.

Bai, Matthew. "Escalations: How Afghanistan Might Be Vietnam — and Obama the Real Kennedy." *New York Times Magazine* 1 November 2009: 11–12.

Black, Conrad. *A Life in Full: Richard M. Nixon.* New York: Public Affairs, 2007.

CBS Reports: Harvest of Shame. Dir. Fred Friendly. Edward R. Murrow. CBS News, 1960.

Cohen, Adam. "*Mad Men* and the Thrill of Other People's Misery in Sour Times." *New York Times* 17 October 2009: A18.

Dowd, Maureen. "Men Behaving Madly." New York Times 7 October 2009.

Edleman, Mark. *Politics as Symbolic Action.* Chicago: Markham, 1971.

Ehrenreich, Barbara. *The Hearts of Men: American Dreams and the Flight from Commitment.* New York: Anchor, 1983.

Felkins, Patricia K. and Irvin Goldman. "Political Myth as Subjective Narrative: Some Interpretations and Understandings of John F. Kennedy." *Political Psychology* 14.3 (September 1993): 447–467.

Freud, Sigmund. "Creative Writers and Day-Dreaming." *The Freud Reader.* Ed. Peter Gay. New York: Norton, 1989. 436–443.

Gilbert, Matthew. "*Mad Men* Just Might Deliver a Little Truth in Advertising." *Boston Globe* 29 August 2009. 8 September 2009. <http://www.boston.com/news/globe/living/articles/2007/08/29/mad_men_just_might_deliver.html>.

Goodwin, Richard. *Remembering America: A Voice from the Sixties.* Boston: Little, Brown, 1988.

Hainey, Michael. "The Man in the Gray (Indestructable) Suit." *Men.Style.com.* 8 September 2009. <http://men.style.com/gq/features/landing?id=content_62.html>.

Handy, Bruce. "Don and Betty's Paradise Lost." *Vanity Fair* September 2009, 268–283.

Heehs, Peter. "Myth, History, and Theory." *History and Theory* 33.1 (February, 1994) 1–19.

Hersh, Seymour M. *The Dark Side of Camelot.* New York: Little, Brown, 1997.

Jameson, Fredric. *Postmodernism or, The Cultural Logic of Late Capitalism.* Durham: Duke University Press, 1991.

Jurca, Catherine. "The Sanctimonious Suburbanite: Sloan Wilson's *The Man in the Gray Flannel Suit.*" *American Literary History* 11.1 (Spring 1999): 82–106.

Kaplan, Fred. "Drama Confronts a Dramatic Decade." *New York Times* 21 August 2009: A18.
Kirkland, Bruce. "Nostalgia as Art." *Edmonton Sun* 18 July 2009. 8 September 2009. <http://www.edmontonsun.com/entertainment/tv/2009/07/18/10178121-sun.html>.
Maier, Thomas. *The Kennedys: America's Emerald Kings.* New York: Basic Books, 2003.
"Matt Weiner Interview." *AMCTV.com.* <http://www.amctv.com/originals/madmen/mweiner-interview>.
McCarthy, Anna. "*Mad Men*'s Retro Charm." *The Nation* 28 August 2007: 1–3.
McNamara, Mary. "Mad Men Creator Matt Weiner on Love, Sartre and Why Men Behave Badly." Multichannelnews.com. 17 October 2007. <http://multichannel.com/blog/TV_crush/7454-_Mad_Men_Creator_Matt_Weiner_on_love_Sartre_and_Why_Men_Behave_Badly.php>.
Nalley, Richard. "*Mad Men*: Season One." *Forbes.* 181 16 June 2008, 99.
McNeill, William H. "Mythistory, or Truth, Myth, History, and Historians." *The American Historical Review.* 91.1 (February 1986): 1–10.
Parmet, Herbert S. "The Kennedy Myth and American Politics." *The History Teacher* 24.1 (November 1990): 31–39.
Reeves, Thomas C. *A Question of Character: A Life of John F. Kennedy.* New York: Prima, 1997.
Rudd, Paul. "Jon Hamm: Talking to *Mad Men*'s Main Man in the Gray Flannel Suit." *Interview* August, 2008. 8 September 2009. <http://findarticles.com/p/articles/mi1285/is_6_38/ai_n27930131/html>.
Schlesinger, Arthur M. *The Thousand Days: John F. Kennedy in the White House.* New York: Mariner, 2002.
"Social Issues: Behind the Times." *Time* 11 November 1991. 4 August 2009. <http://www.time.com/time/magazine/article/0,9171,974226,00.html>.
Sorensen, Theodore. *Kennedy.* New York: Harper & Row, 1965.
Suderman, Peter. "Boys Behaving Badly." *National Review* 3 December 2007: 52–53.
Summers, John H. "What Happened to Sex Scandals? Politics and Peccadilloes, Jefferson to Kennedy." *The Journal of American History* 87.3 (December 2000): 825–54.
Vidal, Gore. "President Kennedy" in *United States Essays: 1952–1992.* New York: Broadway Books, 1993.
Virtual JFK: Vietnam If Kennedy Had Lived. Dir. Koji Masutani. Global Media Project. 2008.
Weinman, Jaime J. "Why We Can't be Mad at *Mad Men*." *Maclean's* 4 August 2008: 8–9.
White, Theodore H. *The Making of the President, 1960.* New York: Atheneum, 1961.
Wilson, Sloan. *The Man in the Gray Flannel Suit.* New York: Four Walls Eight Windows, 2002.

12. Complicating Camelot: Surface Realism and Deliberate Archaism

Christine Sprengler

Toward the end of "The Wheel" (1:13), Don Draper persuades Kodak executives that nostalgia is the best possible tool that they can use to sell their slide carousel. It is not the "glittering lure" of technology but a "deeper sentimental bond" that will attract consumers to this product. He explains that the carousel is a time machine, not a spaceship, as slides of his family life advance across the screen. Don eschews the type of pitch his clients expected to hear, one that would have resonated nicely with the postwar period's fascination with the future. Instead he invents a Greek friend by the name of Teddy to introduce and authenticate his (somewhat inaccurate) translation of nostalgia as the "pain from an old wound."[1] He describes nostalgia as "delicate, but potent," a pain in the heart stronger than only memory. Nostalgia involves a yearning to go home and Don's wistful speech promises that Kodak's carousel has the ability to satisfy this impossible desire.

Don skillfully uses nostalgia to sell his clients on the power of nostalgia and they are instantly seduced. But are we? The snapshots are real, documenting moments of intimacy and reverie in Don's world. He becomes genuinely moved by these images and thus falls victim to his own pitch. And, like Harry, we too are encouraged to see ourselves in these photographs, to reminisce about earlier, happier times. However, something feels a little off about what we see and hear. These snapshots may capture treasured memories of what appears to be a domestic paradise. Yet various cues date them as recent and thus to a time when existential angst and depression were likely already well-entrenched in Don and Betty's respective psyches. Perhaps we are given to wonder if these images, like most records of family life, obfuscate a much grimmer reality.[2] Past episodes would certainly suggest as much. Indeed we may also question if we recognize them not simply as Don's, but as the archetypal nostalgic constructs that populate our cultural landscape, often functioning as visual shorthand for childhood itself. From the subject matter to their aesthetic execution, they are very much part of a visual archive that signifies nostalgia and, more recently, the type of nostalgic construct blamed for manipulating our conceptions of the past. They belong to a genre of images that now encourages parodic or critical readings and are thus no longer exclusively or even reliably indicative of a "kinder, gentler time."

But perhaps what seems most odd about this segment is Don's description of nostalgia. From the vantage of the twenty-first century it sounds antiquated. In fact, by the late 1950s, nostalgia's identification with homesickness had lost ground to what was rapidly becoming its dominant meaning as the captivation with the cultural expressions of previous eras. By 1970, it was recognized as a fully-fledged "industry" that marketed the consumer objects, fashions, and designs of the past (Sloane 171). This is not to suggest that nostalgia as a feeling has been entirely supplanted by nostalgia as an enterprise trading in the aesthetics of pastness. As Paul Grainge suggests, it continues to thrive as both a "mood" and an aesthetic "mode" ("Monochrome Memories" 21). Nor are its mood and mode mutually exclusive. The etymology of "aesthetic" itself reminds us of the affective potential of art. However, as dominant uses of the term in popular and academic writing depend on and reinforce its association with visual pastness, the inducing of sentiment is becoming less and less necessary for its experience. It is in light of this that Don's equation of nostalgia with homesickness seems out of touch. It is also out of synch with *Mad Men*'s own engagement with the phenomenon. Episodes frequently deconstruct tropes central to popular representations of postwar nostalgia and self-consciously foreground period markers well-entrenched in the current retro economy as a way to bring the past into collision with the present.

Though conspicuous, these disjunctions between Don's pitch and the reality of his family life (including his own childhood) and between Don's definition of nostalgia and how it is used in the series are not at all problematic. In fact, I would argue that this scene is incredibly productive and important: it both summarizes the first season and foreshadows subsequent ones, reminding us that what lies at the heart of *Mad Men* is an attempt to complicate nostalgic constructs like "the fifties"[3] and "Camelot" and, in so doing, reveals the complexity inherent in contemporary manifestations of nostalgia itself.

There are a number of ways in which *Mad Men* complicates the heavily mythologized era of Camelot and the heavily theorized concept of nostalgia. My focus here will be on the contributions made by a selection of visual strategies that fall under the rubrics of "surface realism" and "deliberate archaism." I borrow these terms from Marc Le Sueur to talk about aspects of production design,[4] cinematography and casting and to argue that the visual pastness and period details responsible for the series' label as "nostalgic" are not, as some reviewers have claimed, antithetical to its narrative criticality. Instead, I argue that these strategies are integral to *Mad Men*'s demystification of postwar America. As such, *Mad Men* exemplifies the type of engagement with nostalgia that has prompted recent scholarship on the subject to move beyond the Jamesonian view that visual pastness denies us access to our history and obfuscates it in the service of reactionary agendas (Jameson 16–19). Important studies by Paul Grainge (2002), Vera Dika (2003), Pam Cook (2005), and others have demonstrated that screen fictions generically categorized as "nostalgia" have the capacity to be critical: they can offer insight into the relationship between the past and present and between mediated fictions and what is ostensibly real history.

Although I remain deeply sympathetic to the ideological critique at the heart of Fredric Jameson's assessment of postmodern aesthetic modes, I find his wholesale denunciation of the "nostalgia film" somewhat limiting. While some uses of nostalgia do precisely what Jameson claims (e.g. *Forrest Gump* [1994]), many recent examples do not. Consider, for example, how films like *Pleasantville* (1998) use their visual pastness (or "Fiftiesness" as Jameson would say) to initiate trenchant critiques of the kind of nostalgic constructs once central to conservative political rhetoric.[5] Consider too how the fifties itself has been fractured by the cinema into a variety of permutations, ones that acknowledge the complexity and diversity of the period as well as that of its uses in contemporary culture. The Leave-It-to-Beaveresque fifties may continue to fuel conservative fantasies, but it is also pastiched, parodied, and lambasted to a variety of ends. We have seen the Retro Lounge Fifties in *Swingers* (1996), the McCarthyite fifties in *Good Night and Good Luck* (2005), and what we might call the Metacinematic Fifties (films about films from the 1950s) in *Far from Heaven* (2002).

As Grainge argues, many of these films show that "amnesia and historicist crisis" do not necessarily result from constructions of visual pastness, but can "establish and legitimate different kinds of memory" ("Monochrome Memories" 3–6). Moreover they have the capacity to bring to light aspects of the past overlooked by traditional historical perspectives.[6] For Vera Dika and Andrew Higson, pitting visual signifiers central to nostalgic constructs against narratives designed to challenge the authenticity of those constructs can imbue nostalgia films with great critical potential.[7] Reviewers of *Mad Men* echo this logic, proposing that while its sumptuous period details classify it as nostalgic, its story lines, dialogue, and character developments render it "more than nostalgia" (Usborne 32). Some demand that we not see *Mad Men* as "merely nostalgia" because "it's so much richer than that" (Gilbert E1).[8] These assessments certainly help to further entrench nostalgia as a visual phenomenon and acknowledge the critical potential of its representations. However, they also enforce a strict separation between the visual and narrative elements of the series. Each, it seems, is tasked with accomplishing something different. I have argued elsewhere[9] that such an opposition prevents us from recognizing how the visual elements responsible for a film or television series' nostalgia label can also function as the source of its critical consciousness. In what follows I shall develop this argument in order to account for how *Mad Men* mobilizes surface realism and deliberate archaism in both its construction and deconstruction of Camelot.

Surface realism and deliberate archaism were first defined by Marc LeSueur in 1977 in one of the earliest scholarly texts outside psychoanalytic and conservative political spheres to endorse the value of nostalgia.[10] He suggested that the "nostalgic impulse is sometimes associated with very vital and assertive social and political currents, such as revolutions [and] ... to categorize all nostalgia as 'escapist' as is so commonly done, avoids the very important social effects achieved by this sensibility" (188). But his most significant and prescient contribution to the discourse on nostalgia was his identification of surface realism and deliberate archaism as the two "aesthetic approaches" that define "nostalgic art" (192). Surface realism refers to the production of a kind of visual period authenticity through the use of recognizable material objects from the era represented (e.g., clothing, furniture, cars, etc.). Deliberate archaism describes the practice imitating past media forms, of recreating the "appearance of art from [a] distant time" (Le Sueur 194). For example, *The Good German* (2006) was shot in black and white using 1940s lenses to make it appear as though it was produced during the 1940s. *Pleasantville* recreates the look of a 1950s domestic sitcom while *Far from Heaven* recreates the visual style of a Sirkian melodrama. Le Sueur's description of surface realism and deliberate archaism aptly describes many recent nostalgia productions and resonates especially with *Mad Men*'s visual engagement with Camelot.

Though I shall occasionally treat these approaches as distinct (following Le Sueur), I want to focus on instances in which surface realism and deliberate archaism conspire to give the series its critical force. To start, I will explore aspects of production design and cinematography and what the "cinematic" look of the series accomplishes. This will be followed by an analysis of casting practices and the star constructs evoked by the look of the characters enlisted to populate this early 1960s world.

Mad Men's deliberate archaism is more complex than that defined by Le Sueur and less consistent than what we have seen in recent filmic examples. For *Mad Men* to adhere to a strict interpretation of this visual strategy, it would have to look like an early 1960s television drama. This, of course, would imbue it with an aesthetic sensibility far removed from that according to which it operates. Indeed, the aesthetic sensibility of *Mad Men* is effectively cinematic, though only explicitly so in certain sequences. It looks, on occasion, like a film made in the late 1950s or early 1960s. As director of photography Phil Abraham clarifies, *"Mad Men* has a somewhat mannered, classic visual style that is influenced more by cinema than TV" (Feld, Oppenheimer, and Stasukevich 46). This classic visual style is achieved in part through a preference for fixed cameras and the periodic but markedly noticeable uses of slow tracking shots, fades, and dissolves. It is also accomplished by eschewing certain staples of television in favor of cinematic devices.

For example, shots in deep focus designed to capture the full expanse of interior spaces are favored over close-ups which are relied upon to a great extent in most contemporary television drama (Feld, Oppenheimer, and Stasukevich 46). This stylistic conceit is a hallmark of the show and one, I would argue, that serves a number of purposes, not least of which is as homage to its earlier uses in classical Hollywood cinema. It is used to dramatic effect as Joan guides Peggy for the first time through Sterling Cooper, making us privy to the hierarchical organization of space in this Madison Avenue agency (1:1). The frequent use of deep focus renders the public and private spaces occupied by the characters ever-present, serving as a constant reminder of the world and the period they are in. At times characters seem little more than part of the visual texture and palette of the *mise en scene*, mere components in spectacles of visual excess, and thus not as individuals with control over the spheres they inhabit. Consider the establishing shot of Betty in the grocery store in "Red in the Face" (1:7). Here she ineffectually competes for our attention with vibrant displays of fruit and strong graphic designs on the floor and walls of the produce section. She is visually overwhelmed, trapped in an image of consumption, and indeed about to be emotionally overwhelmed after her altercation with Helen.

When close-ups are used, they are noticeably extreme and typically linger on small props to open episodes or transition between scenes. This too has a cinematic feel to it, recalling the visual grammar of mid-century Hollywood and especially Hitchcock's penchant for foregrounding small yet significant objects. But whereas Hitchcockian props served distinct narrative purposes, offering necessary clues to plot development, *Mad Men*'s props appear in the service of surface realism. For example, "5G" (1:5) opens with an extreme close-up on an assortment of period-correct toiletries on a vanity, including a Cutex bottle. "Babylon" (1:6) opens with a series of close-ups alternating between a 1950s toaster, coffee and sugar canisters, glass jug, small ashtray, and gold-rimmed coffee cup on a gold rimmed saucer.[11] In "Long Weekend" (1:10), a thermometer attached to a statuette fills the frame between Don's brief conversation with Sally and a scene introducing the arrival of Betty's father and Gloria. As the ultimate in 1950s domestic kitsch, this object also signals that Betty's temperature is on the rise because of the tensions her visitors are sure to stoke.

These details are central to *Mad Men*'s period authenticity and the subject of extended discussions in the popular press. They are cited as a part of the show's allure and have fuelled demand for mid-century modern artifacts.[12] As a few reviewers have rightly noted, they also do more by adding layers of richness and complexity through their highly specific signifying potential.[13] Weiner confirms the intent of this. For him, "the story is in the details, and those details have their own life.... Not a single prop is an afterthought" (La Ferla G1). Take, for example, *Mad Men*'s cars. Betty's two-tone station wagon confirms her status as a middle-class suburban housewife with a well-paid husband and her adherence to a particular 1950s brand of domesticity and femininity. In "Seven Twenty Three" (3:7), Betty uses her ownership of a station wagon to remind Henry Francis of her status as a married woman. When Henry observes Betty get into her father's car, he suggestively intones that the station wagon is not the car for Betty. In telling him that she has one at home, she clearly rebuffs his advances. Helen's Volkswagen Beetle—and her loose hair—signifies that she is considerably more "modern" than Betty in her values, lifestyle, and views on consumption. The Beetle also figures prominently in "Marriage of Figaro" (1:3) through its print representation in the memorable "Think Small" and "Lemon" ads. Unsurprisingly, Don is unable to appreciate the ways in which this campaign successfully tapped into the shifting attitudes of the age and, in "The Gold Violin" (2:7), buys himself a 1962 Cadillac Coupe de Ville. The Cadillac is thoroughly fetishized by Don (and the cinematography) and thus aptly reinforces the episode's focus on the emptiness of materialism. However, Don's car accomplishes more than this. It may be brand new, but in 1962, the Cadillac Coupe de Ville was already a relic of the 1950s, sporting the type of tail-fins that had begun to shrink a few years earlier. Formed by and inscribed within postwar discourses of conspicuous consumption, planned obsolescence, opulence and optimism, the car, like Don himself, is firmly entrenched in a mythic construction of the fifties. While this reinforces Don's datedness, it also suggests the very real and significant ways in which Camelot was shaped as much by the visual and ideological trappings of the fifties as it was by its promise.

Surface realism and deliberate archaism also collude to productive effect in scenes involving the ceilings of Sterling Cooper. A great deal is made of this by those responsible for *Mad Men*'s creation, for it is yet another way in which the show circumvents the practices of television drama in order to achieve its cinematic feel. That is, we see from low angle shots the space normally reserved to accommodate lighting and other filming equipment. But seeing the ceiling does more than replace a televisual grammar with a cinematic one. It functions as a direct reference to the film cited by Weiner as the greatest influence on him, *The Apartment* (1960), and one in which a vast grid of over-head fluorescent lights is played to almost comic effect. For Abraham, it also embodies the essence of high modernism and thus channels other aspects of visual culture that mediated and interpreted this particular aesthetic: photography, graphic design and architecture. As such, it is an integral part of the show's surface realism. This was the new sleek look for offices, something echoed in the furniture as well. Yet in adhering to the mid-century modernist mantra "form follows function," these ceiling lights, and the objects and spaces they illuminate, achieve something else. They represent a new design aesthetic and, like the cars, a design aesthetic that *meant* something in postwar America, that embodied very specific ideas and ideals about work and gender. In modernist discourse, ornament was rejected as feminine, superfluous, and abject, while geometric simplicity and functionality were esteemed as masculine, rational, and efficient. This was obviously a gendered discourse that aligned a vaunted modernist aesthetic with the public sphere and the decorative with the private and domestic.[14] Thus, like Don's 1962 Cadillac, this aesthetic offers access to the desires and anxieties that the period inscribed in its forms and, in the case of the Sterling Cooper office, it reinforces already well-defined gender dynamics.[15]

The material artifacts responsible for *Mad Men*'s surface realism have the capacity to bring forth the spirit of the age that produced them. Filming them in ways that recall the cinema adds yet another dimension that enriches the complexity of the show. In what follows, I want to deal more directly with *Mad Men*'s deliberate archaism, its multiple sources and, in particular, what its expressly cinematic moments bring to the series. AMC President Charles Collier's reason for endorsing the show's "cinematic quality," as he calls it, is purely pragmatic. For him, it is a "perfect complement to what's at our core: movies" (Strauss 4D). Audiences tune into AMC to see classic films, and *Mad Men* offers both an aesthetic continuity with — and homage to — their regular programming. It is a mutually reinforcing relationship.

Weiner's reason is certainly more personal and stems from his self-professed obsession with the era (High). But having been born in 1965, his obsession is one based on and nurtured by *representations* of the period mined from the cinema and other facets of popular and literary culture. Presumably, it is shaped in large part by his experience of the 1970s nostalgia boom for the fifties. But it is also apparent how *The Apartment* and other similar productions from the late 1950s and early 1960s sourced many of *Mad Men*'s visual, character and narrative tropes. Weiner and his production staff often turned to catalogues and advertising of the period, translating images into sequences and the material reality of sets. For example, a 1950s Sears catalogue provided the inspiration for Don and Betty's kitchen while advertisements served as the basis for their laundry room (Weiner "Shoot"). In the case of the latter, surface realism and deliberate archaism run together once again as the appliances, their staging, and Betty's performance in the space all faithfully reference their source. Of course, in "Indian Summer" (1:11), this image is subverted when Betty discovers that the dryer's vibrations can satisfy her sexual desires. The image of dutiful domesticity so central to late 1950s visual culture is revealed as just that — an image — and one that masks a very different reality and set of needs that cannot be satisfied by conspicuous consumption alone.

Another type of aesthetic sensibility is achieved through the recreation of what Weiner describes as "Edward Hopper" lighting.[16] First used toward the end of "Smoke Gets in Your Eyes" (1:1) when Pete arrives at Peggy's apartment for a secret tryst, it resurfaces in later episodes and especially in scenes set at night. In one instance, as Don disembarks from the late train and walks toward his car, a *Nighthawks*-inspired palette reinforces his isolation and alienation in a way reminiscent of this iconic 1942 painting. This is not the first time Hopper's work has inspired cinematic depictions of postwar anxiety. *Far from Heaven* employs a similar aesthetic in its night time milieus to serve comparable aims.[17] There is definitely more than a passing resemblance between these two productions, reminding us that *Mad Men* relies for its look on both representations produced *during* the mid-twentieth century and representations *of* the mid-twentieth century, and that its visions of the fifties and Camelot are the product of mediations, both past and present.

Whereas postwar appliance advertising provides the visual framework toward the end of "Shoot" (1:9), a reference to an iconic representation of the fifties introduces this episode. As Weiner himself suggests in his commentary, the opening exterior scene of Betty's front yard has a distinct "David Lynchian" feel to it. He is referring, of course, to *Blue Velvet* (1985) and most likely to its opening sequence in which a similarly slow pan downward, use of roses as a motif, and slow formal wave of a hand set the tone for one of the seminal deconstructions of the fifties. But this visual nod does more than simply satisfy a cinephilic interest in origins or delight in recognition. It presents the fifties as a product of suburban fantasies that, over time, has been reconfigured through its appearance in the context of surrealist nightmares (e.g. *Blue Velvet*, *Edward Scissorhands* [1990], and *The Reflecting Skin* [1990]). *Mad Men* certainly prolongs the life and salience of the fifties in this vein by further exposing its fractures and subverting the well-worn tropes of postwar domestic bliss. Through its reference to *Blue Velvet*, "Shoot" thus reinforces the fifties as born from, perpetuated and ultimately changed by its popular representations. We are made acutely aware of both its constructed and changeable nature and, as such, we see the ways in which any given present makes use of—for its own regressive or progressive aims—already mythic and mediated visions of the past.

Mad Men also makes us aware of how mediated representations of the past fuel our conception of it through its mobilization of specific character types that do not always conform to the larger nostalgic paradigms we have come to expect them to inhabit. I would like to turn now to the issue of casting in order to examine how characters function as period markers and what their alignment with recognizable star constructs might entail and imply.

The conflation of *Mad Men*'s characters with well-known star constructs—whether cinematic or political—is reinforced on two levels. We notice that some characters look like Hollywood icons and so do they. We recognize the striking resemblance between Paul and Orson Welles well before Joan points it out in "Nixon vs. Kennedy" (1:12). Likewise, we see that Betty is a doppelganger for Grace Kelly long before Jim Hobart tells her as much in "Shoot." Indeed, by this point in the series, Betty is not just Grace Kelly; she is Grace Kelly the cool Hitchcockian blonde. Whereas some actors call to mind particular Hollywood icons, others simply invoke the various constructs of masculinity and femininity produced through the visual culture of mid-century America. Director Alan Taylor speaks to the importance of this: "Everyone we cast had to be able to do period and that meant being able to be a man in a certain way or be a woman in a certain way" ("Nixon vs. Kennedy").

"Doing period" requires what I call "period casting" and, in *Mad Men*, this means hiring actors who look (or can be made to look) like they inhabited late 1950s and early 1960s Hollywood films, television programs, and print ads. Mark Moses reminded Taylor of Johnny Carson ("Nixon vs. Kennedy") while the young advertising executives were enlisted "based on their face" (Weiner, "Smoke Gets in Your Eyes"). Burlesque performer Ruby Valentine was hired to strip in "Smoke Gets in Your Eyes" because of her body type and, presumably, her capacity to erotically reinterpret Marilyn Monroe's performance of "Diamonds Are a Girl's Best Friend." Robert Morse brings a pastness to Bertram Cooper simply by channeling his former role in *How to Succeed in Business Without Really Trying* (1967) and through his cadence, which, according to Weiner, is real ("Shoot"). Jon Hamm also landed the part when he first "opened his mouth," suggesting that both voice and face played a role in his casting (Littleton 72).[18] Reviewers too have credited *Mad Men*'s authenticity with its actors' abilities to "do period," proclaiming, for instance, that "Hamm and Slattery look like they were born to play roles from that era" (Usborne 32). Likewise, Gilbert observes that "the actors seem to have been cast according to their physiognomies, which recall actors from the 1940s and 1950s. Hamm has a Gregory Peck–like nobility, but with haunted eyes, and his creepily competitive subordinate Pete, has a Farley Granger air about him" (E1).

The close alignment between key characters and well-known star constructs might prompt us to realize that Camelot was populated by mythic figures and ones, for the most part, produced by and disseminated through the popular media. When Betty walks down the stairs to meet Don for their Valentine's Day dinner in "For Those Who Think Young" (2:1), we are encouraged to see Grace Kelly meet Cary Grant or Gregory Peck not only by their costume, hair, and make-up, but also by this scene's deliberately archaic cinematography and editing. As the camera tracks her in slight slow motion, a cinematic score drowns out all diegetic sound and slow dissolves alternate between Betty's demure smile and Don's reaction. It is a brief moment of romantic and explicitly cinematic reverie, interrupted first by Betty's chance encounter with an old roommate now working as a high-class prostitute, and later by Don's sexual impotence. However much they looked the part of the ideal, glamorous Hollywood couple in love, their image concealed a very different reality. Like Joan, Sal, Kitty and Francine, they instead spent Valentine's Day night watching television and, specifically, Jackie Kennedy's tour of the White House.

In a somewhat unexpected twist, Jackie does not function here as the image that her rapt audience will eventually attempt to emulate or as a new model of glamour for Betty to internalize. Neighbor Francine claims that Jackie appeared nervous during the broadcast — almost as if "playing house." In fact, Jackie does lack confidence here; she is not yet the poised, elegant Guinevere at the heart of our conceptions of Camelot. This is Camelot before its creation — before Jackie astutely introduced the metaphor (borrowed from Jack Kennedy's favorite Broadway musical) in her interview with journalist Theodore White just a week after the assassination. Before the appearance of White's article (commonly referred to as "The Camelot Interview") in *Life* initiated a flurry of mythologizing efforts that shaped the early 1960s into the construct we recognize today. In Jackie's televised White House tour she is indeed "playing house," struggling to fulfill the role assigned to her. As this injection of "real" history reveals, even the icons took time to create.

Jackie's tour of the White House also functions as one of many instances where the characters on *Mad Men* are represented as consumers of the visual and popular culture that surrounds them. They watch television, go to the movies, flip through magazines and read books like *Lady Chatterley's Lover*, *Atlas Shrugged*, *Confessions of an Advertising Man*, and *Meditations in an Emergency*. And, like us, they are influenced by what they see, hear, and read, emulating the styles, gestures, and phrases that comprise these cultural texts.[19] We are constantly reminded that their identities, as our own, are formed in part by their practices as fans. They are invested in, and actively identify with, the icons and culture of their age. In "Long Weekend" (1:10), Joan describes herself as feeling "stuck somewhere between Doris Day in *Pillow Talk* and *Midnight Lace*"; who she wants to be is "Kim Novak in just about anything."

Characters also label each other with the familiar and widely circulating constructs of the period. In "Maidenform" (2:6), Paul reduces Jackie Kennedy and Marilyn Monroe to two different archetypes of femininity and becomes convinced that his female colleagues at Sterling Cooper must be either one or the other. Salvatore agrees and explains that this classification is based on whether a woman is a line or a curve. Peggy, however, remains unconvinced and asks which one is she. Ken answers with "Gertrude Stein" in an attempt to deny her what he perceives to be a "proper" postwar conception of femininity, while Don suggests a somewhat older though no less mediated construct in Irene Dunne. However, what this scene ultimately recollects is the age-old misogynistic mother/whore dichotomy and the continued subjection of women to this binary.

Don too can be classified according to particular archetypes of masculinity, but ones which are sometimes at odds with each other. His physiognomy, voice and mannerisms recall 1950s Hollywood icons and, like his clothing and haircut, distance him from the emerging styles of the early 1960s. What he wears remains distinct from the flashier attire sported by younger executives and certainly from the sartorial signifiers of the counterculture modeled by Kurt and, at times, even Paul. Of course the color of the majority of Don's wardrobe ensures his association with Sloan Wilson's (and Nunnally Johnson's) *The Man in the Grey Flannel Suit* (1955; 1956), that icon of mid-century corporate conformity. This adds yet another layer of complexity to Don as he both embodies and rejects this model. On the one hand, he has clearly internalized the corporate ideology of 1950s America. He is, after all, interested in Sterling Cooper's success. On the other, he refuses to sign contracts and is irresponsibly truant when it matters most, slipping out of the office to see a movie or a mistress or out of a conference to experience California. In what follows, I want to suggest that the Fifties that Don represents and inhabits is in some — though not all — ways at odds with the vision of Camelot sustained by our collective imagination. Pitting the two against each other is a key way in which *Mad Men* complicates our understanding of mid-century America. And it is through the various juxtapositions of these two constructs that *Mad Men* engages with the tensions of this historical era.

Don's visual alignment with fifties culture is narratively reinforced in episodes dealing with generational conflict and especially through reference to markers of generational identity. For instance, Don's investment in the cinema is both visual and ideological, recalling the debates on delinquency, health, and morality that pitted film against television and, often times, one generation against another. He questions the value of this "new" medium of television and the worth in Harry's pursuit of a television department for Sterling Cooper. It is cinema that provides Don with his cultural references and functions as the site to which he escapes during the production of the Utz commercial, one featuring a television personality he detests and eventually slugs. He fails to recognize popular programs and scolds his children for sitting too close to the set. In fact, he does not even glance at the television to which his children are glued in the cramped quarters of his Roosevelt Hotel room. To be sure, Don's masculinity, however complex in some ways, is cinematic in origin and at a far remove from that modeled by Ward Cleaver, Jim Anderson or Steve Douglas, all of whom did much to carry forward a specifically fifties conception of patriarchy into the 1960s.

Don may look and act like a cinematic icon, but he identifies himself with a political one and, in the process, brings to light yet another major generational conflict. He sees in Nixon an individual from humble beginnings who achieved something through hard work and determination. In Kennedy, he sees a privileged, Ivy League socialite. Don's observations here are as much about Pete as they are about Kennedy. And though this alignment of Pete with Kennedy may seem sacrilegious to adherents of Camelot, it serves as a reminder that, in 1960, support for Kennedy was far from widespread. WASPs targeted his Catholicism while devotees of a grandfatherly Ike mistrusted his youth. During "Red in the Face" (1:7), Roger chides Kennedy for not wearing a hat and as "a boy too scared to do anything but go on vacation." Pete somewhat snidely observes that Elvis too does not wear a hat. Pete, as we know, is right, revealing an aptitude that Don and Roger lack, namely, a keen awareness of where things are headed and an understanding of why someone like Kennedy might appeal to the young.

Though Don is the protagonist, the age in which he lives is, in some ways, no longer his. What he represents, then, is the persistence of an earlier set of values, desires and anxieties into the 1960s. In doing so, he reminds us that the age of Camelot was as complex as any other, given as much to contradiction as any other, and circumscribed by a very permeable set of social, political, and cultural boundaries. He is both a conservative icon, as Cooper's references to Ayn Rand make clear, and, in terms of his philandering, Kennedy's kindred spirit. He shows little respect for the aims of the counterculture, but continues to be an unlikely participant in the activities of this world. He is clearly a product of the fifties, but not the sanitized version enlisted by Ronald Reagan or George Bush, Sr., to sell their reactionary policies. He embodies the elegance if not the style of Camelot and, at the same time, is evidence that the social justice ideals that this mythic construct have come to represent were far from being realized in any concrete, lived way. In fact, many of Don's younger colleagues are just as racist, sexist, anti–Semitic, and homophobic as those of his generation. Reference to the Freedom Riders, James Meredith, Bob Dylan, and even the fictional "Relax-icizer" may effectively presage the upheavals that would come to define the 1960s, but women and racial and ethnic minorities continue to be marginalized and oppressed.

Of course, racism, sexism, anti–Semitism, and homophobia continue to mar our contemporary moment as they did the 1950s and 1960s. *Mad Men* may evoke bigotry in the service of historical authenticity and in an effort to demonstrate how much attitudes have changed. But these slurs and exclusions are arguably less shocking and anachronistic to those who continue to experience them from individuals, groups, and institutionally-sanctioned discriminatory practices. *Mad Men*'s demystifications and engagement with constructed, mediated images may call to mind the relationship between images and reality and between the past and the present. Its ironic jokes about photocopiers, smoking, child care, Nixon and "new media" (e.g., television) may indeed keep one part of our viewing consciousness planted firmly in the present. However, the question remains as to whether or not its serious critiques of the past — and prompts to re-evaluate the present — go far enough.

Take, for example, this issue of fidelity to historical truth. We know from interviews and commentaries that considerable effort has been expended to manufacture a convincing surface realism, to capture as faithfully as possible the essence of the time. Critics were quick to respond whenever it failed to do so and highlighted the smallest inaccuracy. (Many column inches were devoted to the use of IBM Selectrics by the Sterling Cooper secretarial pool eleven months before their commercial availability.) Like many, the "Nixon vs. Kennedy" episode was the result of painstaking research that peeled away Camelot's veneer to show how the election was actually experienced in 1960. Its authenticity was even reinforced by the integration of historical footage. However, this story line, designed to give us access to a forgotten political truth, contains a scene that takes license with history and in a way that diminishes the force of *Mad Men*'s critique of sexism. Amid the drunken revelry at the prospect of a Nixon win, the junior Sterling Cooper employees participate in a game of "Scuttle." *Mad Men*'s version involves Ken chasing Allison, pinning her down and pulling up her skirt to identify the color of her underwear. The actual version, as described by Helen Gurley Brown in 1991, involved a group of male employees chasing a single female employee in order to remove her underwear entirely. Brown insists that "nothing wicked ever happened. Depantying was the sole object of the game" (A22). Though Ken's actions are deplorable, they are not as shocking as their source, nor as appalling as Brown's dismissal of it in the 1990s as harmless fun. The "real" version may not have made it past AMC's censors. It would have also introduced a profound sense of menace into an otherwise celebratory scene, perhaps upsetting the emotional syntax of this sequence. But in doing so it would have demonstrated the extent to which harassment was tolerated and condoned and the extent to which the casual sexism so pervasive at Sterling Cooper was just one of many ways in which women were subjugated, and one of many that had not yet been acknowledged by the legal system.

The extent of the effectiveness of *Mad Men*'s critique of the era it recreates remains an important question, one that might be easier to answer as the series takes us further into 1960s. In some instances, its critique has been incisive and compelling, in others, disappointingly weak. When Carla feels compelled to turn off the radio broadcast of Dr. Martin Luther King's "Eulogy for the Martyred Children" upon Betty's return to the kitchen in "Wee Small Hours" (3:9), we realize it is because of Betty's lack of support for and general apathy toward Civil Rights. We also understand that the visual and narrative marginalization of Hollis and Carla are meant to show us how African Americans were marginalized in early 1960s America. Nevertheless, another kind of exclusion is perpetuated through the absence of any insight into their experiences and lives outside their workplaces. And yet, the way in which *Mad Men* instills racist, sexist, anti–Semitic, and homophobic attitudes in characters with whom we are otherwise often expected to identify represents an important departure from comparable cinematic offerings like *Pleasantville* or *Far from Heaven*. Such a strategy might remind us, for example, that the Civil Rights initiatives that defined Kennedy as the benevolent king of Camelot did not suddenly eradicate or even diminish expressions of bigotry. Not to mention the realization that those who repeated racist slurs, for example, were not simply unfortunate victims of their age but active participants in the manufacture and preservation of racist discourse. The danger (and unfortunate reality), of course, is that some viewers do identify with these attitudes and see their representation in this way as a vindication of their own prejudices.[20]

When *Mad Men* succeeds in its critique of the past and the present, however, it is because of, rather than in spite of, its operation in the nostalgia mode. Its critical impulse is not something divorced from its visual pastness but dependent on those very things responsible for its label as nostalgic. *Mad Men*'s insights into how the early 1960s preserved the oppressive dimensions of the previous age, including its enduring myths, would be less incisive and certainly less layered without its visual evocation of the fifties. Likewise, the series' engagement with the manufacture and mediation of nostalgic constructs would be less trenchant, and sometimes even impossible, without deliberately archaic moments designed to account for the way practices of representation shape conceptions of the past. The ways in which *Mad Men* makes use of surface realism and deliberate archaism through production design, cinematography, and period casting exposes Camelot for analysis. It is through the deployment of these strategies that we come to realize how designed objects or aesthetic styles, for instance, do more than serve the interests of visual spectacle or the current retro economy. In *Mad Men*, these objects have the capacity to function as conduits to the age that produced them and to the later eras and impulses that recontextualized them.

Mad Men itself participates in the recontextualization and reconceptualization of such objects and, in the process, of what Camelot (and the fifties) can mean. It does so by reinscribing in these broader constructs aspects of history written out by myth-making enterprises, facets neglected for a variety of ideological reasons. Specific tropes too are redefined, accruing new connotations and significance. The mid-century modern office, the housewife in heels, and the image of children glued to the television on an oval rug are widely circulating ones that *Mad Men* has made an effort to retool and reinvent. Like *Far from Heaven* and other critical nostalgic screen fictions, it thus participates in a broader cultural discourse that has at its center these contested tropes and as its central concerns the meaning of mid-century America, the uses of myth, and even nostalgia itself.

By reinterpreting Camelot, *Mad Men* also complicates the two mythic period constructs that both flank and feed it: the fifties and the sixties and, in turn, the 1950s and 1960s. By collapsing the dominant impulses ascribed to each into a single period — and indeed even into a single character (Don) — it foregrounds the artificiality of the reductionism that each has undergone in the service of the culture wars.[21] It recalls for us that the 1950s were conformist and repressive, but also creative, dynamic and the time during which many progressive initiatives first emerged. It reminds us of the vast collective energy that propelled 1960s social movements, but also of the fervent support for reactionary policies that continued to be implemented throughout the decade. Of course the great majority of historical studies acknowledge as much and have revealed Kennedy's Camelot to be as mythic as its source. But this has done little to prevent its continued circulation, cultural potency, or perpetuation through visual and literary representations. In fact, *Mad Men*'s engagement with Camelot could not be timelier given its reemergence as the preferred metaphor to describe the Obama presidency.[22] Certainly there are parallels, both positive and negative,[23] based both on historically significant precedent and mythic invention. Perhaps *Mad Men* will prompt us to acknowledge the complexity of these links, to be aware of our era's self-mythologizing efforts, and to remember to cast as critical eye on the present as we do on the past.

I want to conclude with a brief anecdote that returns us to an earlier presidency and to the question of nostalgia. In 1971, Nixon was asked what he thought about nostalgia after seeing the Broadway production of *No, No, Nanette*. He answered positively, proclaiming: "I personally go for it" ("Nixon Endorses Nostalgia After Seeing 'Nanette'" 1). What he went for was the type of nostalgia defined by its investment in the material and visual culture of past eras, the type branded an "industry" just one year earlier. *No, No, Nanette* was a revival of a 1930s musical that, in an early example of period casting, starred Ruby Keeler. Nixon had nothing but praise for Keeler whom he remembered from her original cinematic performances in 1930s musicals. As such, he demonstrated a rather keen sense of what nostalgia had come to mean in the context of American popular culture. I wonder, however, if Don will too. If Weiner gets his wish to follow Don and Betty up to 1972 (Keveney 6D), will Don participate, like Nixon, in that decade's nostalgia boom? And, more specifically, will he participate in the fifties nostalgia economy by helping to produce its images? Will he do so with or without awareness of his own entrenchment in the fifties? And thus, will the *Mad Men* of 1972 continue to rely as much on the fifties as the *Mad Men* of 1962?

NOTES

1. The term "nostalgia" was first coined by Johannes Hofer in 1688 to describe the homesickness experienced by Swiss mercenaries. He did so by marrying the words *nostos* (a return home) and *algos* (a painful condition). See Hofer 376–91.

2. The jarring disjunction between the Cleavers and the Drapers is made readily apparent when Don's children watch *Leave It to Beaver* (1957–63) in his hotel room during his separation from Betty. This moment emphasizes how Don and Betty's neglectful and risky approach to parenting is at odds with that represented in 1950s and 1960s domestic sitcoms.

3. Despite overlaps and necessary conflations, I will use "fifties" to refer to the nostalgic construct and "1950s" to the actual, historical decade.

4. I will focus specifically on props and set design and touch only brief on costume. To do justice to *Mad Men*'s uses and significance of costume requires a separate study in its own right.

5. For a convincing discussion of how *Pleasantville* accomplishes this see Grainge "Memory and Popular Film" pp. 202–219.

6. Myths too are as important as records of historical facts and events as they give us access to the anxieties and desires of the eras that invented them (Sprengler 64).

7. Dika makes this argument about *Last Exit to Brooklyn* (1989). See p. 142.

8. Reviewers have also cited the mix the program achieves between nostalgia and "slack-jawed horror" (Ahrens D01) and nostalgia and "abhorrence" (Wilson 33).

9. See Sprengler 3.

10. See, for example, Martin 102.

11. I personally recognize these and many other props as the objects that defined my own late 1970s and early 1980s childhood. In my case, the ubiquity 1950s objects was the result of parents who were children of the depression (and thus internalized a depression-era mentality about preservation) but built and decorated their house during the 1950s.

12. See Soll p. 14 for a precise list of the period furnishings and objects in Don's office as well as a list of "modern takes" (i.e., contemporary knock-offs) and where to purchase them.

13. See for example Cooke p. 46 who argues that *Mad Men*'s 1960s interiors and clothes are not "clever distraction[s], but ... fine metaphors (a 'chip and dip' plate signifies a marriage too deeply embedded in social mobility...).

14. However, when a professional designer brings a more "modern" aesthetic into Betty's home in "Seven Twenty Three" (3:7), Betty "ruins" the look by adding an overtly feminine object. That is, she effectively subverts the modernist design logic of her new living room by placing an ornate Victorian fainting couch in front of the fireplace. For an analysis of gender and modernist design see Reed or Attfield and Kirkham.

15. In fact, Abraham purposively tasked his mid-century aesthetic with channeling the essence of its historical moment. He explains: "1960 was on the precipice of change in terms of design and politics, and that was definitely something we were trying to capture" (Feld, Oppenheimer, and Stasukevich 47).

16. In the audio commentary for "Smoke Gets in Your Eyes," Weiner explains that he joked to Abraham that "Edward Hopper is going to see this and sue you."

17. There are other moments in *Mad Men* that appear to have been inspired by Todd Haynes' Sirkian vision of Hartford, Connecticut. The color schemes, quality of light, and style of furnishings in Betty and Don's bedroom recall Cathy Whitaker's well-appointed home. However, it is important to note that Weiner's script for the pilot of *Mad Men* predates the release of *Far from Heaven* by two years (Keveney 6D).

18. Hamm also shares with Jimmy Stewart and Cary Grant the ability to appear much older than his actual age. A further connection with Cary Grant is established through Don's initial introduction in the opening scene of the pilot. Don's reveal is almost identical to Devlin's in *Notorious* (1946).

19. Some of these references may also have unintentional consequences, depending on the familiarity that viewers have with 1950s cinema. Peggy's "basket of kisses" may sound corporately cute, but it might also recall Rhoda's (Patty McCormack) incessant repetition of this phrase in *The Bad Seed* (1956).

20. Consider, for instance, the many blogs that vaunt Don Draper for his unapologetic sexism. "Anti-political correctness" is also celebrated in responses to the show and often in ways that reveal how the term has come to function in reactionary discourse as a euphemism for bigotry.

21. See Marcus for an excellent, in-depth discussion of how the Fifties and Sixties were used in the culture wars of the 1980s and 1990s.

22. Consider, for example, this portion of Caroline Kennedy's endorsement speech: "Over the years, I've been deeply moved by the people who've told me they wish they could feel inspired and hopeful about America the way people did when my father was president. This longing is even more profound today. Fortunately, there is one candidate who offers that same sense of hope and inspiration, and I am proud to endorse Senator Barack Obama for president (Tucker C01). It is little surprise that *The Washington Post* and other publications referred to Obama as Camelot's "New Knight."

23. Despite the promise of advancement in social justice issues, both Kennedy and Obama have been criticized for not going far enough. Kennedy was not always as ardent a supporter of Civil Rights as Camelot makes him out to be. Nor is Obama as supportive of Gay Rights as his rhetoric about change might suggest.

WORKS CITED

Ahrens, Frank. "The Real Mad Men and Women of Washington." *The Washington Post* 21 July 2008: D01.

Attfield, Judy and Pat Kirkham, eds. *A View From the Interior: Women and Design.* London: The Women's Press, 1994.

Brown, Helen Gurley. "At Work, Sexual Electricity Sparks Creativity." *Wall Street Journal* 29 Oct. 1991: A22.

Cook, Pam. *Screening the Past: Memory and Nostalgia in Cinema.* London: Routledge, 2005.

Cooke, Rachel. "The Art of Darkness." *The New Statesman* 16 Feb. 2009: 46.

Dika, Vera. *Recycled Culture in Contemporary Art and Film: The Uses of Nostalgia.* Cambridge: Cambridge University Press, 2003.

Feld, Rob, Jean Oppenheimer and Iain Stasukevich. "Tantalizing Television." *American Cinematographer* 89.3 (2008): 46–57.

Gilbert, Matthew. "Slick Mad Men Visits Madison Ave. at Dawn of the '60s." *The Boston Globe* 19 July 2007: E1.

Grainge, Paul. *Monochrome Memories: Nostalgia and Style in Retro America.* Westport: Praeger, 2002.

_____. "Colouring the Past: *Pleasantville* and the Textuality of Media Memory." *Memory and Popular Film.* Ed. Paul Grainge. Manchester: Manchester University Press, 2003. 202–219.

High, Kamau. "Matthew Weiner's No Madman." *Adweek* 30 July 2007. Web. 12 March 2009. <http://www.adweek.com/aw/esearch/article_display.jsp?vnu_context_id=1003615039>.

Higson, Andrew. "Re-presenting the National Past: Nostalgia and Pastiche in the Heritage Film." *British Cinema and Thatcherism.* Ed. Lester Friedman. London. UCL Press: 1993. 109–29.

Hofer, Johannes. "Medical Dissertation on Nostalgia." Trans. Carolyn Kiser Anspach. *Bulletin of the History of Medicine* 2 (1934): 376–91.

Jameson, Fredric. *Postmodernism, Or the Cultural Logic of Late Capitalism.* Durham, NC: Duke University Press, 1991.

Keveney, Bill. "Mad Men Stands Test of Time." *USA Today* 17 September 2008: 6D.

La Ferla, Ruth. "A Return to That Drop-dead Year 1960." *New York Times* 23 Aug. 2007: G1.

Le Sueur, Marc. "Theory Number Five: Anatomy of Nostalgia Films: Heritage and Methods." *Journal of Popular Film* 6.2 (1977): 187–197.

Littleton, Cynthia. "Smoke and Mirrors: Hamm's in the Gravy ... at Last." *Variety* 29 Sept.–5 Oct. 2008: 5, 72.

Marcus, Daniel. *Happy Days and Wonder Years: The Fifties and Sixties in Contemporary Cultural Politics.* New Brunswick, NJ: Rutgers University Press, 2004.

Martin, Alexander R. "Nostalgia." *American Journal of Psychoanalysis* 14.1 (1954): 93–104.

"Nixon Endorses Nostalgia After Seeing 'Nanette.'" *New York Times* 5 Aug. 1971: 1.

Reed, Christopher, ed. *Not At Home: The Suppression of Domesticity in Modern Art and Architecture.* New York: Thames and Hudson, 1996.

Sloane, Leonard. "Nostalgia for Extinct Pop Culture Creates Industry." *New York Times* 22 Mar. 1970: 171.

Soll, Lindsay, "An Office and a Gentleman." *Entertainment Weekly* 1 Aug. 2008: 14.

Sprengler, Christine. *Screening Nostalgia: Populuxe Props and Technicolor Aesthetics in Contemporary American Film.* New York: Berghahn Books, 2009.

Strauss, Gary. "Mad Men Delves into Gold Age of Ad Men." *USA Today* 18 July 2007: 4D.

Taylor, Alan. "Nixon vs. Kennedy" (Audio Commentary). *Mad Men Season One.* Writ. Matthew Weiner, Lisa Albert, André Jacquemetton and Maria Jacquemetton. Dir. Alan Taylor. AMC. 11 Oct. 2007. DVD. Lions Gate Television, 2008.

Tucker, Neely. "Barack Obama, Camelot's New Knight: The Shining Armor of JFK's Legacy." *Washington Post.* 29 January 2008: C01.

Usborne, David. "Mad For It." *The Independent* 23 Sept. 2008: 32.
Weiner, Matthew. "Smoke Gets in Your Eyes" (Audio Commentary). *Mad Men Season One*. Writ. Matthew Weiner. Dir. Alan Taylor. AMC. 19 July 2007. DVD. Lions Gate Television, 2008.
_____. "Shoot" (Audio Commentary). *Mad Men Season One*. Writ. Matthew Weiner and Chris Provenzano. Dir. Paul Feig. AMC. 13 Sept. 2007. DVD. Lions Gate Television, 2008.
White, Theodore H. "For President Kennedy: An Epilogue." *Life* 6 Dec. 1963: 158–159.
Wilson, Benji. "Smoke and Ire." *The Times* 1 Mar. 2008: 33.

Episode Guide and Cast List

Central Cast

Don Draper — Jon Hamm
Roger Sterling — John Slattery
Pete Campbell — Vincent Kartheiser
Betty Draper — January Jones
Joan Holloway — Christina Hendricks
Peggy Olson — Elisabeth Moss
Paul Kinsey — Michael Gladis
Ken Cosgrove — Aaron Staton
Harry Crane — Rich Sommer
Salvatore Romano — Bryan Batt
Bertram Cooper — Robert Morse
Herman "Duck" Phillips — Mark
  Moses
Trudy Campbell — Alison Brie
Francine Hanson — Anne Dudek
Mona Sterling — Talia Balsam
Sally Draper — Kiernan Shipka
Robert "Bobby" Draper — Maxwell
  Huckabee (Season One)
Robert "Bobby" Draper — Aaron Hart
  (Season Two)
Robert "Bobby" Draper — Jared S.
  Gilmore (Season Three)

1:1   SMOKE GETS IN YOUR EYES

Matthew Weiner, Writer
Alan Taylor, Director
Midge Daniels — Rosemarie DeWitt
Lee Garner, Sr. — John Cullum
Lee Garner, Jr. — Darren Pettie
Dr. Emerson — Remy Auberjonois
Hildy — Julie McNiven

Ivy — Zandy Hartig
Bartender — Jack O'Connell
Busboy — Henry Afro-Bradley
Nanette — Kristen Schaal
Marjorie — Bess Rous
Camille — Emma Roberts
Cleo — Jamie Proctor
Wanda — Heather Klar
Old Waiter — Mark McGann

1:2   LADIES ROOM

Matthew Weiner, Writer
Alan Taylor, Director
Midge Daniels — Rosemarie DeWitt
Helen Bishop — Darby Stanchfield
Dr. Arnold Wayne — Andy Umberger
Waiter #2 — Simon Harvey
Ladies' Room Attendant — Cecelia
  Antoinette
Samuel — Darryl Alan Reed
Waiter #1 — Bob Rumnock
Dale — Mark Kelly
Ernie — Josiah Polhemus
Glen Bishop — Marten Holden Weiner

1:3   MARRIAGE OF FIGARO

Tom Palmer, Writer
Ed Bianchi, Director
George Pelham — Alastair Duncan
Carlton Hanson — Kristoffer Polaha
Helen Bishop — Darby Stanchfield
Chet Wallace — Drew Wicks
Marilyn Farrelly — Jeanne Simpson

253

Joyce Darling — Adria Tennor
Jack Farrelly — Price Carson
Ernie Hanson — Josiah Polhemus
Glen Bishop — Marten Holden Weiner
Andy Darling — Jonathan Nail
Nancy Wallace — Kate Connor
Allison — Alexa Alemanni
Hildy — Julie McNiven
Judy — Jennifer Fitzgerald
Carol — Lauren Hackman
Chinese Man — Michael David Cheng
Conductor — Kent Kasper

1:4   NEW AMSTERDAM

Lisa Albert, Writer
Tim Hunter, Director
Helen Bishop — Darby Stanchfield
Andrew Campbell — Christopher Allport
Tom Vogel — Joe O'Connor
Walter Veith — Randy Oglesby
Dr. Arnold Wayne — Andy Umberger
Dorothy Campbell — Channing Chase
Mrs. Clifford Lyman — Barbara Kerr Condon

1:5   5G

Matthew Weiner, Writer
Lesli Linka Galatter, Director
Adam Whitman — Jay Paulson
Charlie Fiddich — Andy Hoff
Jack Kongi — Jim Abele
Alison — Alexa Alemanni
Judy — Jennifer Fitzgerald
Donna — Sarah Jannett Parish
Dr. Gretta Guttman — Gordana Rashovich
Nick Rodis — Bruno Oliver
Yoram Ben Shulhai — Danny Jacobs
Ginger — Heather Fox
Waiter — George Anthony Alvarez
Abigail — Brynn Horrocks
Poetry Girl — Megan Duffy
Mack Johnson — Morgan Rusler
Dick — Brandon Killham
Hungarian Man — Hrach Titizian

1:6   BABYLON

Andre Jacquemetton and Maria Jacquemetton, Writers
Andrew Bernstein, Director
Fred Rumsen — Joel Murray
Margaret Sterling — Elizabeth Rice
Barbara Katz — Rebecca Creskoff
Lily Meyer — Irene Roseen
Roy Hazelitt — Ian Bohen
Gaudy Hat — Flora Plumb
Delia — Susan Grace
Hollis — La Monde Byrd
Charlie — Doug Hale
Round Mom — Allison Fleming
Waiter (Chop House) — Gary Ballard

1:7   RED IN THE FACE

Bridget Bedard, Writer
Tim Hunter, Director
Helen Bishop — Darby Stanchfield
Dr. Arnold Wayne — Andy Umberger
Carol McCardy — Kate Norby
Kicks Matherton — Teddy Sears
Rosemary — Shayna Rose
Allison — Alexa Alemanni

1:8   THE HOBO CODE

Chris Provenzano, Writer
Phil Abraham, Director
Midge Daniels — Rosemarie Dewitt
Fred Rumsen — Joel Murray
Lois Sadler — Crista Flanagan
Hugh Brody — Bruce French
Elliot Lawrence — Paul Keeley
Judd — Brian Klugman
Roy Hazelitt — Ian Bohen
Archie Whitman — Joseph Culp
Hobo — Paul Schulze
Marge — Stephanie Courtney
Hildy — Julie McNiven
Ross Beresford — Rick Scarry

1:9   SHOOT

Chris Provenzano and Matthew Weiner, Writers
Paul Feig, Director

Ronnie Gittridge — Nathan Anderson
Lois Sadler — Crista Flanagan
Jim Hobart — H. Richard Green
Dr. Arnold Wayne — Andy Umberger
Adele Hobart — Dey Young

1:10   LONG WEEKEND

Briget Bedard, Andre Jacquemetton,
  Maria Jacquemetton and Matthew
  Weiner, Writers
Tim Hunter, Director
Caroll McCardy — Kate Norby
Margaret Sterling — Elizabeth Rice
Eleanor Ames — Megan Stier
Mirabellle Ames — Alexis Stier
Franklin Newcomb — John Walcutt
Ralph Stubbs — Scott Michael Morgan
Gene Driscoll — Ryan Cutrona
Abraham Menken — Allan Miller
Dick — Brandon Killham
Abigail Whitman — Brynn Horrocks
Hollis — La Monde Byrd
Marge — Stephanie Courtney
Dora — Kathryn Taylor
Duane Davis — Barry Livingston
Marty Faraday — Anthony Burch
Joyce (aka Judy) — Rona Benson
Kibby — Anna Campbell
Hildy — Julie McNiven
Donna — Sarah Jannett Parish

1:11   INDIAN SUMMER

Tom Palmer and Matthew Weiner,
  Writers
Tim Hunter, Director
Fred Rumsen — Joel Murray
Dr. Arnold Wayne — Andy Umberger
Adam Whitman — Jay Paulson
Barbara Zax — Rebecca Creskoff
Lee Garner, Sr. — John Cullum
Carl Winter — Aaron Hill
Bob Shaw — Adam Kaufman
Hildy — Julie McNiven
Waiter — Mario Piccirillo
Marjorie — Bess Rous
Vincent — Dominic Testa

1:12   NIXON VS. KENNEDY

Lisa Albert, Andre Jacquemetton and
  Maria Jacquemetton, Writers
Alan Taylor, Director
Lieutenant — Troy Ruptash
Allison — Alexa Alemanni
Hildy — Julie McNiven
Marge — Stephanie Courtney
Mack Johnson — Morgan Rusler
Mae — Heather Seiffert
Abigail Whitman — Brynn Horrocks
Sergeant — Cassius Willis
Doctor — Kevin Symons
Colonel — Stewart Skelton
Young Adam — David Kronenberg
Army Chaplain Lt. Mitchell — Dared
  Wright

1:13   THE WHEEL

Matthew Weiner and Robin Veith,
  Writers
Matthew Weiner, Director
Dr. Arnold Wayne — Andy Umberger
Tom Vogel — Joe O'Connor
Jeannie Vogel — Sheila Shaw
Annie — Katherine Boecher
Dr. Oliver — Gregory Wagrowski
Night Manager — James Keane
Glen Bishop — Marten Holden Weiner
Rita — Mandy McMillian
Nurse Wilson — Maura Soden
Joe Harriman — Ross Mackenzie
Janet — Lisa Lupu
Lynn Taylor — Richard Willgrubs
Victor Manny — Jonthan Walker
  Spencer
Carla — Deborah Lacey

2:1   FOR THOSE WHO THINK YOUNG

Matthew Weiner, Writer
Tim Hunter, Director
Fred Rumsen — Joel Murray
Arthur — Gabriel Mann
Sarah Beth — Missy Yager
Smitty — Patrick Cavanaugh
Gertie — Denise Crosby

Lois Sadler — Crista Flanagan
Chuck — Seamus Dever
Jim — Scott MacArthur
Kitty Romano — Sarah Drew
Juanita — Jennifer Siebel
Greg Harris — Gerald Downey
Doctor Adams — David Bowe
Driver — John Thaddeus
Hildy — Julie McNiven
Carla — Deborah Lacey
Dale — Mark Kelly
Jones — Jeff Grace
Curtis — Frank Novak
Kurt — Edin Gali (Galijasevic)
Nurse — Tess Alexander Parker
Delivery Man — Michael C. Alexander
Older Woman — Norma Michaels

2:2 FLIGHT 1

Lisa Albert and Matthew Weiner, Writers
Andrew Bernstein, Director
Freddy Rumsen — Joel Murray
Lois — Crista Flanagan
Sheila — Donielle Artese
Carlton — Kristoffer Polaha
Dorothy Campbell — Channing Chase
Kitty — Sarah Drew
Katherine Olson — Myra Turley
Anita Olson Respola — Audrey Wasilewski
Gerry Respola — Jerry O'Donnell
Jennifer Crane — Laura Regan
Bud Campbell — Rich Hutchman
Priest (Monsignor Cavanaugh) — Christopher Carroll
Shel Keneally — Vaughn Armstrong
Henry Wofford — Matt Riedy
Eugene — John Patrick Jordan
Hildy — Julie McNiven
Donna — Sarah Jannett Parish
Asian Waitress — Elizabeth Tsing
Gerry Respola, Jr. — Andrew Astor
Judy Campbell — Miranda Lilley
Leroy — Maurice Patton
Sheila White — Donielle Artese

2:3 THE BENEFACTOR

Matthew Weiner and Rick Cleveland, Writers
Lesli Linka Glatter, Director
Freddy Rumsen — Joel Murray
Lois — Crista Flanagan
Sarah Beth — Missy Yager
Arthur — Gabriel Mann
Gertie — Denise Crosby
Jennifer Crane — Laura Regan
Tara — Cameron Goodman
Bobbie Barrett — Melinda McGraw
Jimmy Barrett — Patrick Fischler
Edith Schilling — Jan Hoag
Hunt Schilling — Steve Stapenhorst
Elliot Lawrence — Paul Keeley
Flatty — Nat Faxon
Todd — Brian Norris
Warren McKenna — John Douglas Williams
Waiter (Rob Espierre) — Phillipe Bergeron

2:4 THREE SUNDAYS

Andre Jacquemetton and Maria Jacquemetton, Writers
Tim Hunter, Director
Margaret Sterling — Elizabeth Rice
Katherine Olson — Myra Turley
Anita Olson Respola — Audrey Wasilewski
Gerry Respola — Jerry O'Donnell
Monsignor Cavanaugh — Christopher Carroll
Father John Gill — Colin Hanks
Bobbie Barrett — Melinda McGraw
Jimmy Barrett — Patrick Fischler
Marty Hasselbach — Michael Dempsey
Vicky — Marguerite Morea
Joyce — Julia Carpenter
Tootsie Yates — Cathrine Grace
Brooks — Derek Ray
Gerry Respola, Jr. — Andrew Astor

2:5 THE NEW GIRL

Robin Veith, Writer
Jennifer Getzinger, Director

Fred Rumsen — Joel Murray
Rachel Menken — Maggie Siff
Katherine Olson — Myra Turley
Anita Olson Respola — Audrey
    Wasilewski
Bobbie Barrett — Melinda McGraw
Jimmy Barrett — Patrick Fischler
Dr. Gosman — Donald Sage Mackay
Officer Hahn — Jack Impellizzeri
Tilden Katz — Nick Toren
Dr. Eric Stone — John Getz
Jane Siegel — Peyton List
Ethel — Jennifer Dawson

2:6   MAIDENFORM

Matthew Weiner, Writer
Phil Abraham, Director
Bobbie Barrett — Melinda McGraw
Freddy Rumsen — Joel Murray
Arthur Case — Gabriel Mann
Jane Siegel — Peyton List
Bud Campbell — Rich Hutchman
Crab Colson — Matt McKenzie
Pauline Phillips — Alexandra Paul
Patricia Phillips — Gina Devivo
Len McKenzie — Peter Jason
Chester Rockingham — Edmund L.
    Schaff
Joyce — Julia Carpenter
Judy Campbell — Miranda Lilley
Marcy Patterson — Kim Swennen
Harold Wadro — Jonathan Strait
Griz Patterson — Jesse Henecke
Webb — Greg Felden
William Redd — Benjamin Seay
Mark Phillips — Darian Weiss
Susie Phillips — Sarah Wright

2:7   THE GOLD VIOLIN

Jane Anderson, Andre Jacquemetton
    and Maria Jacquemetton, Writers
Andrew Bernstein, Director
Anna — Melinda Page Hamilton
Bobbie Barrett — Melinda McGraw
Jimmy Barrett — Patrick Fischler
Kitty Romano — Sarah Drew
Jane Siegel — Peyton List

Smitty — Patrick Cavanaugh
Wayne Kirkeby — Adam Godley
Jim Van Dyke — Tom Ormeny
Mr. Wheatley — Gareth Williams
Kurt — Edin Gali (Galijasevic)
Andrew Colville — Gregory Franklin

2:8   A NIGHT TO REMEMBER

Robin Veith and Matthew Weiner,
    Writers
Lesli Linka Glatter, Director
Father John Gill — Colin Hanks
Greg Harris — Sam Page
Anita Olson Respola — Audrey
    Wasilewski
Crab Colson — Matt McKenzie
Petra Colson — Amy Landecker
Phil Mathewson — Christopher Murray
Richard Hanson — Marty Ryan
Hollis — La Monde Byrd
Carla — Deborah Lacey
Hildy — Julie McNiven
Woman — Joeanna Sayler
Bouncer — Angelo Tsarouchas

2:9   SIX MONTH LEAVE

Andre Jacquemetton, Maria
    Jacquemetton and Matthew Weiner,
    Writers
Michael Uppendahl, Director
Freddy Rumsen — Joel Murray
Arthur Case — Gabriel Mann
Jimmy Barrett — Patrick Fischler
Jane Siegel — Peyton List
Sarah Beth — Missy Yager
Carla — Deborah Lacey
Warren McKenna — John Douglas
    Williams
Tootsie Yates — Catherine Grace
Dan Lindstrom — Jonathan Runyon
Kelly Washburn — Carolyn McDer-
    mott
Jim Pastern — Caleb Moody
Wally Kostis — Chet Grissom
Old Waiter — Mark McGann

2:10 THE INHERITANCE

Lisa Albert, Marti Noxon and
Matthew Weiner, Writers
Andrew Bernstein, Director
Helen Bishop — Darby Stanchfield
William Hofstadt — Eric Ladin
Bud Campbell — Rich Hutchman
Gene Hofstadt — Ryan Cutrona
Judy Hofstadt — Megan Henning
Dorothy Campbell — Channing Chase
Viola — Aloma Wright
Carla — Deborah Lacey
Hildy — Julie McNiven
Allison — Alexa Alemanni
Glen Bishop — Marten Holden Weiner
Sheila White — Donielle Artese
Hollis — La Monde Byrd
Gloria Massey Hofstadt — Darcy Shean

2:11 THE JET SET

Matthew Weiner, Writer
Phil Abraham, Director
Joy — Laura Ramsey
Willy — Philippe Brenninkmeyer
Rocci — Justine Eyre
Klaus — Bjorn Johnson
Jane Siegel — Peyton List
Saint John Powell — Charles Shaugh-
nessy
George Rothman — Alan Blumenfeld
Christian — Rudolf Martin
Stu Rogison — Kevin Christy
Carlos — Emilio Roso
Greta — Nina Franoszek
Smitty — Patrick Cavanaugh
Alec Martin — Brandon Hayes
Kurt — Edin Gali (Galijasevic)

2:12 THE MOUNTAIN KING

Matthew Weiner and Robin Veith,
Writers
Alan Taylor, Director
Anna — Melinda Page Hamilton
Greg Harris — Sam Page
Sarah Beth — Missy Yager
Tom Vogel — Joe O'Connor
Kess — Brian Krause

Walt — Josh Braaten
Alice Cooper — Mary Anne McGarry
Ned — Collin Christopher
John Dickenson — Gregg Perrie
Teddy — Charles Weiner

2:13 MEDITATIONS IN AN EMERGENCY

Matthew Weiner and Kater Gordon,
Writers
Matthew Weiner, Director
Father John Gill — Colin Hanks
Gentleman — Ryan McPartlin
Katherine Olson — Myra Turley
Lois Sadler — Crista Flanagan
Saint John Powell — Charles Shaugh-
nessy
Dr. Aldrich — David Doty
Marie — Beverly Leech
Mrs. Conyers — Patti Tippo
Hildy — Julie McNiven
Carla — Deborah Lacey
Alec Martin — Brandon Hayes
Bartender — Joe Roseto

3:1 OUT OF TOWN

Matthew Weiner, Writer
Phil Abraham, Director
Lane Pryce — Jared Harris
John Hooker — Ryan Cartwright
Archie Whitman — Joseph Culp
Carrie — Lauri Johnson
Burt Peterson — Michael Gaston
Shelly — Sunny Mabrey
Morris Mann — Jack Kehler
Hildy — Julie McNiven
Lola — Trisha LaFache
Abigail Whitman — Brynn Horrocks
Evangeline — Kelly Huddleston
Lorelai — Annie Little
Bellhop — Orestes Arcuni
Howard Mann — Jamie Elman

3:2 LOVE AMONG THE RUINS

Cathryn Humphries and Matthew
Weiner, Writers

Lesli Linka Glatter, Director
Lane Pryce — Jared Harris
John Hooker — Ryan Cartwright
Mona Sterling — Talia Balsam
Margaret Sterling- Elizabeth Rice
Allison — Alexa Alemann
Gene Hofstadt — Ryan Cutrona
Judy Hofstadt — Megan Henning
Rebecca Pryce — Embeth Davidtz
Edgar Raffit — Kevin Cooney
Charlie — James Immekus
Brooks — Derek Ray
Ralph Buckland — Jeremy Scott Johnson
Arnold Merriman — Brian Carpenter
Man #1— Mark Brandon
College Boy — Bill Finnigan
Scott — Austin Trace

3:3 MY OLD KENTUCKY HOME

Dahvi Waller and Matthew Weiner,
Writers
Jennifer Getzinger, Director
Olive Healy — Judy Kain
Greg Harris — Sam Page
Gene Hoftstadt — Ryan Cutrona
Smitty — Patrick Cavanaugh
Jane Sterling — Peyton List
Jennifer Crane — Laura Regan
Jeffrey Graves — Miles Fisher
Henry Francis — Christopher Stanley
Ronald Ettinger — Tim Snay
Irene Ettinger — Pamela Roylance
Honey Stolich — Judy Tylor
Carla — Deborah Lacey
Allison — Alexa Alemanni
Hillary — Amy Scott
Rick Stolich — Jamison Haase

3:4 THE ARRANGEMENTS

Andrew Colville and Matthew Weiner,
Writers
Michael Uppendahl, Director
Lane Pryce — Jared Harris
John Hooker — Ryan Cartwright
Gene Hoftstadt — Ryan Cutrona
Kitty Romano — Sarah Drew

William Hofstadt — Eric Ladin
Judy Hofstadt — Megan Henning
Katherine Olson — Myra Turley
Anita Olson Respola — Audrey
Wasilewski
Lois Sadler — Crista Flanagan
Karen Ericson — Carla Gallo
Horace Cook, JR — Aaron Stanford
Horace Cook, SR — David Selby
Herb Emmert — Ken Meseroll
Officer Hinkle — James Howell
Ronnie Santorella — James Giordano
Gary Osborn — Daniel Kountz
Allison — Alexa Alemanni
Ann Margret Type — Kelsey Sanders
Anchorman — Larry Anderson

3:5 THE FOG

Kater Gordon, Writer
Phil Abraham, Director
Duck Phillips — Mark Moses
Lane Pryce — Jared Harris
Francine Hanson — Anne Dudek
Gene Hoftstadt — Ryan Cutrona
Hollis — Le Monde Byrd
Miss Farrell — Abigail Spencer
Nurse Mary — Yeardley Smith
Nurse Elain — Jayne Taini
Dennis Hobart — Matt Bushnell
Bob Adamson — Michael Canavan
Raymond Garvey — Peter Breitmeyer
Hildy — Julie McNiven (off camera
work, no billing)
Allison — Alexa Alemanni
Officer Hinkle — James Howell
Ruth Hofstadt — Lou Mulford

3:6 GUY WALKS INTO AN ADVERTISING AGENCY

Robin Veith and Matthew Weiner,
Writers
Lesli Linka Glatter, Director
Lane Pryce — Jared Harris
John Hooker — Ryan Cartwright
Olive Healy — Judy Kain
Lois Sadler — Christa Flanagan
Greg Harris — Sam Page

Smitty — Patick Cavanaugh
Saint John Powell — Charles Shaugh-
nessy
Guy Mackendrick — Jamie Thomas
King
Connie — Chelcie Ross
Miss Wakeman — Carol Locatell
Hildy — Julie McNiven
Allison — Alexa Alemanni
Kurt — Edin Gali
Dale — Mark Kelly
Harold Ford — Neil Dickson

3:7   SEVEN TWENTY THREE

Andre Jacquemetton, Maria
Jacquemetton and Matthew Weiner,
Writers
Daisy von Scherler Mayer, Director
Duck Phillips — Mark Moses
Lane Pryce — Jared Harris
Connie — Chelcie Ross
Henry Francis — Christopher Stanley
Francine Hanson — Anne Dudek
Carlton Hanson — Kristoffer Polaha
Miss Farrell — Abigail Spencer
Doug — Trevore O'Brien
Sandy — Erin Sanders
Archie Whitman — Joseph Culp
Cynthia Stevens — Jacqueline Hahn
Allison — Alexa Alemanni
Marilyn Farrelly — Jeanne Simpson
Waitress — Dani Repp

3:8   SOUVENIR

Lisa Albert and Matthew Weiner,
Writers
Phil Abraham, Director
Henry Francis — Christopher Stanley
Connie — Chelcie Ross
Mayor Johnson — Mark Metcalf
Saleswoman — Joanne Baron
Gudrun — Nina Rausch
Fabrizio — Federico Dordei
Luca — Giuseppe Raucci
Ed Lawrence — New Vaughn
Hildy — Julie McNiven
Carla — Deborah Lacey

Marilyn Farrelly — Jeanne Simposon
Bellboy — Edoarda Beghi
Ernie Hanson — Josiah Polhemus

3.9   WEE SMALL HOURS

Dahvi Waller and Matthew Weiner,
Writers
Scott Hornbacher, Director
Henry Francis — Christopher Stanley
Connie — Chelcie Ross
Smitty — Patrick Cavanaugh
Suzanne Farrell — Abigail Spencer
Lee Garner, Jr. — Darren Pettie
Allison — Alexa Alemanni
Carla — Deborah Lacey
Marilyn Farrelly — Jeanne Simpson
Kurt — Edin Gali
Joyce Darling — Adria Tennor
Jerry — Jim Hoffmaster
Elsa Kittridge — Ann Ryerson
Marty Faraday — Anthony Burch

3:10   THE COLOR BLUE

Kater Gordon and Matthew Weiner,
Writers
Michael Uppendahl, Director
Lane Pryce — Jared Harris
Rebecca Pryce — Embeth Davidtz
Henry Francis — Christopher Stanley
Suzanne Farrell — Abigail Spencer
Saint John Powell — Charles Shaugh-
nessy
Danny Farrell — Marshall Allman
Jane Sterling — Peyton List
Lois Sadler — Crista Flanagan
Jennifer Crane — Laura Regan
John Hooker — Ryan Cartwright
Alice Cooper — Mary Anne McGarry
Achilles — Hal Landon, Jr.
Carla — Deborah Lacey
Allison — Alexa Alemanni
Harold Ford — Neil Dickson
Marty Faraday — Anthony Burch
Nellie — Shannon Welles

3:11   THE GYPSY AND THE HOBO

Marti Noxon, Cathryn Humphris and
 Matthew Weiner, Writers
Jennifer Getzinger, Director
Carlton Hanson — Kristoffer Polaha
Greg Harris — Sam Page
Smitty — Patrick Cavanaugh
Suzanne Farrell — Abigail Spencer
William Hofstadt — Eric Ladin
Annabelle Mathis — Mary Page Keller
Milton Lowell — Dan Desmond
Marty Faraday — Anthony Burch
Kurt — Edin Gali
Researcher — Troy Vincent
Bulldog Man — Jay Burns
Mutt Man — Mark Doerr
Griffon Woman — Julie Sanford

3:12   THE GROWN UPS

Brett Johnson and Matthew Weiner,
 Writers
Barbet Schroeder, Director
Lane Pryce — Jared Harris
Duck Phillips — Mark Moses
Margaret Sterling — Elizabeth Rice
Jane Sterling — Peyton List
Jennifer Crane — Laura Regan
Karen Ericson — Carla Gallo
Henry Francis — Christopher Stanley
Jean Marie Charcot — Ivo Nandi
Olive Healy — Judy Kain
Allison — Alexa Alemanni
Marty Faraday — Anthony Burch
Carla — Deborah Lacey
Hildy — Julie McNiven
Nellie — Shannon Welles
Kurt — Edid Gali
Brooks Hargrove — Derek Ray
Ethel (Secretary) — Jennifer Dawson
Bandleader — Sewell Whitney
Bruce Pike — Patrick John Hurley
Eleanor Francis — Veronica Taylor

3:13   SHUT THE DOOR, HAVE A SEAT

Matthew Weiner and Erin Levy, Writers
Mathew Weiner, Director

Lane Pryce — Jared Harris
John Hooker — Ryan Cartwright
Smitty — Patrick Cavanaugh
Saint John Powell — Charles Shaugh-
 nessy
Connie — Chelcie Ross
Archie Whitman — Joesph Culp
Henry Francis — Christopher Stanley
Kenneth Dillon — J. Patrick McCor-
 mack
Allison — Alexa Alemanni
Carla — Deborah Lacey
Kurt — Edin Gali
Young Dick — Brandon Hall
Abigail Whitman — Brynn Horrocks
Farmer 1 — Bobby Hall
Farmer 2 — Kevin Scott Allen
Cooperative Head — Leonard Kelly
 Young

4:1   PUBLIC RELATIONS

Matthew Weiner, Writer
Phil Abraham, Director
Bertram Cooper — Robert Morse
Henry Francis — Christopher Stanley
Joey Baird — Matt Long
Candace — Erin Cummings
Bethany Van Nuys — Anna Camp
Mark Kerney — Blake Bashoff
Pauline Francis — Pamela Dunlap
Frank Keller — Jack Laufer
Jack Hammond — Chris McGarry
Jim Hartsdale — Ron Perkins
Bob Finley — Paul Bartholomew

4:2   CHRISTMAS COMES BUT ONCE A YEAR

Tracy McMillan and Matthew Weiner,
 Writers
Michael Uppendahl, Director
Bertram Cooper — Robert Morse
Henry Francis — Christopher Stanley
Allison — Alexa Alemanni
Joey Baird — Matt Long
Freddy Rumsen — Joel Murray
Mark Kerney — Blake Bashoff
Deborah Lacey — Carla

Trudy Campbell — Alison Brie
Faye Miller — Cara Buono
Geoffrey Atherton — John Aylward
Megan — Jessica Paré
Lee Garner, Jr. — Darren Pettie
Jane Sterling — Peyton List
Jennifer Crane — Laura Regan
Phoebe — Nora Zehetner

4:3 THE GOOD NEWS

Jonathan Abrahams and Matthew
    Weiner, Writers
Jennifer Getzinger, Director
Allison — Alexa Alemanni
Candace — Erin Cummings
Greg Harris — Sam Page
Anna Draper — Melinda Page Hamilton
Patty — Susan Leslie
Stephanie — Caity Lotz
Dr. Emerson — Remy Auberjonois
Sandy Schmidt — Bayne Gibby

4:4 THE REJECTED

Keith Huff and Matthew Weiner,
    Writers
John Slattery, Director
Allison — Alexa Alemanni
Tom Vogel — Joe O'Connor
Faye Miller — Cara Buono
Megan — Jessica Paré
Joyce Ramsay — Zosia Mamet
Joey Baird — Matt Long
Abe Drexler — Charlie Hofheimer
Miss Blankenship — Randee Heller
Jeannie Vogel — Sheila Shaw

4:5 THE CHRYSANTHEMUM
AND THE SWORD

Erin Levy, Writer
Lesli Linka Glatter, Director
Bertram Cooper — Robert Morse
Henry Francis — Christopher Stanley
Joey Baird — Matt Long
Carla — Deborah Lacey
Bethany Van Nuys — Anna Camp
Faye Miller — Cara Buono

Phoebe — Nora Zehetner
Smitty — Patrick Cavanaugh
Edna Keener — Patricia Bethune
Ted Chaough — Kevin Rahm
Ichiro Kamura — Sab Shimono
Jean Rose — Amy Sloan
Walter Hoffman — Christopher Shea

4:6 WALDORF STORIES

Brett Johnson and Matthew Weiner,
    Writers
Scott Hornbacher, Director
Joey Baird — Matt Long
Faye Miller — Cara Buono
Megan — Jessica Pare
Stan Rizzo — Jay R. Ferguson
Danny Siegel — Danny Strong
Ted Chaough — Kevin Rahm
Duck Phillips — Mark Moses
Wallace Harriman — John Aniston
Jim Anderson — Tim De Zarn
Doris — Becky Wahlstrom

4:7 THE SUITCASE

Matthew Weiner, Writer
Jennifer Getzinger, Director
Joey Baird — Matt Long
Mark Kerney — Blake Bashoff
Trudy Campbell — Alison Brie
Faye Miller — Cara Buono
Megan — Jessica Pare
Stan Rizzo — Jay R. Ferguson
Danny Siegel — Danny Strong
Anna Draper — Melinda Page Hamilton
Stephanie — Caity Lotz
Miss Blankenship — Randee Heller
Anita Olson Respola — Audrey
    Wasilewski
Gerry Respola — Jerry O'Donnell
Katherine Olson — Myra Turley
Duck Phillips — Mark Moses

4:8 THE SUMMER MAN

Lisa Albert, Janet Leahy and Matthew
    Weiner, Writers
Phil Abraham, Director

Henry Francis — Christopher Stanley
Joey Baird — Matt Long
Bethany Van Nuys — Anna Camp
Faye Miller — Cara Buono
Stan Rizzo — Jay R. Ferguson
Greg Harris — Sam Page
Miss Blankenship — Randee Heller
Francine Hanson — Anne Dudek
Ralph Stuben — Peter Lewis

4:9   THE BEAUTIFUL GIRLS

Dahvi Waller and Matthew Weiner,
  Writers
Michael Uppendahl, Director
Faye Miller — Cara Buono
Megan — Jessica Pare
Stan Rizzo — Jay R. Ferguson
Joyce Ramsay — Zosia Mamet
Abe Drexler — Charlie Hofheimer
Miss Blankenship — Randee Heller
Leonard Fillmore — David Warshofsky

4:10   HANDS AND KNEES

Jonathan Abrahams and Matthew
  Weiner, Writers
Lynn Shelton, Director
Henry Francis — Christopher Stanley
Trudy Campbell — Alison Brie
Faye Miller — Cara Buono
Megan — Jessica Paré
Lee Garner, Jr. — Darren Pettie
Frank Keller — Jack Laufer
Toni Charles — Naturi Naughton
Robert Pryce — W. Morgan Sheppard
George Casey — JD Cullum
John Gibbons — Casey Sander
Agent Norris — Ray Proscia
Agent Landingham — Rob Nagle
Dr. Howlett — Jim Jansen
Mother — Susan May Pratt

4:11.   CHINESE WALL

Erin Levy, Writer
Phil Abraham, Director
Freddy Rumsen — Joel Murray
Faye Miller — Cara Buono

Megan — Jessica Pare
Jane Sterling — Peyton List
Stan Rizzo — Jay R. Ferguson
Joyce Ramsay — Zosia Mamet
Abe Drexler — Charlie Hofheimer
Tom Vogel — Joe O'Connor
Jeannie Vogel — Sheila Shaw
Danny Siegel — Danny Strong
Ted Chaough — Kevin Rahm
Cynthia Baxter — Larisa Oleynik
Ed Baxter — Ray Wise
John Flory — Tommy Dewey

4:12   BLOWING SMOKE

Andre Jacquemetton and Maria
  Jacquemetton, Writers
John Slattery, Director
Henry Francis — Christopher Stanley
Trudy Campbell — Alison Brie
Faye Miller — Cara Buono
Geoffrey Atherton — John Aylward
Megan — Jessica Paré
Stan Rizzo — Jay R. Ferguson
Danny Siegel — Danny Strong
Ted Chaough — Kevin Rahm
Midge Daniels — Rosemarie DeWitt
Perry Demuth — John Ales
Dr. Edna Keener — Patricia Bethune
Raymond Geiger — John Sloman

4:13   TOMORROWLAND

Jonathan Igla and Matthew Weiner,
  Writers
Matthew Weiner, Director
Henry Francis — Christopher Stanley
Carla — Deborah Lacey
Faye Miller — Cara Buono
Megan — Jessica Paré
Greg Harris — Sam Page
Stephanie — Caity Lotz
Joyce Ramsay — Zosia Mamet
Francine Hanson — Anne Dudek
Frank Keller — Jack Laufer
Carolyn — Cassandra Jean
Henry Sloan — Lawrence Pressman
Marvin Woodman — Jay Seals
Art Garten — Jon Manfrellotti

About the Contributors

Brenda Cromb recently completed a master of arts in film studies degree at the University of British Columbia, where she served as associate editor of *Cinephile*, UBC's graduate journal of film studies. Her thesis was on the ambivalent melodramas of Pedro Almodóvar. Her research interests include the politics of gender, genre, and affect in postmodern cinema, particularly as they touch on melodrama and camp.

Diana Davidson is an instructor in the Department of English and Film Studies and the interdisciplinary Writing Studies Program at the University of Alberta, Canada. She earned a PhD in literature from the University of York, England, in 2003. Her publications include essays on AIDS narratives in *The Journal of Commonwealth and Postcolonial Studies*; the anthology *Spectral America: Phantoms and the National Imagination*, and the forthcoming *Transplanting Canada: Seedlings*. She has published a memoir essay on her volunteer work with the UK AIDS Quilt. She is researching recent representations of motherhood in literary and popular cultures.

Jennifer Gillan is an associate professor of English and media studies at Bentley College in the Boston area. Her essays in television studies have appeared in numerous books, including *Teen Television* (McFarland 2008), and *Grace Under Pressure: Grey's Anatomy Uncovered* (Cambridge Scholars Press 2008). She has also published in *Cinema Journal, American Literature, American Drama, African American Review,* and *Arizona Quarterly,* among others. With Maria Mazziotti Gillan, she coedited *Unsettling America* and *Identity Lessons* and *Growing Up Ethnic in America* (Penguin 1994, 1999, 1999) and *Italian American Writers on New Jersey* (Rutgers 2004). Her *New Media and the Networks: The Circulation of American Must Click TV* is forthcoming.

Maura Grady's research focuses on the intersections of gender, work, popular fiction and film. She earned a PhD in English with a designated emphasis in gender studies from the University of California, Davis, in 2008 and currently is assistant director of core writing at the University of Nevada, Reno. Her latest research projects have focused on masculinist power hierarchies in corporate structures as depicted in twentieth-century American popular fiction, film and television. She has presented at many conferences including those of the National Popular Culture/American Culture Association.

Melanie Hernandez is a doctoral candidate in the Department of English at the University of Washington. She holds a BA in psychology from New York University and an MA in English from California State University, Dominguez Hills. Her current research focuses on miscegenation and hybridism in nineteenth-century American frontier literature. Prior to graduate school, she worked as a television writer and producer in New York City.

David Thomas Holmberg is currently pursuing his doctorate in English at the University of Washington, after receiving his MA from the University of Montana and his BA from the University of California, Los Angeles. He has published in the *Rocky Mountain Review of Language and Literature* and *The Great Plains Quarterly*, the latter of which he also co-edited for a special edition devoted to HBO's *Deadwood*. He is researching American national mythologies and sports culture in antebellum and early modernist American literature.

Tonya Krouse is an associate professor of English at Northern Kentucky University. Her publications include *The Opposite of Desire: Sex and Pleasure in the Modernist Novel* (2009) and articles in *Journal of Modern Literature*, *Virginia Woolf Miscellany*, and *Doris Lessing Studies*. She teaches courses in twentieth-century fiction and film, as well as courses in literary theory and theories of gender and sexuality. She is the president of the Doris Lessing Society.

Tamar Jeffers McDonald is a lecturer in film studies at the University of Kent, England. She read English at Somerville College, Oxford, and received a master's degree from the University of Westminster and a PhD from the University of Warwick. Her research interests are on Hollywood films of the 1950s and 60s (especially the representation of virginity); romantic comedy; and film costume. She wrote *Romantic Comedy: Boy Meets Girl Meets Genre* (Wallflower Press 2007) and *Hollywood Catwalk: Exploring Costume in Mainstream Film* (I. B. Tauris 2010). An edited collection, *Virgin Territory: Representing Sexual Inexperience In Film*, is forthcoming.

Meenasarani Linde Murugan is a recent graduate of the New York University Tisch School for the Arts in the MA program in cinema studies. She completed her BA in film studies at Wesleyan University, where she was also a Mellon Mays Undergraduate Fellow. She read a paper, "*Duel in the Sun*, Female Sexuality, and the Impact of Race on Gender," at a Women & Society Conference at Marist College. She also presented "Maidenform: The Temporality of Fashion, Femininity, and Feminism in *Mad Men*" at the 2009 Southwest Texas Popular Culture and American Culture Association Conference.

David P. Pierson is an associate professor of media studies at the University of Southern Maine. His research interests are the aesthetic and discursive dimensions of cable and broadcast network programming, and the relationship between American television and history. He has published book chapters and articles in the *Journal of Popular Culture* and *Film & History* on *Seinfeld*, the Discovery Channel, and Turner Network Television made-for-TV westerns. He is completing a book on the 1960s TV series *The Fugitive* for Wayne State University Press.

Sara Rogers received a master's degree in American studies from California State University, Fullerton, in 2010. Her research interests include the significance of place in America — specifically, how built environments shape and reflect both the confinement and liberation of women. Sara has served as editorial assistant for the *American Quarterly* (spring 2009) and is co-chair of the American Studies Association Student's Committee (2009–2011).

Christine Sprengler is assistant professor of art history at the University of Western Ontario. She received her PhD in film studies from Birkbeck College, University of London, in 2004. She is the author of *Screening Nostalgia: Populuxe Props and Technicolor Aesthetics in Contemporary American Film* (Berghahn 2009) and of articles and chapters on British and American film and television. She is currently working on a new book on representations of 'the fifties' in popular visual culture since the 1970s.

Scott F. Stoddart is the dean of the School of Liberal Arts at the Fashion Institute of Technology, State University of New York. He served as provost at Manhattanville College and an associate professor of liberal arts at Nova Southeastern University, where he taught American literature, cinema studies, and musical theatre history. He has published on the fiction of Henry James, E. M. Forster, and F. Scott Fitzgerald; the musical plays of Stephen Sondheim; the films of the Coen Brothers, Jane Campion, Jack Clayton, John Ford, Oliver Stone and Martin Scorsese; and the image of the president in Hollywood film and television. In addition to working on the *Love/Lust* television program for the Sundance Channel, he is editing two collections, *Regal Reels* and *The 9/11 Western*, while writing his next book *"Queer Eye" for a "Straight Dick": Contextualizing the Queer Villain in Film Noir*.

Index